Ken
Purdy's
Book
of
Automobiles

Ken Purdy's Book of Automobiles

Ken W. Purdy

Galahad Books · New York City

Contents

CONTENTS

CONTENTS

Foreword

Ken W. Purdy is widely regarded as the dean of American motoring writers. He has written seven books on the automobile. His book *Kings of the Road,* was in print for seventeen years, and his biography of Stirling Moss, *All But My Life*, has been called one of the best automobile books ever written. Purdy has probably published more articles on motoring in magazines of general circulation than anyone else using the English language. His The Day They Dug Up Babs was judged the best automobile article published in 1970. He is the author of the Encyclopaedia Britannica's section on the historical development of the automobile. Purdy has also written automobile oriented fiction.

One of Ken Purdy's short stories, Change Of Plan, first published in the *Atlantic Monthly* in 1952, has appeared in a dozen anthologies here and abroad, beginning with *The Best American Short Stories of 1953*. He has contributed more articles and short stories to PLAYBOY—a total of seventy-five—than anyone else and is a three-time winner of the annual Playboy Award for the best short story or article of the year.

Purdy, formerly editor in chief of *Victory, Parade, True,* and *Argosy* magazines, has been a freelance writer since 1954. He has extensive interests apart from the automobile and has written on subjects as diverse as hypnosis, karate, the carillon, the crossbow, and the history of liqueurs.

THE EDITORS, PLAYBOY PRESS

Preface

The automobile peculiarly fascinates the male animal, we must presume because it was the first device that made individual freedom of movement available to him, a benison the horse and carriage, for technological and economic reasons, had been unable to confer. This fascination appears to be nearly universal: a Volkswagen agency dropped into the middle of the Australian Outback would almost surely flourish, and the remark that nothing could be better calculated to undermine Soviet political discipline than the decision to have Fiat set up a Russian branch factory was made not wholly in jest. Men who are indifferent to what they wear, and not terribly concerned with what they eat, as long as they do eat, will make absurd sacrifices to possess an automobile. A sociologist once noted that the first topic of conversation among American men was not sex, not politics, not money, but the automobile. And that was at a time when the automobile's image was rather pedestrian, before the sports-car boom of the 1950s convinced millions that the automobile had a second function, that it was an instrument of sport, a notion that has made auto racing the second-biggest American spectator sport, drawing 40 million-plus devotees a year, more than baseball, football, or basketball. (Horse racing, because it's a betting game, is first.)

I was first aware of the sports-car phenomenon, a cloud on the horizon no bigger than a baby's hand, in 1934. I was laboring on the staff of a Massachusetts newspaper for a weekly stipend which would not today persuade a high-school boy to mow a lawn when I was exposed to what the British motoring magazines refer to as The Sport. The publisher of our little gazette, a Harvard graduate of recent vintage, undertook to stage a roadrace as a promotional device. To this end he summoned from Yale and Harvard, then the twin hubs of what little American roadracing there was, a covey or pride of sports-car owners. All were members of the Automobile Racing Club of America, which was dominated by three young men, Barron, Sam, and Miles Collier, sons of the advertising eminence Barron Collier. The club had first raced on a course laid out on the driveways of the Collier estate in Pocantico Hills, New York.

They stormed into town on the stated weekend, driving or towing their exotic machinery. Even the tow-cars were extraordinary: I remember an immaculate twelve-cylinder boattail Auburn speedster pulling an Alfa-Romeo. It was the first Alfa I had ever seen, and small wonder: I doubt there were a dozen in the country at the time.

The types in the drivers' seats were new to me, too. They were *sportif,* to say the least. They were of a race apart. They spoke only to each other, and in their native tongue: "I shouldn't turn that much over five thou, old boy, the big-ends simply won't stand up to it." They treated their mounts like newborn children. I remember standing in one of the garages, mouth agape, as a Bugatti owner heated a gallon and a half of pure castor oil on a portable electric burner. He had a candy thermometer in the reeking stuff, and he peered steadily at it. Just as it rose to the temperature he wanted —80° centigrade, as I recall—he snatched the instrument out, grabbed the kettle, and turned to me to say, "Do stand aside, please, the oil mustn't cool before I get it into the engine." He had about three feet to cover before reaching the filler-pipe, and I marveled at his fear that the temperature of the oil would decline half a degree before he could decant it.

A couple of cars away, a crisis was flowering: the driver needed four gallons of water to refill his radiator, and no one, it seemed, knew where to find four gallons of water—pure distilled water, that is.

Alas, all was in vain: at the last moment the city fathers in their wisdom forbade the race on the ground of danger to the populace.

It must have been one of those same sophisticates whom I saw, a few years later, standing outside the Time-Life building in New York beside a brand-new MG Midget. The dashing *pilote,* pulling on a pair of pierced-back chamois driving gloves, was about to board when one of the staring yokels (an MG would draw a crowd in New York in those days) asked him what the letters MG stood for (Morris Garages of Oxford).

"MG?" he drawled, affecting surprise. "Why, 'Mighty Good,' of course."

"Where can you buy one?" the fellow said.

"You *can't* buy one," he was told. "They're available only as gifts." He smiled condescendingly and blasted off.

I encountered this gambit on other occasions. It was not uncommon. Alarmed at the growing interest of the peasants in their hobby, many sports-car owners refused to divulge price or dealer's name. All very well, of course, when a dealership might be housed in a one-room office high in a skyscraper, without a showroom to its name, but it couldn't work for long. The bug had bitten, and farsighted entrepreneurs were soon on hand with the vaccine.

The obvious snob's target was the Detroit automobile, and I contributed my share, and then some, to that assault. Detroit had it coming, in those days. The 1948 family sedan, for example, was not a very good automobile, and those of us who had access to the public prints denounced the men who made it in terms that might perhaps have been better reserved for wife-beaters and poor-box looters. Whether our jeremiads had anything to do with it or not I cannot say, but Detroit's automobiles *did* change, and for the better, if infinitely slowly. The Volkswagen was thought to be hilarious idiocy, but came the day, twenty years later, when The Big Four hurriedly cranked out lines of little cars designed to be stuffed into the holes in the dike through which VWs, Renaults, Toyotas, Fiats were leaking in consequential numbers.

There are still valid accusations to be nailed to Detroit's door, but the American car remains splendid value for money, and it does superbly well what it is designed to do. Granted, a Cadillac can't follow a Mercedes-Benz up an Alpine pass, much less down the other side, but it isn't meant to. And while U.S. cars are built for obsolescense, that can be defeated: if you have it Ziebart rust-proofed when it's new, maintain it absolutely by the book, wax it four times a year, wash it once a week, keep it out of the hands of garage-repair *banditti* even if that means driving twenty miles to have Honest Eddie change the plugs, put in an engine-heater if you live in severe climate, so that it never starts cold—if you do all this, the thing will run like a watch until you're sick of the sight of it.

Most of the attitudes that make up the sports-car mystique were imported from Britain. One of them has it that the owner of an open car shouldn't put the top up in anything short of a blizzard. I know a man who bought an XK-120 Jaguar off the showroom floor fifteen years ago and has *never* put the top up, and he never will. I knew a gentleman of similar persuasion who gave his wife two black eyes in observance of the convention. It wasn't that he struck her, he wouldn't dream of that. He just drove 250 miles on a cold autumn day with the top down *and* the windshield of his MG folded flat. The wind-buffeting blacked her eyes. He felt sorry for her, but she had forgotten her goggles, so what could he do? The matter was out of his hands.

The incident should not be classified as an extreme example of British *sang-froid*. The Frazer Nash club is a society devoted to the preservation of the sports car of that name, an exotic chain-driven device, and the annual Christmas party of the club is one of the notable events on the British motoring calendar. I went one year in the company of two gentlemen of some prominence in the métier. I wouldn't say they were really eccentric, although one of them, Derek, kept a Bugatti in the front hall of his house, next to a cabinet full of rare Delft china, and Martin had been heard to say of a friend who, given the choice of spending a weekend driving a Lamborghini Miura or in the company of a ravishing and compliant lady, had chosen the lady, that the poor man was obviously losing his buttons. The venue of the meeting was some ninety miles out of London, and we started at dusk in a pouring rainfall. Derek and Martin were traveling in Derek's Brescia Bugatti, and I was to follow in my Porsche. The Bugatti had no top and no windshield. Martin wore a Royal Navy surplus oilskin; Derek, as I recall, a tweed jacket.

It was a memorable journey. As we poked along through the outskirts of London I was driving negligently, heater and radio on full blast. Instantly we were clear of town, things changed radically: the Brescia's tail lights, about the size and color of a pair of ripe raspberries and throwing all of three candlepower each, suddenly disappeared into the haze. Derek had counseled that I tag along closely because he proposed avoiding traffic: "We'll go along the back doubles," he had said. Since I'd be hopelessly lost in minutes without him, I turned the radio off and got down to it, and for most of the rest of the trip I was fully occupied. The pattern repeated itself insistently: the little red lights would pull away, then suddenly I'd be on top of them as Derek dove into some hairpin corner. He carried no stoplights and no rear bumper. I'd be in danger of losing him one minute and on the point of crumpling the rear end of an irreplaceable 1923 Bugatti the next. Derek was a famous competitor in vintage-car races, and in anything less handy than a Porsche I doubt I could have stayed with him. I marveled at the way the Brescia fled along the back roads we were using, twisting and turning as only British country roads do, throwing rooster-tails of water high into the air behind it.

In the fulness of time we arrived, parked the cars in the hotel court, and made straight for the bar. Derek and Martin ordered double whiskies. They were standing in spreading puddles. They looked as if they had been walking on the bottom of a lake.

"You two seem to have shipped a little water," I said.

"Dampish," Derek said.

"Splendid motorcar for this kind of going," Martin said. "Absolutely splendid."

Indeed, there were some odd types in The Sport. I have seen a man mumble and flush when it was pointed out to him that he had wrongly placed his left leg in entering a vintage racing car. Poor fellow, he had thought the idea was to squirm into the narrow seat in whatever fashion was effective, when what he had done was equivalent to mounting a horse on the offside. A man of genuine *sang-froid* would have carried it off by saying something like, "That's all very well for the 3½-liter, old boy, but *this* is a 4-liter, you know."

I remember seeing this ploy effectively implemented by an Englishman who came into a filling station after a trial run in a friend's classic Alfa-Romeo. In most Alfas of the period the accelerator pedal was mounted between the clutch and the brake, instead of to the right side. The car came into the station very fast and, just when it should have braked, the engine howled and it leaped forward. The driver managed to stop it six inches short of a brick wall. As he jumped out, he said to the owner, standing there white and shaking, "That throttle return-spring sticks badly, old man. You really ought to have a look at it." It was perfectly obvious that he had stepped on the accelerator thinking he was hitting the brake pedal, but no one had the temerity to accuse him of the gaffe.

The sports car, and the racing of it, gestated a heady sense of freedom and a disdain for convention that sometimes took outrageous forms. One bright Sunday morning a friend, a racedriver, picked me up at a railroad station. He was driving a Cadillac-engined Allard, a formidable competition car. Waiting beside us at a traffic light was an open Buick convertible, behind the wheel a man who looked almost too big for his car: he would have weighed 220 or so, his shoulders bulged in a blue flannel blazer bright with brass buttons, and his size-twenty neck was graced with an ample paisley foulard. My friend looked at him, smiled, and, just before the light changed, said, "Tell me, Agnes, did you tie that thing—or did your mummy?"

He let in the clutch and we blasted off. I turned around. Hard behind us came the monster, purple-faced, a fist the size of a pineapple shaking over the top of his windshield.

"This'll be *funny,*" my friend said, banging into second gear. "I'm going to put the silly son of a bitch right through the schoolhouse."

Two blocks ahead of us, a T-junction, a red-brick school dead in the center on the far side of the road. We howled up to it, my friend stood on the brake, dropped two gears, and went through the right-angle corner at an absurd rate, the tires chirping as they tried to find a bite on the pavement.

The last I saw of the poor innocent in the Buick, he had the wheels hard over, the brakes locked, he was sliding string-straight up the lawn. He stopped before he hit the schoolhouse—just.

Mad free spirits of that stripe were not so often seen as the 1950s closed down. There were racedrivers, even of the first rank, who were notable wenchers and drinkers, uninhibited to a degree, but most of them were killed. Mike Hawthorn, champion of the world in 1958, was a swinger who knew few inhibitions. He went into another driver's hotel suite, before a race in France, and found the man's wife in the tub. He promptly joined her. He was widely criticized, most of his peers agreeing with the affronted husband, who said, "No gentleman gets into a lady's bath without at least taking off his hat, it simply isn't done." Both men died at the wheel not long afterward. Automobile racing is indisputably the most dangerous game men play and it has defied all efforts to make it safe. Today's drivers tend to be cold, detached, planning men, they no longer uncomplainingly drive 190 miles an hour over a circuit bordered with trees two or three feet thick or so roughly surfaced that it can tear a wheel off a car. Few smoke, almost none drink. Jackie Stewart of Scotland, present champion of the world, will take no drugs, aspirin included. Today's drivers have business managers and investment counselors, they plan to leave the sport rich—and alive. They shudder to think how men they knew well and remember dressed to go to work: cotton T-shirt and slacks, perhaps, if the day was hot, with nothing underneath, boxers' shoes, gloves, a cloth helmet. The form today is long underwear of Nomex or some other fire-resistant fabric, socks, gloves, coveralls, and facemask of the same stuff, a full-face helmet of fighter-pilot standard, shoulder, lap, and sometimes thigh-restraining safety harness. Thus armored, they may stay conscious in a crash, and they can survive thirty seconds or so in the flame of burning gasoline at around 2500° F. Still they die, even the best and most expert of them—five of that category, one a world champion, within roughly the last year of this writing. Nowadays, men of the first rank rarely die through error in judgment: someone else's mistake kills them; that, or something breaks on the car, negating their skills, however great. A careful estimate suggests that by January 1, 1972, 885 drivers will have been killed since motor racing began. And when one goes, ten rush to fill his place.

Periodically, insistently, strong voices—the Vatican's, for example—are heard demanding that automobile racing be outlawed. So far, only one nation has listened: Switzerland forbids all forms of motoring competition, even the comparatively innocuous rallying and hill-climbing. With that exception, the prohibition attempt has always broken against the argument that a man's right to risk his life is inviolate, so long as in the doing he doesn't risk another's. Spectators die, too, but they have been warned, as if they should need to be, that proximity to a vehicle running 220 miles an hour is risky, and most circuits are now protected against a horror like Le Mans-1955 when a car jumped a barrier and killed at least eighty-eight people. (The true figure is hard to establish, and may have been as high as 118.)

Racing has always been under attack, and so has the automobile itself. Men still living remember when a motorcar on British roads had by law to be preceded by a man on foot carrying a red flag of warning. Today the portents of restriction are clearly in view. Only a few years ago one could drive on the open road in Europe at whatever speed one liked: 100, 125, even 150 mph. First England imposed a 70-mph limit; Sweden, France, Germany followed. Switzerland will be next, and Italy, where 180 mph is today a perfectly legal speed, will of course be last. A case can be made for the proposition that the rising population of the world and the consequent overcrowding of the roads will sooner or later impel society to legislate the automobile into three or four standard forms, severely limit its use even in those forms, and force most people to use rapid public transport, admittedly much more efficient, quicker, safer, and less environmentally damaging than the number of private automobiles needed to move an equivalent number of people.

So it may come to pass. One hopes not, because while the automobile has shown us very cruel sides of its nature, injuring and killing millions of us, smothering the cities and threatening to lead us to bury under paving a shocking fraction of the earth's green surface, it has been a boon as well: a world without automobiles since, say, 1920, seems unimaginable.

And it may not come to pass—the prophet must ever peer into a hazy future. The men who in 1905 predicted the speedy disappearance of the horse would be boggled to know that 1972 America supports thousands more horses than it did when the animal was the standard and indispensable prime mover.

I for one hope that the automobile, a little less lethal, a bit more civilized, will long be abroad in the land. I should hate to think that all the pleasure I've had of it, and anticipate having, would not be known to my children and my children's children. I would be the poorer if I couldn't recall the delights of running along a country road on a bright autumn day in a Mercer Raceabout, even with the wind whistling up my trouser-leg because the accelerator lived outside the car, or the midnight ride I gave a friend in a Grand Prix Bugatti. The back roads we took were dark and empty, we ran on and on at highly illegal speeds, too far gone in euphoria to pay the least attention to direction until finally we were hopelessly lost. Or the night a friend and I left Le Touquet at six in the evening, in identical Porsches, for Monaco, running through the night, nearly all the way across France, as fast as we could go. I remember the thrill of discovery in finding some splendid cars: a Mercer, three Bugattis, a Frazer Nash, three Rolls-Royces, a Packard roadster, a Morgan Three-Wheeler—and the pangs of regret over having sold some of them. I remember watching many new automobiles come painfully into existence—the Tucker, for example. Most of them failed and not always because they didn't deserve to succeed.

I should hate to lose the memory of Jean and Cameron Argetsinger's postrace parties at Watkins Glen; or the long porch of Kenilworth Lodge in Sebring, the still night air heavy with the scent of the citrus groves; or the Chateau de Segrais near Le Mans, a seventeenth-century pastel frozen in amber; or the Steering Wheel Club in London; or René and Maurice Dreyfus' Le Chanteclair in New York, a restaurant that is a second home to everyone who thinks of the automobile as more than mere transport.

I have found scores of people in the métier rewarding to know, many of them drivers—Stirling Moss, Fon Portago, Jimmy Clark, Graham Hill, Erik Carlsson, Carel de Beaufort, Richie Ginther, Dan Gurney, Eddie Sachs, Phil Hill, Bob Bondurant, Jim Hall, Derek Bell, Jonathan Williams, Masten Gregory, David Piper, John Miles, Eric Glavitza, Peter Huber, Michael Parkes, Jo Bonnier . . . It still strikes me as curious that these competitive men showed, once out of the automobile and relieved of the terrible tensions of their profession, an extraordinary courtesy and consideration, some of them, indeed, a *politesse* almost Edwardian. I have never observed its like in any comparable company.

The pieces that make up this book have been arranged roughly chronologically, with no attempt at categorization, because in putting them together I have found it most enjoyable to begin reading wherever my hand fell, and I suspect others will do the same.

The year in which each piece was written is appended to it. Many of them have, in detail, been overtaken by events, and the temptation to update was strong in some instances. But this book is, after all, an anthology, and the individual articles that make it up must honestly reflect the state of affairs at the time they were written. Updating is easy, but it's cheating, too.

Ken W. Purdy
Wilton, Connecticut
10 November 1971

Ken
Purdy's
Book
of
Automobiles

Stirling Moss: A Nodding Acquaintance With Death

A pretty, pink-cheeked English nurse pushed him into the room; he was riding a high-backed, old-fashioned–looking wheelchair, a small man, heavily muscled, laughing, slit-eyed. It was his forty-sixth day in the hospital, and for thirty-eight of those days he had been unconscious, or semiconscious, or in amnesia, but he was tan and he looked strong. The left side of his face was raddled with rough, red scars all around the eye, as if someone had been at him with a broken beer bottle.

"That was a funny story, boy, in your last letter," he said, "that story about the clam-digger . . . what's this, what's this?" An enchanting *gamine* thing in faded levis, red-brown hair, and dark glasses was handing him an envelope, her photograph. "I *like* that!" he said. "Put it over there, stand it up, you've met, you two, this is Judy Carne?"

We had met. He stared at her, smiling, as if he could pull himself out of the wheelchair with his eyes. He grabbed her wrist. "Did *you* see the *Daily Sketch* yesterday?" He turned to me. "Did you see that, boy? We were sitting in the garden, this bloke poked a telephoto lens over the wall, the bastard was twenty yards away, Judy was brushing a bread crumb off my chin when he shot it, 'an admirer' the caption said . . . "

"I like *that,*" Miss Carne said. " 'Admirer'!"

"Are you suing?" he said.

"I can't," she said. "I'm going to Hollywood tomorrow."

He smiled again. He looked much as he had when I saw him four days before he went off the course at 120 miles an hour and slammed into a wall at Goodwood: the forty-odd stitches had been taken out of his face; the left cheekbone, stuffed full of support from inside, didn't betray that it had been shattered, and his nose didn't really look as if it had been broken eight times. His bare left foot lay immobile on the wheelchair rest. His leg was bandaged, but the plaster cast was on the windowsill, sliced in two. There were marks on the pink top of his head. He looked beat up but whole. What he could move, he did move: his head, his right arm, his left arm less, and he talked. He picked up a cellophane bag of red roses someone had left on the bed.

"They're from Germany," he said. He read the name. "I don't know who that is," he said. The door opened behind him. "Viper?" he said. He looked around the back of the wheelchair. "Viper, you went off with my fountain pen." Valerie Pirie, his secretary, a pretty, calm girl. She gave him his pen. He made a note on the card and dropped it on a neat pile of cards and letters. "So-and-so and so-and-so are outside," she said. "I told them not to come, but . . . and the man from Grundig is coming at 4:30, about the tape recorder." Tape recorders are important to Moss. He has done five books on tape recorders.

An orderly brought in another bunch of red roses. As he left, a tall blonde came in, and behind her, another, taller. Kiss-kiss. Judy Carne was lying on her belly on the bed, her chin in her hand, staring at him. "I'll tell you, boy," he was saying, "nothing that has happened to me since I came here, except when they broke my nose again, hurt like that clot's shaving me. I had seven days' growth of beard. He swore he knew how. I can't think where he'd learned, it was like pulling it out . . ."

Another nurse, with tea, bread and butter, jam, clotted cream. He talked. Valerie said, "Drink your tea, Stirling." He drank it and she gave him another cup. He made each of the blondes eat a piece of bread and butter and jam. Neither wanted to, they were dieting, but they couldn't think of answers for the persuasions that poured out of him.

He talked very well, but he didn't stop. He said to me, "You know, I'm not supposed to put any weight on this left leg, under penalty of death or flogging or something, but I'll tell you, the other night I went from there, to there, the washbasin, *and* back; actually, coming back I passed out. I didn't go unconscious, I get dizzy now and then, I just fell down, but it was so funny, the reason I had to do it . . ."

For some time after the accident his speech, when he spoke in delirium, was thick and slurred because of the brain injury, and there was some reason to doubt he would ever speak clearly again. Worse, a close friend had said, "I have the impression that he cannot form an idea of his own, but can only respond to ideas that are fed to him." Now he spoke the crisp quick English he had always used, and ideas came as fast as he could handle them. And he went on and on. It wasn't that he talked incessantly, or compulsively, although he did come close to it. He would stop and listen. He had always been in my opinion a good listener, polite, attentive, absorbed, and retentive. But he would listen now only exactly as long as someone spoke and had something to speak about. Then he would begin instantly to talk again. There were no pauses. I think he was happy to find himself *able* to talk again, and in any case excitation is common in recovery from severe trauma. But it was also plain that he wanted no silences in that room.

I remembered something he had said that last time I'd seen him, in a long dark afternoon of talk in the little apartment in Earl's Court Road: "When I go to bed tonight, I hope to be tired, very tired, because I don't want to think. I don't want to think."

Valerie Pirie had said to me, when he was still in coma, "Do you know, last night he was speaking in French and Italian, as well as English, of course—but his accent in French and Italian was very pure, much better than it's ever been when he was conscious. Why's that, do you think?"

"Disinhibition. What did he say?"

"He was talking about girls, a lot of the time. Once he said, '*E molto difficile per un corridore—molto difficile.*' "

("[Life] is very hard for a racedriver—very hard.")

A hard life? Stirling Moss is one of the best-known men in the world, and beyond any doubt the best-known sports figure. Only Queen Elizabeth, by actual line count, gets more mention in the British press than Stirling Moss. Six weeks after his last accident the Sunday *Times* of London considered his appearance in the garden of the hospital worth a four-column picture and a long story—on page one. He makes $150,000 or so a year. He knows the world as few men can imagine knowing it. He travels constantly, once flew to London from South Africa just for a date, flew back next day. His present injuries aside, he is as healthy as a bull, iron-hard, capable of fantastic endurance. He's expert at every sport he has ever tried, rugby, swimming, water-skiing, whatever. He was a better show-rider and jumper at sixteen, his sister Pat says, than she is today, and she's on the British International team. (The two of them once cleaned out an entire horse show: between them they won every prize offered.) Moss is highly intelligent, easily roused to intense interest in almost anything, from astronomy to Zen. He is one of the most pursued television and radio guests in Europe.

He is a witty and amusing speaker. He has written five notably successful books on racing, and about eight hundred magazine and newspaper articles have appeared under his by-line. He subscribes to no clipping service, but he has forty-two full scrapbooks, nevertheless. His mail averages ten thousand pieces a year (400–500 a day when he's in the hospital) and he answers every letter, and promptly. Most men like him. Women find him irresistible, nine times in ten. He has picked a girl out of the crowd standing in a corner at a race circuit, waved to her every time around, made a date for that evening in pantomime, and won the race, too. He sometimes dates three girls in a day.

Most importantly, he has work to do that he likes doing, and he is better in his work than any other man alive, better in the common judgment of his peers. He is, if the last accident has not destroyed him, the greatest racedriver living. In matched cars he would beat any other driver in the world. More, he is probably the greatest racedriver of all time, the greatest who has ever lived. He has been champion driver of Great Britain ten times. He has won so many silver cups that he estimates they could be melted down into an ingot that would weigh 300 pounds. (The ingot, he thinks, would make, in turn, a striking coffee table.) Of his store of other medals, awards, oddities, there is no counting. I remember his coming through New York after a race in Venezuela carrying the Perez Jimenez Cup, a lump of solid gold so heavy it was unpleasant to hold in one hand.

For years he has been universally considered the fastest driver alive and that he has never won the championship of the world is one of the major curiosities of sports. He has been three times third in the world rankings, four times second. The championship is decided on the basis of placement in, usually, about ten major races throughout the world. The 1958 champion, Mike Hawthorn of England, won only one of these races, while Moss won four; But Hawthorn, driving an Italian Ferrari, finished in more races than Moss, whose insistence on driving, when possible, privately owned cars (factory-owned models are always faster) of British manufacture has severely handicapped him. (Now British cars are fastest; in the 1950s they were not.) But Moss has beaten every man who has held the world championship for the past ten years. Those very few of whom it can be said that they do one thing, whatever it is, better than anyone else has ever done it are marked forever, and in his profession Moss is an immortal. And he is thirty-two, well off if not rich, healthy, popular, talented, a citizen of the world.

E molto difficile per un corridore—molto difficile?

Yes. Very difficult. The essence of the difficulty is that racedriving on the highest level, in the fastest, most competitive company, Grand Prix driving, is the most dangerous sport in the world. In one recent year the mortality rate was 25 percent. The list of drivers killed in the decade 1951–1961, *counting major figures only,* totals fifty-six names.

If the game is so dangerous, why does anyone play it?

Because it's also the most compelling, delightful, sensually rewarding game in the world. In a racedriver's view, endeavors like tennis and golf and baseball are exercises, pastimes; demanding, yes, if you like, but still, games that children can play. Some games, like court tennis, are both physically and intellectually demanding, but a split-second miscalculation in court tennis will cost only a point, not a life or crippling or sixty days in the hospital. Bullfighters, mountain climbers, skin divers know something of the racing driver's ecstasy, but only a part, because theirs are team sports.

What is a racedriver? Is any man who has learned how to drive 150 miles an hour through traffic reasonably skillfully, a racedriver? No, he isn't. Hear Moss: "If you habitually go through the corners one-fifth of a second slower than your maximum, you can make a reputation, you can earn a living, you can even win a race now and then—but you are no racedriver."

There are some such. Also there are many drivers who will deny that there is anything esthetically or sensually rewarding about motor racing. But they betray themselves when they say, and they all do, "I drive because I like it," or, "I like the life." They feel, but they are inarticulate.

The full terror and the full reward of this incredible game are given only to those who bring to the car talent honed by obsessive practice into great skill, a fiercely competitive will, and high intelligence, with the flagellating sensitivity that so often accompanies it. In these men, a terrible and profound change sometimes takes place: the game becomes life. They understand what Karl Wallenda meant when he said, going back up on the high wire after the terrible fall in Detroit that killed two of his troupe and left another a paraplegic, "To be on the wire is life; the rest is waiting." This change is irreversible. A man who has gone through it will never come back across the fence to the herd. Once the game has become life, and life has become a vestibule, unimaginable courage is required to renounce the game —because renunciation is suicide. Tazio Nuvolari, for decades called the greatest master of racedriving who ever lived, could not find the courage to leave the game that had broken every major bone in his body and had more than once caused doctors formally to announce his impending death; he drove with blood running down his chin because the exhaust fumes made him hemorrhage; he drove when he was so weak he had to be lifted, inert, from the car at the end of a race; he drove until he could not drive; he died in bed, hating it.

No, Grand Prix racedriving has nothing to do with other games, just as driving a Grand Prix car has nothing to do with driving a Chrysler on a parkway, even at, say, 100 miles an hour. ("It has not to *do* with it," Moss says. "That kind of driving is not even remotely the same thing. It's night and day, fire and water.")

Juan Manuel Fangio, five times champion of the world, retired and left the game in 1958 because he was slowing and because he was lonely and depressed, so many of his friends had been killed. Today, if he were standing in front of the pits on a practice day and someone were to point to a car and say, "Juan Manuel, that is your car, made for you to your measurements, ready for you," I think the struggle within the man would be a hard one. Successful, wealthy, loved, respected, still he knows that he has gone to live in the vestibule.

Men like Nuvolari and Fangio, or the *matador de toros* Juan Belmonte, retiring with the marks of seventy-two bull gorings on a frail body, share a common mold: skill, obsession, courage, sensitivity. Courage doesn't count most. Skill is basic, and sensitivity, and always the obsession. When the obsession is great enough, the man will find courage to sustain it, somehow. The American racedriver Frank Lockhart, killed at Daytona in 1928, nearly always vomited before he got into the automobile, but he got into it.

Once a man has gone over, the terror of his nights will be, not mortal death, which he will have seen many times, and which, like a soldier, he believes is most likely to come to the man next to him, and the risk of which is in any case the price of the ticket to the game, but real death—final deprivation of the right to go up on the wire again. Then, like Moss, he'll do anything to get back. In the hospital, Moss would accept any pain, any kind of treatment, anything at all that he could believe would shorten, if only by a very little, his path back to the race car, never mind the fact that it took a crew of mechanics thirty minutes with hacksaws and metal shears to cut the last one apart enough to make it let go of him. When he was finally lifted free his face was slashed in a dozen places, his left arm was broken, his left leg was broken at knee and ankle, he had cracked ribs, torn muscles, a broken cheekbone, and a broken nose—and his brain had been so massively bruised that the left side of his body was paralyzed. "Recovery from the brain damage is likely to be a slow process," specialists said, "and there is a possibility that full recovery of function in the arm and leg will not take place." His vision was disturbed. Moss laughed at the doctors and in the night, and whenever he could, pushed the broken leg against the footboard of his bed to exercise it.

How does a man come to this terrible place?

By an ordinary road, usually.

Moss's father, Alfred Moss, is a prosperous London dentist. He was a racedriver, although never approaching the first rank. Still, he ran at Indianapolis in 1924 and 1925, finishing sixteenth the first time and thirteenth the second time. He did some barnstorming in the United States. Stirling's mother, Aileen, was a well-known British rallydriver, and in 1936 she was woman champion of Britain. She drove a Marendaz, one of the specialist cars for which England is famous, made from 1926 to 1936. She was a noted horsewoman. Stirling was their first child, born September 17, 1929.

Stirling was not a flaming success as a student. He was bright, but indifferent to the academic appeal. He was the kind of problem student who requires teachers with skill and special sympathy. He was often ill. His medical record shows appendicitis as a child, scarlet fever, and a serious, prolonged case of nephritis. He and the academic life abandoned each other; he tried apprenticing himself to hotel administration and to farming and was bored.

He could drive an automobile, in the sense of steering it, when he was six. He had a car of his own when he was fourteen. It was a device called a Morgan Three-Wheeler, beloved of two generations of Englishmen. The Morgan had two wheels in front and a third, chain-driven, in the rear. The engine was usually a big motorcycle racing engine, and it rode out of doors, in front of the radiator. The Morgan attracted Englishmen because a whimsy of British law, involving chain drive and weight, classified it as a motorcycle, to its tax advantage; being light and overpowered, it had remarkable acceleration; also—and this was what brought one to Stirling Moss—you could legally drive a Morgan before you could drive a four-wheeler.

Moss's father was well off, but the Morgan wasn't really a gift. "My parents taught me that I could have what I wanted if I paid for it. I always managed to get what I was after, but in order to do that, I had to get rid of everything else. I could have a motorbike if I sold my radio and my chemical set and this and that and the other and when I wanted to move on from the bike I had to flog off my tent and my camping kit and the bike itself and this and that . . . I was taught that everything is attainable if you're prepared to give up, to sacrifice, to get it. I think my parents gave me, gave me as a gift, one might say, this belief that *whatever* you want to do, you can do it if you want to do it enough, and I do believe that. I *believe* it.

"I believe that if I wanted to run a mile in four minutes I could do it. I would have to give up everything else in life, but I could run a mile in four minutes. I believe that if a man wanted to walk on water, and was prepared to give up everything else in life, he could do it. He could walk on water. I am serious. I really do practically believe that."

When Moss decided that he wanted to be a racing driver, his parents objected. His father argued on practical grounds: "*I* couldn't make a living at it, and I tried years ago, when it was easier. " But they only objected, they didn't refuse. Neither is the kind of parent who wants to live life over again through a child, but as former competition drivers they didn't consider the métier as dangerous as some parents might, nor as unrewarding. They were outdoor people. They considered physical risk a part of life. After all, Stirling and his sister Pat, five years younger, had been riding show horses and jumpers since they'd been old enough to say "horse" and no harm had come to them. So, after the Austin 7 and the Morgan and the MG and such traditional school cars of the British competition driver, Stirling graduated, at sixteen, to a solid, reliable, medium-fast German sports car, a BMW (Bayerische Motoren Werke) 328. In 1948, when he was eighteen, and legally could drive in competition as well as on the roads, he got his first race car, a Cooper.

The Cooper then (the firm is famous now) was made in a garage that has been described as approximately the size of a big kitchen. It was a Formula III car: 500 cubic centimeters of engine, which usually meant a rear-mounted 1-cylinder J.A.P. or Norton racing-motorcycle engine, propelling it at speeds up to 120 miles an hour. The car was tiny and light. Steering was so quick as to be instantaneous and the engine delivered usable power only when it was turning very fast: if the speed dropped it would promptly stall. It was best as a sprint and hill-climb car. Moss put in an entry for the famous Shelsley Walsh hill climb and was not accepted: nobody had ever heard of him. He tried again, for a hill climb at Prescott, the famous venue of the Bugatti Owners Club, was listed, and on the scheduled day he loaded his Cooper into a horse box and set off.

Prescott was then 880 yards of twisty, narrow road. Cars start on the flat, run over a rubber contact timing device, scream up the hill, and break an electric-eye beam at the finish. Every great driver in Great Britain has run at Prescott. Moss's first assault on the hill was ragged. But each car is given two tries, and his second run was a record for the 500 cc class. It didn't last long, it was broken three times in the course of the day, but still it was a fact: Stirling Moss broke a course record the first time he ran in competition. Knowledgeable people at Prescott that day, noting the speed with which he learned the circuit and seeing that he made no mistake twice, marked him as one to watch, and one perceptive journalist so cited him in print. The next time he ran in a hill climb he won it. He entered in an airport race and won that, in pouring rain. He went to Goodwood, one of the best-known racing circuits in Britain, and won there, in fast company. All in all, in his first year, a boy, he entered fifteen events and won eleven of them.

For the next year he bought a bigger Cooper, with a 2-cylinder engine. He kept on winning. His father, reluctantly supporting his campaigning, serving as his manager, conceded that there would be no return to the hotel business. With mixed feelings, he began to suspect greatness in his son.

Moss was invited to run on the Continent, a small race at Lake Garda in Italy, and offered fifty pounds in starting money. The Italians thought he was amusing, a boy, a pink-cheeked *Inglese* with curly hair, and too much of it. Some laughed at him and his funny-looking Cooper. He won his class, going away, and was an astonishing third overall to a pair of Ferrari drivers, one of them the formidable Luigi Villoresi. He began to form his own style of driving, patterning the attitude, which today identifies him as far as he can be seen—relaxed, limp as *pasta,* arms straight out to the wheel—on Dr. Giuseppe Farina, onetime champion of the world.

Since then Moss has run 494 races. He won 222, was second in 54, third in 26, fourth in 20. At what may have been his peak, from 1945–1961, he won 134 out of 268 starts, that is, he won every 2.15 races entered, almost one out of two. For comparison in another field, the jockey William Hartack, one of the greatest, had his best season in 1957, when he won 27.5 percent of his races. Moss has had more than his share of mechanical breakdowns that have prevented his finishing races, but he has finished 366 of them in first, second, third, or fourth place, and that is 78.9 percent placements. Moss aside, the three greatest drivers of all time were Tazio Nuvolari, Rudolf Caracciola, and Juan Manuel Fangio. No one of them approaches his record, except that Fangio, when he retired at the age of forty-seven, had won twenty-five races of the first category, while Moss has so far won fifteen. In 1961 he started fifty events and won twenty-three of them. This year, when he had won the Grand Prix of New Zealand in a spilling, solid, tropical downpour, and had lapped every man in the field to do it, including former world champion Jack Brabham, another driver said, "I wouldn't mind, if he was a human being!"*

What kind of driving is this that Moss does, and the other fifteen or twenty men who are classified in any one year as drivers of Grand Prix stature? It is hard to understand, because it relates to ordinary driving in about the same way as mountain climbing relates to riding up a flight of stairs on an escalator. Basically, the idea is to drive so fast that the car barely maintains adhesion to the road, runs just a hair this side of a tremendous skid and loss of all control. Richard Seaman, a great British driver who was killed at Spa in Belgium in 1939, said that the sensation of driving a Grand Prix car on dry concrete produced exactly the same sensation as driving a fast sports car on a frozen lake. The fastest driver is the one who can come closest to the point at which the car's tires will break adhesion to the road and let the machine go into an uncontrolled slide. ("Uncontrolled" is the

---

*On the basis of 167 of his most important victories, the authoritative *Guinness Book of Records* [1972] calls Moss the most successful racedriver of all time.

key word. Much of the time, the driver has deliberately broken the car loose and is letting it slide.) Since this speed varies with the individual car, with the kind of tires and their state of wear, with the weather, and may change every few yards all around a 5.6-mile course, a fantastic degree of skill is required. Moss will decide in practice, for example, that the car will slide off the road in a certain corner at 97 miles an hour. He will go through the corner in the actual race at 96.5 miles an hour, over and over again, perhaps 100 times. Other good drivers will go through at 95 one lap, 96.3 the next, and so on in a slightly varying pattern. Moss will beat them. Another will try the corner at 98. He will go off the road. This exercise is mildly complicated by the fact that no race car carries a speedometer. The information it gives is not sufficiently precise. The driver judges car speed by feel and by engine speed, which is important: "4500 rpm in third gear."

That is the basic skill required, to estimate, almost instantaneously, and always correctly, that the four little oval patches of rubber that alone hold the car to the road will give up and let go of it, here at 49 miles an hour, there at 103, there at 158, and, having made the estimation, to keep the car within a fraction of those speeds, steadily and consistently.

Next, one must be able instantly to modify the entire equation in the event of rain, or sand, or oil on the track. (American oval track racing stops in the rain; Grand Prix racing does not.)

Then, one must be able to maintain speed in traffic, among cars going faster in some places and slower in others; one must be able to handle odd little emergencies, such as coming around a corner to find another car spinning in front of one; or having a wheel break off; or having the car catch on fire or lose its clutch or its brakes. (Total loss of the clutch, making clutchless gear changes imperative, or total loss of the brakes, is not supposed to stop a first-class driver. When Moss and William Lloyd won the 12-Hour Race at Sebring, Florida, in 1954, Moss drove the last four hours or so, from 8 P.M. to midnight, without the clutch and without a trace of braking power. After the race Moss asked a writer to get into the car and put the brakes on full; he then pushed the car down the track at a dogtrot with one hand. During the race he had avoided a couple of stark emergencies by sliding the car sideways.)

Moss runs in no rallies now (his sister Pat does; she is indisputably the greatest woman driver living), but he did earlier in his career. He holds the most coveted of rally trophies, the golden *Coupe des Alpes*. The average speeds imposed by point-to-point rally organizers are usually so high that the cars have to go flat out most of the time, and it is a matter of record that Moss once *made up twelve minutes going downhill in the Alps*. A competent professional observer has recorded his emotions while sitting in the back seat of a sedan Moss was driving at 90 miles an hour on black glare ice in the mountains. They were mixed.

"We're just as likely to go off the road at 30 as at 90," Moss said, "so we may as well press on."

It is my own belief that these skills in their highest orders are not available to men of normal physical equipment. Whether they are or not, Moss's physical equipment is demonstrably not normal. His reaction time is from 2.5 to 3 times faster than normal. Like Joe Louis at his peak when, he has said, he often found that he had hit a man before his eyes had had time to record the opening, Moss has often braked, accelerated, or changed course before his brain could record the reason for the action. His vision, before the Goodwood accident, was startlingly abnormal. Denis Jenkinson, one of the most reliable of observers, tells of an occasion when Moss identified a driver by name at a distance at which Jenkinson, who has normal corrected vision, could barely tell the color of the man's car. Moss's visual accommodation is fantastic: He can change focus from, say, one mile to thirty inches to one mile again virtually instantaneously. His perception approaches the extrasensory: he can reduce his time over, say, a 2.5-mile course by a second a lap exactly; he can add or subtract a fifth of a second to the time he takes to go through a corner; he can tell, running flat-out, if one tire has a pound less air than the other three; he can gauge the amount of tread left on a tire, in millimeters, at a glance.

Until Easter Sunday and Goodwood, it was usually held that no one had seen Stirling Moss make a major error of judgment. Off the road enough to bash a fender on a hay bale, yes, or run up on the curb, that sort of thing, yes, but serious, no. No one knows what happened at Goodwood. Thousands saw the accident, but no one knows what caused it, least of all Moss, who has the amnesia typical of his injury. Driving a Lotus, he was in fourth place in the ninth lap when the gearbox stuck in fourth gear. He came in, and the mechanics took five minutes to fix the gearbox. Almost any stop at all will ruin a driver's chances in today's G.P. racing, and when Moss went out again, he was three laps, or 7.2 miles, behind Graham Hill, leading. He had absolutely no chance to win, but typically ("One's a race-driver or one's not") he began to drive at the absolute limit. Last year, at the Zandvoort circuit in Holland in a similar situation, with no chance to win, he broke the lap record seven times in succession. He broke the course record at Goodwood, too, and made up an entire lap, 2.4 miles. He came up behind Graham Hill at around 120 miles an hour, out of a fast bend called Fordwater into a slower one called St. Mary's. It is not a stretch in which drivers ordinarily attempt passing. He shifted from fifth to fourth gear at the proper place, but at this point Graham Hill, looking into his mirror, was astounded to see that Moss's car was not slowing, but was coming on; observers on the ground saw him pull abreast of Hill's car and then go almost straight on sixty yards or so into an earthen bank. He did slow the car down to something around 60–80 miles an hour before he hit, but he did not spin it, which would have been logical.

The possible explanations were various: (1) He had finally made a major error in judgment and was trying to overtake Hill at a point in the circuit where it couldn't be done. There is always a first time. The great Italian driver Achille Varzi never had a real accident until the one that killed him at Bern in 1948. (2) When he lifted his foot off the accelerator after shifting from fifth to fourth, the throttle stayed down. This had happened to him in the same car the week before, but as he would be expected to do, he had managed. (3) The engine had suddenly cut out. When this happens, the car can go instantly out of control.

Laurence Pomeroy, a world authority on the racing car, was near. He considers that the behavior of the car was typical of a throttle jammed wide open, and that Moss had one second, or one second and a half at the most, in which to assay the situation, decide what to do, and do it. Most of Moss's retirements, and nearly all of his accidents, have been due to mechanical failure of the automobiles. He can't remember how many times he has had steering failure, completely lost the brakes, the clutch, the transmission, run out of oil, water, gasoline, been hit by other cars (one jumped completely over him and took the top out of his crash hat—without hurting him). He lost one race because when he hit the starter button he found the battery dead—in a car that had been two weeks in preparation for that one race! "I can't believe the number of races that I've honestly seen thrown away by something really stupid!" he says. Among the uninformed he has a reputation as a car breaker. It is totally undeserved. The same was said of Nuvolari, who asked only that a car do what it was supposed to do. The ranking race manager of all time, Alfred Neubauer of Mercedes-Benz, for whom Moss drove with great success in one of his two efforts with non-British cars—the other was with Maserati—jeers at the notion that Moss is hard on cars. So does Rob Walker, for whom Moss drives now. So does Enzo Ferrari, who knows more about automobile racing than anyone now active in the sport.

It is commonly said that had Moss been driving for Ferrari the past few years he would have been champion of the world three times at least. Instead, he drove British cars during the postwar years when they were not really in contention. When British Grand Prix cars, Lotus cars, and Coopers running Coventry-Climax engines did begin to demonstrate superiority over Continental machines, Moss drove privately owned models, always a year behind, and a few miles an hour slower, than the ones the factory teams raced.

The only legitimate professional criticism that can be made of Moss is that he has not been a good judge of race cars. He will concede the point.

He has picked the wrong cars either because he didn't know they were the wrong ones, or because they were British and privately owned. He is fiercely patriotic, in the old-fashioned way. "Everything else is a suburb of London," he will say, and he means it. He has been on Queen Elizabeth's Honors List (Order of the British Empire) and he's proud of it.

In 1951 Enzo Ferrari offered Moss a place in his team for a race at Bari in Italy. When Moss appeared for practice the first day he asked which was his car, and was told that he had no car. *Il Commendatore*—Ferrari, an arrogant and capricious man—had decided to assign it to the veteran Piero Taruffi. Moss felt that he had been grossly maltreated and that, through him, his country had been insulted. He announced, profanely, that Ferrari had seen the last of him.

For ten years Moss raced against Ferrari cars, and beat them when he could, which was often enough. But, toward the end of that time, in sports-car and touring-car *(gran turismo)* events, he began to drive Ferrari automobiles, but never for the factory, only for private owners. The reason he did was simple enough: they were best. Ferraris have been very successful in long, hard races, like the Sebring 12-Hour Race, and the 24-Hour Le Mans. They are strong, reliable, hard to break, qualities attractive to Moss, who has had so many fragile horses shot under him.

Enzo Ferrari once drove. Later, when he was a race manager, Nuvolari drove for him. He could not be indifferent to ability on Moss's soaring level. Nor could Moss withhold respect at least from a man the product of whose hands came so near perfection. The climate around them began almost imperceptibly to better, and in April of this year, just before the Goodwood crash, Moss flew to Italy to see Ferrari. Ferrari sent a coupe to Turin for him to drive the 100 miles to the factory at Modena. Although he has been known to keep waiting for two hours a customer anxious to buy $50,000 worth of cars, Ferrari came to greet Moss immediately. He showed him through the Ferrari factory, one of the industrial wonders of Italy and considerably harder to enter than the Vatican. He showed him this year's cars and he showed him, incredibly, the drawings for next year's models. He gave him lunch and told him that he was as great a driver as Nuvolari had been, and greater than Fangio. He asked Moss to come to Italy and drive Ferrari cars. People who had long known Enzo Ferrari could not believe their ears when they were told of the conversation. "I need you," this harsh, imperious, gifted man said to Moss. "Tell me what kind of car you want, and I will make it for you in six months. Put it on paper. If you drive for me, you will tell me on Monday what you did not like about the car on Sunday and by Friday it will have been changed to your taste . . . If you drive for me, I will have no team, just you and a reserve driver. With Moss, I would need no team . . ."

They were together, with George de Carvalho of *Time* magazine, for four hours.

"It must have shaken you," I said to Moss a few days later.

"It did indeed," he said. "It was fantastic. Because Ferrari *could* make a new car in six months, you know. A British company might take two years, but he really could do it; and he could, and I think he would, change anything you wanted changed from Monday to Friday, as Mercedes-Benz would . . . but, I don't know, I think it might be anticlimactic, winning the world championship on an Italian car after all these years . . ."

"He'd be world champion tomorrow if he'd sign with Ferrari," Moss's manager, Ken Gregory, said. "But he won't."

"I admit I like being the underdog, coming from behind, doing things the hard way," Moss said.

I think he may go to Ferrari, if and when he goes back to racing. And if he does I think it will be the ruggedness of the Ferrari that will draw him. No matter how resilient a man may be, no matter what reserves of spirit he has to draw on, it's hard to go to the rim of death and stay there in suffering for six weeks because a silly piece of steel broke in two.

But, arguing against joining a factory team has always been the necessity for Moss's conceding that someone else would be chief. Moss likes to run his own show. He drives Formula I, Grand Prix cars for Rob Walker, who is his friend. He drives sports cars for British Racing Partnership, which is himself, his father, and his manager. And he freelances. As the biggest drawing-card name in the business—motor races in Europe often pull 250,000 spectators—his starting-money fee is as high as $3000 paid for appearing and moving the car off the starting line, even if it dies 100 yards down the course.

Moss is as much a tycoon in his way as Ferrari. To an extent undreamed of by drivers before him, he has made racing a full-time business. His income from accessories and endorsements alone is important. One reason for the ferocity of his efforts to cure himself when he has been hurt is that he wants to get back to the mainstream of his life; but another is that when he is not in the car the major source of his income stops. He is not profligate and he is not penurious, but he likes money and he likes to live well. He dresses carefully. Five feet eight, he has the slim waist and wide shoulders that tailors like and last year he was listed one of the ten best-dressed men in Great Britain. The last time I lunched with him he was wearing a jacket made without side pockets, so that he wouldn't be tempted to carry anything that would spoil the line. His choice of food is pedestrian, but his taste in restaurants is not. His house in London will be a showplace, and he is planning a beach house in Nassau, where he has a home. He moves among interesting people. When King Hussein of Jordan visited Prime Minister

MacMillan and was asked whom he would like to have as a guest for dinner at 10 Downing Street he asked for Moss. *Il Commendatore* Ferrari cannot confer status on Stirling Moss, but he has other gifts to offer, and I think Moss may wish to think about them, once his curiosity about his Goodwood crash has been satisfied.

He is very deeply curious, and more than curious: if he believed that he crashed through his own error he would consider racing again irresponsible and he would retire. I suggested to him that when he is well enough to stand the shock he have himself put under hypnosis and let himself be taken through the accident. Of course, he may not have been able to determine, in his second and a half, what was putting the car off the circuit into the bank, but if he did know, then the information is there, buried in his subconscious under the protective amnesia, and he could recall it in hypnosis, in the view of a pioneer in this form of therapy, a world authority whom I consulted. If Moss's memory does not return in the ordinary way—and it almost certainly will not—he is going to do this. He has had an interest in hypnosis for years, as in so many other things. If the process is successful I believe Moss will recall that the symptoms preceding the accident were those of a stuck throttle. If so, he'll be glad that he can still say that he's never had an accident that wasn't caused by someone else or by something's breaking on the car, but he'll be depressed, too, that he wasn't able, in that second and a half, to do more about it. He has done more, other times and other places.

For example, in 1957 he started the Mille Miglia, the thousand mile open-road race in Italy, abandoned now. The last running was in 1957, the year Portago was killed. Moss started in a big Maserati, the last car to leave the line at Brescia for the run to Rome and back. With him was Denis Jenkinson, his navigator in the 1955 Mille Miglia, which they won at the all-time record average speed of 97.9 mph. They had barely started, they were only a few miles out, when they had what Moss calls not an accident but an incident: the break-pedal shaft broke in half. He told me about it in a letter a few days later:

". . . I was approaching the corner at approximately 130 mph in fifth gear. I estimated that the corner could be taken at about 90, therefore it was a fairly sharpish curve, to the left. I lifted my foot off the accelerator and put it on the brake, and on increasing pressure on the pedal it suddenly shot forward and broke off. More or less at the same time I was dropping the car down into fourth gear. [Usually, in this situation, the driver applies the brake with his toe and works the accelerator with his heel.] I pulled the hand brake on, which was useless; pushed the car into third gear, immediately followed by second. I remember the car fishtailing a little. At the same time as all this I attempted to put the car into a bit of a broadside to lose a little speed. I managed to get the car around the corner and then dropped it into first gear. Finally Denis and I had to jump out and stop it manually! When I tell you there were absolutely no brakes at all it is no exaggeration . . ."

That is how Moss considers an emergency should be managed. He had pulled the car down from 130 miles an hour to 2 or 3 mph, in a brutally short distance, without enough braking power to stop a child's tricycle, in a corner, on a narrow road lined on both sides with people standing shoulder to shoulder, and he hadn't so much as brushed one of them. On a closed-course circuit, with room in which to maneuver, he would probably have kicked the pedal to one side and gone on without brakes.

He and Jenkinson turned the car around by hand, so as not to let it roll into the ditch, and roared back to Brescia. Moss came out of the car in a rage, waving the broken brake pedal over his head. There was talk of sabotage, but it wasn't true. The pedal shaft had been made of a flawed piece of metal.

Moss was the more annoyed because he would like to have topped his running of the 1955 Mille Miglia for Mercedes-Benz, a classic performance, one of the greatest motor races ever run. Not only that, it was probably the best-reported motoring performance of all time, because Denis Jenkinson, Moss's codriver, is uniquely equipped as a journalist. An ex-motorcycle sidecar champion of the world, he is completely tranquil at any speed; he is a profound student of the behavior of the automobile at high speeds, knows exactly what is happening at all times, and is an excellent writer.

Moss had asked Jenkinson if he would try the race, because he believed that with someone of Jenkinson's ability and temperament it might be just possible for a non-Italian to win the race. As a rule the Mille Miglia was held to be an Italian monopoly, because no one not an Italian could hope to learn the road. (Moss was the first Englishman to win it, and the second non-Italian. Caracciola won it in 1931 for Germany.) An Italian like Piero Taruffi, who won in 1957, having driven Brescia–Rome–Brescia scores of times in his fifty-four years, *knew* which way the road went. (He was also a famous mountain driver.) Moss realized that neither he nor Jenkinson nor any other Englishman could memorize 1000 miles of Italian road—but he thought it might be possible to plot or map 1000 miles of road, if he could find a man cold enough to sit beside him, read the map, and *tell* him which way the road went after every curve.

Moss and Jenkinson ran the course in practice again and again, smashed two cars (one of them against an Italian army truck full of live bombs), and put it all down on a strip of paper seventeen feet long, rolled into a plastic tube. They then made up a set of hand signals, since the car was an open one and conversation would be out of the question. A signal might mean "right-hand bend, flat-out in fourth gear, straight afterward." Finally, Moss developed so much confidence in Jenkinson that he could unhesitatingly accept Jenkinson's signal that the road went straight after a blind brow ahead; he could hold his foot flat on the floor, go over the crest at 170 miles an hour, let the car fly through the air for fifty yards, and press on. They went into *cities* at 125–150 mph. It was what Jenkinson termed "nine-tenths and ten-tenths motoring"—absolutely flat-out, nothing left. He told of their 300SLR Mercedes-Benz passing low-flying airplanes; of Moss, going down a steep hill in third gear, shifting up to fourth, and standing on the accelerator pedal. "It took a brave man . . ." he wrote later. Jenkinson was burned by the hot gearbox; the sideways *g* forces in the turns made him vomit; he lost his glasses overboard in the slipstream, but in ten hours, seven minutes and forty-eight seconds of driving he made not one mistake and missed giving only one signal, when a full tank sloshed a pint of gasoline down his neck. Afterward he found it extremely difficult to express his admiration for Moss's mastery of one of the fastest cars in the world over 1000 miles of ordinary Italian roadway. As for Moss, he said, "I might have finished the race without Denis Jenkinson, although I doubt it, but I couldn't possibly have won without him."

Moss went to the festive victory dinner in Brescia. Then, noticing that he wasn't really tired, although he'd driven 1000 miles since morning, he got into his own car and drove to Stuttgart, Germany, and on from there to Cologne, where he took a plane to England.

In Germany, in 1961, he had another legendary triumph: he won the German Grand Prix on the Nürburgring in a car that was demonstrably twenty miles an hour slower than the favored Ferraris. The Nürburgring, in the Black Mountains, is one of the most frightening and difficult of circuits, 14.2 miles to the lap, with up- and downhill grades as high as one in five, and 174 bends and corners. It is a "driver's circuit," which is to say that the driver is more important than the car; skill counts on the Nürburgring, and the courage to put your foot flat on the floor can never be decisive, although you can't win without it. A virtuoso can do wonders on the Nürburgring. In 1935 Tazio Nuvolari beat the combined Mercedes-Benz and Auto-Union teams of Germany, held to be absolutely unconquerable except by each other, and he beat them in an aging Alfa-Romeo that was twenty miles an hour slower than they were. Moss's 1961 run on the Nürburgring, in an aging, outmoded, privately owned Lotus running against Phil Hill, champion of the world, leading the factory Ferraris, was the first to be seriously compared with Nuvolari's victory of twenty-six years before. Moss beat the Ferrari team by twenty-one seconds, which is a long time as Grand Prix racing goes today.

The car he used was the same Lotus with which he had won the 1961

Grand Prix of Monaco earlier in the season, another race held to be an imperishable example of his skill, a classic. Again, he did it on a driver's course: the Monaco G.P. is run through the streets of Monte Carlo. The knife-edge corners of marble buildings, shop fronts, trees, and the deep water of the harbor wait for the driver who makes one small mistake. This year, the trees killed one driver, and flying debris from another crash killed a track official. Only *virtuosi* can do 100 really fast laps through the streets of Monte Carlo. "To go flat-out through a bend that is surrounded everywhere by level lawn is one thing," Moss has said, "but to go flat-out through a bend that has a stone wall on one side and a precipice on the other—that's an *achievement!*"

"Last year at Monte Carlo," Moss told me, speaking in what was for him an oddly slow and sober fashion, "I was absolutely flat-out *at my own rating.* That is very unusual. One doesn't very often run a race flat-out—ten-tenths. Nine-tenths, yes. But at Monte Carlo every corner, every lap as far as I remember I was trying to drive the fastest I possibly could, to within a hairsbreadth of the limit. Driving like that is tremendously tiring, just tremendously tiring, most people have no idea what it does to one." (On a hot day cockpit temperatures may reach 150° F; a man may lose five to eight pounds; on some confined circuits, Monaco is one, crash-causing carbon monoxide poisoning from the car just ahead is a real danger.)

Three-quarters of the way through the 1961 Monte Carlo race, Phil Hill, lying second, signaled the Ferrari number two man, Richie Ginther, running behind him, to take up the attack on Moss. Ginther, a tiger, drove the race of his life and Moss beat him by three seconds and a bit. The Monte Carlo crowd, sophisticated in motor racing, was hysterical; the knowledgeable people in the pits, knowing Moss was doing something that really could not be done, were transfixed. Rob Walker, who owned the car Moss was driving, and who used to drive as an amateur, said, "The last few laps I stopped watching; I couldn't look anymore, I couldn't stand it."

This year, 1962, Moss didn't run at Monte Carlo. He watched the race on television in his room in Atkinson Morley's Hospital. There were the last few laps to run, and Phil Hill, champion of the world, was increasing his lap speeds fantastically in an attempt to catch Bruce McLaren, winning, when the BBC shut the program off in order to accommodate a serial. Moss was furious, but his primary concern, characteristically, was to get a radio going in time to hear the end of the broadcast. He has a curiously equable temperament for one so volatile. Racedriving sometimes makes short tempers. I have seen wrenches thrown, and the French driver Jean Behra, killed at Avus in 1959, once punched a Ferrari team manager, but Moss has never gone past the gesture of fist-waving, which is merely a convention, at a driver who balks his passing. A good boxer and beginning judo player (green belt), he hasn't had a fight since he was a boy in school. He is never rude and rarely cuttingly sarcastic, but he will occasionally defend himself with a short answer.

Bone-deep toughness and a curious tendency to return to dead-center egotism have marked every man and woman I've ever known who had accomplished much, or who had come anywhere near the aura of greatness, whether statesman, artist, writer, film producer, or whatever. Moss is of this pattern, as he must be, and differs from the norm only in demonstrating less overt ego and more humility than any other great accomplisher I've known. I remember saying to a bullfighter, years ago, before I knew better, "You are the most completely egotistical bastard I've ever met." He said, "You don't understand. When I go in there, if I don't really and truly believe I am the best in the world, I had better not go in at all." That is part of it, that and the obsession. Everyone who accomplishes greatly is obsessed with one purpose, nearly blind to all else; he can only with difficulty tear his mind away from the one thing that is important to him to consider lesser matters —and everything except his central purpose in life is a lesser matter. In the light of the obsession I know he has to live with, I am inclined to marvel at Moss's gaiety every time I see him. I know very well he forces it, but still, it's there.

I amuse myself, when I have an appointment with him, by being punctual. He is unfailingly punctual, and he is the only person I know who really appreciates punctuality. Just before Easter I had an appointment with him for four o'clock one afternoon. I have an accurate watch, and I opened the door of his office within five seconds, plus or minus, of the hour. He looked at his own watch. "God, that's wonderful!" he said. "You're spot-on time!" He was as pleased as if I'd brought him a present. He was ready to go, but an emergency had come up, he had to make one phone call. He had to hire a carpenter, the crew working on his new house was a man short. The house is in Shepherd Street in London's West End, a building he had gutted and redone to his own design. He has some ability as a designer. There are offices on the ground floor, living quarters on the next three: a garden, a penthouse, sunken bath with bedside controls, television set in the ceiling of the master bedroom, closed-circuit TV to the front door. He was living there in a jungle of electric conduit, wet plaster, and sawdust. In a two-car garage on the ground floor next to the office there was a yellow Lotus Elite and we got into it. I asked him how he liked it.

"There's nothing like it," he said. "There is no other motorcar, this side of a race car, that handles like an Elite. Coming back from Snetterton the other day I *averaged* 60 without ever going over 70, and I think that's remarkable. It's the best thing of its kind in the world."

We ran out into the traffic of Park Lane. He drove fast, but not conspicuously or spectacularly so; there was nothing remarkable about his driving except the machinelike precision with which he shifted gears.

A couple of girls in a Mini-Minor ran up beside us and looked in and smiled. "Crumpet to port," I said. "I see," he said. We smiled at them. "The one driving is nice," Moss said. He let them pass and in the next block passed them. If he had stopped, they would have pulled up behind him. Moss's stunning effect on many women demonstrates no technique, but derives from his brute energy, his profound interest in what goes on around him, and his civility. He is essentially kind. Last year he saw on television a man who was paralyzed and who needed, for business, a small truck. Moss bought one, had it fitted with hand controls, and delivered—in the strictest secrecy. Nothing was known of it until the story leaked following the Goodwood accident. Also after the accident two brief letters from spectators were printed in a motoring magazine, remarking that before the race began, a time when most drivers are apt to be edgy, Moss had found time to take a man in a wheelchair on a thirty-minute tour of the paddock area to show him the cars; and had taken someone else, similarly immobile, on a complete tour of the circuit in a car, pointing out the various corners so that the announcer's comments would be more graphic to him. He then found the man a good vantage point from which to watch the race, and took him to it. In talking about him women insistently remark about his force, his impact, and his kindness, which they usually cite as thoughtfulness— and those of them who know they are listed in a series of little black books, with coded reminders, are not much the less moved. Oddly, though he may complain that the day is ruined if he comes into London airport at midnight and doesn't have a date waiting, Moss is psychologically out of phase with the Don Juan role. He was perfectly faithful to his wife during his marriage and indeed for some time afterward. Fidelity to one woman would be his free choice, but it was suggested to him that it's possible to forget one woman with many. I don't know if, another time, he'd have stopped and let the two girls in the Mini-Minor stop behind him, but he has driven alongside a girl before this and made a date without much more than slowing down enough to be heard. At any rate we turned off abruptly and lost them.

We went into the little ground-floor apartment in Earl's Court Road. I unlimbered a tape recorder, plugged it in, and tested it carefully. There was an electric fire in the grate. It was cold outside; a heavy, wet wind leaned on the side of the building and shook it.

Unlike some drivers, for Moss the automobile has no compelling fascination. He won't say so, but obviously automobiles bore him. He is like a painter asked about brushes. One tool is much like another.

"It's odd, how many commonly held ideas are all wrong," he said. "The notion that you need a lot of raw courage to race, for instance. Actually I don't think courage is any advantage at all except in certain special circumstances. It's a disadvantage. If a driver has too much courage it's difficult for him to discover his limitations until perhaps it's too late. We've both known people who had more courage than judgment and they are no longer with us.

"I would say courage comes into the equation, oh, let's say you're driving a car of a team and a wheel falls off a teammate's car and you see it at the side of the road and you have to keep going, in a sister car, identical. That takes a certain amount of courage.

"It took courage as far as I was concerned to do the record attempt with the MG on the salt flats in Utah [where he set five world records] mainly because they buttoned me into the thing and I knew it took three miles to stop it and there wasn't a hope in hell of getting out of it if it caught fire. That I didn't like. I had quite a long time to think about it, while the car was building up to 100, 150, 200, 250 miles an hour, and the whole situation was made worse by the fact that when you've gone through the measured mile you cut the ignition and put your foot flat down on the accelerator to suck any flames through the engine and out the pipe and when you did that you got a smell of fuel, of fumes throughout the car . . . you wouldn't get out because, to start with, the cockpit lid came down from the front, you knew wind pressure would hold it down even if you could undo it; there was a release inside, but if the thing went on fire you'd be all thumbs. That sort of thing takes a certain amount of courage.

"My greatest recollection of fear? There were two times, one was at Monza [in Italy in 1958] when the steering sheared on the big Maser, the wheel just came loose in my hands; I had time to think about it, but there was nothing I could do. I stood on the brakes, which were nothing, they were sports-car brakes, you couldn't even feel them. The car was doing 160 miles an hour; I thought maybe I could steer it by holding the bare steering shaft between my feet, which was silly of course; I knew I just had to sit and wait and I knew damned well I had to be killed. I was sure we were going over the top of the banking and I didn't think the retaining wall would hold the car and of course it didn't; I ripped steel posts out of the concrete for more than fifty yards. That Maserati slid for a quarter of a mile, blowing its tires, buckling the wheels . . . when it stopped, and still right side up, I was surprised to find myself alive, I can tell you that.

"The other time was when a wheel came off the Lotus at Spa [in Belgium in 1960]. I was doing about 140 when the car suddenly went into a very violent oversteer condition; first I thought I had hit oil, then I saw the wheel roll past me. I knew I was going to crash, I jumped on the brakes and tried to spin the car around. It's best to hit going backward, it distributes the shock more evenly over your body. I took about 50 miles an hour off it before I hit. I was thrown free, which I much prefer to staying in the car. I was lying on the side of the road and I couldn't see and I couldn't breathe, and that frightened me. I was in great pain around my chest and I was afraid I had broken ribs and that they would puncture my heart or my lungs, which was how Bobby Baird died. I was more afraid of that happening than I had been when I knew I was going to hit the bank at around 100 miles an hour."

The Spa incident made minor medical history. Moss had two broken legs, a broken nose, a broken ankle, three broken ribs, and three broken vertebrae. But he had normal pulse and normal blood pressure! Belgian doctors told him he would be in a plaster body cast for six months. He insisted on being flown to London, where a specialist he trusted told him that he could heal easily and slowly in plaster or painfully and quickly without it. He elected the quick, hard way in St. Thomas' Hospital in London. Three weeks after the accident I telephoned him from New York.

"How are you really?" I said. "I hear all kinds of things."

"I'm in good shape," he said. "I'm going bike riding tomorrow."

"You mean on a stationary bicycle?"

"No, I mean a real bike."

"You're out of your mind. What happens if you fall off?"

"I don't intend to fall off."

Punch ran a Russell Brockbank cartoon showing Moss careening across a Thames bridge in a hospital bed with an engine on it, an ambulance in mad pursuit. Five weeks after the accident he went to the Silverstone circuit to see if the crash had taken anything from him. He broke the course record. Two weeks after that he won the Swedish Grand Prix and set a new record. Eight weeks after the accident he ran in the Portuguese Grand Prix. His car stalled and officials objected to his pushing it downhill to start it. "I can't very well push it *up*hill," he told them, "after all, dammit, both my legs are broken."

"I remember feeling some fear in Portugal that time. I was driving the same car I'd crashed at Spa and that circuit is tree-lined and I remember going through a really fast corner, 130 miles an hour or something like that, and the idea flashing through my mind, what would happen if a wheel came off *here?* All one can really do is put it out of one's mind. One's just got to conquer that. It isn't courage, it's just a case of overcoming whatever it is that worries you.

"People think courage is required for things that don't need it at all. For example, people say to me how do you dare take your hand off the wheel to wave to someone in a corner, maybe they've heard me on the subject of one-hand driving on the road, which I think is so stupid. What they don't know is that once a car is presented to a corner, all things being equal, that is, avoiding oil on the track or something funny happening, that car has a sort of line of destiny, a line on which the damned thing is going to go no matter what; once a car is set up for a corner, it should hold its line. I remember doing a demonstration in a Healey, in about a 90-mph wide right-hand sweep, where I started on the left, set the car up, and then told the student to watch the steering wheel, and I would go from the very left verge, clip within a couple of inches of the apex, and go out to the exit to the very verge within say three or four inches, without moving the steering wheel a fraction of an inch over, say, 250 yards. Of course you do compromise with the throttle, but I think once you've got it set up you should be able to go to nine-tenths motoring anyway. It's only when you're right on the ragged edge, at ten-tenths, that you do need quite a lot of steering to keep the thing exactly in balance, but one doesn't go beyond nine-tenths all that frequently. And so, once you've got the thing set you can let go with one hand or the other, it doesn't make much difference."

A racing car, at racing speeds, spends quite a lot of time going sideways, "drifting" with all four wheels sliding equally. This is generally held to be the fastest way through a bend, although there is some indication that modern suspension techniques are altering the picture. When the car is going fast enough, and it must be going very fast, the driver will provoke a drift by turning the steering wheel sharply and abruptly—but always smoothly—and by hitting the brakes hard, once. The car's adhesion to the road is broken, and it is thereafter steered with the gas pedal, more gas increasing the angle of drift, or slide, nose pointing to the inside of the bend, and less gas decreasing it. Going through a series of S-bends very fast, a driver can be extremely busy with the steering wheel, and a layman sitting beside him would be quite unable to tell what he was doing. He would be altering not so much the *direction* of the car in the sense of steering the front of it, as altering the whole attitude of the car relative to the road, pointing it now this way and now that way in various sliding positions, breaking and restoring adhesion of the front wheels separately, the rear wheels or all four together. Going through a long S-bend at, say, 125 miles an hour, a driver of Moss's caliber may change the whole direction the car is pointing on the road as many as six times. Maintenance of inch-by-inch control of a car doing perhaps 150 miles an hour partially forward and partially sideways is the essence of the difference between racedriving and ordinary driving. It is a difficult skill to acquire, since it can't be learned with the car going at a safe slow speed. Also the sudden appearance of a patch of oil, sand or water can fatally upset the requisite balance.

At the Sebring circuit in Florida, top speeds can get to 150 or so, but there is one acute-angle corner that can't be taken at much over 30. The French journalist Bernard Cahier was standing beside this bend drinking a Coca-Cola when Moss came by and gestured that he wanted one, too. Cahier handed it to him next time he came around and got the empty bottle back the following lap. A couple of bystanders with stopwatches made the curious observation that Moss was no slower in the lap during which he drank the Coke than in the one before or the one after it.

"It's those two extra arms he puts on when he gets into his car," someone said. Another time at Sebring, banging a sedan through two right-angle corners flat-out, he was seen to wave to a friend and almost simultaneously crawl over the seat back to slam a loose rear door.

At a teaching session Moss was demonstrating spins to a succession of students. A photographer who knew him focused on the spot he had stopped the first time and made a dozen more pictures without moving. Moss would come screaming down the track, throw the car sideways, spin it like a top, and put it almost into the tire marks it had left the time before. Said another photographer: "I've checked. The man doesn't cast a shadow."

Moss likes to teach novice drivers and does it well. He learned a great deal from Juan Manuel Fangio when they both drove for Mercedes-Benz, and apparently feels he should pass on what he can. When Innes Ireland, now an internationally ranked driver, was failing to qualify for the Grand Prix of Monaco, Moss told him, "Come around behind me. Just get on my tail and stay there." Moss shrewdly judged the maximum pace Ireland could sustain, Ireland followed his line, his attack in every corner, and qualified. Moss is not wildly popular with other drivers perhaps largely because he is so obsessively concerned with the job, but their respect for him is unlimited: "He never stops trying." "He never has an off day." "He is absolutely dedicated." "Some people can drive only Grand Prix cars well, or sports cars, or something else, but Moss can drive anything that has four wheels and a place to sit." No one has ever accused him of anything remotely approaching dirty tactics, although, like all "real" professionals, he knows how much of the road is his, and he will fight you for it. If other drivers find it hard to accept the fact that he earns perhaps ten times the average top-line driver's salary, they do not say so. There are drivers running today who can give Moss a very hard time, but there are many others who can be hanging on the ragged edge of disaster, going just as fast as a stout heart will allow, when Moss runs up from behind, immaculate in white, utterly relaxed, and blasts on by with the invariable wave of the hand in thanks for moving over, and perhaps at the same time a big smile for a friend beside the road . . . "He makes it look as if you're not *trying*," one said. "That's got to bug you, when you think you're flat-out."

At Silverstone in 1960 Moss hit an oil slick at 140 miles an hour. The car went into an uncontrolled spin. It had spun six times when the crowd heard the blip of the engine as Moss dropped down one gear, and on the seventh spin, as the car came around with its nose pointing the right way, he put his foot down and screamed away, waving to acknowledge the frantic hand-clapping he could see if not hear. One had to go back to 1939, and Nuvolari steering across a pool of oil through a gaggle of wrecked cars at Donington to find a *tour de force* with which to compare it.

One measure of Moss's virtuosity is his stated preference for a wet course. Many drivers will concede a sinking sensation when they know they will have to drive in the rain; Moss drives as fast in pouring rain as in sunshine, or tries to, and since most others will not, he's more likely to win. He is as fast in the wet as Caracciola was, and Caracciola's eyes were so peculiarly constructed that he could drive at top speed in a pouring rain without goggles, and in fact preferred to. In addition to being physically insensitive, oculists said, Caracciola's eyes admitted abnormal amounts of light. So do Moss's obviously.

Nuvolari is said to have contributed to racing the idea of the controlled four-wheel drift; Moss brought to it a radical concept of braking. It has from the beginning been held basic to the driving of any automobile that the brakes should never be applied in a corner. Brake before the corner, accelerate coming out of it, is holy writ. Braking while actually in the corner was supposed to bring automatic disaster—and it did often seem to. Moss upset all that. He applies brakes when the car is in the actual corner, turning, and then instantly bangs on full acceleration, so that the car is always under either heavy braking or severe acceleration, and spends no time merely coasting. The difference can amount to useful fractions of seconds, and in the frantic world of Grand Prix racing, a tenth of a second in each of ten corners can make the difference between winning desperately or winning almost tranquilly.

Moss can make an impression of serenity and tranquillity, although he has probably not known a moment's tranquillity in his life, but sooner or later the extra nerve endings will show through, and the sandpapering on them: he was telling me how he had momentarily "lost" the car during the last New Zealand Grand Prix.

"A driver senses the loss of the vehicle before it becomes apparent to anyone else, through the steering wheel. It's a funny thing, it's practically a noise. When you lose the back end of a car you just feel it go. When you lose the front end you feel a "growl" through the steering wheel. You hear a sort of rumble. There *can't* be any sound, you'd never hear any sound, you're wearing earplugs and the engine is screaming away just behind your head, but I can assure you that you nearly hear this sensation, this growling rumbling sound as the thing is losing adhesion. When you lose the whole bloody vehicle you don't get either of these sensations, I suppose the two together just cancel each other out, you just know the car is moving sideways more than it should be at that moment; say it's moving eight feet sideways per eighty feet forward, and that may be exactly what you want, but if the rate rises to nine feet sideways per eighty feet forward you know somewhere inside you that this is not right, and if you've worked out the equation quickly enough, you know there's not going to be enough road . . . I wish I could explain that phenomenon of the noise better. I cannot."

The complexity of Grand Prix driving is so great, one marvels that so many survive it. For example, no Grand Prix car has fewer than four gears; many have five. If he is to stay in contention, a driver must keep the car under power as much of the time as he can, therefore he makes gearshifts with stunning speed, as nearly instantaneously as he can. If he cannot correct this situation within half a second or so the car may go out of control and off the road. He may shift gears 500 times in the course of a race. He has only to miss once, he has only to lose the braking effect of one downward shift going into a corner, to kill himself. Race cars used to be strong and substantial, a factor that was sometimes of use to a driver in a crash. The Bugatti of the 1930s had a chassis frame that was a girder seven inches deep at one point. Today's G.P. cars weigh less than 1000 pounds, and the most advanced design, one that will surely be widely copied, has no chassis or frame of any kind: it is not inaccurate to describe it as three long, very stiff gasoline tanks with an engine bolted to one end, steering gear bolted to the other end, and a reclining seat in the middle. It is conceded that damage to this car in any kind of crash is likely to be substantial—but it's forty or fifty pounds lighter than competing models, and that's important. Seeing thirty gallons of gasoline poured into the thing, a sober citizen might not wish even to sit in it with the engine running. Its driver will be expected to work it up to 180 miles an hour on some courses, and to run it within six inches of another car if that is necessary. If he declines, he will not be asked a second time. Many are waiting for his seat. But he won't decline. If he can get 185 out of it, he will.

E molto difficile . . .

"You see people who go in over their heads too early and they're not with us anymore. Or you see others do it, like John Surtees, but he has so much sensitivity and ability and sheer feeling for a vehicle that he gets away with it; you have a feeling that even if he loses it he'll get the thing straight before he hits what he's going to hit and he'll hit it with the right end of the car and all that. And others you just know if they can hit in the wrong way they'll bloody well hit in the wrong way and the wrong place. You see drivers who have tremendous accidents and sometimes they're not as bad drivers as you think; and others like poor Pete Collins [killed at the Nürburgring in 1958] have a slight one and he's not with us anymore—and Pete didn't really drive over his head.

"Someone whose judgment I respect told me that he believes that the accidents happen before the man gets into the car. In many cases I'm inclined to agree with him. Attitude of mind and mental condition and *knowing* when you're dropping off in effectiveness . . . physical fatigue comes on slowly, slowly, it could be measured with a micrometer, you're giving energy gradually but continually, and then quite suddenly you're into your reserve, you're a fifth-second slow in reacting to something, and perhaps that's when you leave us . . .

"I don't know what makes one go on. People often ask, do you think of giving up racing when someone's killed, a close friend perhaps? Yes, surely. You must think, there but for the grace of God . . . but you hope, of course, that you have a little more experience or a little more ability or a little more luck or a little more something and so it's not going to happen to you. If I were killed racing I wouldn't want any driver to give up racing or even pull out of the race it happened in . . . it's not going to do me any good. [Talking to Walter Cronkite of CBS, Moss said, "I never say to anybody, 'See you next week.' If they say it, I say, 'Well, I hope so.' "] I understand racing. I know it may happen, and if I knew any way to lessen the chance I would do it—as I think I do now. I race as safely as I know how—with the possible exception that I drive cars that are more likely to fail than others, they are less robust, and in that I'm foolish, and I know it. But other considerations enter there—my wish to drive nonfactory cars, and British cars, and so on . . .

"But there's not much point in looking into the past. I won't do it. I will not allow myself to live in the past, not the slightest bit. The only way I know what I did yesterday is to look it up in my diary. I keep a full diary, and I do it every night no matter what. And do you know, sometimes I find it difficult to remember, at night, what I've done that day, never mind yesterday. I upset my friends. I said to David Haynes, you must see this terrific film and he said, look, old boy, we saw it together last Thursday. I said to him, by God next year you must come with me to South Africa and he said, you know, we got back only a week ago . . . he understands, it's just that there's so much going on today and tomorrow and next week, and I *must* think that way, because there are so many heartbreaks for me in racing that if I worried about yesterday . . . as it is now I can lose a race, I can lose the world championship on Sunday and I can be out enjoying myself on Monday, and I *mean* enjoying myself. Nothing is sillier than this notion that racing drivers have a death wish. Most of them enjoy life infinitely more than the average man, and it's nothing to do with eat, drink, and be merry, for tomorrow we die, either. I've been accused of living a

27

twenty-nine-hour day and I plead guilty, with pleasure. I live for the day. If I won the world championship on Sunday, Sunday night I'd be swinging but Monday morning I'd be back in the office.

"You could say it's an odd life and I'd agree, but it's like a story I remember your telling me in a letter a long time ago, about the man who was told the roulette game was crooked, and he said, yes, I know, but it's the only game in town.

"I think racing destroyed my marriage, but I'm not really sure, sometimes I think I don't know what did do it. I live in a suitcase and an office and at race meetings, and that's hard for a woman to accept. Secondly, I have no privacy. I've had reporters phone me at three in the morning many times, I don't know how they get the number so easily. I've been called on the radio at 4 A.M. in the Australian bush. I've been called at 6 A.M. in Bangkok, from London, to be asked one quite silly question—and, by the way, that means going to the central post office to answer, you don't just pick up the phone on Bangkok. Then, a woman doesn't like being put on exhibition every time she goes out for a drink or to the theater. And the strain of racing is terrible for those who *watch*. It makes me very nervous to watch my sister Pat race, I'm far more nervous watching her race than I could ever be before a race myself. A driver's wife goes through all that, again and again . . . and there is the endless press of things that must be done, nagging little details. Of course you can avoid much of that, if you'll compromise. I think that if a driver is prepared to be number two, is willing to be number two, then I think the life is easy. But if you're not prepared to be number two . . . then it's hard. Katie was everything to me. I was shattered when we parted. I very nearly came unstuck."

Moss met Katie Molson, an extremely wealthy Canadian girl, pretty, gentle, brown-haired, in 1953 and again in 1956. They were married in 1957 and parted in 1959. Moss thought of Katie as very much a woman, a lady, and a tomboy as well. She was in Nassau when the marriage collapsed. Moss did not return to their apartment in London; he said he could not go through the door again, and he never has. He insisted that the failure of the marriage was his fault, must be his fault. His friends told him that it was not his fault, and not Katie Moss's fault, and not any one person's fault, but a complex of events and circumstances. I don't know if he has come to believe it. He missed no races, though.

"In the end, finally, one has one's work. The major satisfaction in my life is racing, obviously, and I enjoy it even when I'm frustrated: sometimes I think maybe *most* when I'm frustrated, I think, God, I can't damned well win, I've lost five laps in the pit, it's impossible to win now, mathematically impossible, but then I begin to think, well, my God, even if I can't win I'm going to damned well go, and then I can enjoy really fast motoring, for the exhilaration of it and because I'm trying to prove something to myself; they may have five laps' lead on me, but I'm going to take one back, you know; and the lap record is always there to be broken, and you can say to yourself, let's really get going, let's try to drive the perfect lap, all the way around and not one mistake, not one mile an hour slow or 100 revs down, and this to me is an interesting thing. Often I turn to myself and say, well, let's try to turn one perfect lap. Invariably something, somewhere, isn't just quite right, and you say, well, that's finished, now let's try another, try again. I've never made a perfect lap, of course, although people have said I have.

"You go through a corner absolutely flat-out, right on the ragged edge, but absolutely in control, on your own line to an inch, on top of everything, and the exhilaration, the thrill is tremendous; you say to yourself, all right, you bastards, top that one, match it, even, and you feel like a painter who has just put the last brushstroke on the *Mona Lisa* or something, after years of trying . . . it's rewarding. And you must grant that it's not monotonous. No art can be monotonous, and I believe that driving, as practiced by some very few people in the world, is an art form, and is related to ballet. It is all discipline, rhythm, movement. It is like skiing, too, very much like skiing . . . the same but never the same, never monotonous . . .

"Monotony in life would drive me mad in no time at all. I can't bear inactivity; I get disheartened sometimes when I stop moving. If you turned to me right now and said, we've finished, you're to go home and sit down and think for a while, I wouldn't dream of doing it. I would find that very bad. I fill every moment. When you leave me here Ken Gregory and some people are coming for a meeting. After that I'm going out to dinner. Then I'm going dancing. [An earnest exponent of the Twist, Moss has been known to dance from early evening until dawn—nonstop.] I don't know how long I'll stay out, but one thing I'm sure of, when I go to bed tonight I hope to be very tired, because I don't want to think, I don't *like* thinking, unless it's about a specific, solvable problem. As far as life is concerned, and what life is going to offer me, I find it terribly depressing. When I look at the future I find it terribly depressing."

He spoke so vehemently that I was surprised. "Do you really?" I said.

"Yes, terribly, because I can't see in the ultimate, what there can be of happiness. I know that to some people achievement in business, in work, is happiness. To me it's not, it's a fulfillment, but not necessarily happiness. It's a pleasure, but pleasure isn't happiness. My idea of happiness seems utopian to me and it may seem absurd to you; it is to be married, and have two or three children, and a house in the country if you like, and to go away for two weeks on holiday—and, most of all, most importantly, to be able to *accept* that life as happiness. Do you understand? To be able to *accept* it, that's the whole heart of the matter. I cannot at the moment. I'm hoping that with maturity I will be able to, or that at least some form of compromise with it will be possible. I'm not unhappy. I'm in a state of suspended animation, in a transition period which is tolerable, and which keeps me from being depressed . . . I dance, I run about, I do a bit of designing and this and that, it's activity, I keep my finger in the dike, it's not going to patch the bloody thing but at least it's stopping the water pouring in. I'm waiting for maturity to come to me, and I'm doing what I can to bring it. I don't know if one ever feels happiness, or if contentment is the maximum we can hope for. As I said, I'm not *un*happy. If I were to be killed tomorrow I wouldn't feel that thirty-two of my thirty-two years had been unhappy . . ."

We talked, and the thin brown tape silently took it down. Dusk sifted out of a wet London sky. I had told Moss I'd need three hours, and at five minutes of seven the tape ran out. He made me a drink, Scotch. He couldn't find a bottle opener for the orange squash he wanted and I fiddled the top off with my knife. We talked about some other people for a few minutes. He phoned for a taxi. I told the driver to go to Charing Cross. As I opened the cab door I looked back. Moss was standing in the middle of the little room, looking through the window. I waved to him. He waved, and moved across the room. He looked grim, and, somehow, weirdly, sheathed all in gray, or white. I was suddenly and inexplicably immersed in a crushing sadness and in pity for him. (As a matter of curiosity I should record that as the taxi moved away I fell into the most profound depression; I was hopelessly in tears before we were halfway to Charing Cross station. Three days later, on Easter Monday, I was in Belgium. Before breakfast I told my wife I was going out to get a newspaper. "I want to find out what happened to Stirling," I said. "Why do you put it *that* way?" she said. I had no idea until I saw the headlines, the notion that he was going to be hurt had never consciously entered my mind. The incident was one of three incontrovertibly valid psychic experiences I have had, and it is the only one involving prescience, although I use the term loosely since I was obviously only subconsciously aware of an impending happening. The other two were also inexplicable and overwhelming depressions involving people, one a child, one a woman, to whom I was close. They were timed, as nearly as I could afterward determine, to the second with events occurring hundreds of miles distant.)

I didn't see Moss again until early June, when I went to Atkinson Morley's Hospital. I stayed for a couple of hours. Judy Carne did a scalding imitation of a Hollywood manicurist phoning a boyfriend. I told the old story about Beatrice Lillie, Lady Peel, and the butcher's wife. Moss explained how he had gone about convincing a nurse that a urinal should be called something else. The Grundig man came, tacking shyly into the room against a gale of laughter. I left.

"Come back soon," Moss said. "I'm not going to hang about here forever."

A year after the Goodwood accident, Moss decided that the time had come to try himself, to decide, on the basis of hard fact and his own judgement, whether he could go on with his career, or not. He was in good physical condition, he moved easily and quickly, and only those who had known him well for a long time saw that he limped slightly. The left side of his face showed the plain traces of radical plastic surgery. On the road, he drove as well as he had ever done, but he knew how little that meant, in terms of the métier. To test himself truly, it would be best, he thought, to go back to Goodwood. He asked Ken Gregory to arrange, in absolute secrecy, for the use of the circuit for one day. And on that day . . .

At noon on the First of May, Moss left London for Goodwood, where Ken Gregory and Tony Robinson were waiting for him with a Lotus 27. He drove the fifty-odd miles in a Mini-Cooper, two friends with him, and he went flat-out the whole way, constantly remarking the behavior of the car under the various stresses he put on it, obviously seeing the trip as a mild warm-up for what lay ahead of him. It had rained all morning, but the circuit was drying when Moss came to it, drying in some places, deeply puddled in others. The loudspeakers were silent, but there must have been armies there for him; the mild May air must have rung with their shouts and with the howl of engines ripping across the flat land under the pale lemon-colored sun. The first significant British race meeting after the war had been at Goodwood, in 1948, and Moss had won the 500-cc event, in his first Cooper. He was nineteen then. How many times he'd run at Goodwood since, how many nights at the Fleece Inn, he couldn't begin to remember.

He dropped himself into the car. It had occurred to him that, coming out of Fordwater into St. Mary's for the first time, running fast, some vagrant memory, the thin wedge of a clue might come to him, something that would explain the accident. No. It was just a bit of wet road. He felt nothing.

He was alone on the course. The little knot of people who had known of his plan—Gregory, the mechanics, a private photographer, three friends —could hear the engine scream across the circuit; they could follow the car by noting the shift points. Back in sight, he hit a pool of water, lost the car, recovered it quickly—but not as quickly as he once would have done.

He lapped the circuit for half-an-hour and more, running fast but, at his own rating, at only around eight-tenths. At the quickest, he said afterward, he was three seconds over what he would consider competitive time.

He had suspected what he would find, and he found it: "I had to think," he said. "I had to give orders to myself: here I'll brake, here I must change down, and so on . . . and the other thing, I used to look at the rev counter without taking my eyes off the road; not only that, I could see the rev

counter *and* the road *and* a friend waving to me, all at the same time
. . . I've lost that, that's gone."

He drove back to London. Ken Gregory called the press, the bulletin
went on the wires: "I've decided to retire. I will not drive again." It was
fifteen years, almost to the day, from the date on which Stirling Moss had
run his Cooper up Prescott, in the Bugatti Owners Club event which had
been his first official competition.

—1962/1963

Change
of
Plan

Pietro Lonetti sat in his car, a little man, very erect,
well back from the wheel. He looked confident and
happy, and so he was. In about one hour and a half
he intended to kill himself. The decision had calmed
him; it had put an end to the torments of the five years
that lay leaden behind him; it had restored the lilting
serenity, the certainty that all was for the happy,
happy best, that he had, as a younger man, worn like
a feather in his hair. Pietro Lonetti felt very well
indeed.

He looked around. Most of these people were new
to him. Lots of them had still been driving sports cars
when the war started. He knew Pierre Marten, in the
Ferrari, an old competitor. He knew Lyon, of course,
with his bull neck and wrestlers' arms, and Ignace
Manelli. Manelli had one of the new Alfa-Romeos.
But so many of the others were young and new. The
boy next to Lonetti, for instance, in the blue Talbot.
Maurice Lascelle, called "Popo." He had been a great
hero in the French Resistance. He drove very hard,
but with no style. The Englishman, Danton, in an old
E.R.A. That pink skin, Lonetti thought, that bland
blue eye. A thin old man of about twenty-nine sum-

mers. He looks a bit like Dick Seaman, but Seaman is a dozen years dead, burned in a Mercedes-Benz at Spa. Varzi, too, dead in a skid in the rain. Rosemeyer long dead, Christian Kautz dead, Ted Horn dead, Hepburn dead, Lonetti dead . . . the dour little man grinned to himself. Not yet, he said, not quite yet. Lonetti will die when he wants to. And not in bed, no matter what the damned doctors say. And after he has won this one. And in no accident.

The sixty-second gun boomed out and one engine fired, coughed, and settled down to an undulating roar as the driver gunned it up and down; another started, then two, three, another, two more, until the hot July air was pulsing with the sound of thirty open exhausts.

Lonetti hunched his shoulders a bit and stared at the fat man who was the starter. The fat man held the bright flag over his head as he counted off the seconds on his stop watch. He will be late, Lonetti thought. He loves himself and what he is doing and he will do it for as long as he can. In thirty years of watching starters, Lonetti had learned to read their little minds, he was sure of that. This one would hold the flag for a bit too long, and before he dropped it, he would lift it a bit, to get a wider, more spectacular swing. Lonetti would go on the lift and make a fifth of a second for himself.

He ran the engine up. The fat starter's shoulders bulged, the flag imperceptibly lifted and started down. Lonetti let in the clutch, bore down on the gas, and got away in a rush. He was a clear half a length ahead of the blue Talbot. It was enough. He grabbed the Maserati's crooked gearshift, banged it into second, and wound the engine up tight, snatched third and ran it up to 7000, slid through the first corner with the ease of a boy pulling a toy around the floor on a string, and settled down into the first straight, three miles long. He stood on the throttle and locked his knee. There was 175 mph in the car under him and Lonetti wanted all of it.

It was a good French road, string-straight, and lined with poplars that had watched two wars. The trees slid past in a smooth and solid wall and the road rushed hysterically under the bellowing Maserati like something in a nightmare. Lonetti knew every pebble in the road. He had carted plenty of silverware, plenty of francs, away from this circuit before the war. They had called the race something else, in those days. Now it was the Grand Prix Robert Benoist. Benoist, another hero of the Resistance, like Lascelle. He had driven in Bugattis before the war. The Germans killed him. Lonetti remembered him well, a big, pleasant man. He would win Benoist's race now, and a few of them would mutter about it: "Why did it have to be Lonetti?" Lonetti shrugged. He would not be around to hear them. He shot a quick look into the left-hand mirror. The Talbot was fifty yards behind him, the Alfa hard on its tail. Lonetti grinned. "Driving Lessons Given Here," he said to himself. A right-angle turn, one of the nasty ones, loomed ahead. Lonetti braked at the last possible tenth of a second, yards past the normal point. The engine screamed as he kicked it into third. He put the right wheel six inches from the grass and kept it there, to a hair, as the car cornered in an insanely fast four-wheel slide. He flicked it straight and roared at the hill ahead. He had doubled his lead on Lascelle and he screamed with laughter and pounded on the side of the car. They'll write about that one all right, he thought.

". . . at the second corner, Lonetti clearly demonstrated that his fifty-first winter had taken nothing from his legendary skill. He laid the elderly Maserati into the bend at an incredible rate of knots, causing grief to the novice Lascelle, who foolishly imitated him and lost vast yardage in the subsequent skid. *Il Maestro* slid the corner in his patented position and was obviously looking at 8000 rpm as he urged his ancient mount up the hill, steering with one hand and beating happily on red tin with the other . . ."

The red car left the ground at the top of the hill and sailed like a bird for fifty feet. It came down square and straight and Lonetti grabbed fourth gear and rocketed away. He felt wild exhilaration and he screamed again.

". . . at the twentieth lap, Lonetti had increased his lead to twenty-two seconds, but the little man was obviously in distress. He was seen to be coughing continuously, and blood began to show on his sleeve as he drew it across his mouth. He held the comparatively slow Maserati in front by dint of black wizardry and a refusal to entertain any regard whatsoever for the welfare of the machinery. Manelli and Lascelle, in faster vehicles, were able only to stay in sight and pray earnestly that the Maserati would disintegrate under the punishment . . ."

The brass-bright July sun was hot enough, but the shadeless grass beside the road looked cool to Pietro Lonetti, because the car was a moving furnace. There never was a cool one, Lonetti thought, they all roast you to death. Or gas you. The noxious smell of burning gasoline and half-burnt oil was sweet to him; it opened the door of his memory on all the good and happy things that had ever come his way; it meant more than the remembrance of violets in the hair of one's first girl, or the longed-for smoke of boyhood's chimney, or the crystal scent of rain in autumn. The smell was the warp and woof of his life, but the stuff itself was killing him. He coughed, and felt the bleeding, and he leaned out to gulp clean air, but it was no use and he knew it. Still, he had lasted the first hour and he would last the rest of it.

The faster cars had lapped the others now, and there were only signals from the pits to tell position. Lonetti didn't need signals. Until somebody passed him, he was first. He waved as he went by for the thirtieth time, and came up fast on the car ahead. He thought of passing him in the corner,

35

but it was Danton, the Englishman, and Lonetti backed off and let him go through the corner alone. He could take him at will on the long straight, and he would humiliate him there if he could, but he would not take a chance on crowding him in the corner. Lonetti was not notorious for his sportsmanship, and in the old days he would crowd any man in a corner if he felt like it, but he did not feel like it now. They said he hated Englishmen, and so he did, maybe, but he was not going to kill one on the road. He blasted past Danton in the straight, staring at him.

He flew on. He knew he would win. He was happy. He sat up straight, so proud of what he knew was being said of him that he could almost hear them talking. For twenty years Lonetti had been the standard by which other drivers were judged. There were many serious men who said that he had been born great, that he was the only authentic genius motor racing had ever produced, that his skill could not be explained in rational terms. Lonetti believed them. He believed that he could tell, for example, exactly how many pounds of a car's total weight rested on any single wheel at any time, cornering or straight, braking or accelerating. He believed that he could drive at 150 miles an hour through a slot an inch wider than the car. He had done it, so he believed it. Other men had to practice in cars, get used to them, feel out their peculiarities. Not Lonetti, *Il Maestro*. They were all one to him, so long as they had four wheels, something to steer with, and a loud pedal that could be held flat on the floor.

He put it down hard now, to try to pass the two cars looming up ahead. One was Marten, a notorious road hog, the other was old Lyon. They were having a private race for the corner, and when Marten saw Lonetti coming up behind he moved over imperceptibly, blocked him off, and let Lyon get around first. The three cars went around nose to tail in a hellish howling racket and slid into the straight like triplets. The others drew away there. Lonetti put the whole weight of his body on the throttle and shook the wheel in rage, but the tachometer needle would not go up where he wanted it: past the red danger line. He moved to the right-hand side of the road. The pits were only a couple of miles ahead.

He stopped the car where they waited for him and old Giorgio threw up the bonnet, the question in his eyes. "Plug," Lonetti croaked.

Giorgio savagely swiveled out the plugs. Nobody could do it faster, but he couldn't do it in twenty seconds, and Lascelle and Manelli roared past him. They were out of sight when the bonnet banged down and he was pushed off.

Lonetti had never been beloved by other drivers; he gave them good cause now to hate him. He drove as if he were alone on the road. He passed them in bunches as they braked for the corners, slamming through them flat-out to stand viciously on the brake for a second and then drift through the corner in his own weird slide. He went into every corner with the nose of the car pointed dead wrong for the entrance but right for the exit, stealing yards and seconds from the lesser men who had to do it by the book.

He went into one corner behind Marten, caught him in it and slid around him, staring arrogantly out at the six inches that lay between the two cars and instant death. He was coughing constantly now; the blood ran unheeded down his chin and he grinned wickedly at Marten as he left him. He had terrified the man, he knew it, and he ran away from him roaring with mirth and pounding the side of his car like a maniac blacksmith. Manelli he passed at pits, his Alfette blowing out a fog of blue smoke, and he could see the Talbot ahead. He had two laps in which to take it, and as he passed the stands he pointed ferociously ahead, his big white teeth stripped. Let no one miss this, he thought. We will see now how much resistance is in this hero, he thought. We will separate the men from the boys here. We will motor a little bit now.

Lascelle saw him coming and he tried everything he knew. On the straights he took every ounce of power the car had, and held his own, but it was either slow up for the corners or crash, and the insane Italian behind him crept closer with every bend in the road. Lascelle wanted to win. It was the first big race in which he had had any luck; it would make his reputation. Too, he had served under Robert Benoist, and the idea of an Italian taking the cup away made him want to kill again. But every time he looked into the mirror Lonetti was a little closer to doing it.

At the beginning of the last lap, on the long straight in front of the stands, it finally happened. Foot by foot, the red Maserati pulled up beside him. Lonetti held the red car dead alongside, and when Lascelle looked over the little man grinned wolfishly at him. There was blood all over his shirt. As they went past the stands, locked together, Lonetti bowed graciously to the people, and suddenly then, in horror, Lascelle knew why he had not pulled on past: he intended to amuse them with the spectacle of two cars running suicidally together into a corner that was, at that speed, but one car wide. He was going to make him quit, brake, and pull over. Lascelle knew, and everyone knew, that Lonetti had done this a hundred times in the past, and that in the end, and always, it had been the other man who had felt terror slam his foot down on the brake. Lascelle decided, suddenly, that he would be the one who did not quit. Live mouse, dead lion, he thought. He kept his foot down. After all, he just might live through it.

Pietro Lonetti was surprised, fifty yards from the corner, to find the Frenchman still with him, but he drove the bend the way he had intended to, coming out of it slightly faster to clear the road, since he knew that otherwise nothing in the world could keep Lascelle from sliding into him. As it was, he felt the cars tick, nose to tail, when the blue Talbot moved behind him. It seemed to him that he heard the scream of the rubber, in two great howls, as the Talbot spun; and when he topped the hill he saw in his mirror the orange burst of flame as the car exploded against the great trees beside the road.

He had it won, now. It was all over, they would give him the flag as he swept past, the crowds would scream his name, the journalists would pound their typewriters, he would take his victor's lap and at the end of it, as he had so long planned, he would fold his arms, proudly lift his head, and smash himself to death against the wall in the exit road, where everyone could see that it was no accident, and no one could come to harm by it. That had been his plan. That was why he was in the race. But suddenly now it didn't seem so much of a plan. It was empty. It was nothing.

Pietro Lonetti lifted his foot and let the red Maserati run along the side of the road at a bare 50 miles an hour. He felt as if he could get out and walk. He could see the separate blades of grass, each petal of the flowers along the ditch. He coughed and was surprised to taste the blood. His arms trembled and for the first time he felt the blisters on his palms. Everyone went past him. They roared by like a long freight train. He coasted into the pits. None of the din was for him. The photographers were elsewhere.

"Jesus and Mary!" Giorgio screamed at him. "What happened? What broke? What let go?"

"Nothing let go," Lonetti said. "I took my foot off, that's all."

"Man, man, you threw it all away!" Giorgio said. "For what? For that kid, that dumb Frog? For what, for Christ's sake!"

Lonetti looked up at him. "Take off the steering wheel, Giorgio," he said. "Take it off, and get me out of here. I want to go home."

—1952

Three
Wheels
are
Enough

There have been some strange and wonderful automobiles unleashed on the world's roads—the French have one that folds up like a collapsible baby carriage, and a visit to the James Melton Museum in Norwalk, Connecticut, will show you America's only remaining example of the two-wheeled motorcar—but most of these departures from the orthodox don't stay with us long. Four wheels, engine in front, drive to the rear: that's the standard prescription and few of the designs departing from it have lasted. There are rear-engine designs of fairly long term, it's true, and the front-wheel-drive Citroën is a youngster when set beside the most successful unorthodox automobile of all time: the Morgan Three-Wheeler. For the Morgan has been built steadily since 1911 and is still going strong. So is the man who built the first one and is still at it: Henry Frederick Stanley Morgan of Malvern Link, Worcestershire, England.

The virtues of the Morgan, the "Mog" to its devotees, are soon stated: it weighs next to nothing (896 pounds) so that its forty or fifty horsepower can accelerate it in a very convincingly lively fashion; it's small and nimble, and in its homeland is rated as a motorcycle and licensed as one, an important advantage in view of the severity of British taxes. Disadvantages: well, it's likely to rattle a bit, and the brakes won't really pitch you through the windshield. Aside from those trifles and the fact that it steers like a truck, there's nothing much to worry about. Nothing at all, in the view of most Morgan owners—a singularly devoted lot—nothing even to think about.

Some forty thousand Morgan Three-Wheelers have been built since 1911, and of this impressive total there are at the moment only four known to be in this country, a proportion that almost certainly qualifies them as the rarest cars in America. They are unlikely to become more common: the secondhand market for Morgans in England is strong, and the 1952 three-wheel production will not exceed twenty, most of the small factory's output being the Morgan Plus-Four, a standard four-wheel sports car comparable with the MG.

The Morgan came into being strictly by accident—or as the result of an accident. In 1908, Mr. Morgan bought a V-twin Peugeot engine in France with the intention of making a motorcycle for himself. But his father, the Reverend Prebendary H.G. Morgan, was a stern man, and because Morgan Jr.'s previous motorcycle had somewhat bent both itself and rider as a result of a bit too much speed downhill, he forbade the project. His son therefore announced a change in plan: he would make a tricycle, than which nothing could be safer. The finished product weighed 336 pounds and went like mad. Three years later a production model was exhibited at the annual motor-cycle show in London. It had an 8-horsepower engine, one seat, and was tiller-steered. About thirty were sold—no vast number even by the standards prevailing in those days, when the horse was still supreme—but enough to put the Morgan works in business.

By 1912 the Morgan had a passenger seat, wheel steering, and independent suspension—a couple of decades before Buick announced to a startled world that this arrangement had at last been made possible. It was not original with Morgan, by the way. The French Decauville had had it in 1899.

Morgan's placement of the V-twin engine was unique: he hung it out in front of the front axle, connecting it to the driveline with a leather-faced cone clutch. Final transmission, then as now, was by chain, with two speeds forward, and the single rear wheel was suspended in a pivoting fork with quarter-eliptic leaf springs to keep it on the ground a certain percentage of the time. The steering was direct, and was a notable muscle builder. The accelerator was a lever mounted on a spoke of the steering wheel, and it was just as well that the wheel had a limited movement, because to accelerate the lever was moved *up,* to decelerate it was moved *down.* This worked splendidly as long as the wheel moved through a small arc, but had the steering ratio been normal, say four turns lock to lock, the accident would have been over and the streets strewn with cadavers before the driver could make up his mind which way to push the lever in a crisis.

From the beginning, the Morgan's success was built on success in racing competitions. It was a *quick* little car. Mr. H.F.S. himself entered one for the 1912 London-to-Exeter Trail and took the highest award put up. No wonder—the car weighed 550 pounds and had a big hairy V-twin motorcycle engine banging it along. Oddly enough, it had not been the maker's intention to evolve a particularly fast car. He had intended to get great economy (and did, on the order of ninety miles to the gallon!) but of course terrific performance came with it. In 1912, Morgan put fractionally less than sixty miles into one hour on Brooklands Track, then a record, and in 1913, W.G. McMinnies won the cyclecar International Grand Prix at Amiens, France, in a hot Morgan. From that point on, until the last of the big V-twin-engined cars were produced in 1948, the Malvern-made three-wheeler was a serious factor in competitions from one end of Europe to the other.

Like most British manufacturers, the Morgan people have not indulged in frequent model changes. There were three basic models in the 1911–1948 outdoor-engine line: the Grand Prix, the Aero, and the Super Sports. They were all dashing looking buckets, although purists have decried the placement of the spare wheel on the Super Sports: it plugs up the hole made by cutting the boat-tail rear end off square. It still lives there in the current F Four and F Super models, the first, as the name indicates, a four-seater. These cars are powered by the British Ford four-cylinder engine, and although they lack the punch produced by the old twins, they make up for it in tractability. The J.A.P., Blackburne, Anzani, and Matchless engines required a bit more attention than most contemporary motorists care to provide their powerplants.

Morgan got around to three-wheel brakes in 1926. Up to that time, both hand and foot brake worked on the single rear wheel, and there were no crash stops provided from, say, 80 miles an hour, which any stock Morgan in good shape would do. The braking system never was hooked up so that all three wheels could be held on one application: the pedal applied the front-wheel binders and the hand-lever the single rear. The steering ratio was changed, as well, giving about 100 degrees of movement at the rim. It is brutally quick steering, of course, but great for sudden maneuvers once you're used to it.

If the driver stopped worrying about the brakes and stuck his foot well into a thoroughly prepared hot Morgan Three, he could do some astonishing things with it. Clive Lones, who won more than 500 events in Morgans, lapped the Brooklands track at 103.2 miles an hour, getting 110 on the one short straightaway and carrying a passenger to boot. Gwenda Stewart, one of the all-time great woman drivers, put 101 *into* the hour with a Morgan at Montlhery in France, and held 72 miles an hour for twelve consecutive hours. Even the softer contemporary Morgans, with their 1172 cc engines worked up a bit according to standard U.S. speed-shop practice, would turn out fantastic speeds, and of course the Morgan has always been just the thing for fun and games on getaway from traffic lights.

The contemporary Mog two-seater has a seven-foot eleven-inch wheelbase and four-foot two-inch track, with an overall length of eleven feet. It will top 70 in stock form, comes as a roadster only, and costs $756 at the factory, plus tax. The four-seater is a trifle bigger and is priced at $798.

Mr. H.F.S. Morgan is in his seventy-third year just now, and shows no sign of a wish to retire. His sons run the Malvern factory, but twice a week he hops into his Bentley and runs the 120 miles from his home to the factory at a good clip, usually hitting 100 somewhere along the route. He has owned a good number of Rolls-Royce and Rolls-Royce-built Bentley automobiles. "Next to a Morgan," he likes to say, "a Rolls-Royce is as good a car as you can buy."

—-1952

Classics
of
the
Road

Long-distance, hell-for-leather, town-to-town automobile races began in Europe soon after the first horseless carriage chugged doubtfully out of a dank garage into the bright sunlight. These races, beginning around 1900, were so popular that some of them still rank among the best-attended sporting events of all time.

The automobile had tremendous appeal for the sportsman of the day: it was the fastest vehicle at man's bidding; it was new; much about it was unknown. It offered a great challenge. And, since the motorcar was designed to transport people over ordinary roads, it was logical to test it for speed in that fashion.

To the manufacturer, turning out perhaps a few score automobiles a year, racing was the best kind of advertising. Because it was a brand-new sport, the newspapers gave it extensive news coverage, and the manufacturer whose car had won an important race on Saturday could be sure of a full order book by the following Monday evening.

So hardy is the appeal of racing automobiles that there are still three great cross-country races run today, in spite of many difficulties—heavier traffic, higher speeds, reluctance of authorities to cooperate. The two races are the Mille Miglia in Italy and the Carrera Panamericana in Mexico. The Mille Miglia, usually run in April, is a circuit race centering on the Italian city of Brescia. The Mille, one of the maddest sporting events in the world, is usually enlivened by pouring rain and by the insouciance of the Italian citizenry, who may or may not keep bicycles, hay wagons, and trucks off the road, and who in any case like to watch motor racing from close up. A Lancia won last year at an average speed of 86.7 miles per hour. The Panamericana usually is run in November, in five one-day stages, over a route nearly 2,000 miles long. It is a hard race to watch. The cars come past only once, and they're traveling at anything from 100 to 150 miles an hour. The Targa Florio, the oldest closed-circuit race—first run in 1906—is disputed over 467 miles of Sicilian road.

Difficult and dangerous as these events are (it took an average speed of 134 miles an hour to win the last leg of 1954's Panamericana), the dedicated fanatics who drove in the earliest town-to-town races would be likely to find them mild enough in comparison. True, the cars go faster today, but they have brakes that will actually stop them, and the fracture of an axle or the loss of a wheel will not cause them to disintegrate into an armful of junk metal and splintered wood. Furthermore, no one runs today on dirt roads so dusty that a driver, doing perhaps 90 miles an hour, can steer only by watching the tree tops on the not always valid assumption that they consistently border the road.

They ran the Paris–Madrid Race more than fifty years ago, and to this day no one knows how many people were killed. But the toll of spectators as well as racers was so heavy that the French government stopped the race at Bordeaux, impounded the cars, had them towed by teams of horses to the railroad station, and shipped them by special train to Paris. The Spanish authorities were no less obdurate, sending word that the cars would absolutely not be allowed to cross the frontier.

In 1903, even veteran drivers (a man who had driven for five years was a real veteran) did not know what today's bright schoolchildren know about the effects of high-speed crashes. And most people had literally no conception of speeds beyond those that could be made by a good horse. The spectators' inability to understand how quickly an automobile covered ground was a great trial to early racing drivers. Paris–Madrid contestants complained that they had constantly to drive on pie-shaped pieces of road, the edges black with a wedge of people opening reluctantly to an apex a little way down the course.

On that May 24, 216 cars lined up at Versailles, ready to go off at timed intervals. There were automobiles of every size and description, little and big, fast and slow, but nearly all shared two characteristics—they had been made as light as possible, and their engines were better than their chassis, their brakes, or their steering arrangements. For this was early in the game, and little was understood of the qualities that make for roadability, road-holding qualities, in an automobile.

Most of the heavy cars were stark: a straight chassis, simple wagon-type springs fore and aft, a steering wheel, a gas tank, and a couple of bucket seats. In some cases, there was only one seat, the mechanic sitting on the floor and clinging to the car as best he could. Wheels were wood-spoked for the most part, tires were hopelessly unreliable, and the brakes (on the rear wheels only, of course) were of negligible value, particularly at speeds above 40 miles an hour.

Charles Jarrott, an Englishman, driving a De Dietrich, started first from Versailles and held the lead for thirty miles or so out of Paris, being passed finally by De Knyff and then by Louis Renault, driving one of his own cars. Louis's brother Marcel was farther back in another Renault. Jarrott was driving with one hand, using the other to haul tight a strap connected to a jerry-built clutch lever; it was the only way he could keep the car running. His mechanic, Bianchi, sat on the floor, pumping oil to the thirsty engine with both hands. Jarrott had his foot well down but he could not catch Renault, who was getting 90 miles an hour out of a 30-horsepower automobile.

For all but the leading cars, the dust was incredibly dangerous. It hung in the air like fog, impossible to see through. Cars traveling close behind others were driven by blind men steering by instinct, their faces, often enough, raw and bleeding from the barrage of small stones thrown up by the furiously spinning wheels ahead. It was the dust that killed Marcel Renault. He had caught up with Thery, in a Decauville, and had drawn level with him. Then for three miles in the dust they fought side by side, inches apart, until Thery, probably imagining an obstacle in the dust curtain ahead, swerved slightly. Renault twitched his steering wheel automatically, skidded, spun out, and crashed into a tree.

Meanwhile, Gabriel, the eventual winner, was whistling down the road in a Mors car at an average of 65 miles an hour to perform one of the epic feats of motor racing in his time or any time. Gabriel had started 168th. He had run 342½ miles in five hours, thirteen minutes, and thirty seconds. This was a most respectable accomplishment in itself, but he had passed 167 automobiles to do it, and passed them in spite of the dust, the weirdly high-crowned road, and the wreckage littering the course. It would be years before anything comparable would be done in motor racing.

After the Paris–Madrid tragedy, France, Italy, Germany, Austria, and Spain put up bars against that kind of race. England had never allowed racing on open roads and has not to this day. Many driving contests in the future would be of the rally type—events in which touring or sports cars attempt to maintain a rigid average speed for four or five days and nights of tricky driving. Still other races of the so-called circuit type filled the gap left by the big town-to-town events.

The circuit races, dismal as they seemed to men who found their greatest excitement in a race run from point to point, were exciting enough. They were laid out over country roads, closed for the occasion, and a typical one might be run for six laps of a fifty-mile circuit. The purists thought it less than sporting to run over the same ground six times, but they had to make do with what they had at hand. At Le Mans, France, they have run a twenty-four-hour circuit race over the same route for the last thirty years. The Le Mans circuit is 8.4 miles long. Sixty cars start at four o'clock in the afternoon and race with alternating drivers until the same time the next day, by which time the leaders have covered more than 2400 miles.

It was inevitable that someone would attempt to combine the cross-country race with the rally, and 1908 saw it done. The conception was big, indeed probably too big: a race from New York to Paris via Siberia, but to be run by touring, not racing, automobiles. The thing was so palpably mad that comparatively few entries were received. Those who did sign up, though, were iron men, and they came to New York with no illusions.

At ten o'clock in the morning, on a cold and snowy 12 February 1908, six automobiles lined up in 43rd Street, between Broadway and Seventh Avenue, and awaited the fall of a signal flag. Their impatient drivers—three Frenchmen, an Italian, a German, and an American—nervously gripped the steering wheels, ready to jump for any advantage, as though they were starting a fast run for money to 110th Street. But their goal was not 110th Street, it was Paris. Under the sponsorship of *Le Matin* of Paris, and the *New York Times*, they proposed to drive their hard-sprung, unsheltered, dubiously reliable horseless carriages from New York to Albany, Buffalo, Cleveland, Toledo, Chicago, Omaha, Cheyenne, Granger, Ogden, Reno, Carson City, Goldfield, Daggett, Mojave, Saugus, Santa Barbara, San Jose, San Francisco; thence by sea (with a brief road run in Alaska) to Vladivostok, and on to Harbin, Irkutsk, Tomsk, Omsk, Tyumen, Ekaterinburg, Moscow, Novgorod, St. Petersburg, Berlin—and Paris.

Last year, this year, ten years ago, such a race would have been madness, and few men could have been found to embark upon it, no matter what the rewards. But this was the year 1908. To the automobilists of the day, a trip of twenty miles was an event, one of fifty, an adventure. Even in the heavily populated eastern states, the roads outside the cities were kidney-wreckers, tooth-pullers, bone-shakers, little more than cart tracks, even in the middle of summer—and this was snowy February. The temperature was in the low thirties, and there was heavy ice in the rivers.

The cars were open, of course, all of them: the Thomas, the three French cars—De Dion, Moto Bloc, Sizaire et Naudin—the Italian Zust, and the German Protos. None of these makes has survived. But in February 1908, every one of them was a potential world-beater.

There were 250,000 people in Times Square that February morning, and the streets were black with derby hats. Three hundred policemen were busy holding a clear path for the cars. At eleven o'clock the six chugged away.

This was a race that was not really a race; it was more properly an endurance contest, and everyone concerned had predicted that the cars would proceed at a fairly decorous rate at the beginning. They did not. Once clear of New York City the fever got into the drivers and they began to motor in earnest. They were soon hard at it, driving as if Paris were no farther away than Albany. They were a hard-bitten crew, three men to the car. George Schuster and Montague Roberts drove the Thomas Flyer, and George Miller from the Thomas factory joined them when they reached Buffalo. The Thomas, incidentally, was certified as a stock car, having been selected from others at the plant six days before the race began.

The fast run out of New York was too much for the smallest car in the race, the ambitious little one-cylinder Sizaire et Naudin, and it dropped out. The Thomas, the De Dion, and the Zust ran ahead, with the Moto Bloc and the Protos falling steadily behind. At Erie the American car was well ahead of everything else. The Thomas ran the 220 miles from Erie to Toledo, Ohio, in a day, but there was snow ahead, and the next day saw a bare eighty miles logged to Corunna. The Thomas crew could find no accommodations for the night in Corunna, so went on to Kendallville, seven miles away. It took them fourteen hours of snow fighting to make it, and that was typical of the whole run from that point to snowbound Chicago, the Thomas a day ahead of the Zust, and the De Dion, Protos, and Moto Bloc three days behind. The Thomas hadn't made the whole distance on its own, though —$1000 had been spent on towing charges in Indiana.

Iowa was solid mud, hub-deep, from end to end; mud frozen hard in the morning, so that the big touring car bounced on it like a pony cart, mud sun-thawed soft by noon, stuff in which a four-mile-an-hour walking pace was a good rate of travel. In Nebraska it was cold: real, bone-snapping, Plains Country cold. The Thomas was in Omaha three days ahead of the two closest competitors, still the Zust and the De Dion. In Wyoming there were no roads at all, just unmarked plains, and rivers to be forded. Nevada was sand, and California was hot, but the Thomas was in San Francisco on March 24—3832 miles in forty-two days, and twelve days ahead of the nearest competitor, of which there were only four now, the Moto Bloc crew having given up halfway across Iowa.

The cars were to be transshipped by steamer from San Francisco to

Valdez, Alaska, via Seattle. The Thomas docked at Valdez on April 8 with an altered crew: George Schuster, driver; George Miller, mechanic; Hans Hansen, an arctic explorer; George McAdam, a *New York Times* correspondent. Incredibly, the original itinerary of the race called for the cars to be driven from Valdez to Nome and thence shipped by boat to Siberia. The Thomas crew, having fought its way already through much terrain certified by natives as impassable, persisted in the plan until a Valdez stagecoach operator took them a little way out of town in a horse-drawn sledge. Once clear of the twelve-foot drifts in the town itself, it took the horses very little time to bog down completely, and the Thomas crew thereupon allowed cooler heads to prevail, and booked ship passage back to Seattle. The car was in Seattle on April 17 and in Kobe, through the good offices of the S.S. *Shawmut,* on May 12. They spent four days in crossing Japan and sailed for Vladivostok from Tsuruga.

Considering the size and the complexity of the undertaking, the New York-to-Paris race was singularly free of the quarrels and jurisdictional arguments that might have marred it, but at this point there was some small trouble. The De Dion and Zust cars had arrived in Seattle and shipped out by boat before the Thomas had returned from its investigation of the Alaskan snowdrifts. This advantage, of course, they had obtained at the expense of the Thomas's side trip of 1100 miles. Further, the Protos crew, still in Idaho, and broken down, had decided to put the car aboard a railroad train for Seattle, there being no other way to move it. This should have disqualified the Germans, but the race committee decided instead to penalize them thirty days: the twenty-three days they were behind, plus seven days for the 1100 miles they had done by rail.

The Protos shipped to Vladivostok directly, skipping Japan, and there, with the other surviving cars, waited under instruction from race headquarters for the Thomas to arrive. The cars would start even again, but in order to win, the Protos, at least, would have to be in Paris thirty days before the Americans. Considering the terrain to be covered, this was by no means impossible. While they were waiting, the De Dion and Protos crews cornered the gasoline supply of Vladivostok. The Americans liberated some launch-engine fuel and ran on it until gasoline could be found.

Running out of Nikolskoe on May 25, a day behind the Americans, the Germans elected to forgo the prescribed race route and took to the Trans-Siberian railroad tracks. The Thomas ran on the Siberian roadway, so-called, for 100 miles and then gave up in a sea of mud, returned to Nikolskoe, and took to the tracks behind the Protos. Both cars rode the rails for 420 miles.

Their wheel tread did not fit the wide-gauge Russian railway, of course, and the ties were unballasted much of the way, which meant a four- or five-inch climb and drop over each tie for each of the four wheels, repeated thousands of times a day. It is hard to believe that any present-day automobile, much less a 1908 40-horsepower, $3000 touring car, could take such a drubbing. But aside from one breakdown which the crew repaired with the limited facilities they carried, and which cost a five-day delay, the Thomas came off the tracks in Harbin in practically as good condition as it had been when it went on them in Nikolskoe, nor did either car have to dispute the right-of-way with a train. Fortunately, the Trans-Siberian runs through flat country, and the infrequent trains could be seen and heard a long way off.

From Harbin the cars took to the Manchurian plains, the Protos now five days ahead. There were virtually no roads. Gasoline and oil had to be carried in the cars, and the Thomas sometimes had as much as two barrels aboard. The Thomas was seventy-two days in Siberia, and the crew had five nights of rest in bed during the whole time. The only major difficulty came just before Ekaterinburg, on the boundary between Asiatic and European Russia, when two teeth were stripped from a gear in pulling through mud. George Miller repaired the part in a blacksmith shop. They had passed the Protos, but a few days later the gear gave way again, and a trip by horse and wagon to Kazan, 227 miles away, had to be made before they were able to get a new one.

The Zust and the De Dion cars were now hopelessly out of the running, but the Germans, beaten on the face of it by their thirty-day handicap, were still driving as hard as possible. The lead changed back and forth. All other hazards aside, merely finding the right road was terribly difficult. The existing maps were wildly inaccurate; signposts and road markers could hardly be expected where there were no roads; and passing peasants gave directions as various as such helpful fellows always do.

The Germans made St. Petersburg first, and Berlin first, and Paris first, four days before the Thomas Flyer's arrival on July 30. But it availed them nothing. The Thomas had come the whole way, where there was land to run on and excluding tows, under its own power, while the Protos had done 1100 miles by rail.

The Thomas came back to New York for a triumphal run up Broadway, a Mayor's reception, and a visit to President Theodore Roosevelt. The car had covered a distance equivalent to halfway around the world—estimates varied between 12,116 and 13,341 miles—had beaten the Protos by twenty-six days, the Zust by fifty-three, the De Dion by fifty-six. It had gone the whole way on the same set of spark plugs.

Alone of the cars that made the run, the Thomas is still in existence today. Battered and beat-up and unrestored, it lives at Austin Clark's automobile museum in Southampton, Long Island. Some day, perhaps, it will be put back into running order, its proud brass polished, its body painted gray again.* And the day the job is done, someone is sure to suggest gassing it up and trying one more round-the-world junket. Perhaps this time it could be done in less than 170 days of elapsed time and 112 days of running time—and maybe it would take a lot longer.

—1955

*The car is now in Harrah's Automobile Collection in Reno.

Blood
Sport

The big skyrocket startled Stephanie Marshall. It wasn't really a skyrocket; it was a sort of aerial bomb —a "maroon" the British called it—whooshing a hundred yards into the brass-bright August sky to burst with a flat, echoing boom. It meant that there were ten minutes left.

Stephanie was alone. There wasn't much point, for her, in being with someone, trying to talk, at a time like this. She walked along the oil-stained concrete, an aloof little figure in black slacks, black Shantung blouse, a green kerchief over her head. She was blond, pale, and the palms of her hands were wet with perspiration. Stephanie was giving up a man she dearly loved, rehearsing what she would say, moving in the wash of babble and shouts in a half-dozen languages, in the crackling, ripping bite of the exhausts of one car after another being warmed up.

She moved past the crowded pit structures, their counters stacked with tools, stop watches, cans of oil, and the rest of the paraphernalia of racing, and came finally to Dennis Marshall's place; 26, the big sign over it read Ferrari. Dennis was talking with someone she didn't know. He smiled the man away and turned to Stephanie.

"Hi, darling," he said. "You look ravishing. You look a dear, good, sweet, passionate girl, and I adore you. Except that decorum must prevail, I'd certainly kiss you." He kissed her gravely on each cheek. Her hands moved to his shoulders and held him. He looked into her eyes.

"I know, baby," he said. "You're scared green. Shatters me. Here am I, about to have three hours of delirious fun, and maybe pick up two thousand pounds to boot, and you, poor Steph, poor Steph, are worried." He shook his head dolefully and a second rocket boomed in the air. "Five-minute gun," he said. "Where's m'hat?" He pulled a white-billed helmet from under the pit counter. "Run over to the bar, Steph," he said. "Have a nice vermouth cassis or something until the cars get sorted out. It's the beginning of these things that shakes one, you know. Go on, now, there's a lamb."

He kissed her and casually walked out to the lean, mean-looking red car standing with the others on the starting grid. She watched him go.

Dennis Marshall wasn't a big man, five-nine, perhaps and only twenty-five years old, but there was more of the virile essence in him than most men ever know. He had a rock-hard body and he moved it with that grace no one's given and few care to buy, the price of self-discipline being what it is. He'd been born with fast reactions and 20/5 vision. The rest had been sweat and planning. He was one of the three top-ranking automobile racing drivers in the world and in a good year he could make $150,000. He was intelligent, courteous, serene. *He's my lover,* Stephanie told herself, *and I'm his mistress, and tonight I'll say good-by to him, and all this.*

She didn't go to the bar. She stood beside the pit counter and waited. All the cars were manned now, twenty-odd of them. She knew most of the drivers. They were strange men. She thought Dennis was the only reasonably oriented one in the lot. They were the gayest possible companions, when they weren't talking shop, but they were all mad. She saw Dennis jump out of his car and run over to shout something into Hilary Martin's ear. Martin looked up at him. He was a round little man, completely preoccupied for hours before a race.

There was Aldo Caducci, tall, shiny-bald, very gay, and a legendary lady-killer. Next to him, Van Groot, a Hollander. She saw Patrick Munoz, a Brazilian, twice champion of the world, a man so relaxed that he appeared, in the car or out of it, to be just on the point of falling asleep. There was Borros Spohk, an American who believed that if a man tried hard enough he could live thirty hours a day; and a Swedish count, Helmut Ovden, who had been a devotee of what he called "the blood sports" since his fifteenth birthday. There was the Frenchman, Maurice Delafont, a perfectly normal, ordinary man, except that he was fifty, owner of a prosperous business, married to a beautiful woman, had three delightful children, and still he went motor racing all year long.

The starter's flag was in the air and Stephanie twisted her hands tightly together and waited. The exhaust noise rose steadily to a shattering roar. The big flag fell and the cars started to move, slowly for the first few feet, many with blue smoke rising from spinning rear wheels, the rubber burning; and then, unbelievably as you watched, they were away, up to 60 miles an hour in the time it took to draw a long, deep breath, then 90, 100, all in a solid multicolored pack, mere inches from each other; they howled into the first long curve and were gone. In a bit over five minutes they'd be back. Stephanie tugged at the clasp of her purse, dredged out a cigarette and lighted it.

In the next pit a bottle crashed on concrete and a woman's strident voice said, *"Ah, c'est dommage!"* Floating over everything, the impersonal, professional excitement of the public-address system.

These few minutes of the first lap were almost the hardest of all for Stephanie. She looked in at the pit. Everything was neatness and order now, the little squares of the graph paper on which the lap charts were kept, the four Swiss split-second watches in their mahogany case, the orderly rows of pencils. The voice of the crowd rose and began to mount to a shout; the cars were in sight.

Stephanie leaned around the pit and stared down the long straightaway to the distant corner where the first car would show itself. It came now, a red one, sliding the corner so that she could see the whole length of it, straightening out with a wicked-looking, tremulant tail wagging, and then seeming to swell in her eyes, without moving, as she looked straight at it. Half a breath and it was level with the pits, and she felt the shocking "Whack!" as the driver shifted into top. It was Munoz, lifting a limp hand to wave to his pit; twenty feet behind him a green Vanwall car, little Martin, tight and tense; then another red car, Dennis, sitting so far back that his arms were out almost straight in front of him. Once she'd seen Dennis, Stephanie paid no attention to the rest of the cars as they rasped past. Silence again.

Stephanie felt quite apart from the other women who had committed their men to what she thought of as the unspeakable hazards of the race. She was sure she was more in love than any of them were; and she knew exactly what was happening on the 7.7 miles of the road circuit, two cars wide, its blacktop softened by the sun. Like many women, Stephanie had a poor graphic imagination; but she did not have to depend upon it to know what the men were daring. Once she had let Dennis show her, in Italy, the car, a big two-seater open Ferrari of the type called a 4.9.

The road was straight where they started, after Dennis had told her to expect to be frightened, but to force it down; if she could not, she was to slap his thigh and he would slow the car.

They smiled at each other. He ran the engine up, let in the clutch, and Stephanie's head snapped back. She tried, unsuccessfully, to pull herself forward against the surge of the car's acceleration. Dennis's arms were bare, the muscles standing in ridges. The steering wheel shook in his hands, the uncovered metal of the body vibrated, the noise of the engine was unbearable, and Stephanie wanted to scream in sheer terror. The big needle riding the tachometer dial spun around: 3000, 4000, 5000, 6000. Dennis's left hand grabbed the gearshift lever, his left foot hit the clutch, his right stamped on the accelerator pedal, and with a crack like a long fat whip being snapped across the sky, the engine bit again. The tachometer needle climbed again to 6000 and again his feet danced on the pedals, and the soft evening air was split as 400 horsepower slammed into the clutch.

Stephanie was rigid with terror. Ahead of them, the road ran out in a right-hand corner. It is impossible to explain how a corner looks running up to a car nearing 200 miles an hour. The car seems to stand still, and the corner rushes into one's face like a train in a nightmare. Stephanie knew they were going to die then and there. The car would sail through the corner and a mile into the woods beyond it. She couldn't bear to look and she couldn't close her eyes either. She turned to Dennis. He was staring ahead, the brown skin crinkled around his eyes. His toe hit the pedal, and the brake-pads, tight in their calipers, shrieked as they bit into the discs. His heel came down on the throttle and his left arm flicked as he dropped a gear; the engine screamed, fell off; again the wail of the brakes and the monstrous howl of the engine as he caught third gear.

He flicked the wheel back and forth and the car drifted through the corner, nose pointed in, tail in the middle of the road. Dennis kicked it straight, flattened the accelerator, and again Stephanie felt the whole weight of her body thrust inexorably into the leather of the seat back behind her. She endured it all for three laps of the circuit. She smiled wanly at Dennis as he helped her from the car. She staggered in his arms to a chair. After a while the memory of the physical beating faded. What remained was the face of death hanging to the flying car like its own exhaust smoke.

"There are three sports," she remembered Helmut Ovden saying. "Bullfighting, motor racing, mountain climbing. All the rest are recreations."

The leaders came by again: Munoz, Martin, Dennis, Caducci. The other cars were stringing out behind them. There was no silence now. Every few seconds a car came past, or two or three. Stephanie walked through a narrow place between two pit counters, and she felt sheltered immediately, separated from the circuit by the pits, by the odds and ends piled up behind them—tins of oil, cases of mineral water, camp chairs, stacked spare tires. There were parked cars, too; motorcycles, bikes, scooters. Looking a long way across the field, she could see another leg of the circuit; little toy cars sliding along it, too far away, too quiet, and too small to matter. She felt removed and safe.

Still she was oddly bound to do what Dennis had asked her to do, and she looked for the candy-striped tent of the bar. She would have the vermouth cassis he'd suggested, although she didn't want it. She had an uneasy, unspoken conviction that to refuse him anything, just before or during a race, might be fatally unlucky. Fear of his being killed with some small favor ungranted terrified her. She stirred the purplish, bittersweet drink.

By the time the race was half over, an hour and a half gone, it had settled into a deceptively simple pattern. Of the twenty-some cars that had started, four had retired with mechanical trouble, one had been disqualified for accepting help from spectators after going off the road. Munoz, Dennis, Martin, and Caducci were all driving on the absolute limit, and they traded the lead back and forth among them. Only the professionals present, and a few knowledgeable spectators, marking the way the cars slid the entire width of the road going into bends and shuddered and danced under maximum acceleration coming out, knew how bitterly the first four places in the race were being contested.

Stephanie knew, and so she marveled at some of the other women, bright, twittering little things, no more concerned than they'd be at a horse race. She had little to say to them and they had nothing for her. When she wanted to talk with someone she looked for Madame Delafont, who always came to the races with her husband. Stephanie found her sitting behind her husband's pit in the shade of a beach umbrella, a bottle of wine in a tiny tub beside her chair. She was knitting.

"Sit down, my dear; sit down, Stephanie," she said. "Have some wine."

"Thanks, Julie," Stephanie said. "I just finished a vermouth. I'll wait."

"How does it go with our heroes?" Julie Delafont said. "I haven't looked at the chart for half an hour now."

"Munoz first, then Dennis, Caducci, Martin, a few minutes ago," Stephanie said. "I think Maurice is farther back."

"He was eighth," Julie said. "He knew the car was not going well this morning, and then, too, of course, it isn't a factory car."

Stephanie stretched her legs straight in front of her. "The sun is good," she said.

"This is no sun," Julie said. "Wait until you get to Nassau."

"I shan't be there," Stephanie said.

"Dennis isn't running?" Julie Delafont asked.

"Oh, yes, he's running," Stephanie said. "It's just that I'm not going."

They heard a shout and a double screech of brakes hard on as a car came too fast into the pits. Both looked and saw a flash of it. It was green, not blue, not red, so they paid no attention.

"I think I will have a little drink, if I may," Stephanie said. "I guess I'm getting jumpy. I'm getting so I hate all the noises. The only noise I like to hear anymore is the pop of the champagne cork when they open the bottle for the winner; just that one pop and all the blessed silence, not a single damned engine running." She took a little sip of wine.

"Don't be thinking like that; don't run off down that alley, Stephanie," Julie Delafont said, "or you'll find yourself giving up the whole thing, and Dennis too."

"That's just it," Stephanie said after a bit. "I am giving Dennis up. I'm going to give him up."

"I see," Julie said. "I must say you've surprised me." She spilled wine into her glass. "Tell me, how long has it been now that you and Dennis have been together?"

"July a year ago," Stephanie said.

"That isn't very long, is it?" Julie said. "A pity, too. It's a sad thing to fall out of love."

"Don't tease me, Julie," Stephanie said. "I haven't fallen out of love. I adore Dennis. There cannot be anything else like him in this entire world. But I'm going to leave him because I can't stand the life he has, that's all, I can't stand watching him make a bet with his life practically every week. Do you know how many times Dennis ran last year? Forty-one! Look, Julie, I know what it's like out there, I know what goes on out there, and I can't take it. If I keep on, I'll ruin both our lives."

"My girl," Julie said, "I think you're mad. Look. All this you are talking about—the racing—this is nonsense. The fact of the matter is that you love him; by which I mean, you like him, you admire him, you desire him. That is reasonable love. You may not find it again. Therefore it doesn't matter what the man does—whether he is a garbage collector, a banker, or the public hangman. Don't you see that?"

"No, I don't think I do," Stephanie said.

" 'The beauty of the young is God's apology for their stupidity' " Julie said. "Look, Stephanie, the only men worth having are the ones who are passionate for the world, for their work in the world. These are the only good ones, and there are not nearly enough of them to go around. With a man like Dennis or Maurice, it is possible to have a life; not an existence, a life, something that is not just cabbage soup and winter rain on the roof. You don't give up a man you love because he will die! What an idiocy! You are making me angry."

"I'm sorry if I am," Stephanie said. "But don't you see, what good am I, what use to Dennis, when I can't even keep him from seeing how frightened I am? Today, just before the start, he took one look at me and he knew. I'm sure he always knows. In time he'll hate me for it. Right now, I hate myself for it."

"The essence of the thing is so simple," Julie said. "It's impossible for me to understand how you miss seeing it. Look; you are afraid of only one thing, really. That he will die. Don't you think he's afraid too? Every one of them is; it's the main reason they do these madnesses—to see the fear of dying rise up in themselves and then to push it down again. He is going to have to do this dying, if it comes that way, not you. Give some thought to him. And for yourself, think only how dear he is, what he means to you. And every time he gets into a car, kiss him good-by; that's all, kiss him good-by!"

"You do that?" Stephanie whispered.

"Certainly I do that. I kiss him good-by. I pat his dear fáce; I walk away saying to myself, Ah, my Maurice, he was the dearest and bĕst of all men who ever lived in this world! Sometimes I even think of how I will tell the children. I say good-by to him. I tell myself calmly that he is dead. And then—every time so far, at any rate—I am lucky. The noise, as you say, is over and Maurice is back with me. So I can kiss him again, and wash the oil from him and take him in my arms again and comfort him. What else should we do but meet our men as they come down from the mountain, and comfort them until they have to go back again? And when they go back, kiss them good-by!"

Stephanie sat silent for a long time.

"I'm sorry, if I have disturbed you, Stephanie," Julie Delafont said finally. "If I was too rough, I am sorry. It's just that that's how it seems to me to be, that's how I have been so happy all this time."

"No, no, you weren't too rough," Stephanie said.

"At any rate we have drunk up all the wine," Julie said. "And there's only a half hour of this foolishness left. Let's walk down to the corner and watch these crazies for a few minutes, and then we can come back and see the finish. I love to watch the finish. That idiot with the big flag, seeing how close he can stand without having his feet run over. I do hope I'm watching, the day somebody gets him!" She giggled like a girl.

They walked together behind the pits to the first corner. The sun was low now, butter-yellow on the drivers' faces as they came down the long straightaway and into the corner, the air was cooling, night was coming in. There were fourteen cars left. Caducci was out, Perdita in a Maserati was running fourth behind Munoz, Dennis Marshall, Spohk. Dennis was within two car lengths of Munoz, and had been hanging to him like that for more than a hundred miles. Spohk was well back, driving magnificently with his characteristic indifference to hazard, but his car was not fast enough to bring him up to the leaders and everyone was watching the fantastic Munoz-Marshall duel. Their two cars ran as if tied together. Twenty-five times a lap each driver watched the other accept a chance to make a mistake, and none were made. A trifling error by Munoz would suffice to let Dennis pass him; one by Dennis, and Munoz could run hopelessly far ahead. But they came around like a train.

"They're so incredibly good they make it look dull," Stephanie said.

"They'll finish that way," Julie Delafont said. "I think they're reconciled. Maurice, as you can see, he is not."

Maurice Delafont was lying seventh overall, and second in his class to Stehrs, in a Gordini. Stehrs had been well ahead, but his car was slowing, and Delafont was closing hard on him. He was pushing, delaying his braking to the rim of disaster, whipping the wheel madly back and forth as the car slid, spinning his back wheels as he bored out of the corner.

"Look how excited," Julie Delafont said. "Like a damned wet-nose schoolboy. You would think he'd been driving for six months, instead of God knows how many donkeys' years."

Excited or not, Delafont was hurrying, and every time he came around he had made a few more yards. A man standing behind Stephanie and Julie was timing the interval. "Delafont will catch him," he told his friends. "If he keeps on at this rate, he'll catch him with two laps to spare." Stephanie and Julie turned to look at the man; he held his watch up to show them the interval, and they both had their backs to the circuit when they heard the rubber shriek and the shouts. They snapped their heads around. Blue car and white car; the white one swerving to the side of the road, its driver fighting to hold it out of the ditch; the blue one flipping end for end down the course, like a clown's toy. A man flew out, tumbled through the air. To the people standing at one side it seemed that he would miss the telephone pole. No, he hit it high and fairly and face-on in a terrible embrace; just for a second the body stuck there; then it fell backward, arms piteously outstretched. The white car had got around; there was nothing else in sight; nothing to be heard but the soft thud of the body hitting the ground, the quick sigh from the crowd. This much Stephanie was sure of; then Julie was gone, out into the road, tugging at the body, people pulling her away, a man tearing off a yellow sweater to wave it madly at the cars still coming.

When she dared, Stephanie ran across. That was when Julie began to scream. She screamed rhythmically, methodically; her chest working like a bellows, in breath, out in a long, bare-souled animal howl. Her eyes protruded, she knew no one; the veins in her forehead purpled and she screamed. In the fifteen minutes it took for an ambulance to come, she destroyed her voice.

Stephanie was helpless before the ambulance came, but afterward she could at least admit it, and she left and walked alone back to the pits. Munoz had won, Dennis behind him. He was waiting for her, his face black with oil and rubber, except for the egg-shaped patches around his eyes where the goggles had ridden. His shoulders sagged with fatigue.

"He's dead?" Dennis asked.

"He's dead," Stephanie said. "I was there. So was Julie. They've given her a tremendous dose of morphine or something."

"What a pity she had to see it," Dennis said. "What a miserable thing for her."

"I really thought she was losing her mind," Stephanie said. "I suppose it was only hysteria. Only! The odd thing was, we had been talking about it just a little before—the chances drivers take—and she said she was always reconciled to Maurice's death. Every time he went out she gave him up all over again, and felt only lucky when he came back to her. And then, when it happened, she went completely to pieces."

"That was because she saw it."

"No, I think she always knew she would," Stephanie said, "but she made up that other fiction, and for all those years they lived in it and were happy."

"The poor sod," Dennis said. "One trip to the well too many. After all, the man was over fifty!"

"Let's go home, Den," Stephanie said. He threw his kit into the little car behind the pits and they bumped off across the field to the roads, solid with traffic now in the gray twilight. Dennis ran alongside the road, cutting in and out with easy virtuosity. The hotel was eight miles distant.

"You said you were going to tell me something tonight, Steph," Dennis said.

"No, I'm not going to tell you anything, darling," Stephanie said. "I'm going to soak you in a tub, and give you tea and rum and take you to bed; those are the only plans I have for you."

"Those plans will do," Dennis said. "They'll do very well."

—1957

The
Marvel
of
Mantua

Seventeen times they pulled Tazio Nuvolari out of the wreckage of motorcycles or automobiles and carried him into a hospital in serious condition or worse, and seventeen times he walked out. Even the eighteenth time he came out alive, although it was only to go to his home in Mantua in Italy and there to die, on August 11, 1953, sixty-one years old, a legend in his own lifetime.

Tazio Giorgio Nuvolari was unique: indisputably he was supreme in his own sport, better than any other man who had ever lived. Nuvolari was a racing automobile driver so fabulously skilled that lesser men were hard-pressed even to understand how he did the things they watched him do.

"I tell you honestly," a contemporary said, "in a match race with the devil himself I would bet all on Tazio."

Nuvolari for twenty-nine years drove against the toughest competition in the world and died in bed— incredible in itself. He ran in 172 recorded races and finished first in sixty-four of them. Of the 200 most important races between 1906 and 1939, Nuvolari won thirty although he didn't start driving until 1921.

He finished second just sixteen times and third only nine times, for Nuvolari's racing plan was simple: win, or break up the automobile.

To watch the little man from Mantua—he was five-feet-five and weighed 137 pounds—excited even those who knew nothing about motor racing. Flying down the circuit in a blood-red Alfa-Romeo, he sat proudly upright, bright in white cloth or red leather helmet and yellow sweater. He was well back from the wheel, his hairy arms straight out, and he would sail through the curves in long, flaring slides, stare arrogantly over his tremendous jutting jaw at the cars beside him, then flick the machine straight and run away. Sometimes he would throw back his head and scream with exuberance, pounding the side of the car like a manic blacksmith.

Rules of form were revised for Nuvolari. If his car were as fast as anything else running and stayed together, he would probably win. If it were 10 miles an hour slower, still he might win. He once beat nine of the best cars in the world, and beat them twice in the same race, driving an Alfa that was 20 miles an hour slower. That was in the Grand Prix of Germany, held on July 28, 1935.

The German Mercedes-Benz and Auto Union cars of the 1930s were the fastest racing machines the world had seen to this day. The German Grand Prix of 1935 was supposed to be a private contest between the four Auto Union entries and the five from Mercedes-Benz. The Auto Unions would do 180 mph, the Mercedes were 5 mph slower, and Nuvolari's Alfa-Romeo was 20 miles an hour off the pace. The German cars were handled by some of the world's best: Rosemeyer, Von Brauchitsch, Stuck, Geier, Fagioli, *and* Caracciola and Varzi, the only two drivers automobile men ever attempt to compare with Nuvolari—*il maestro, il campionissimo.* The course was the Nürburgring, a mountain circuit, fourteen miles to the lap, 175 curves—a driver's course.

In ten laps Nuvolari moved his obsolescent Alfa-Romeo through the pack from sixth place to first. Still leading in the twelfth lap, Nuvolari came in for fuel. An Auto Union had just refueled in forty-nine seconds. It took Nuvolari's excited crew two minutes and fourteen seconds, and when he came screaming onto the track again he was back in sixth place. The Germans in the crowd relaxed. But in the next lap, the thirteenth, Nuvolari raced past four cars with absurd ease and lay an incredible second to Von Brauchitsch's Mercedes. The Mercedes pit gave their man the flat-out signal and he responded—indeed he broke the Nürburgring lap record. But he was over-revving his engine and wearing down the thinning tread of his tires to do it. Inevitably the big red car appeared in his mirrors, grew bigger and bigger until, halfway through the last lap, a rear tire blew out and Nuvolari blasted past to win by thirty-two seconds. It was the greatest individual triumph in the history of automobile racing.

A courteous, soft-voiced man, Nuvolari, unlike many drivers, was tranquil before a race, but he was often afraid. He had reason to be. It was said that he had broken every major bone in his body at least once, two vertebrae in his neck included. He once drove with a leg in a plaster cast, so that he had to manipulate clutch, brake, and accelerator with one foot. "It doesn't matter," he said. "I never use the brake anyway." He won a motorcycle race so encased in plaster that he had to be derricked onto the cycle and held up to start. His doctor walked away. "You are a dead man if you fall, Nivola," he said. "I don't want them even to call me."

Nuvolari's small stature probably explained everything about him—his terrifying competitive instinct, even his marvelously unorthodox style. When Nuvolari was at his peak, the cars were brutes, the most dangerous they have ever been and, compared with today's cars, very hard to handle. "I found out early," Nuvolari said, "that I didn't have enough strength to horse them around the curves like the other drivers. So I worked out my own methods. I let the car go, I let it slide. I found I knew where it was, always." He swore he knew to a pound the weight on each of a car's four wheels, running straight or sliding. He could drive on spilled oil. Again and again he drove safely through when catastrophe was all around him. "Nuvolari's reactions in emergency," said a British authority, "were so nearly instantaneous as to appear to be pure instinct."

Beyond the fact that he had abnormal reactions, the little man from Mantua can be explained only in terms of will to win. He loved winning and he loathed losing. Nuvolari was a competitor, a killer. He would not give an inch of roadway to his dearest friend.

Running in the 1930 Mille Miglia—he won this insanely dangerous 1000-mile roadrace two times—he was behind Achille Varzi, his great rival. Varzi was well ahead, and Nuvolari knew that if Varzi saw him coming he would never catch up. It was night. Nuvolari switched off his lights. He drove over the winding roads of Italy for sixty miles, howling along in the blackness flat-out, his mechanic sitting beside him stiff with fear, until he was just behind Varzi. He threw on the lights then, rode past, and won.

Essentially frail, Nuvolari was ill during the years of World War II, apparently of incipient tuberculosis. Tuberculosis took both his sons, one at eighteen, one at nineteen. Most of the men he had driven against were dead, a dreadful list: Brilli-Peri, Antonio Ascari, Arcangeli, Tenni, Bordino, Varzi, Materassi, Fagioli, Compari, Rosemeyer, Wakefield, Von Delius, Fane, Kautz, Seaman—dead at the wheel almost to the man. "Nivola is a sick man," a close friend said, "sick, and heartbroken too." Still he began to drive again as soon as he could, and he raced seven times in 1946, winning the Grand Prix of Albi.

He ran in 1947 too and won twice for Ferrari, but the penultimate blow had fallen: the fumes of racing fuel had become unbearable. A few laps of breathing the stuff on which his life was founded and he would begin to hemorrhage. He tried wearing masks. He had his tonsils removed. Nothing helped. Still he came within an ace of winning the Mille Miglia again, this time in an absurdly small Cisitalia, beating the roaring hundreds of cars to within sight of the finish and then losing only because a rainstorm soaked his magneto and cost him twenty minutes. Even so, he finished second. He tried again in 1948, driving a Ferrari. He came into Rome thirty minutes ahead of the pack, but the car was breaking up. At Florence the bonnet was gone and a spring had broken. He wouldn't let his riding mechanic get out to check the car. He stalked arrogantly once around it, spitting blood, and climbed back aboard. Still leading near Modena, where the Ferrari is made, the car broke down, quit cold, and that was that. Nuvolari sat quietly in the rain, in tears, as the others screamed past in the dark, until finally a priest came and persuaded him to come into the parish house.

As late as 1950 he ran a little 1100-cc Abarth at Monte Pellegrino. He had to be lifted out of the car. As the winner's wreath was given him he moaned and fell unconscious to the roadway. He was fifty-eight, he had done what he had to do for all his lifetime and he could do it no longer. When his friends came to the hospital he told them, "The man you came to see is dead."

Finally he did die, speechless in a paralytic coma, on a hot day in August. They buried him in his cloth helmet and his yellow sweater, the good-luck turtle brooch the poet D'Annunzio had given him so long ago pinned to his breast, and a steering wheel beside him. They raised a marble tomb over his body, and that year the Mille Miglia was changed so that the cars could run through Mantua.

—1957

The Life and Death of a Grandee

A year ago, on 12 May, a Ferrari automobile running in Italy's Mille Miglia race crashed in the village of Guidizzolo near Brescia. The car had been making something over 150 miles an hour and it killed nine of the spectators lining the long straight road. It killed the codriver, Edmund Nelson, and it killed the driver, a Spaniard named Alfonso Cabeza de Vaca y Leighton, Carvajal y Are, 13th Conde de la Mejorada, 12th Marquis de Portago. He was twenty-eight.

In the days after Portago's death, a standard picture of him was quickly established on the front pages of the world's newspapers: an immensely wealthy aristocrat, charter member of the international set, an indefatigable pursuer of beautiful women, and a man obsessed with the wish for an early and violent death. Portago would have laughed, I am sure, reading his obituaries. Two months before he died he had laughed when I had repeated a columnist's remark about his "death wish."

"It's so ridiculous. I'm sure I love life more than the average man does. I want to get something out of every minute. I want to live to be a very old man. I'm *enchanted* with life. But no matter how long I live, I still won't have time for all the things I want to do,

I won't hear all the music I want to hear, I won't be able to read all the books I want to read, I won't have all the women I want to have, I won't be able to do a twentieth of the things I want to do. I want to live to be a hundred and five, and I mean to."

But Eddie Nelson, who had been Portago's friend for years, and who was to die with him, had a different belief. "I know Fon says he'll live forever," Nelson remarked, "but I say he won't live to be thirty."

Nelson didn't say that because he believed Portago had a "death wish." He knew better than that. He felt that simple percentage would kill Portago: he didn't believe that anyone could go on exposing himself to hazard as Portago did and survive. Because he tried so hard to wring every drop of juice out of every moment of his life, Portago was always in a hurry, and he had no patience with time-consuming caution. Normally it takes ten years to become a top-ranked Grand Prix racing driver—ten years, that is, for those few who can do it at all. Portago never drove a racing automobile until 1954, but by 1957 he was ranked officially among the world's first ten drivers. He believed that he would be champion of the world by 1960. I for one would not have bet against it. He had been, briefly, an airplane pilot —he apparently believed that the primary function of aircraft was to fly under bridges—a jai-alai and polo player. He was a superb horseman and, typically, he was interested only in jump-races. He was the world's number-one amateur steeplechaser in 1951 and 1952. When he was invited to go down the St. Moritz bobsled run he said he'd be glad to—if he could steer. Told that he'd have to learn the run first in a good many trips as a passenger he said he'd rather skip all that and learn it straight off. He steered the first time he went down. Later he was captain of the Spanish bobsled team in the Olympics, and he set one-man skeleton-sled records on the Cresta run, too. He was a tremendous swimmer, handy and willing in a street fight, with a very short jolting punch. He was not a big man, not heavily muscled, but he had unusual strength, great endurance, abnormally sharp eyesight, an almost incredible quickness of reaction. He could catch knives thrown at him, pulling them out of the air by their handles.

Because he was so flamboyant, and because he had disdained the confinement of the schoolroom early in his teens, most people thought that Portago's interests were entirely physical. It was not so. "During most of the eight years I was married to Fon," Carroll Portago told me, "I think he read a book a day. He read history and biography, and little else. I don't believe I ever saw him reading a novel, a modern novel, although he did like Robert Graves. He thought most novels a terrible waste of time. One day, coming back from a race in Nassau, I read *Peyton Place* on the plane. Fon muttered about it all the way home. He said it was idiotic to waste time on such books."

Portago did have pronounced views on the well-rounded life. "The most important thing in our existence is a balanced sex life," Portago once said to me. "Everybody knows this is true, but nobody will admit it —of himself, that is. But if you don't have a happy sex life you don't have anything."

"It's the first thing historians suppress when they write the lives of great men," I said, "and often it was an astonishingly big factor in their lives."

"Of Course," Portago said. "Look at Nelson, look at Napoleon."

"Well, look at George Bernard Shaw," I said. "He gave it up altogether, and married on condition that his wife never mention sex to him."

"A freak," Portago said. "A very untypical writer. Look at Maupassant. A prodigy, in more ways than one. Well, as for me, making love is the most important thing I do every day, and I don't care who knows it."

On his father's side Portago was born to one of Spain's ancient titles. His mother, a Briton, had been married before and she brought to Portago's father, the 11th Marquis, an enormous American fortune. The last king of Spain, Alfonso XIII, was Portago's godfather and namesake. As a baby, and as a child, he was close to beautiful. In his teens he looked petulant, and in maturity he was simply tough. Sometimes he looked like a hired killer, sometimes he looked like what he was—a Spanish grandee to the bone. One of his friends said, "Every time I look at Fon I see him in a long black cape, a sword sticking out of it, a floppy black hat on his head, riding like a fiend across some castle drawbridge." Portago himself said that had he been born in another century he would have been a Crusader, a free-booter, a knight errant. I'm sure he often thought of that, and probably with longing. A determined lust for adventure, plus an inclination toward government, runs through the Portago line, and Spanish history is studded with the name. In the sixteenth century one of Portago's forebears, Cabeza de Vaca, was shipwrecked on the Florida coast. He *walked* to Mexico City, recruiting an army as he went. Another conquered the Canary Islands, another was a leader in the fight to drive the Moors out of Spain. Portago's grandfather was governor of Madrid, his father was Spain's best golfer, poloist, yachtsman; he was a fabulous gambler said to have once won $2 million in Monte Carlo, a soldier, and a movie actor. He died of a heart attack on the polo field, playing against his doctor's orders.

Portago's childhood was in the standard pattern of the wealthy European nobility: a melange of governesses, tutors, Biarritz, lessons in the graces— dancing, horsemanship, and so on. In the inevitable early pictures—six-year-olds at a birthday party, ranks of nannies in the rear—he is easy to pick out, and not only because he is usually close to the camera. There is a calm arrogance about the child, and he seems to be just on the point of moving. Portago kept a careful record of his life almost to the end of it. He collected pictures, he was a paper-saver, he recorded almost literally everything he pictures, he was a paper-saver, he recorded almost literally everything he did. He kept six huge leather-bound scrapbooks, so big that three of them make a load too heavy to carry comfortably. They are full of photographs and newspaper clippings, obviously cut with ruler and razor blade and pasted in dead straight and level.

Why had he gone to such trouble? Ego? Certainly. That, plus the wish to be sure that his children would be able to form a firm portrait of him. And I think he thought of the record of his life as something quite apart from himself. He was proud of his lineage, and he did not want the life of the 12th Marquis de Portago to be less well-recorded than the other eleven had been. And, as he said, he looked forward to a long life. And a full one.

I asked him if he intended to go on driving until he was as old as the present champion of the world, Juan Manuel Fangio, now in his middle forties. I knew that he would say no.

"Never," he said. "Certainly not. In any case I'll stop when I'm thirty-five, and if I'm champion of the world, sooner."

"And then?"

"I'm ambitious for myself," he said. "I wouldn't be racing automobiles if I didn't think I could get something out of it, and not only the championship. I haven't told this to a great many people, but—well, you see, Spain has had no national hero for many years. That's what the championship of the world means to me."

Portago never attempted bullfighting, the sport in which the Spaniards have been accustomed to find their heroes. Few Spanish aristocrats ever do. "I have thought about it, of course," he said. "I like to watch bullfights. I suppose that's natural since I'm Spanish, but I've never thought of trying it because I couldn't start early enough. To be any kind of *torero,* you must begin almost as a child, you must live with bulls, learn how they think. Racing cars don't think. When I give up racing I'm going to Spain and go into politics."

"You seem hardly the type," I said.

"Maybe the word is wrong," he said. "Maybe I should have said 'government' instead of 'politics.' In any case, if you want to know what I mean, I mean that I think I could reasonably hope to be foreign minister of Spain."

Later, from Paris, he sent me a photograph of himself and Fangio and the Pretender to the Spanish throne. On it he had written, "With Fangio and Don Juan, the *future king* of Spain."

When he found automobile racing, Portago knew that he had come to his real métier and he abandoned all other sports.

Portago had driven midget trackracing cars in Paris, but it was not until 1953 that he found out what automobile racing was really like.

"I met Luigi Chinetti, the New York Ferrari representative, at the Paris auto show in 1953, and he asked me to be his codriver in the Mexican Road Race—the Carrera Panamericana. All he wanted me for, of course, was ballast. I didn't drive a foot, not even from the garage to the starting line. I just sat there, white with fear, holding on to anything I thought looked sturdy enough. I knew that Chinetti was a very good driver, a specialist in long-distance races who was known to be conservative and careful, but the first time you're in a racing car you can't tell if the driver is conservative or a wild man, and I didn't see how Chinetti could get away with half what he was doing. We broke down the second day of the race, but I had decided by then that this was what I wanted to do more than anything else. I used to think that flying was exciting, and for a long time riding seemed very rewarding. I rode, mostly steeplechases, twice a week at least for two years. But those things can't be compared with driving. It's a different world. So I bought a 3-liter Ferrari."

When Portago began to drive in earnest, early in 1954, no one took him seriously. He was almost universally considered to be just another rich dilettante. He and Harry Schell, an American living in Paris who is now ranked number six in the world listings, took the 3-liter Ferrari to the Argentine for the 1000-kilometer sports-car race. Said Portago: "Harry was so frightened that I would break the car he wouldn't teach me how to change gear, so when after seventy laps [the race was 101] he was tired and it was my turn to drive, I did three laps, during which I lost so much time that we dropped from second to fifth place, before I saw Harry out in the middle of the track frantically waving a flag to make me come into the pits so he could drive again. We eventually finished second overall and first in our class. I didn't learn to change gears properly until the chief mechanic of Maserati took me out one day and spent an afternoon teaching me." Portago had driven all his life, of course, since childhood in fact, but changing gears on a passenger car bears little relation to shifting on a 175-mile-an-hour competition car, when a miss on a shift from fourth to third, for example, can wreck engine or transmission or both and perhaps kill the driver as well.

Schell and Portago ran the 3-liter in the 12-Hour Race at Sebring, Florida, in 1954. The rear axle broke after two hours. He sold the Ferrari and bought a 2-liter Maserati, the gear-shifting lesson thrown in, and ran it in the 1954 Le Mans 24-Hour Race with Alejandro DeTomaso codriving. They led the class until five in the morning, when the engine blew up. He won the Grand Prix of Metz with the Maserati—"but there were no good drivers in it"—and ran with Louis Chiron in the 12 Hours of Rheims, Chiron blowing up the engine with twenty minutes to go while leading the class. He ran an Osca in the G.P. of Germany, and rolled it. "God protects the good, so I wasn't hurt," he said.

In 1954 Portago broke down while leading the first lap of the Mexican Road Race, a murderous affair run the length of the peninsula. He won three races in Nassau that year. He broke an automobile occasionally, and he was often off the road, but he was never hurt until the 1955 Silverstone race, in England, when he missed a gear-shift and came out of the resulting crash with a double compound break in his left leg.

The crash had no effect on Portago's driving; he continued to run a little faster on the circuit and to leave it less frequently. At Caracas in Venezuela in 1955 he climbed up on Juan Manuel Fangio until he was only nine seconds behind him, and he finished second. He was a member of the Ferrari team in 1956, an incredibly short time after he had begun to race. The precise equivalent of his rise in this country would be for a man to be a first-string pitcher for the Yankees two years after he had begun to play baseball. He won the Grand Prix of Portugal in 1956, a wild go-round in which the lap record was broken seventeen times; he won the Tour of France, the Coupes du Salon, the Grand Prix of Rome, and was leading Fangio and the great British driver, Stirling Moss, at Caracas when a broken gas line put him out of the race. After Caracas that year I asked Moss how he ranked Portago.

"He's certainly among the ten best in the world," Moss said, "and as far as I'm concerned, he's the one to watch out for."

Running in the Grand Prix of Cuba in 1957 he was leading Fangio by over a minute when a gas line broke again, and afterward, when they gave Fangio the huge silver cup emblematic of victory, he said, "Portago should have it."

He ran at Sebring in '57, driving alone nearly all of the twelve hours and finishing seventh; he ran at Montlhery in France breaking the track record for *gran turismo* cars, and then went to Italy for the Mille Miglia. It was a race he did not like. Few professional drivers do like it: a thousand miles over ordinary two-lane roads, across two mountain ranges, beginning at Brescia, down the Adriatic coast, across the boot of Italy, and back to Brescia through Florence. The Mille Miglia is probably the world's most dangerous automobile race. The weather is usually wet, there are hundreds of cars running, from tiny two-cylinder runabouts to Grand Prix racing cars barely disguised as sports models and capable of 185 miles an hour. "No matter how much you practice," Portago said to me, "you can't possibly come to know 1000 miles of Italian roads as well as the Italian drivers, and, as Fangio says, if you have a conscience you can't drive really fast anyway. There are hundreds of corners in the Mille Miglia where one little slip by a driver will kill fifty people. You can't keep the spectators from crowding into the road—you couldn't do it with an army. It's a terrible thing, the Mille Miglia."

To make matters worse for him, the illness of another driver on the team forced Portago to take a car he loathed and mistrusted, the 3.8 Ferrari. As a rule he was indifferent to the cars he drove, had no affection for them, could barely tell one from the other, but the 3.8 he considered to be somehow malevolent. He told a reporter that he was intent only on finishing, that he was, in effect, going to take it easy. But when he slid down the starting ramp at Brescia with Nelson hunched enigmatically beside him, he forgot all that, his bitterly competitive instinct took over, and he began to go. He was fourth overall at the first check-point. Peter Collins, lying third, broke a half-shaft, and when Portago was given this information, he knew that he could finish third without any trouble at all. It wasn't enough. He knew too that he might finish second, that he might even win. He ran the car at the absolute limit of road adhesion. At the Ferrari depot in Florence, he refused two new tires, grudging the forty-five seconds it would have taken to put them on. He had run nearly the whole 1000 miles, he was within twenty minutes or so of Brescia and the end of the race when a tire blew out, or a half-shaft broke, on the straight at Guidizzolo and the car lifted its wheels off the road and left him helpless as it flew through a telephone pole, went into and out of one ditch, and came to rest finally in another.

Portago's widow, Carroll McDaniel Portago, left their New York apartment with the children, Antonio, four, and Andrea, seven, and went to Italy to take her husband's body to Spain. The world's newspapers duly ran the funeral pictures and that was that.

Portago married Carroll McDaniel, a South Carolina girl, in 1949. He had been living in New York for some time. He met her at a party, told her two hours later that he intended to marry her. They spent most of their eight years of married life in France. A beautiful and enchanting woman, Carroll Portago brought to her husband a social stability that was new to him. She became an intimate of the Duke and Duchess of Windsor and she could move with grace in any circle. "Carroll, in a sense, tamed Fon," one of their friends has said. "To the degree that anyone could, she brought him into the twentieth century. I think he regretted not having been born in the 1600s, lots of us thought that, and I believe that Carroll helped him fit into his own time."

Portago was volatile, violent, headstrong, almost desperate in his determination to take every sensation out of every minute of his life. Carroll Portago is tranquil, firm-minded, strong-willed in her own right, and their life together produced some heady moments. If Portago felt that a man had impugned his honor, the debate was apt to be short and terminated by a right cross to the jaw, and among the people to whom he publicly demonstrated this side of his nature was a columnist who has not even yet forgiven him. Portago's airy indifference to the maxim "Never, but never hit a reporter" ensured that his attentions to women other than his wife, and they were many, would have maximum coverage in the public prints. And at least one of the women concerned demonstrated a semiprofessional ability in publicity on her own right. Just before Portago's death, columnists were frequently predicting that he and his wife would be divorced.

"Like so much else that was printed about Fon," Carroll Portago told me, "that has no connection with reality. Fon's attitude toward divorce was very Catholic: to him divorce was anathema, it was impossible, unthinkable.

"Another thing: there was very little that was sneaky about Fon. He moved quite beyond commonplace deception. I knew him, I think, better than anyone else, and there was very little indeed in his life that I did not know about. We could talk about anything, and we did. I can assure you that some of the explanations, excuses, that he gave me at one time or another when we talked about something that he had done were strange and wonderful, often hilarious, even, but you could not laugh at him because he was absolutely sincere. All one can say about it, really, is that he was unable to resist a beautiful woman, any more than he was able to resist any other kind of challenge. He could not be changed. It was a facet of his nature, and not by any means the most important, either. Most of his attachments were completely casual. One was not, but even that had ended before his death.

"After all, the essence of Fon's whole personality was his maleness. He was totally a man, and he was almost ferocious in his determination to live by his own rules."

What was he, really? He was the absolutely free spirit.

"If I die tomorrow," he told me the day before the 1957 Sebring, "still I have had twenty-eight wonderful years."

I cited to him the Spanish proverb "In this life, take what you want—but pay for it."

"Of course," he said. "Of course, that's exactly it. You must pay. You pay . . . you try to put it off, but you pay. But I think, for my part at least, I think the game is worth the candle."

When Portago died, I wrote for the magazine *Sports Cars Illustrated* an appreciation of him. Nothing that I have learned about him in the months since inclines me to change it:

He was not an artist, he left nothing of beauty behind him and nothing of use to the world. He moved no mountains, wrote no books, bridged no rivers. He saved no lives, indeed he took innocents with him to death. He could be cruel. If he wished to indulge himself he would do it, though the act hurt and humiliated others who had done him no harm nor in any way earned his malice. Yet it would be a flinty heart that did not mourn his death. At the very least he was an adornment in the world, an excitement, a pillar of fire in the night, producing no useful heat or light perhaps, but a glory to see nonetheless. At most he was an inspiration, for, with the mere instruments of his life set aside—the steeplechasing, the motor racing, wealth, women, world-roaming—he proved again what cannot be too often proven: if anything at all is meant for us here, we are meant to live life, there is no folly like the folly of the hermit who cowers in his cave, and a dead lion is a greater thing than a live mouse.

—1958

The
Brothers
Chevrolet

Louis Chevrolet is remembered as a man who designed a wine-pump and an automobile. The wine-pump didn't amount to much and he made little money from it. The automobile, the Chevrolet, became one of the legends of the century, a fountain from which billions of dollars flowed, but not much went Louis's way. He was a racing driver, too, Louis, and so were his brothers Gaston and Arthur.

The Chevrolets were Swiss who moved to Burgundy in France from La Chaux de Fonds when Louis was an infant. As a young man he ran a bicycle shop, he invented his wine-pump and he came to America in 1900 to represent a French manufacturer. He lived in Brooklyn and he worked as a mechanic for a foreign-car dealer, E. Rand Hollander. Gaston and Arthur had come across the Atlantic with him, hot with pride and energy, full of hope. France was the world capital of what was called automobilism in those days, and the three Chevrolets all wanted the same thing: a wheel, a ride in somebody's racing car. Hollander introduced Louis to Alfred Reeves, a race promoter who was looking for new boys to throw into the pit against the great Berner Eli Oldfield, a converted bicycle racer who'd been blowing off everybody with Henry Ford's "999," handle-bar steering and all. Louis was a hungry tiger and he went. He beat Barney Oldfield three times in 1905, once in a ten-mile race at Brunot's Island, Pittsburgh, once at Hartford, Connecticut, once at Morris Park, New York. Walter Christie, inventor of the front-wheel-drive Christie racing machine, was in the Morris Park field. Louis drove a 90 Fiat in those races.

He made the Fiat team for the Vanderbilt Cup race of 1905, and he wrote off the first car assigned to him, a 110 Fiat, laying it into a telephone pole. He took another car for the race itself, a 90, and was in eighth place at 150 miles when he hit a second phone pole. He was a heavy-footed driver, Louis, and so were his brothers. In the opinion of Peter Helck, whose view of the period is authoritative, all the Chevrolets were rough on the machinery.

The Chevrolet driving style attracted a man who moved in much the same fashion in his own field: William Crapo Durant. Durant, a promoter who operated on the principle that $1000 was the smallest unit of U.S. currency, thought it would be nice to have a Chevrolet for a chauffeur. In 1908, when this notion occurred to him, Durant was head of General Motors, a company he had organized. He had been head of his own insurance agency when he was twenty-one, and a millionaire carriage tycoon before he was out of his thirties. Promoters behind the Buick car being made in Flint, Michigan, asked Durant to come and take over. He gladly did so. He raised Buick capital from $75,000 to $1,500,000. He sold $500,000 worth of stock himself—in one day. Price of the stock quadrupled in four years, and the Buick plant couldn't keep up with orders. Everybody seemed in line for a killing except David Dunbar Buick himself, an inventor of fabulously diverse talent who was said, when he died a poor man, to have made at least fifty fortunes for others.

Durant decided to organize a really impressive holding company and call it International Motors, including Reo, Ford, Buick, and Maxwell-Briscoe. Ford and Ransom Olds wanted too much money, so the deal collapsed, but Durant and Briscoe went ahead. They asked J. P. Morgan & Co. for $500,000. The Morgan lawyer didn't like Durant's attitude (almost *nobody* liked Durant's attitude) and besides he didn't see any future in the horseless carriage, so he recommended refusal. The decision cost the house of Morgan around $200,000,000. Durant went ahead anyway, and organized General Motors with a capital of $2000. Twelve days later he made it $12,-500,000. Sixty days later he bought Oldsmobile for $17,279 in cash and some GM stock and was on his way. He told the Oldsmobile engineers what kind of car to make. In fact, he showed them: he had the body taken off his Buick and sawed into four equal parts. Then he ordered the sections moved apart from each other. "Make a bigger Buick," he said, "with an

Oldsmobile radiator and hood, and raise the price $250."

This, then, was the tycoon who in 1908 offered to audition Louis and Arthur Chevrolet for the post of chauffeur. He took them to the dirt track behind the Buick works and got into a car himself. Louis won and was somewhat surprised when Durant announced that the chauffeur's job was Arthur's. Louis had been faster, sure, but Arthur had taken fewer chances. However, there was a nice consolation prize: the Buick company raced its cars, as every contemporary manufacturer of any prominence did, and Louis found himself in the big leagues.

He began to run on the one-mile dirt tracks, and he won a fair share of the events he entered. Journalists of the time usually ranked him just after Oldfield, Earle Kiser, and Jay Webb, the top drivers of the day. He ran a Cleveland in the 24-Hour race at Brighton Beach in 1908, and again in the same race in 1909 and 1910, placing fourth both times and sharing the wheel with Arthur in 1910. He ran in the 1908 Vanderbilt, and won the Cobe Trophy at Crown Point, Indiana, in June, 1909 on a stock 30 HP Buick, 396 miles at 49.3 He led during nine of the seventeen laps. He won a ten-miler at Indianapolis in 1909, again for the Buick team. At Lowell, Massachusetts, in September of 1909 he won the Yorick Trophy for 158 miles by a full twenty minutes. Trying for the Lowell Trophy on the same circuit he broke the Buick's frame after making the fastest lap of the day. In the same month he won his class at the Riverhead, Long Island, Motor Derby, doing 113 miles at 70 mph, which was really flying for the time. He led the 1909 Vanderbilt until a cylinder head cracked on the fourth lap, and in the 1910 running he led for seven laps and then had total steering failure while in fourth place. He wasn't hurt, but his riding mechanic was instantly killed. Arthur was running in the Buick team that year, too. Louis was in a two-mile event at the Atlanta, Georgia, Motordrome in 1909, and a 200-miler as well, averaging 72 in a Buick.

Meanwhile, back at the foundry, Durant was making big automobiles and big decisions. In 1909 he bought Cadillac. Henry M. Leland, who owned it, was a man who knew his mind. His first price was $3,500,000, take it or leave it in ten days. Durant didn't get around to it for some months, when he was told that the price was now $4,125,000, take it or leave it, ten days. Durant procrastinated again and when he went around with the $4,125,000 he was told that the market was up again: $4,500,000, take it or leave it, ten days. Durant scratched up the extra $375,000 in a hurry that time.

He tried to buy Ford for $8 million (cash, Henry wouldn't touch anything else, and as a matter of fact, suggested *gold* cash) but couldn't raise it, the far-seeing New York bankers goofing again with the opinion that this represented a ridiculous overevaluation of the Ford assets. He did acquire about two dozen automobile and accessory companies, though, grabbing them off like a mad squirrel harvesting nuts in a blizzard. Among them was something called the Heany Lamp Company, which cost $7 million in GM stock. Heany was one of Durant's mistakes. John Heany had a patent on tungsten incandescent lights which would have up-ended General Electric and everybody else in the business. But GE went to court and had the patent declared void. Durant's $7 million had bought nothing. It was too much of a blow, and the board of directors began to bay. They thought Durant needed $7 million. Actually the company was $12 million down and nobody would lend it. Finally a New York syndicate agreed to help out. In these days of the Securities Exchange Commission and the other such instruments of enlightenment with which Franklin Roosevelt prevented American capitalism from cannibalizing itself it's a little hard to believe what bankers of the happy 1900–1914 period could and would do once they got a hammerlock. The banks agreed to loan GM $15 million at 6 percent per year interest. Of this, the firm actually got $12 million. The other $3 million never left the vaults. That was for openers. Then, as payment for having arranged the loan, the banks took $4,169,000 in GM preferred stock and $2 million in common. All in all, the syndicate stood to make a 75 percent profit on the deal, *plus* interest. The final condition was that Durant resign, which he did, on November 15, 1910.

Durant had not left GM without mad money, and he used some of it to buy the Flint Wagon Works. Here he set up the Little Wagon Company. (This was not a synonym for a Small Cart, the president being named William H. Little, once general manager of Buick.) Louis Chevrolet, naturally loyal to the man who'd given him his chance, proposed to design a small car, a *voiturette* such as Ettore Bugatti had first shown the world in the Bébé Peugeot. Durant thought it was a good idea, providing the car was beefed up enough to cope with American rural conditions, and Louis went ahead.

The first car the Little Company made was a 4-cylinder priced at $700. In 1911 the Chevrolet Company appeared with Louis's design, pretty big by now, a five-passenger touring car at $2150. It was a notable success, and 2999 units were sold. Louis was a principal in the Chevrolet Company, and Arthur and Gaston were in as well on lesser elevations. In the next two years Chevrolet sold 16,000 cars and made a profit of $1,300,000. New models poured out, such dazzlers as the Royal Mail roadster, at one time as much a part of a doctor's outfit as his stethoscope, the Amesbury Special, the 490, and the Baby Grand. But Louis wasn't convinced and in 1913 he dropped out. Durant bought up his interest in 1914 and Louis went off on his own.

The Monroe racing car was Louis's design, and it won at Indianapolis in 1920, Gaston Chevrolet at the helm, beating full teams of Ballot and

Duesenberg machines. Louis had designed the Frontenac, too, and the Frontenac was big for a while, and the brothers must have thought, now and then, that the Fronty would be the golden egg. Race-car oriented, they couldn't know that they'd left the golden egg back in Flint. Frontenacs ran seventh and ninth at Indianapolis in 1919, Louis and Gaston up and Arthur in the pits. They won at Sheepshead Bay, a big-league circuit indeed in those days, in July and September of 1919, a 100-miler at 110 mph, 150 at 109 mph, Gaston up both times. On the same day in July, the 4th, that saw Gaston win at Sheepshead, Louis won at the Tacoma Board Track in a Frontenac, 80 miles at 100. They had a good car, and it had run fast from the beginning, but it wasn't going anywhere. Louis won at the Uniontown Board Speedway, 112 miles at 102, as early as December 1916.

Frontenac cylinder heads turned the T-Ford into quite a hairy machine for its time, and for a while "Fronty Ford" was something you heard a lot about, and that looked like money to Louis, too, but the appearance of the Model A killed it off.

Chevrolet and Durant prospered, though. Durant steadily built the company up, planning and scheming for one day, one hour. He set up Chevrolet in Delaware, he affiliated with the Du Ponts. He began to buy GM stock in big bundles. It was easy: the stockholders were sore because the bank controlling the company had seen the profits run to $58 million in three years but hadn't declared a dime in dividends! On September 16, 1920, Durant walked into the GM annual meeting, lackeys laden with bundles of proxies staggering behind him, and said, quietly, "Gentlemen, *I* control this company."

He did, too. He ran it in a big way. He paid Walter Chrysler $500,000 a year to run Buick, a salary that represented a $494,000 raise in two years for Chrysler. He brought in Delco and Hyatt Roller Bearing and Kettering and Sloan and Fisher Body and Frigidaire. But he couldn't stop expanding, juggling. He finally got too far out on the wire, the company's accountants guessed about $30 million too far out, and the GM doors shut behind him again. This time, there was no Chevrolet to ride back in.

In the same year that saw Durant out of GM for the last time, Gaston Chevrolet was killed driving a Monroe at the Los Angeles Speedway. Louis had stopped driving in 1923, and Arthur even before that. Arthur had never really liked it anyway, and he doesn't often show in the record: 1910 Vanderbilt Cup, Marquette-Buick, out at eighty-eight miles with a broken chain, 1910 G.P., Savannah, out at 130 miles with a broken crankshaft while running eleventh.

Louis tried boat racing in 1925, won at the Miami Regatta. He worked for Stutz for a while and then in 1929 he and Arthur organized the Chevrolet Brothers Aircraft Company, intending to make airplane engines. It didn't work out, the brothers quarrelled and there was recourse to law. Louis won, but it was a case of winner take very little. In 1934 he went back to work for Chevrolet, stayed until 1938 when the illness which was to cause his death forced his retirement. He had a small pension from GM. He died in 1941. During World War II Arthur Chevrolet worked for Higgins in New Orleans as a master mechanic. In April, 1946, when he was sixty-one, he hanged himself.

Durant lived longest of the four. He died in 1947. He was running a chain of bowling alleys and a grocery store in Asbury Park in New Jersey. Not just a bowling alley, a chain. Not just a grocery store, a supermarket. Characteristically, he was in early on a couple of things that were booming. He was thinking big, and all he needed, probably, was a little more time. But at eighty-six, he didn't have it.

—1959

Elisabeth and the Racing Mog

"You are a genius," Elisabeth Harmon said. "Not only that, but you are a good man, kind and true."

Her husband smiled indulgently. "It's possible, just possible," he said, "that you are too generous."

"No, Peter, I mean it," Elisabeth said. "And I do want to apologize to you. When I think how mean I was about your buying that old Mercer Raceabout—why, I said terrible things to you."

"Oh, I don't know," Peter Harmon said. "Trifles, really. You said I was taking the food out of the children's mouths, that I was untrustworthy, and a liar—things like that. Nothing to get excited over."

"You should have beaten me with a stick," Elisabeth said. "I hated you for all the time you spent fixing that old car, and I laughed at you when you said you'd keep it only a year and then sell it for a lot of money. I never thought you'd give it up at all, much less make money on the deal. And now—wow, a check for six thousand dollars!" She held the little slip of blue paper to the light, and her big brown eyes peered lovingly at it.

"Actually, it's five thousand," Peter said.

"No dear, it's six," Elisabeth said. "See: 'Six thousand and no/100 dollars!' " She frowned ever so slightly and stared curiously up at her husband. "Why did you say it was for only five thousand?"

Peter poured another dollop out of the shaker of martinis compounded up for celebration. "It's a little complicated," he said. "The check is for six thousand dollars, that's right; but it actually represents only five thousand, because I've sort of spent a thousand of it. See?"

His good wife stopped in the act of buttering a cracker with gooey cheese. "You sort of spent a thousand of it?" she said. ":Already? Without telling me? Peter, I thought that sneaky kind of business was all in the dim and distant past . . . What did you buy with it?"

"Another car, what else?" Peter announced calmly.

"You beast!" Elisabeth said. "You dreadful, two-timing sneak. Without even telling me? Without a word . . ."

"Steady, girl," Peter said. "That is no way to talk to a genius, a good, kind man, I think you were saying a minute ago?"

"A minute ago I thought you'd reformed," Elisabeth said. "Now I know better. It was just a passing phase. Did you buy another Mercer? Are you going through all that again?"

Her husband stood up and offered his hand. "Come with me," he said. He led her through the hallway, down the steps to the sidewalk. She could hear a sound like a low-flying airplane, an ominous crackling and booming noise. It grew louder, and she ducked under Peter's arm to peer up the street as he was doing. The thing came around the corner, scuttling like a big green beetle. It looked vaguely like an automobile, like an open two-seater, and it took Elisabeth a second or two to realize that its strange, truncated air was due to the fact that it had only one wheel in the rear. It had no top, what appeared to be the engine hung out in front of the radiator, and a strange man peered through the tiny windshield as it screeched to the curb. The noise stopped abruptly.

"Here she is, Mr. Harmon," the driver said.

"Thanks, Mike," Peter said. "My wife. This is Mike Donovan, dear."

Elisabeth nodded vaguely. "What *is* it?" she said.

"This, pet, is a Morgan Three-Wheeler," her husband said. "There are only six others in the whole country."

"I'll bet there's a good reason," Elisabeth said. She leaned in to look at the dashboard. She screamed and jumped backward, grabbing for her knee. "The damned thing bit me!" she yelled.

The Mike person grinned idiotically. "That exhaust pipe gets pretty hot," he said, pointing. A shiny snake of chrome ran down the side of the car, right beside the rim of the doorless cockpit. "There's one on the other side, too."

"Darling, I'm sorry," Peter said. "I should have told you not to get so close."

"You won't have to worry in the future," Elisabeth said. "If you'll excuse me now, I'll just run into the house and call an ambulance. I have every reason to believe I'm burned to the bone." She spun on her heel and limped convincingly up the walk.

Donovan treated Peter to another of his vapid grins. "She don't like it," he said.

Peter nodded sadly. "I'll drive you back to the garage," he said.

The house was ominously quiet when Peter returned. He found Elisabeth reading, a cup of tea beside her.

"How's the leg?" he said brightly.

She looked up. "Oh, it's you," she said. "The leg, as you put it, is all right. Just a small, deep, third-degree burn. I suppose it will infect."

"Darling, look," Peter said. "I . . ."

"A weird coincidence has just taken place," Elisabeth said. She held up her book. "I was rereading *Mrs. Miniver*, and Jan Struther mentions a Morgan Three-Wheeler. 'A two-cylinder roller skate,' she calls it, 'with overhead valves and partially exposed viscera.' Isn't that cute?" She closed the book. "Tell me, in simple terms: Why did you buy that thing?"

"I bought it because I wanted it," Peter said. "And because it's rare, and unique, and it's fun."

"You are the soul of logic," Elisabeth said. "How did you know there *was* such a thing?"

"The Morgan Three-Wheeler," Peter told her, "was built in England from 1911 to 1951. They made 40,000 of them."

"The British are mad eccentrics," Elisabeth said, "but you have no excuse. You're thirty-six years old, you're married, you have two children and a position of some trust in an ad agency. You have no business driving a two-cylinder roller skate. You look like an aging juvenile delinquent in that thing. You'll be a local joke."

"Hah!" Peter said. "You'll see. I'm going to fix it up and enter it in shows. I may even race it. What do you think about *that?*"

Elisabeth rolled her eyes. "Oh, boy!" she said. "Go to bed, hero-driver. You might as well start training right away."

The first cop who stopped Peter Harmon on the road didn't want him for speeding, which he was doing—he wanted to ask if the Morgan was homemade. Gaspump attendants soared to new heights of witticism when the Morgan pulled in. Peter drove it to the station a couple of times, but commuters are notoriously a crude group, and he decided finally that the car shouldn't stand unattended in the parking lot all day—someone might pick it up and take it home for the kids. The gibes of his fellows otherwise only hardened his resolution. He met small but numerous bills for chrome-plating, for upholstery, for paint, for new tires. No doubt about it, he had the best-looking Morgan Three-Wheeler in New England. The only one, too. He overheard Elisabeth talking about it on the phone one day, satisfying one of her girl friends' morbid interest.

"Oh, it gives him something to do," she said in the condescending tone peculiar to women talking about their husbands. "I've told him he looks like a teen-ager running away from home in something he made in the back yard, but he doesn't care. I guess it's harmless. I don't think the thing would go fast enough to be dangerous, and it could be worse: it could be blonde. And speaking of blondes . . ."

Peter slipped the extension phone quietly into its cradle. What the dear girl doesn't know can't hurt her, he told himself. But Elisabeth's ignorance was short-lived. The blow fell at a cocktail party. It was an ordinary, standard Connecticut countryside cocktail party: three advertising men and their wives, a lady novelist, a plastic surgeon, two television writers, a stray textile tycoon, an English artist just off the boat, and a ceramist. It was the Englishman, answering to the name of Dennis Mulford, who spilled the beans when someone introduced Peter as a Morgan owner.

"Didn't think there were any Mogs over here," the fellow said. "Yours an early one?"

"Nineteen thirty-three," Peter said.

"Oh, a Super-Sport," Mulford said. "They're great fun, if a bit chancy. J.A.P. engine, I suppose?"

"That's right," Peter said.

"Lots of luck, old boy," Mulford said. "I ran one like that. Dreadful thing. That hand throttle has killed more people than the plague. Sticks, you know, usually at full chat. You'd be wise to convert it to foot feed. And I suppose you've noticed how she lifts the near wheel in a left-hand corner? Always trying to turn over. Beastly habit. Lost my best friend that way, just before the Hitler war."

Peter looked at Elisabeth out of the corner of his eye. She was missing nothing.

"Nice to have seen you," he said to Mulford, looking over his head.

"Do watch that rear tire, too, old boy," Mulford said. "Never run it over 7500 miles, no matter how good it looks. Throw it away. You just can't have a tire failure in the rear, you know. I remember seeing a Morgan blow a rear tire at Brooklands, doing just on 100, I should think. Remarkable. I don't suppose there was a piece of it left bigger than one's hand. Broke every bone in the poor chap's body, of course."

"Hope I see you again," Peter said. He dragged Elisabeth away.

"Oh, quite," Mulford said. "Bags of luck, now!"

"Mr. Mulford seemed to know quite a bit about Morgans," Elisabeth said on the way home.

"Probably never even sat in one," Peter said. "He looked like a total fraud to me. Sounded like one, too."

Elisabeth ignored his estimate of Mulford's character. "So in addition to being silly-looking, and perfectly useless," she said, "a Morgan is approximately as dangerous as a maddened cobra. *That's* your new toy, is it? That's what you're going racing in?"

"Nonsense," Peter said. "Propaganda. Folklore. Foolishness."

"Peter," Elisabeth said. "You will kindly sell The Thing tomorrow morning. If you have to die of overwork, very well. If the 8:11 meets the 7:02 head-on some foggy morning, very well, that is fate. If you fall on the field of battle, I can accept it with some grace. But I am *not* going to be widowed by a stupid two-cylinder roller skate, and that is that!"

"Stop shouting!" Peter said. "This is a residential area. Somebody will set the police on us."

"In the morning," Elisabeth said. "And I mean it."

"No."

"Why don't you grow up?" Elisabeth snapped. "You're not a downy-faced boy any more. You don't have to prove that you have exotic tastes and the courage of a Cossack. Buy a nice little MG or something. After all, *I* like sensible sports cars myself."

"No."

She was silent the rest of the way home. They were in bed and the lights were out before she spoke again.

"I suppose I shouldn't be so cross with you," she said, her voice full of resignation. "It's a congenital defect in men: they never can see anything from a woman's point of view."

"Look, pet," Peter said. "Listen to me. Now—"

"Shut up," she said. "I'm thinking."

She didn't answer when he said good-night.

Peter brought flowers when he came home next day, and he came early, too. It was a Friday, and he had made big, conciliatory plans. There was no one in the house but Mrs. Hobart, the cleaning woman.

"Mrs. Harmon said to tell you she wouldn't be home tonight," Mrs. Hobart said. "She went to a place called Lime Rock. The children are with Mrs. Schwartz."

"Lime Rock?" Peter said. "Lime Rock? That's a race course. Why in the world would she go there?"

"I have no idea," Mrs. Hobart said. "She left at noon, she and her friend."

"What friend?" Peter said wildly.

"I didn't catch his name," Mrs. Hobart said primly. "He was English, though; he had an English accent. They took your little three-wheel car.

They had to strap your wife's helmet on the back of it; there was no room inside."

"*Helmet?*" Peter said. "What helmet? Are you out of your mind? Elisabeth hasn't got any *helmet!*"

"Well, I beg your pardon, Mr. Harmon," Mrs. Hobart said, "but she said it was her helmet. A big red thing, like a football helmet. And it has her name painted on the back: 'Liz's Lid,' it says."

Peter reeled toward the refrigerator. He felt the need of a restorative.

"I'm going now," Mrs. Hobart said. "There's a casserole in the oven, and your wife left a note for you upstairs."

That much was true, at any rate. "Dear Peter," the note read. "Dennis Mulford and I have gone to Lime Rock. I asked him to teach me to drive the Morgan—I mean, drive it really fast, you know. I called John Fitch and he said we can use the track today and tomorrow, and it won't really cost much. Wasn't that nice of him?

"You see, I've decided that if you're going to live dangerously, so am I. As you've so often said, the governing principle of a good marriage must be share and share alike. And after all, lots of women race: Denise McCluggage, Eve Mull, Margaret Wyllie, Averil Scott-Moncrieff. No reason, I shouldn't, too.

"Please don't worry. After all, you said yourself that the Morgan is perfectly safe.

Love, Elisabeth.

P.S. Did you know that the world's speed record for Morgans was held by a woman? Gwenda Hawkes, 116 mph. Do you think I could do 120?"

If I really stand on it, Peter thought, and I don't get arrested, I can be in Lime Rock in an hour and a half. He ran for the garage and made Lime Rock before sunset. At first he thought the place was deserted. He ran the station wagon across the bridge into the infield, and as soon as his feet hit the ground he heard the Morgan somewhere on the backstretch. Then he saw Mulford leaning against a post on the straightaway.

"Where is she?" he yelled as soon as he was close enough.

"Ah, there you are," Mulford said. "Elisabeth? Just into the downhill leg, I should think. She'll be coming round the bend any second now." He listened critically. "Very nice downshift," he said. "The girl's a born driver."

Peter stared up the straight. Another howl of the engine heralded his helpmate's appearance, the Morgan drifting wickedly, the rear end reaching for the edge of the road, then straightening out suddenly. The engine note dropped as she got into third gear, and then she was past, an incredibly tiny figure under the absurdly big red crash hat. He watched, openmouthed, as she made the corner at the far end.

"My God," he said. "She must have been getting 85 past here."

"Every bit of that, I should think," Mulford said. "That Mog is quicker than most."

Peter turned on him. "Why, you birdbrained Limey," he said. "What about all that stuff you were giving us the other night, people getting rolled into a ball at Brooklands and all that? That's my *wife* out there, you idiot. I'm going to belt your brains out!"

Mulford regarded him calmly. "Shouldn't do that if I were you, old boy," he said. "I'd have to hit you back, and one of us ought to be on his feet, you know. Only sensible. I mean, the girl's alone on the circuit and all that."

Peter glared at him. He started for the edge of the track. "Wait'll I get her in here," he muttered.

Elisabeth waved prettily as she went by the second time, and a couple of minutes later she pottered slowly up to them and stopped. She took her helmet off and shook her hair out.

"Peter!" she said. "What are you doing here?"

"Turn that thing off," Peter said, "and get out of it."

She punched the ignition button and smiled up at him.

"I want to talk to you, Elisabeth," he said.

"All right," she said. "There's a nice inn not far away. Bring Dennis with you in the wagon." She blasted off.

"By the way," Mulford said, "if you still want to have a go with me, I suppose it's perfectly all right now. No reason why not."

"Get in the automobile," Peter snarled.

The gathering at the inn was tense. Elisabeth insisted that Dennis have a drink with them, but as soon as he had finished it he pushed his chair back.

"Must make a couple of phone calls," he muttered.

"Funny thing about men," Elisabeth said. "As I was saying last night, they just don't have the imagination to put themselves into a woman's place. They *have* to be shown."

"You said something else the other day," Peter said. "You said I ought to beat you with a stick. I'm going to."

"How cute! You *were* worried about me, weren't you, darling?"

"Why should I be?" Peter said. "It's a perfectly ordinary, everyday situation: wife and mother of two stashes the children with a neighbor and zips off to go blasting around a race course. What's to worry about?"

Elisabeth covered his hand with hers. "Okay, chum," she said. "I'm sorry. I was a louse. I admit it: I put on this whole production just to frighten you. I didn't even intend to drive the Morgan fast when I came up here. But then Dennis took me around a couple of times, and you know something? It's fun! I love it!"

"It's dangerous, too," Peter said glumly. "Only the maddest of the mad British race Morgans any more."

"You were going to."

"Maybe."

"But not now?"

"Not now."

"Order another drink, Peter," Elisabeth said. "I've just had a bright idea. Why don't we buy something sensible and go in rallies together, for fun? Then maybe later on we could try some racing—nice little short races for you and nice little ladies' races for me."

Peter beckoned to a waiter. "I've heard much worse notions," he said. "After all, neither of us wants the other to drive the Morgan, so we'll get a nice orthodox car with four wheels."

"We ought to sell the Morgan first, though," Elisabeth said.

"Sure," Peter said. He was watching Dennis coming back from the phone, and he felt Elisabeth's shoeless foot nudging his shin under the table.

"Dennis, old boy," Peter said. "Just to show you that there are no hard feelings, I'm going to do something for you. I'm going to let you buy that Morgan."

"You are?" Mulford said.

"That's right, you lucky fellow," Peter told him. "No, don't try to thank me. I want it to be yours, and I'm going to give it to you for exactly what I have in it."

Mulford smiled gratefully. "Done," he said.

Peter looked across the table at his dear, flint-hearted wife. How pretty she is, he told himself, sitting there drunk with power, inflamed with triumph. She's right, though—in a way that hasn't occurred to her. Why should I have been cheap with myself? A Morgan Three-Wheeler for $1000, indeed. I'll get the check back from her on some plausible subterfuge, and then I'll shoot the whole six grand on something really worthwhile for her—say a 4½-liter Blower Bentley. It seemed to him now that nothing was too good for her. He thought, I could get an almost-mint Bentley for six thousand, and felt the overwhelming pride of a benefactor. Elisabeth was a wonderful girl.

He smiled at his wife, and she smiled back, and he felt her hand tighten trustingly on his.

—1958

Diesels

A friend of mine bought a new automobile recently. It came equipped with numerous useful accessories, and one not so useful—it has a built-in problem of conscience.

The car is a Mercedes-Benz 190D. The "D" is significant, for it denotes the presence of a diesel engine, and it is the diesel engine that has upset the proud new owner. His home is heated by an oil-fired furnace, and every time he thinks of the 300-odd gallons of fuel oil resting in his cellar tank, temptation smites him, and an angel-versus-devil debate rages within him. For a Mercedes 190D will run just as well on furnace oil at ten cents or so a gallon as on diesel oil at twenty-six cents.

A diesel-engined automobile knows nothing of the snobbery of its gasoline-burning fellows. Not for the D-car are the golden or purple or pink gasolines drawn from their gaudy pumps at up to forty cents a gallon. A D-car doesn't care if men of distinction use only Scarlet Pimpernel Petrol. A D-car takes smelly fuel oil and burns it without so much as the help of a spark plug, simply by compressing it so tightly that the generated heat sets it off. It is not true that a diesel engine will burn drawn butter or melted candle ends, but it is remarkably unfussy, just the same. And so the temptation to drain a bucket or two at the oil-burner tank, rather than hunt up a filling station that displays a sign "Diesel" or "Trucks," is strong. After all, sixteen cents a gallon is—well, sixteen cents a gallon. And when the fact that a 190D will run thirty-five miles on a gallon is thrown into the equation, I suspect the devil often wins.

The diesel-engined automobile is, comparatively, a newcomer in this country, although Mercedes-Benz put the first one on the market in 1949. The highways are full of diesel trucks, but diesel passenger cars are still uncommon—so uncommon, in fact, that the various states haven't got around to setting up measures to defeat the owner whose cupidity overcomes him. The governor of one New England state did personally telephone the first Mercedes-Benz diesel owner in the municipality to ask him to state where he proposed to buy his fuel, and officials of another commonwealth for a time considered making diesel owners sign an undertaking, under penalty of *peine forte et dure,* not to run it on furnace-oil siphonings. The project was finally abandoned, however, apparently on the ground that it might well have the effect of informing people of a good thing who might otherwise never know about it.

Adequate law is already on the books, of course, since the use of furnace oil instead of fuel oil constitutes tax evasion. But strict universal enforcement would be a tricky business. A Mercedes-Benz 190D looks very much like a Mercedes-Benz 190 gasoline burner. It sounds a bit different, if one gets close enough, and its exhaust has the characteristic diesel pungency (it produces fewer harmful contaminants, by the way). And one can, by looking narrowly, see the small chromium "D." But a snooping enforcer armed with police powers could not make a case by siphoning something out of the tank: the two oils look the same. Ultimately, I suppose, if enough diesels appear on the roads, diesel fuels will be colored, and presence of white fuel in one's tank will constitute *prima facie* evidence of malfeasance. Until that time, diesel owners will wrestle with their consciences—sometimes winning, sometimes losing.

—1960

Classic
Cars
of
The
Thirties

In 1991, thirty years from now, will Cadillac El Doradoes and Pontiac Bonnevilles and Humber Super Snipes be sought after and restored and lovingly tucked up in museums? I am assaulted by doubt when I consider this proposition. But when we look in the other direction, and contemplate the scene thirty years behind us, we see the streets of the world's great cities dotted with automobiles that were obviously destined for immortality, and deserving of it, too. Why is this? What differences have grown in these three decades?

We are talking now about gentlemen's carriages built to serve two basic purposes: to transport four people, at most, in elegance over city streets and boulevards, and to carry them, in comfort and at high speed, over the roads from one city to another, or from the city to the seashore, the mountains, or the lake country. These were not multipurpose cars in the modern manner. Emphatically, they were not designed to be easy for Mom to drive to the supermarket, with trunk space big enough to accommodate the deer Dad lays low on his annual hunting trip, and upholstered with plastic wonder-fabrics proof against upended chocolate ice-cream cones. The men who laid down these cars had in mind a clientele for whom a butler ordered the groceries, whose venison was slain by a gamekeeper, and whose squalling young were in the charge of a nanny who would expect to be drawn and quartered if one of them got anywhere near an ice-cream cone. Certainly persons less fortunately situated bought these cars now and again; but so did those who conformed to the designers' specifications, and they were pleased with them.

These were the cars that dominated the mad years between the end of the bull market in 1929 and the beginning of World War II, when many who had kept their money saw the deluge ahead and were inclined to say, "I can't take it with me, and I'll be damned if I'll leave it here."

Gaiety counted; gaiety and movement. Mayor Jimmy Walker of New York so accurately reflected the acceptable attitudes of his day that he became almost a cliché; his sins, which were notable, were forgiven, indeed were hardly termed sins at all, because the citizens of whom he was the nominal servant so ardently wished they could behave as he behaved. "Keep your hands to the plow, dear friends," he would say as he terminated ten minutes of attendance at a City Hall meeting and skipped down the steps to the waiting Duesenberg town car and told the driver to which of the currently fashionable speakeasies he wished to be hurried.

It was not a time for stay-at-homes. It was a time for travel and sensation-hunting and moving as quickly as possible from place to place. There was plenty of room on the roads and some of the automobiles available were splendid.

These were the motorcars the Americans call Classic, the British, Vintage and Post-Vintage Thoroughbred: cars of the breed of the SJ Duesenberg, the 8-liter Bentley, the Hispano-Suiza Boulogne, the Marmon 16, the P. II Continental Rolls-Royce, the Types 41, 46, 50, and 57SC Bugatti. Some were quicker than the others; some more comfortable, more reliable, more beautiful; but looking at them today, sitting in them, driving them, riding in them, one is struck by one universal characteristic: privacy. Nearly always, the coachbuilders placed upon these great chassis bodies that offered privacy of a kind today's motorists, sitting in mobile greenhouses of tinted glass, know nothing about. Sedans, limousines, four-passenger coupes, *berlines de voyage,* coupes de ville, sometimes even open double-cowl phaetons offered rear-seat passengers shielding from public curiosity that ranged from a discreet shadowing to total privacy behind heavy silk curtains. Modern attempts on this concept have nearly always failed in elegance and taste because they were makeshift and they required arbitrary blanking off of large areas of glass, as when the late King Ibn Saud ordered twenty Cadillac limousines at $12,500 each, all five windows and the chauffeurs' divisions made of Argus glass, mirror-side out. The women of his harem could thus see and not be seen, but the automobiles must have glittered like circus wagons under the bright Arabian sun. The coachmakers of the thirties did it better: I know a coupe 8-liter Bentley built with a rear quarter all blind except for a six-inch oval rear window of beveled plate. The saddle-brown leather of the seat is soft and smooth as only well-worn and cared-for leather can be, and there is room on it, and to spare, for two people, but not for three. That wasn't the idea. There are ashtrays and lighters and a mirrored vanity case holding perfume atomizers and the like; a small walnut cabinet on one side of the front-seat back holds a picnic set, a matching cache carries three cut-glass carafes for spirits. A foot-square table unfolds over each cabinet. A long way ahead, past the fellow driving, and his *petite amie,* is the short, straight windshield, and one can look a little to one side and see out the front windows, but why bother?

This 8-liter Bentley was the last gasp of the original Bentley company of Great Britian, a gauntlet thrown in 1930 into the face of the approaching financial hurricane. W. O. Bentley, one of the giants of automobile design, had produced the heavy, immensely strong, and quite fast 3- and 4½-liter Bentleys that dominated sports-car racing in the late 1920s. Bentleys won the 24-Hour Race at Le Mans in 1924, 1927, 1928, 1929, and 1930. In 1929 they did it in a style that has not been seen since: four Bentley cars were entered, and twenty-four hours later four finished—first, second, third, and fourth! Bentleys were sought after in those days, but they were expensive to buy—and to make. The company never really rolled in money, and the 8-liter, with its twice-normal-size engine, was designed to intrude into the profitable luxury-carriage trade. The 220-horsepower engine was available in one of two wheelbases: twelve or thirteen feet; the lightest model weighed three tons, and the chassis cost was just under $10,000. Mr. Bentley's purpose in design was to create a car that would carry luxury coachwork at 100-plus mph in silence. By the standards of the day he succeeded admirably. One hundred 8-liter chassis were produced and variously clothed by the many custom coachbuilders of the time. The 8-liter was a formidable automobile. As late as 1959 an 8-liter Bentley was breaking records with speeds in excess of 141 mph.

Eight liters of engine ran another *voiture de grand luxe* of the period, the Hispano-Suiza Boulogne. The Hispano-Suiza Company was made up of Spanish capital in the person of St. Damien Mateu and Swiss talent in the person of M. Marc Birkigt. Birkigt was gifted in the extreme, and had he had the flamboyance of Ettore Bugatti or Gabriel Voisin, he would have been as widely known as either of them. He was respected, indeed, among professionals. The firm began in 1904, and "Hisso" aircraft engines were much used by the Allies in the war of 1914–1918. Birkigt's concepts of luxury motorcars came to full fruition in the 1920s, when he designed the big Boulogne. The model was named after a race won by one of the proto-types, but nearly all the fifteen chassis produced were bodied as gentlemen's carriages. André Dubonnet of Paris, sometimes irreverently called the *Apéritif* King, commissioned a Boulogne that is still in existence and is still among the world's half-dozen most spectacular automobiles.

Dubonnet believed that a Boulogne would make an ideal mount for an early Targa Florio race. No one else thought so. The Targa was a long and brutal race on rock-studded roads through the Sicilian hills in which small, tough, hard-sprung sports and racing cars usually did well. But Dubonnet had the weight of gold on his side, and he ordered an alloy and tulipwood body from the aircraft company that built the famous Nieuport fighters. The alloy frame was handmade, and two-inch strips of tulipwood were riveted to it. Wood and rivets were then sanded and polished. The body was beautiful, and suitably light, but M. Dubonnet did not win the Targa Florio. He finished sixth, though, and the tulipwood car is now in England. The original mudguards were metal, but the car's present owner, a Mr. L. G. Albertini, found a Thames boatbuilder who knew about tulipwood and ran him up a set in exactly the style of the body.

The Model 37.2 Hispano-Suiza was at one time the most expensive automobile in the world, at $11,000 for the bare chassis, but the V-12 of 1931, which cost less, was a better automobile, indeed it must be included in any list of the best automobiles of all time. It was quite stable on the road, would move from 0 to 60 mph in twelve seconds—still, thirty years later, an entirely respectable figure—and would exceed 100 carrying almost any kind of coachwork. Further, it handled much like a modern automatic-transmission automobile: the engine had so much torque that top gear could be used from 4 miles an hour up!

Pride of place among American-built automobiles of this genre goes to the Duesenberg, and, among Duesenbergs, to the model SJ; and among SJs, to the double-cowl phaetons, in popular opinion but not in mine: I incline to Murphy Beverlys, Rollston convertible Torpedo Victorias or Opera Broughams, or Hibbard & Darrin convertible town cars, automobiles fit for fast passage over rain-swept autumn roads, with the dusk coming down like violet smoke, and a long way to go before midnight, and what of it?

Fred and August Duesenberg made Duesenbergs to be fast. They were: an SJ Duesenberg would do 104 miles an hour in second gear and 130 in top. After all, the car should have been quick; its first fame came as a race car. For years Duesenbergs were a fixed part of the scene at Indianapolis, and Jimmy Murphy won the French Grand Prix in a Duesenberg in 1921.

Only about 470 J and SJ Duesenbergs were built. Their basic price range was $14,750 to $17,750. A very few ran up to $20,000 and perhaps half a dozen cost $25,000. (Only two were sold to American customers at that figure.) However, some owners gilded the lily. For example, a maharaja carpeted the rear of his Duesenberg with a Persian rug which had, he said, cost him "several times" the price of the car.

There was something about the Duesenberg, long, lean, narrow, wholly elegant, that brought out the sybarite in most people. A man of means was likely to expand in the matter of interior luxury. Duesenbergs were done in raw silk, silver, and ebony. They were done in alligator and sandalwood, in patent-leather and ivory. Sometimes the back seats were arranged as two overstuffed chairs, covered in West of England cloth and filled with down plucked from the breasts only of a fleet of geese. A good many bespoke coachmakers working on this side of the water stood ready to fit out Duesenberg chassis: Murphy, Rollston, Willoughby, Derham, LeBaron, Judkins, Weymann, Walker, Brunn, Holbrook. Of all these, only Derham is still in business, but doing more modifications than from-the-ground-up work. There are only three left of the great British firms, and two of those are affiliated with Rolls-Royce and thus busy. The first-line French and German houses are nearly all gone, and the Italians, now the world's paramount coachmakers, have so prospered working for their own great designers, and making specimen cars for Detroit, that they do not want bespoke business, even at the prices they charge: say $40,000 for a completely executed body to an original design. Even the oil pashas of the Arabian peninsula blink a bit at estimates in that range.

Designers of the big classic motorcars kept the coachbuilders in mind when they laid down their specifications: long wheelbases, heavy chassis, engines remarkably powerful for the time. The Marmon 16-cyclinder produced 200 horsepower. It was intended as a riposte to the Cadillac V-16 and the Duesenberg. It was a splendid automobile, and the 12-cylinder Marmon of 1934 was even better.

An item cataloged by Messrs. Rolls-Royce as "The 40–50 H.P. Continental Touring Saloon" was a kind of super Rolls-Royce, a Phantom II model modified to be faster than standard, and in other ways. The chassis was short, the steering column was low, and the springing and shock-absorbing arrangements were made for fast touring over dubious roads. The Continental cost about $12,250 in 1933, with the standard four-passenger sedan body.

Ettore Bugatti of France clearly felt that he was approaching the ultimate in a gentleman's carriage when he designed a coupe de ville, or town car, on his own Type 41 chassis. The Type 41 Bugatti, one of the biggest automobiles ever built—its wheelbase equaled a London bus's, and the engine was twice as big as a Cadillac's—was conceived as transport eminently suitable for kings. There is some reason to believe that M. Bugatti did, at the beginning, consider actually restricting the sale of the model to kings. He relented, and Types 41, or Royales, were made available to any ordinary tycoon who was willing to spend $20,000 for the chassis and half as much more for the body—providing M. Bugatti approved of the man. Only six Bugatti Royales were made.

The market for $30,000 motorcars slackened, so Bugatti made a slightly smaller version of the Type 41, the Type 46, a standard big straight-eight-cylinder automobile. It offered useful scope to the coachbuilders of France (Bugatti himself liked the Type 46 so much that he kept it in production until World War II closed the factory), and so did the Type 50, a similar model carrying a more powerful engine. The Paris firm Million-Guiet built bodies for Types 46 and 50 Bugattis that might have been called *ménage à trois* coupes: they carried three people, driver and one passenger in front, the other passenger sitting sideways in the rear, with a splendid view out the slotlike rear window, and a big triangular cushion on which to rest her feet.

The Type 57SC Bugatti, the peak of the company's models, the result of collaboration between Ettore Bugatti and his son Jean, was put on the market toward the end of 1937. It produced about 200 horsepower, had a top of 130 miles an hour—fabulous for the time—and was remarkably secure and roadable at high speeds. The chassis invited low, lean coachwork. A 57SC Bugatti was one of the thirties' most desirable possessions.

Packard and Pierce-Arrow, who made such impressive limousines and touring cars, didn't offer many coupes, but both built lovely victorias and convertible sedans on V-12 chassis. So did Lincoln, also on a V-12, and there were splendid big Lincoln double-cowl phaetons.

The Pierce-Arrow Silver Arrow, aluminum-bodied, was much in advance of its time. Packard offered an interesting range of custom bodies, set out in a catalog so lush that it cost the company fifty dollars a copy to produce it. One of the last phaetons made by an American manufacturer was a Packard, turned out in 1939 for Franklin Roosevelt and armored to be proof against anything up to 50-caliber machine-gun fire. Its cost wasn't released, but a Manchurian warlord, Chang Tso-lin, paid $35,000 for an armored Twin-Six sedan.

Gabriel Voisin made a unique approach to the 12-cylinder engine, unique in the precise meaning of the word: nobody else ever did what he did, which was to put 12 cylinders *in line* in a production car. (One 12-in-line Packard was built, but never put into production.) This double-6 engine was so long that it protruded into the driver's compartment, but the required length of hood enchanted the bodybuilders, and some noble carriages were laid down to take advantage of it. Voisin made V-12s, too, and his Sirocco sports sedan on that chassis, low, squared, flat-topped, knife-edged, was a soaring expression of the squared-off style.

Few now alive have ever seen a Bucciali, more's the pity. It was made in France, but in the thirties, too late in the century. The pinch of depression was on the rich English, the maharajas, the Rhineland steel-masters. French tycoons were inclining to something comparatively unostentatious when their *petites amies* needed new cars. It was a time of stress. Even the Hungarians were slowed down, and mad young things in Budapest were saying, "*Szeretnèm ha megengedhetnèm magamnak hogy ugy èljek mint ahogy èlek!*" or, "If only we could afford to live the way we do!" Still, the big Bucciali cars stunned the Paris Salon. The power plant was a V-16 of aluminum and it glistened under the lights, engine-turned, like the inside of a cigarette case, everywhere. Even the blades of the fan were engine-turned. The Bucciali was very long indeed, and very low, the biggest front-wheel-drive motorcar ever built. There was nothing lithe or graceful about it, and one viewer is supposed to have said that it looked like "a band-vault on wheels."

Daimler of England made a V-12 car of the same genre: tremendously long bonnet, blind rear-quarter coupe body, high wheels, a 150-inch wheelbase, and the roof of the car just three feet, six inches from the ground! A good many Mercedes-Benz looked like that, too, built on the 540K chassis, a big straight-8 equipped with a "demand" supercharger, one that cut in and out at the driver's whim, and blew, when it was blowing, *through* the carburetor, with a shrill zombie scream. The 540K was heavy and there was nothing astonishing about its acceleration, but once under way it would cruise all day, solid as a battleship, in the 80s and 90s, and it would do 106 mph with a little runup. It had the edge, there, on such American classics as the Cadillac V-16, most of which would not show 90 miles an hour, or the famous first-model Cord, the L-29, which was reluctant to do much more than 75, for all its dash.

The V-16 Cadillac ran as high as $7850 in price, and still it's doubtful that General Motors ever made a dollar's profit on one of them. The car was a prestige item. For some, it was even more of a status symbol, or a more satisfactory one, than a Duesenberg: When one said Cadillac 16, one was offering an almost palpable rating; the owner of a V-16 clearly outranked a V-12 man.

The Models 810 and 812 Cord—the round-nose, disappearing-headlights ones—were among the most beautiful automobiles ever built in America. The Cord was short-lived: a hundred hand-built models were made for the 1935 Auto Show and the firm was out of business by 1937. The rarity of the car was early established: More than twenty of the first hundred hand-mades were stripped and burned immediately after the show, on the ground that the cost of finishing them would have been too great. The Cord looked as if it had been born on the road, one admirer said, and even today the entry list of almost every *concours d'élégance* held in this country will show one or more Cords looking as new as they did the day they left the showroom.

The German firm of Maybach had made engines for the great raiding airships of World War I, and the 12-cylinder Maybach Zeppelin was another of the massive carriages of the 1930s, solid, beautifully made, comparatively rare, like the Horch. The Italian Isotta-Fraschini was another, and the Minerva of Belgium. A few years ago I saw a Minerva limousine so big that it ran on doubled rear wheels, like a truck; and the jump seats, usually little folding things, were overstuffed club chairs.

There were smaller cars of the 1930s that wore a great air of chic: Delage, Delahaye, Talbot, Darracq, Hotchkiss, Stutz, Lagonda (made in England and named after a river in Ohio), but they had already begun to move away from the lushness of the golden times toward simple utility. There are cars being made today that are vastly superior in comfort and controllability to anything the 1930s knew: the Rolls-Royce, the new Lincoln Continental, the Mercedes-Benz 300, for example. The Jaguar XK-E, the Chrysler 300G, the Ferrari 250 GT, the Maserati 3500, the Aston Martin DB4 are all faster than anything made before World War II. But no one of them, shining with glass, can, for all its virtues, replace one of the shadowed, high-riding gentlemen's carriages of three decades ago, stiffly sprung, to be sure, a handful to drive, yes, but fascinating still for what they were and for what they recall of the vanished age in which they moved.

—1961

The
Lincoln

Continental has for more than thirty years been a classifier indicating a desirable, sought-after automobile. Rolls-Royce used to make a Continental, a special high-speed grand touring car. When the postwar Bentley Continental came on in the 1950s it was priced at $26,000 and Messrs. Rolls-Royce urged, indeed ordered, dealers to restrict its sale to high-speed drivers of demonstrable competence. But it is of the Lincoln Continental that most Americans think when they hear the term; not the $10,000 Mark II of 1955, but the prewar model, the Continental that Edsel Ford originally designed for himself and his sons alone to have.

There were only 5320 of these cars built, and probably fewer than half of them survive today. (Some of the 500-odd members of the Lincoln Continental Club own three or four cars.) They were not expensive. Before World War II a Lincoln Continental could be bought for $2640, and afterward for $4260. In the classic-car market today, rough examples can be had for $500 or $600, a fine one will bring $2500, and one particularly lavishly restored specimen is alleged to have changed hands a few years ago for $10,-

000. The Lincoln Continental is one of the very few automobiles, of the 5000-odd makes the world has known, that will apparently be wanted as long as there are roads to run upon. If anyone foresaw such a turn of events when the car was being designed and when the first models were being built he kept his opinion tightly to himself. From 1938 to 1948, when production ceased, ownership of a Lincoln Continental conferred a certain prestige. It was an endorsement of one's taste. (It carried no connotation of the love of speed—mechanically the car was indifferent.) For the next seven years, after 1948, the Lincoln was just a good mass-produced car like any other, but in 1955 the new Continental Mark II appeared, offering what its makers hoped was the ultimate in status appeal: a $10,000 automobile so precious that even in transit it wore a fleece-and-plastic envelope. About 3000 Mark IIs were sold in two years. Its successor is the current Lincoln Continental, which looks a little bit like the 1938 classic, a little like the 1955 tycoons' chariot, and has been engineered in terms of the excellence that marked the great Model KB of 1932 and 1933. The new one, the 1962, may be the best of the lot, but still it will never be *the* Continental. That was Edsel's car.

Edsel Ford was with his father in 1922 when Ford bought Lincoln from Henry and Wilfred Leland. Edsel signed the contract, sitting under a bunting-draped picture of Old Abe. The picture's being there was not a public-relations man's idea. There weren't any public-relations men around: neither Henry Ford nor Henry Leland believed in them. The picture was legitimately present: Leland called his car the Lincoln because the first time he'd voted, in 1864, he'd voted for Lincoln. Leland admired Lincoln and he liked to think that he imitated Lincoln's rigid ethical standards. The big cars he made were good ones. For example, it was common practice among other fine-car builders to break in their engines, before installing them in chassis, by hooking them up to electric motors. Leland tested his on gasoline and under load. They were broken in on the road, too, and Lincoln buyers who wanted to run past the first motorcycle cop they saw after leaving the showroom could do it with an easy conscience, at least as far as injuring the engine was concerned.

Lots of Lincoln owners did hurry. When the newspapers of the day reported "the killers made good their escape in a big black touring car," they were often talking about Lincolns, and they were much favored by the police as well. A Model KB Lincoln would do 95 miles an hour, handle well in the bends, and stop in twenty-eight feet from 30 miles an hour, the latter something that not many cars have ever been able to do. The KB's V-12 engine was justly famous for reliability and long life. It was an expensive car, expensively made, but by 1933 the world market for it, and for the smaller, companion KA, had dwindled so markedly that they were replaced by a standard production model, and in 1935 that was in turn replaced by the famous Lincoln Zephyr.

The Zephyr's designer, John Tjaarda, intended the car to be rear-engined. The first one was, at a time when the only heavily produced rear-engine car in the world was the Czechoslovakian Tatra. (The Zephyr also had a torque-converter transmission, handmade at a cost of $40,000.) The Zephyr was planned by the Briggs body people, like all other Ford cars. Henry Ford was almost indifferent to "styling." He wanted his cars to be cheap to make and he wanted them to run and to last long enough but not too long; if they looked neat and orderly and were painted black he was pleased. Edsel Ford's primary interest was design, and by 1938 he had persuaded his father to let him cancel out Briggs and set up a Ford design department. The 1938 Zephyr was the first project, and as far as Edsel was concerned, the Continental was the second.

The design conception of the Continental was Edsel's own. One of the reasons for the good looks of the Continental, its design integrity, is that it *was* a one-man idea. Most good cars have been. Bugatti, Voisin, Bentley, Royce, Porsche were men inclined to make their own decisions. Many of the worst automotive abominations that have cluttered our roadways were committee creations. Edsel Ford's authority, in 1933, was strong, and he did not have to accept any dilution of his design. After all, the car was *not* a company project, it was not to be made to be sold, but for Edsel's own use. He could have what he liked. Only one fairly serious attempt at change was made. Edsel heard strong suggestions that the rear-mounted exterior spare-wheel carrier be deleted from the design, and the spare put inside the trunk like everybody else's. Unerringly, the committee-oriented designers had fastened on the one characteristic that everyone who ever saw a Continental would remember, the one that was held to be so important that it was incorporated into the brutally expensive Mark II. Edsel said the spare had to stay in the open and he made it stick.

The first Continental was a convertible and so were numbers two and three, which were made—with Henry Ford's permission—for Edsel's sons, Henry II and Benson. Edsel took number one to Florida in 1939 and returned with 200 blank-check orders, although he'd made no effort to sell the car. Its own looks had done that. (And only its looks: in every other particular of manufacture it was a standard mass-produced Lincoln.) It went on the market in December 1939, and it was an instant success.

The immediate public acceptance of the Continental was a remarkable tribute to the esthetic, even the artistic soundness of its body design, which was, in 1951, to be given the imprimatur of the Museum of Modern Art. The engine was no better than it should have been and perhaps not that good. If the car were driven as it looked as if it should be driven the engine was sure to make trouble, and many collectors, despairing of keeping it running, replaced the engine with a sturdier unit. (The vogue now is to replace the replacement with an original V-12). But the clean, smooth flow of the Edsel Ford Continental was intriguing to anyone of taste: the fine hood, the beautifully proportioned, squared-off doors, the graceful pontoons over the wheels. Some of the body units were standard Lincoln, the sheet metal hand-stretched and fitted by skilled workmen in custom-coachwork tradition, but few buyers knew this and none cared, because everything looked exactly right.

It was the handwork on the car that killed it; by 1948 the rising cycle of prices would not allow more than cursory handwork on a car selling for only $4620, and the Continental was dropped. But so secure had it become, so important was it in the American consciousness that I am sure a substantial number of the 1938 cars could be sold today, without a line being changed in the body. Even the trunk, which had to be loaded with a derrick over the spare tire, could be kept, for the car in its whole attitude and outward voice, conveyed elegance and purpose and privacy then and it would today. Mechanical concessions would have to be made. The suspension would have to be improved—although the Continental was reasonably roadable and some present-day owners think it more comfortable for a long trip than a standard 1962 automobile. It would have to be given a modern V-8 engine, strong enough for the work, reliable—and driving through an automatic transmission. I agree with Stirling Moss: a street automobile running anything but an automatic is silly.

Lincoln did try to bring back the Continental in 1955. Although the car was called the Mark II, because it seemed a good idea to someone to imitate the terminology of wartime, when military hardware from dishwashers to rockets was tagged Mark this-and-that, it was indisputably an imitation of the Edsel Ford Continental. It was a good car, and good-looking, and it offered flaming proof of the immutable fact that successful creation cannot be an act of will alone. The good and earnest and intelligent men, who staffed the separate division of the Ford Motor Company set up to make the Mark II, were determined that it would be so very good as to be irresistible, and the doors to the money bins were left open day and night to that end. The hood of the new car was long, as the old one had been, and there was a suggestion of the blind rear quarter that had marked the old one, but it was only a suggestion, it was not the real shield, the solid curtain against the peering eyes of the world that the original Continental had had.

Ford let it be known that more than the credit standing of a prospective Mark II owner might be questioned; his social stature, his moral and ethical principles might well be quietly examined. But snobbery is hard to establish artificially. Some people did want a Mark II badly enough to submit to almost anything in order to get it, but there weren't enough of these. William Clay Ford's automobile was a very much better car than Edsel

Ford's had been, but that was all it was—an automobile, not an artifact, possession of which magically enlarged a man in every dimension.

A wealthy man said to me:

"I know the old Continentals were not the best cars you could buy in 1939 and 1940, but I bought three just the same, and I still have one of them, well into its second hundred thousand miles. It's got a Ford engine in it, it's been repainted twice, and it's wearing its third top, and I still drive it in preference to anything else on the market—and I can buy anything else on the market. The Continental is a *practical* classic: it has a heater, a defroster, and no service problems, or few at any rate. I don't drive it because I like nostalgic reminders of my life twenty years ago, and I don't drive it because I want to establish a reputation for quaintness and eccentricity. I drive it because it's *individual*. I think of it as damned-near *alive*."

That's about as close to articulation as most Continental owners get. Understandably, for they're not talking sense, they're talking about a love affair. They won't be much more moved by the new Continental, the 1962 (though a younger generation of quality-seekers may), than they were by the Mark II, in all probability, despite the fact that it's one of the finest automobiles available today, competitive with any luxury car, and at only about $6500 with everything aboard, air conditioning included. The magazine *Road and Track* has cited the new Lincoln as one of the seven best-made cars in the world, and it is the only American car on the list.

Extreme care is taken with the Lincoln from beginning to end of the manufacturing process. It probably more closely approaches the legendary "handmade" ideal than any other American car presently in production. One Continental body a day is pulled off the assembly line and checked against a master jig which will reveal any errors of fit that have crept in; one body out of every ten is taken off the assembly line and spot-checked; one body a week is minutely examined inside and out and torn to pieces in the process. It is tossed on the junk heap when the inspectors are through with it.

The finished car is given a short but exhaustive road test on public highways, its skilled driver being responsible for checking scores of points. This driver is under no pressure of time, and anything he complains about will be fixed, rebuilt, or replaced. When the car goes to the customer even the tone of the horn will be exactly right.

The newest White House state car is a Continental with a few extra features designed into it: it's armor-plated, the rear seat can be raised ten and a half inches, to give spectators a better view of the President, it has three different tops and two two-way radios. *And* a pair of old-fashioned running boards for Secret Service men to stand on. Specialties aside, President Kennedy's car looks much like any other Continental built in the last couple of years. As far as the Continental is concerned, company policy is inclining to the "continuity" concept that has served Rolls-Royce so well for so long; only trained eyes can tell a 1962 Continental from a 1961. The company is probably right. The Continental's is a good design, winner of an Industrial Design Institute award this year. Why change it?

Still, every day in the year, somewhere in the country someone takes pen in hand, and asks, of a newspaper, or a magazine, or Ford in particular or Detroit in general, "When are you going to get sensible and make another car like the original Lincoln Continental?"

—1961

The
Bugatti

Ettore Bugatti was an Italian who lived his life in France among Frenchmen, and he was, they said, *un type,* or as we say, a character, an exotic, one of a kind, greatly gifted, proud, unswervingly independent, indifferent to any opinion but his own, amused, aristocratic, impractical, profligate, a connoisseur, a gourmet, a *bon vivant.*

He died in 1947 after sixty-six years of life full of frenzy and creation. There are many photographs of him. He is in one of his racing cars in 1925, his two sons crowded into the cockpit with him, one fourteen, one three, Bugatti is smiling at the photographer and waving, his hand gloved in what looks to be immaculate chamois. Another, he is sitting, six feet off the ground, in a car he built for the Paris–Madrid race of 1903. Another, he is wearing goggles and a helmet. The helmet is odd looking. M. Bugatti has been amusing himself. He has taken a knife or a scissors to the brim of a bowler, and made a helmet of it. He didn't cut it all off: he made a neat little bill in front, to shade his eyes. Another, he is twenty-five or so, and apparently about to go riding. He's wearing a cap, a flaring short coat, pipestem breeches he must have put on barefoot, a hard collar four inches high, on his left wrist a watch and a massive bracelet showing under an inch of cuff, altogether a figure of shattering elegence and *sang-froid*.

Bugatti made about fifty different models of automobile. One that he liked particularly was the Type 46. It wasn't his most inspired design, and nagging little things often went wrong with it. A Parisian brought his 46 back to the factory time after time. One day M. Bugatti, *Le Patron* as he was known in deference, came upon the fellow in a corridor.

"You, *monsieur,* I think," he said, "are the one who has brought his Type 46 back three times?"

The man admitted it, full of hope.

Bugatti stared at him. "Do not," he said, "let it happen again."

King Zog of Albania, visiting in France, wanted to buy a Bugatti Royale, a ducal motor carriage priced at $20,000—for the bare chassis. The body came separately and expensively. Bugatti did not care to sell a Royale, a Type 41, to anyone who merely happened to have $30,000 or so, even if he was a reigning monarch. The aspirant customer was always invited to spend a little time at the Bugatti château in Molsheim, in Alsace, so that *Le Patron* might, covertly, estimate his character. Zog came, saw, was seen, and heard, in due course, that there was not, alas, a Royale available, nor could one say, unfortunately, when the factory would be able to make one.

"Never!" Bugatti told one of his assistants. "The man's table manners are beyond belief!"

"My dear fellow," Bugatti told a customer who complained that his car was hard to start in cold weather, "if you can afford a Type 55 Bugatti, surely you can afford a heated garage!"

Ettore Bugatti had earned the right to be arrogant. The Type 55 might not start first push on a January morning, but it was the fastest two-seater on the world market in 1932, and the most beautiful, and while its 115 miles an hour is no great figure today, half-a-lifetime later, it's not slow, and its fender line is still the loveliest ever put on a motorcar. No one else ever attempted anything like the mammoth Royale, its dashboard fittings of solid ivory, a Jaeger stopwatch in the center of the steering wheel, where men of lesser imagination put a horn button.

Bugatti's Type 35 Grand Prix car appeared in 1924. In 1925 and 1926 it won the incredible number of 1045 races. In 1936 a Type 57S ran 135.42 miles in sixty minutes, and it was twenty years before any other stock passenger car went faster. And then there's the Type 50, and the 44, the 37, the 51, the 57SC . . . there have been 4000 makes of automobiles, and of them all, is the Bugatti the most intriguing, the most enchanting, the farthest ahead of its time in its own day, and the most venerated now? Very probably.

Enter the devotees:

The man whose notepaper carries, not his name or his monogram, but the scarlet oval Bugatti radiator badge, engraved in miniature.

The man who wears the Bugatti Owners Club tie seven days a week.

The man who was suddenly presented, in 1957, with an opportunity to buy a brand-new Type 46, miraculously preserved through World War II, seventy-five kilometers on the odometer. The only way he could raise the money was to sell his house, so he promptly sold his house.

The young lady of Paris, whose boyfriend swore he'd go out of his mind if he didn't have a Bugatti. The year was 1934, and money was tight. Her father had it, though, and in cash. She killed him, took it, and bought the car. Her name was Violette.

It's just a car, surely?

No, it isn't, in the sense that it is very like other cars. The Bugatti was so unlike most other cars of its day as to become, almost, a different kind of object. This is true almost in equal measure of the Ferrari today. It's no use trying to convey to a man who has been driving a new Cadillac for six months the experience of driving a 250 GT Ferrari. He won't understand because he doesn't have the frame of reference. Even people who did have the frame of reference were startled by exposure to some Bugattis, as Mr. C. W. P. Hampton, a British connoisseur, writing in 1937:

"I had a trial run up the Barnet bypass with Williams, the Bugatti works demonstrator, who had brought over a Type 57S electron coupe Atlantic. It was simply terrific: 112 mph still accelerating over the crossroads past the Barn—and the roads cluttering up with usual Friday evening traffic. Along the next stretch we did 122 mph, and I thought, under the circumstances, that was enough . . . thereafter we cruised along at a mere 90–95 mph, once doing just over 100 in third gear . . . the speed constantly maintained was prodigious . . . along almost every yard of the crowded thoroughfare . . ."

("Williams" was never called anything else during the years he spent with Bugatti as a demonstrator and a team-driver. No one knew anything about him except that he was young, British, seemed to have spent all his life in France and could pass as French. When World War II broke out he dropped into the Resistance, worked successfully for a long time, then disappeared at the hands of the Germans. It is now known that his name was William Grover and that he held the rank of captain in a branch of the British armed forces, presumably Intelligence.)

The truly creative make their own worlds and populate them with people of their own choosing. Ettore Bugatti did that, and most of the people around him were, like "Williams," anything but ordinary.

Says René Dreyfus, champion of France and Bugatti team-driver in the

1930s, "It was easy to believe, in those golden years, that we were not living in France at all, but in a little enclave, a little duchy, Molsheim, quite independent . . ."

Bugatti came to Molsheim, now the department of Bas-Rhin, then in Alsace-Lorraine, in 1906. Thereafter he worked in France, and thought of himself as French to the bone—he called his Italian birth "that accident" —but he did not take French citizenship until the year he died. He had been born in Milan, in 1881, son of one artist, Carlo, brother of another, Rembrandt. He first intended to be an artist as well, but he judged his brother's talent superior to his own, and it was not in Bugatti's nature willingly to be second to anybody in anything. Bugatti was apprenticed to the firm of Prinetti & Stucchi of Milan, and in 1898 he built a motor vehicle of his own, and raced it, probably a modification of a Prinetti & Stucchi motor tricycle. In the same year he made a four-wheel car from the ground up, and then another, which won an award given by the Automobile Club of France and a gold medal at an international exhibition in Milan in 1901.

Bugatti's gold-medal car so impressed the French firm of De Dietrich that they hired him as a designer. He was still a minor, so his father had to sign the contract in his stead. For the next few years Bugatti designed for De Dietrich, for Mathis, for Deutz, for Isotta-Fraschini and, later, for Peugeot. While he was working for Deutz, in Cologne, Bugatti designed and built, in the basement of his home, the small car which he called the Type 13. He left Deutz in 1909 and on Christmas of that year he came to Molsheim, with Ernest Friderich, a mechanic who had been his friend and associate since 1904. He rented an abandoned dye works, Friderich installed the machinery and staffed the place and in that year five cars were made. By 1911 there were sixty-five employees, and Friderich, driving a tiny 1.4-liter Bugatti, won his class in the Grand Prix du Mans and was second overall, just behind a mammoth 6-liter Fiat. The disparity in size between the two cars made the victory most impressive, and Bugatti was famous from that day onward. His cars were to win so many races, rallies, sprints, hill climbs that no one now remembers them in their thousands, but this was the first one and it mattered the most.

Fantastically, Bugattis are *still* winning races, although the last of *Le Patron*'s own designs was built in 1939. Of course, twenty-year-old cars can't compete with brand-new ones, but there are many races for old cars today. For instance, the famous circuit at Bridgehampton on Long Island schedules such an event every year. There were seven Bugattis entered in the last Bridgehampton, among many other makes contemporary with them. They completely dominated the event, coming in first, second, third, and fourth. Indeed, when the winning Bugatti, D. H. Mallalien's Type 51 Grand Prix car came down the straight, the very first time around, there was nothing else in sight behind it.

In July 1961, Mickey Thompson, who has driven faster than anyone else living today, broke six international records in a series of runs at March Air Force Base. One of them was a mile record that had stood for thirty-one years. It had been made by a Bugatti.

When World War I broke out in 1914 Bugatti had to leave Alsace, of course. He designed a straight-8 aircraft engine which was built in France and in the United States, under license, by Duesenberg. The Duesenberg engine, heart of the most luxurious automobile we have made, was clearly derivative from this Bugatti design. Bugatti was interested in airplanes, as he was in everything that moved by mechanical means. He built at least one airplane, and Roland Garros, one of the great French aces of World War I, was his close friend, indeed he named his second son for Garros. Garros was a pioneer in development of the machine-gun synchronizer which allowed firing through the propeller arc.

(The first American soldier to die in line of duty in World War I was an aircraft mechanic, part of a crew sent to France to assay Bugatti's airplane engine. The man stepped into the propeller while the engine was running on a test bed, *hélas!*)

After the war had been won, Bugatti went back to Molsheim and settled into a pattern of life extraordinary for an industrialist, indeed extraordinary for anyone. Ettore Bugatti made a small world for himself, and he lived at the peak and center of it. It was a world of many parts which he arranged to fit neatly together. There was the factory, first. It was a model factory. The cleanliness of the place was startling. Bugatti bought soap and scouring powders and cleaning rags in such quantity that his accountant swore the firm was supplying every home in Molsheim.

"It doesn't matter," Bugatti would say. "Things must be kept clean, very clean."

He probably did come near to employing someone from every family in Molsheim, when the payroll ran 1000 individuals. Out of 3000 families he knew a great many of these individuals by name. Indeed, for a long time he knew by name every man who worked for him, and thus could deliver compliment or reprimand with proper force. He was severe with people who mistreated tools. Every machine tool in the place, vise, lathe, shaper, whatever, was polished and engine-turned, like the inside of a cigarette case, and *Le Patron's* choler would spiral at the sight of a hammer scar or file mark on one of them.

He toured the factory on a bicycle or in an electric cart, both of his own design and manufacture. The French, among whom he lived, and the Italians, among whom he was born, prided themselves on their production of the world's lightest and finest bicycles, but Bugatti thought them all heavy and graceless, and so made his own. When he made his morning tour of the establishment he would often be in riding habit. His stables were extensive, and he had a covered riding hall. (The graceful lines of the Bugatti radiator, the most beautiful ever put on an automobile, are thought by some to derive from the horseshoe.)

He alone carried the master key that opened all the doors of the factory, all identical doors of brass-bound varnished oak.

There was one formal title on the Bugatti table of organization, and that was Bugatti's own. His subordinates had no titles. One man was in charge of purchase, another was chief accountant, another was head of the racing department, and so on, but no one had a title. M. Bugatti was chief and the rest were little French Indians. Such a system will work under one condition: the chief must be able to command devotion by reason of innate dignity, ability, force of personality, *not* merely by the fact of his being boss. This Ettore Bugatti could do. The soaring range of the man's imagination, his power of creativity, his sheer *drive* were clearly evident.

The Bugatti château was a stone's throw from the factory, and between these two places were the rest of the units that made up the establishment: the stables, the riding hall, the kennels housing thirty or forty fox terriers, the dovecots; the museum for the works in sculpture of Rembrandt Bugatti, and the museum housing historic horse-drawn carriages; the distillery in which Bugatti produced his own liqueurs, the powerhouse in which his own electricity was made. Farther away, but still definitely a part of the establishment, Bugatti's hotel, Le Hostellerie du Pur Sang, where clients of the house would find food, drink, and lodging fit for the gentry, and where one's standing with *Le Patron* could be gauged: some clients were given bills on departure, some were not, and some bills were more than others.

Each of these buildings reflected M. Bugatti's iron-hard view of the properties. The powerhouse, for example . . . Living as he did, Bugatti did not always have a great deal of cash on hand. He was not, after all, Henry Ford. His lifetime production of automobiles was a week's work for a Detroit assembly plant and not a big week's work, at that: 7500 cars. So his bills sometimes ran on. He shared the attitude of the Edwardian aristocrat: he considered reminder of indebtedness an affront. The Strasbourg utility company once made this *gaffe*. Bugatti paid the bill and simultaneously drew up plans for a powerhouse of his own. When it was completed, beautiful in white tile, mechanically *le dernier cri* in every way, he summoned the representative of the Strasbourg company and gave him a conducted tour. When he had finished he said, "So you see, *m'sieur,* I shall no longer have need of your firm's services." So saying, we must presume, he strode to the master board and pulled the main switch. Bugatti's life was full of such gestures. Indeed, his whole life was a gesture, a sweeping, magnificent gesture.

Even Bugatti's failures were notable. In 1922 he produced a team of round-bodied, tublike racing cars that were so ugly they were unreal. The next year he rolled out a team of motorcars notable only because they were uglier than the 1922s: they were slab-sided, slope-topped monstrosities of such short wheelbase that the back of the engine protruded into the cockpit, and they would not handle, besides being revolting to look upon. But in 1924 came the first of the Type 35s, then, and now, the most beautiful racing automobiles ever built, and, at least until the post–World War II Alfa-Romeo and Ferrari machines came along, the most successful.

The Type 35s made Bugatti and it was of their time, and the time immediately following them, that René Dreyfus and others of the entourage think when they talk of the golden times. Every weekend during the season the little blue cars would leave Molsheim for a circuit in France or England or Italy or Germany or Spain, where they would probably win. On Monday or Tuesday they would be back, dusty and oil-stained, and the mechanics would tear them down and make them as new again. Meanwhile, the drivers, the aristocrats of the establishment, could amuse themselves as they pleased, eating well, drinking well in the company of pleasant people. Of course, there were times when there was no money, but in Molsheim one did not, if one were a driver, need money in order to live well, and if an imperative necessity *did* come up . . . René Dreyfus once wrote, in the magazine *Sports Cars Illustrated,*

"When I had not been paid for a while, and needed money, it would not occur to me to ask for it, and of course it would be unthinkable to approach M. Bugatti. If one were not paid, it meant only one thing: there *wasn't* any money just then. So I would go to see M. Pracht, the treasurer, and we would have a bright little conversation, moving around the subject for a while and then getting down to cases. In the course of the next day or two I would pick up a chassis, or two chassis, and take them to Robert Benoist, a former team-driver who had a Bugatti agency in Paris. I would sell them to Benoist and be in funds again.

"If M. Bugatti did not often reward his employees with money, he had other means. Like the head of any state, he instituted a supreme decoration, a sort of Bugatti Victoria Cross. This he conferred rarely, and it was much coveted: a wristwatch made by Mido to Bugatti's own design. It was very thin, very elegant, and the case was formed in the familiar horseshoe shape of the Bugatti radiator. When a driver had made a notable win against heavy odds he might be given a Bugatti wristwatch. Even a customer might be given one, if he were a notably *good* customer, say one who had bought eight or nine cars and made no complaint if some little thing went wrong with a couple of them. One was summoned to *Le Patron's* presence, perhaps in his château on the grounds, and there, with all due ceremony, the plushlined box would be presented. It was a great honor, and no one would have conceivably equated a watch from M. Bugatti's own hands with mere money . . ."

Dreyfus tells, too, of a typical Bugatti *beau geste* which arose when he built his first *automotrice,* or rail car. He had conceived this idea when he found he had twenty-three huge 300-horsepower engines on hand, and the Depression of 1929 just getting under way. Why not make fast, self-powered railway cars? Why not, indeed? Bugatti ordered a big shed built on the factory grounds and began to draw up plans (the cars to have two engines, or four, to have speeds up to 120 miles an hour, running on rubber-mounted wheels, and stopped by cable brakes; the chauffeur to sit, not in front, incongruous among the passengers, but in a little cupola on the roof, alone, undistracted, and with a proper view). But when the first *automotrice* was finished, it was evident that *Le Patron* had, as it were, made an oversight. The railway station was a mile distant, and there was no track. Indeed, M. Bugatti had not even had the *automotrice* built on track. It had been built on the floor. And it would by no means go through the gate in the wall that solidly surrounded the factory.

Bugatti was not disturbed. He spoke to one of his supervisors. "Knock down the wall, if you please," he said, "and ask 800 or 900 of the men if they would be good enough to push the car down to the station for me tomorrow night."

It was done, the car riding on rollers so that the flanged wheels would not destroy the road, hundreds of men pushing, dozens carrying torches, the women bringing the wine. The *automotrices* were a great success. They really did run 120 miles an hour, their strange cable brakes did stop them, and the records they set—Strasbourg–Paris, Paris–Nice—stood for years after World War II.

They were Type 41 engines, made for the Royales, the kings' coaches. When the Depression came down on France, Bugatti had built only six Type 41s, his answer to the soft challenge of a British dowager at dinner: "Ah, M. Bugatti, everyone knows you build the greatest racing cars in the world, the best sports cars. But for a town carriage of real elegance, one must go to Rolls-Royce or Daimler, isn't that so?"

He went from dinner to the drawing board, the story goes, and laid down the first line then and there: a huge automobile, long as a London bus, seven feet from windshield to radiator cap, the engine running in nine individually water-cooled bearings, all working parts machined to zero tolerance, plus or minus nothing. Daimler, indeed!

Even at a ferocious $20,000 without a body, the Type 41 was in a seller's market, until the Depression broke, and certainly two or three of the most spectacular motorcars ever set on the road were 41s. There was a two-seater roadster, for example, a thing to dwarf every other roadster ever built.

Bugatti himself used a *coupe de ville,* or *coupe Napoleon,* a tiny cabin for two, an open cockpit for chauffeur and footman, and all that engine out in front. He had as well a *berliner de voyage,* or double berline, looking something like two medieval coaches put together; there was a convertible with German coachwork, a straight limousine, a sedan, a touring car.

The Type 46 was a smaller version of the 41. It was usually offered as a sedan or a big coupe, but for that usage I think the Type 50, which has a detuned racing engine, double overhead cam, supercharged, and producing more than 200 horsepower, is to be preferred. A listing and description of all the Bugatti models is not for this place, but the most interesting, aside from the Royale and the children's racing car he built first for his son Roland and then in limited series for the get of the very rich, are Grand Prix cars, the various 35s, the intermediate 51, the Type 59, a 170-mph car with which Bugatti attempted singlehanded to stem the tide of the Nazi-backed German race cars of the late 1930s and the 185-mph 4.7-liter; the Brescia and "Brescia Modifie" cars of the early 1920s; among the passenger cars, the Types 40, 43, 44 (considered by J. Lemon Burton, an eminent British *Bugattiste,* to be one of the best of all), 50, 55, 57, 57C, 57S, 57SC.

Wide variation exists even in this truncated catalog. The 44 is supposed to have come about because Mme. Bugatti taxed her husband with the noisiness and harsh springing of his sports models. Accordingly he designed the 44 as a lady's car. A good one will do 80 miles an hour, it's reasonably quiet, starts easily, is pleasant to shift, and has the softest clutch I, at least, have ever laid foot to. The 43, on the other hand, is a detuned version of the racing 35B given, ususally, an open four-seater body. It's a harsh, brutal, fast automobile. The 55 was race-bred, too, a Grand Prix Type 51 engine in a Type 54 chassis, while all the 57s were smooth passenger cars of varying speed capabilities up to 130 miles an hour, rare today, fantastic in the 1930s. Bugatti made something for everyone.

The history of the Bugatti is extensive, many tens of thousands of words have been published about it in many languages, and even the basic text, *The Bugatti Book,* runs to 375 pages. The Bugatti Owners Club, the oldest and biggest of the single-make clubs, has been publishing a magazine treating Bugatti matters for nearly a quarter of a century.

The BOC itself is unique if for no other reason than its possession of a seventeenth-century manor house as headquarters. This is Prescott, near Cheltenham in Gloucestershire, ninety miles from London. The house is a big one, built of Cotswold stone. It was, until 1871, the seat of the Earl of Ellenborough. The driveway leading up from the public road is more than a thousand yards long and has been made into one of the most famous hill-climb courses in the world. In 1949 a wrought-iron gate was installed in the garden wall at Prescott as a memorial to Ettore Bugatti and his son

Jean. Jean, who showed signs of great brilliance as a designer, died in 1939, at twenty-seven, in avoiding a drunken postman who had come, on a bicycle, onto the Molsheim circuit. Bugatti came around a corner at high speed and elected to go off the road rather than hit the man. Ettore Bugatti died, in 1947, at the end of a victorious struggle to retain control of the factory in the upheaval of postwar France. Because he was still an Italian citizen during World War II, he had been able to bluff the German occupying authorities to a certain extent, but still he was technically an enemy alien when peace came. And there had been, even before the war, grave labor difficulties at Molsheim. During the war the Germans made torpedoes in the factory. The Canadians seized it from the Germans and burnt much of it in an accidental fire. The Americans took it over, hid away all the machine tools and equipment before the Battle of the Bulge—and lost the papers. Pierre Marco, one of Ettore Bugatti's oldest collaborators, traveled tens of thousands of miles through France, much of it in a creaking, charcoal-burning automobile, searching for the red-monogrammed Bugatti tools. He found most of them, too, took them back to Molsheim, rounded up many of the old workers, and put the factory back to work. At first he did anything. He would make stove lids if the price was right. Ultimately a few cars were produced, Type 101s, which were not really new, and in 1955 a racing car, the Type 251, again not really new, and a competitive failure. Today the factory is flourishing, making industrial and marine engines and so on, but no automobiles. Roland Bugatti survives, his sisters survive, the second Mme. Bugatti survives, but without Ettore Bugatti, nothing marches as before.

He was a man of parts. He was marked in many ways, by his determination to live like a duke, his belief that a mechanical device should be artistically beautiful as well as technically correct—he wouldn't employ a draftsman who couldn't draw in perspective, in the round—by his ability to project himself twenty years ahead of his time. He was imperious, stubborn, supremely creative—he died holding hundreds of patents covering such things as motors, fishing reels, sail rigs, Venetian blinds—and fallible. Some details on his cars were outrageously impractical: Bugatti water pumps, for example, are hard to lubricate and keep in service, and some, indeed most, of his engines are so complex that even experienced Bugatti mechanics must quote figures like $1500 as overhaul cost.

But, taken all in all, good with bad, his cars have magic. This is not to say that there is nothing as good as a Bugatti on the world market today. That's nonsense. There are dozens of cars as good as a Bugatti, and better, cars faster, more roadworthy, more reliable, cheaper, more comfortable, and so on down a long list. But they are not the *same*. There is an indefinable, impalpable quality of *life* in a good Bugatti that does not exist in lesser machines. Of course, much of the charm of the Bugatti automobile lies in the aura of splendor that lay around its creation: *Le Patron* stalking the factory corridors in pongee and yellow corduroy, a brown bowler on his head and a Malacca stick in his hand; a champagne gala at the château; the little blue cars screaming across a finish line in one-two-three order; Benoist flying down a country road away from the pursuing Nazis in a Type 57; a reigning beauty of the Paris stage posing beside her Type 46 at a Deauville *concours d'élégance* . . .

Within the week just past as I write this, I have driven, and for some little distance, two great contemporary high-performance automobiles: a 3500 *gran turismo* Maserati coupe, $13,500 worth of Italian *mácchina,* and a Bentley Continental Flying Spur, at just under $27,000 one of the most expensive motorcars ever built. I've also driven a Type 50 Bugatti a hundred miles or so. The Maserati will run away and hide from the Bugatti, and the Bentley makes it sound like a cement mixer in full cry. Máserati and Bentley performances peak, like a needle on an instrument, and that is that. The Bugatti never seems to peak. There's nothing imperturbable about a Bugatti, it may exceed every expectation, or it may inexplicably goof off, but whatever it does, the impression that *more* is possible, *more* is available, remains with the driver. The car seems to be willing to try, and try again, and keep on trying forever.

This may be the essence of the quality that Ettore Bugatti tried to put into his cars. Thoroughbred—*pur sang*—was a phrase he liked. He believed that his cars had breeding. He said, and it was true, that from 1909 to 1939 no driver was killed or even seriously injured through material failure of a Bugatti automobile. Perhaps this was because he knew how to design an automobile to endure great stress, or because he used only the best materials on the market—special Sheffield steel, for example—but Bugatti did not think so. He thought it was an indefinable thing, really breeding. He may have been right. Who is to say he was not?

—1962

Italian
Line

The Italians were building fine carriages around 1550, and they still are. Buy a *gran turismo* automobile today, one of the first rank, a 130-mile-an-hour car, a Ferrari, Corvette, Maserati, AC Cobra, Aston Martin, E-Jaguar, and you'll be buying a body either designed and made in Italy or massively influenced by the Italians. Buy a small car, a Japanese-made Datsun, a German BMW 1800, a British Sunbeam, and the story is the same. The much-admired lines of the Buick Riviera are clearly reflective of the best Italian practice. The Italians are few, in proportion to the weight they bring to bear on the automobile industry: a dozen designing companies, twice that many top-line creative men, a few thousand workers to put the drawings into wood and clay and metal, to shape and give being to "the Italian line."

Like all esthetic concepts, the Italian line, the Italian idea, is hard to lay down in words, but at the root, in its highest form, it means plain metal, unadorned or very nearly unadorned by brightwork; a smooth, flowing, natural line, an intelligent modification of the fish shape that is nature's solution to the problem of high-speed passage. In the interior, evidence that great care has been taken to provide the *driver* with comfort, stability and convenience: ideally, a bucket seat that holds him firmly—hip and shoulder —gear lever and steering wheel set for the straight-arm style of driving, instrument panel directly in his gaze, individual gauges canted toward him if need be; in fine, everything placed to give him a long, level look at the road, to keep him in full control, to let him know the subdued and hedonistic wonders of first-cabin private travel.

Italian domination of automobile body design and fabrication as nearly approaches the absolute as does Paris's domination of the *haute couture:* now and again there is a flurry of activity and a fanfare of trumpetry on behalf of a new *couturier* in New York or Dublin or wherenot, but in the end it is to Paris that the world turns. Every year or so Detroit or Coventry or Stuttgart will proclaim a revolution, but nearly always it is no revolution, only gimmickery, and the designers and the panel beaters of Milan and Turin press on with their work, unmoved. They are perfectly secure, and they know it.

If success in automobile bodywork could be found in the first instance, and thenceforth maintained, by the creation of beauty of line alone, it would be hard enough to gain; but the Italians cultivate their exotic art in much greater depth than that. In the 1920s and 1930s, the heyday of true custom, one-at-a-time coachwork, general practice was to take a chassis from the car manufacturer, build on it a strong and rigid framework of ash or hickory or some such timber, and lay over that the hand-hammered, hand-filed-and-fitted metal. The end product would be good-looking in proportion to the designer's talent, and as nearly unique as one's purse could manage. It would also be very heavy, as a rule. It had to be, to accept the driving stresses that would be put through it. This kind of *carrosserie* was best suited to majestic touring cars and sedate, town-bred limousines. It wouldn't do for race cars, for sports cars, for the *gran turismo* machine intended for a career of mountain-storming.

The Italians have designed and fabricated, to button over race-car chassis, whole bodies that weighed less than sixty-five pounds, complete with seats, windshields, rearview mirrors, and St. Christopher medals. Long ago, houses like Touring were hammering out coupe and short-sedan bodies that a strong teen-ager could lift over his head—bodies, what's more, that would stay squeak- and rattle-free indefinitely, because they were designed to do nothing but give the passengers a place to sit out of the wind and the rain: they were completely protected from any trace of driving stress. A structure of pencil-thin tubing had been built up on the chassis, and the body panels hand-fitted over this, and at the same time insulated from it. The car might go into and out of foot-deep holes in the road all day, but this adventure could not affect the fit of the doors. Some builders refuse to weld or drill panels to fit them together, contending that both systems are weakening. They *fold* the ends together and hammer tham flat!

The history of Italian coachwork is full of such innovation. Pininfarina was making quad headlights fifteen years ago. It is difficult to think of a useful device applicable to bodywork still unexploited by the Italians. Hooded dashboard instruments, red warning lights that go on when the doors are open, rear-window wipers are all ancient notions. The door extending into the roof of a very low car, the pillarless sedan, the pillarless windshield, the faired-over headlights—all are old, well-used Italianate ideas.

Individual custom creation is a rarity today. Even Pininfarina does not care to do more than half a dozen of these a year, and the clients thus favored will be selected with great care. Merely to have the money isn't enough; they must be persons of distinction whose possession of the car will be noted. Heads of state are favored—but not just any states. Most coachbuilders say that it's impossible to charge an individual client more than 25 percent of the real cost of the car; thus each unit represents a 75-percent loss. Custom cars today are made for corporations, used in ways that allow the tremendous costs involved to be written off: as exhibit cars, as design inspirations, and so on. Some idea of the cost of these items can be formed from the eighteen months of work that Ghia put into the Chrysler Norseman, the car that went down with the *Andrea Doria.*

The category called *elaborazione*—elaborations—occupies much time in the smaller houses, adept at giving a standard car a new look at prices the owners can face without shuddering; but it is the creation of designs for the big manufacturers that returns reputation and profit. The national origin of an automobile gives no real indication of the origin of its body design: German, French, British, Swedish, Japanese cars by the dozen wear Italian. Of cars designed *and* built by individual *carrozzerie,* a production of thirty to fifty a day is thought to be a good many—the biggest, Pininfarina, turned out 14,132 last year—but the total of cars built around the world to Italian design would run into the millions. They may range in price from under $2500 for a VW Karmann-Ghia to over $20,000 for a Ferrari Super America.

There are a dozen Italian designers and coachbuilders famed around the world—Michelotti, Viotti, Scioneri, Savio, Boneschi, Moretti, besides Ghia, Vignale, Touring, and the rest—but it is Battista Pininfarina who means the most. His name was changed in 1961 with the warm and paternal consent of the Italian government: "The President of the Republic . . . in consideration of the high social and industrial merits of Battista (Pinin) Farina, has entitled him to take the surname 'Pininfarina,' this being the prestigious name of the industry created by him, well known and appreciated in Italy and throughout the rest of the world." Battista Pininfarina is today laden with honors, friend of presidents and kings, member of the Royal Academy of Arts. He has retired from the active direction of his firm—his son, Sergio, and his son-in-law, Renzo Carli, are in charge—but his stamp is large in the history of the automobile. Among a score of his works which may be cited, there is his 1951 Cisitalia, chosen to represent the best of all postwar designs in the now-legendary first Museum of Modern Art show.

It was Pininfarina who formulated the law that a motorcar body should have, first, elegance of line, second, comfort, and third, good penetration— an efficient aerodynamic shape. Almost anyone can create a car body (and before and just after the last war, almost anyone did) that will be striking-looking at first glance (but not five years afterward), and perfectly comfortable for a bald man five feet tall. To evolve a body that is permanently beautiful, comfortable, and that will of itself add 10 miles an hour to the speed of the chassis it is given—this is something else again.

Pininfarina has stated that matter succinctly: "The interrelation between the body of a beautiful woman and that of a Farina-designed car is that both have simplicity and harmony of line, so that when they are old one can still see how beautiful they were when they were young."

—1964

The
Ferrari

Years ago I was looking at three cars in the Ferrari pits at Sebring. It had rained in the afternoon and the Florida sun, dropping to the rim of the great plain, shone red in the black pools of water on the circuit. There were only a few cars running in practice, howling separately in the distance, out of sight most of the time. The blood-red Ferrari cars would go a few laps as soon as the mechanics finished with them. These were stark, open two-seaters. Their paint was flat and crude. The bucket seats were upholstered in wide-wale corduroy. Everything else in the cars except the wood-rimmed steering wheels was bare unpainted metal, much of it roughly finished. Heavy weld-seams joined the thin tubes of the frames. Shiny streaks here and there showed where oil had been mopped up. A man next to me turned, remembering the old pilots' gag: "You wouldn't send the kid up in *that!*" he said. A small, dark, red-eyed mechanic got into one of the cars. An ignition key looped in a piece of sisal wrapping twine stuck out of the dashboard. He leaned on it with the heel of his hand and a bare-metal clanging and clattering began. You wanted to move away before the thing exploded. It fired suddenly, all of a piece, and pumped out a gout of blue smoke that drifted low over the wet grass of the infield. The mechanic sat there with his foot on it for five minutes. There was somebody in each of the other cars, and they were running, too. Juan Manuel Fangio materialized, pear-shaped in a rain jacket. He looked sleepy, he looked bored, he looked indifferent, until one noticed the incessant flickering of his eyes. The mechanic yelled something into his ear. Fangio let him see a sad smile, he shrugged massively. He got into the automobile, stared briefly at the instruments, and then he went away and the other two, Eugenio Castelotti and Luigi Musso, howled after him, down the straight and under the bridge and around the corner out of sight. We could hear them through the esses and into the Warehouse Road and then not again until they showed up on the back straight, the three of them in echelon astern, the howling of the engines squeezed down by distance to a thin buzz, their progress across the horizon apparently so leisurely that you wondered why this should be called racing. They were running around 140 mph. They went down through the gears for the hairpin turn, a 180-degree reversal, the rear wheels spinning or trying to, and then suddenly they were in the hole at the bottom of the finishing straight, drifting up to the edge of the concrete, coming past the pits, Fangio first, sitting there limp as *pasta,* then Castelotti, then Musso, all of them turning 7000 revolutions a minute, and then one after the other they shifted up a gear, three successive explosive *whacks* as the engines bit, and they were gone again. They ran over the five-mile circuit a dozen times like that, tight together, so stable they seemed locked to the ground like buildings, but flying past light as deer at the same time. Wet with rain, the hurried-on paint glistened like oven-fired enamel as the cars screamed down the shiny concrete chute, the drivers sitting back from the wheels, their arms straight. These were beautiful objects, perfect of their kind, there was nothing of crudity or starkness about them now. It was hard to believe that any of the other sixty cars that would start the race the next day could run ahead of the red Ferraris, and, in the event, none of them did.

Enzo Ferrari of Italy may make a dozen such cars a year, full racing cars, Grand Prix cars, now that the times have swung away from the so-called big sports cars, and he will make 350 or 400 passenger cars for the entire world market. His clients will wait from three to eighteen months for delivery and they will pay from $12,600 to $17,800 per car. Some of them, perhaps wishing something out of the ordinary, may find it politic or necessary to go to Modena to see *Il Commendatore.* They may wait an hour for an audience. They may wait three days. After all, these may be the best automobiles in the world, and not many of them are made. Sometimes desirable possessions must be paid for in more than money.

Since he began to build motorcars, in 1947, under his own name and the black prancing horse that is his trademark, Enzo Ferrari has laid down about forty models of sports and Grand Prix cars and about forty passenger models, properly *gran turismo* or "fast touring" cars. There is no annual or seasonal model change. The Ferrari catalog is changed when the *Commendatore* thinks a change is due, and not before and not afterward. At the moment, six models are offered, some of them rather tentatively. They are the 250 Granturismo coupe, with body by Pininfarina, $12,600 in New York. This, one of the most enchanting automobiles ever built, will be discontinued and replaced with a four-passenger coupe on the same chassis, also by Pininfarina, also selling for $12,600. This is the first four-passenger car Ferrari has made. The Berlinetta, slightly better suited to competitive use than the 250 GT, has a shorter wheelbase, the same engine in a higher state of tune, and a body by Scaglietti, who specializes in lightness. All three of these use essentially the same engine, a 12-cylinder, 3-liter (180-inch) specimen which some authorities consider the most nearly perfected high-performance engine in the world. The models Super America and Super Fast, built to order only, use bigger 12-cylinder engines, one of 4.1 liters, one 4.9, or as big as a Studebaker V-8. These are 170-mph cars and they cost a minimal $17,800. Extant as a prototype with body by Bertone is a *small* car, with a 1000-cubic-centimeter, 75-horsepower engine, called the "mitra" (machine-gun) by the factory people, or the "Ferrarina." The car has been tentatively priced at $4500.

The new car will be fast for its size, but it will of course not be comparable with the standard model. A Ferrari 250 GT will do, depending on gearing, from around 125 miles an hour to around 150. So will a Chevrolet Corvette, for one-third the price. The Ferrari will accelerate from 0 to 60 miles an hour in 6.0 seconds, the Corvette in 6.6. Is six-tenths of a second worth $8000? Hardly. Is the Ferrari's road-holding better? Yes, but the difference is critical only in the uppermost ranges, where few drivers are capable of going, areas few should enter on an open road in this country.

Is the Ferrari better made? Probably, since it is largely made by individual men working with individual machines and micrometers, but against this must be laid the incomparable General Motors experience and the easy availability of Chevrolet spare parts. A windshield-wiper arm can fall off a Ferrari, too.

Is the Ferrari esthetically superior to the Corvette? Here I think there is little room for discussion. Ferrari Granturismo coachwork is from the hand of Pinin Farina, whose firm is now officially Pininfarina, and the bodies are chaste and beautiful, simple, unadorned. They are full of enchantments for the eye. For example, seen from the driver's seat, the hood of the GT is not a flat expanse of metal, dull to the view. Two tunnellike effects run along the side of the hood, to culminate in the headlights, and Farina has contrived to make them appear to be, not parallel, but converging strongly, thus creating the illusion that the hood is not only narrower than it is in fact, but that it comes to a directing point. Is it worth $8000, then, to have a car beautifully appointed, cunningly made comfortable for the passengers, and appearing to the onlooker so conservative in line and unspectacular in ornament that only the sophisticated will recognize it as an imported high-performance automobile? Yes—for some tastes, a few, this is worth $8000. For most, no.

What, then? Why pay $12,600 for a 250 GT, $17,800 for a Super America?

To buy the only thing of its kind in the world, of course.

The Corvette, the Aston Martin DB4, the 5000 Maserati, the Alfa-Romeo, and the Mercedes-Benz 300SL are comparable with the Ferrari in speed, in roadability, in interior comfort. In a lower category, only because they have not been demonstrated in competition, are the Chrysler 300G and the Chrysler-engined Facel-Vega of France. What sets the Ferrari distinctly apart from these seven great motorcars? Breeding and greatness, beauty and performance. Sitting beside the curb, moving away from a stop light, many cars look as good as a Ferrari, but when the last twenty-four-hour race was run at Le Mans, *six* of the first seven cars to finish were Ferraris. When the 1000-Kilometer Race of Paris was run this year, Ferrari 250 GTs came across the line first, second, third, fourth, and fifth. These were not racing cars, they were passenger cars that anyone can buy. Stirling Moss won the last Tourist Trophy in a 250 Berlinetta, running merrily around the course with the radio playing. The ability of Ferrari components to take the pounding of long-distance, big-money European roadraces sets the car apart from every other automobile in the world. The formulas of weight distribution and geometry and springing that keep the car hanging limpet-like under maximum power to a rain-soaked Alpine road set it apart. Luigi Chinetti, the American distributor for Ferrari, remarked to me that he liked the balance of the four-passenger Ferrari better than the *gran turismo,* citing the fact that he had been able to make the run from Geneva to Paris over a rainy night at an average of 75 mph without often running faster than 100, when in the GT he had to use 112 mph a good deal of the time and 125 occasionally in order to make that average.

I consider Chinetti to be objective, and his judgment in such matters must be regarded as definitive: he is among the best long-distance drivers who ever sat in an automobile. He has won the Le Mans 24-Hour Race twice, in 1932 with Raymond Sommer, in 1949 with Lord Selsdon. In 1949 he and Selsdon won the Spa 24-Hour Race as well, and in 1948 the Paris 12-Hour. In 1951, driving with Piero Taruffi, he won the Carrera Panamericana, a race over the length of Mexico.

Every owner of a fast car is used to hearing the skeptical "Yes, but where can you use that kind of speed in this country?" One answer is "You'd be surprised where you can use it." Another might say that having that kind of performance in reserve is something like having a lot of money in the bank: it contributes pleasantly to your sense of security even if you *don't* wear it in your hatband.

And this kind of traveling can be done in easy comfort, in an esthetically lovely carriage, the best of Italian bodywork covering a chassis so tough and capable that a day and a night of flat-out whip-and-spur running will not begin to overstress it.

A 1961 250 GT engine has no choke. To start it from cold you switch on an electric fuel pump to fill up the three big carburetors. (The pump is also an insurance against vapor-lock in hot weather.) When the clicking has stopped you can shut if off, twist the key and the engine will start with its characteristic metallic rasping. Once the 12 cylinders have begun to fire, a discreet nudge on the accelerator pedal now and again for the first thirty seconds will keep everything turning at a decent 1500 revolutions per minute or so and thereafter the engine will run steadily until it's warm. You can hurry the warm-up by winding up a shutter in front of the radiator. The engine will idle around 700 and you can put the transmission into first gear and let out the clutch at that rate and the car will move off like a Cadillac.

The GT Ferrari is so soft that it is possible to motor an elderly innocent around town on a shopping tour all afternoon without the car's once demonstrating any essential dissimilarity with a Cadillac. (All Ferraris now have four- or five-speed stick-shift transmissions. Although it is absolutely necessary for competitive driving today, the manual transmission will eventually be obsolete. I'll be stoned for saying this, but I look forward to the inevitable automatic-transmission Ferrari. That, I think, will be the ultimate piston-engine automobile.) It is this characteristic, perhaps more than any other, that is astonishing in a car capable of outperforming anything else in the world. One is reminded of Dan Mannix's descriptions of the feats possible to virtuosi among Roman animal-trainers, who could school a lion to retrieve a shot hare, accept a pat in reward, then kill a bear or a man, and come back to be patted again. The 250 GT Ferrari is a trained and tamed lion.

However, it is certainly not everybody's lion. A driver coming to a Ferrari from a schooling only on high-powered domestic passenger cars, Corvettes and Chrysler 300s excluded, should proceed with care. He will find that speedometer readings of 70 and 80 come up frequently on roads over which he has previously held himself to 50 mph, and 100 is likely to appear to be merely quick, not really adventuresome. Why's this? Because everything about the car is smooth and quiet: the engine, until it gets up around 5000 and begins to rave, the steering, the Porsche synchromesh transmission, and the ride—smoother the faster the car moves.

Extremely deceiving to the driver newly acquainted with such things is the Ferrari's flat ride. There is minimal roll in corners and curves, and sometimes there seems almost to have been a repeal of the law of gravity, because one's tendency is to stay put while the car corners, instead of bobbing from side to side. Up to rates of speed illegal in every county in the land, there are no mainroad curves in a Ferrari's path. The car irons them all out straight. The driver used to gauging speed by seat-of-the-pants reaction in curves will be deceived to the point of wondering if the speedometer is wild.

The Ferrari's brakes contribute to the deception. They are servo-assisted Dunlop discs, and they will, under severe usage, produce the sensation that the car has run into a wall of dough. In ordinary practice they'll pull the speed down precipitately and unobtrusively.

All of these things that I have talked about as deceptive for a new driver are enchantments for one used to the car. A trip I make frequently, and count quickly done in seventy minutes, I did in fifty-five in a GT Ferrari, under a sluicing rain, and without anything spectacular to call attention to myself. Only in a car like this is it possible safely to go quickly from point to point: without prodigious acceleration and braking power and impeccable roadholding it is dangerous and silly really to hurry.

You can hurry in the 250 GT Ferrari, a not-very-big car at eight feet six inches of wheelbase, unchromed and unfinned, a model of taste, two big form-fitting leather seats, a little odd space behind, radio, heater, every amenity, a large trunk in the rear, and that 180-mph speedometer glowing in a dim blue light. Among all the automobiles available today there is nothing exactly like this, and only once in the sixty years of the automobile has there been: the Bugatti of the 1920s and 1930s, another ivory-and-steel passenger car that could go out and set records.

Enzo Ferrari, who puts his name on these cars, and on the sports and Grand Prix cars that have won so many races in the past dozen years, will be sixty-three soon. He is a tall, spare man. He does not smile frequently. He lives quietly in Modena, ten miles from his factory in Maranello. He is conservative, moderate, unspectacular if one excepts the fact that his concern with his work amounts almost to obsession. He is distant, austere. He is apparently unhappy, like most creative people. He has said, "I feel lost in the cruelty of destiny." The death of his son Alfredo in 1956 profoundly depressed Ferrari. He had intended his son to carry on the work, and when he died in his twenties, of leukemia, Ferrari saw much point and purpose go out of his own life. (The subsequent series of race cars was called "Dino" after the affectionate diminutive of Alfredo.) Ferrari's temperament is sombre. He has a strong sense of dignity and his own worth, and if his ego is a sturdy, well-nourished plant, it should be: in a very short time as such things go he has cut his name into the record beside Royce, beside Ford and Bentley and Bugatti and Porsche and the rest. Fame has come to some automobiles with time's aid, like ivy growing thicker on a wall, but a child born when Ferrari made his first car isn't out of high school yet.

Ferrari knows automobiles and he knows his business and he knows that it is a rough business. "If a man really calculated the risks he would never drive a racing car," he has said. "Also he would never build one." He was an old-time racing driver and before that he was a mechanic, early in the service of a good house, Alfa-Romeo. He drove first for Alfa-Romeo. Ascari the elder and Campari were on the same team. On June 17, 1923, Ferrari won the Circuit of Savio race at Ravenna, setting a new lap record in the process. The prize that meant most to him that day was nothing the race organizers had to offer; it was a heraldic device, a black horse rampant on a yellow field, given him by the parents of Major Francesco Baracca, the leading Italian pursuit pilot of World War I. Baracca, victor over thirty-six enemy planes, had been shot down on June 18, 1918, so Ferrari had won his first race almost on the fifth anniversary of his death. He was much moved by the gift, part of the Baracca coat of arms, and has used it as a personal emblem ever since. The only other award that has meant as much to Ferrari came a few months ago when he was given an honorary degree in engineering by the University of Bologna, one of the oldest universities in the world. A holder of the same degree was Guglielmo Marconi, who invented the radio.

Enzo Ferrari was not a driver of the very first rank, but now and then he was good enough to beat some who were—he beat Tazio Nuvolari on three occasions, and Nuvolari was the greatest of his day and perhaps the greatest of all time. When, in December 1929, the Alfa-Romeo factory withdrew from racing, the team cars and equipment were turned over to Ferrari's management, and for the next few years ran as the Scuderia Ferrari. It was a successful team. Ferrari recruited the best drivers in Europe, and, until the Germans appeared with the monster Mercedes-Benz and Auto Union cars, Ferrari had notable successes. Nuvolari won the 1930 Millé Miglia driving for the Scuderia, and his legendary victory at the Nürburgring in 1935, when he beat full teams of Mercedes-Benz and Auto Union cars, was in a Ferrari Alfa-Romeo.

Ferrari put together a car in 1939, the engine built up out of two Fiats, and when the war put a stop to racing he made machine tools. His Maranello factory was hit by eight American bombs in a 1943 daylight raid, and shortly afterward the Germans came along and picked up what equipment was worth taking. Four years passed before Ferrari could get back on his feet and produce the first car wholly of his design and manufacture, a 12-cylinder, 1.5-liter supercharged racing model.

Ferrari is unique in that his passenger-car operation is secondary to his racing, and not the other way around. Mercedes-Benz, probably the most successful of all racing organizations, taken by and large over the past half-century, bases its racing operation, which is intermittent, on a huge commercial business, and this is the usual rule. Factories producing both racing and passenger cars usually expect to lose money in competition, and to write it off as publicity and advertising and research. Ferrari needs $40,000 or $50,000 a year in prize money to stay in business. He races for keeps.

The intensity with which Ferrari approaches racing has contributed a good deal to the prevailing image of the man. He never sees a race, or almost never. He stays in Modena and waits by the telephone. His tendency to personalize his automobiles and to become emotionally involved with his drivers would create, he feels, an undesirable level of excitement which would communicate itself to the team. He has been severely criticized in recent years because of the deaths of so many ranking drivers at the wheels of Ferrari cars. The toll is in fact impressive, including all the front-rank drivers Italy had—Ascari, Castelotti, Musso—plus the Britons Collins and Wharton and the Spanish Marquis de Portago, to mention only the leading lights. After Portago's Mille Miglia crash, which took fifteen lives, the outcry was particularly vehement. There was nothing wrong with the automobiles. Their list of successes indicated the correctness of their design, and as for material, Ferrari is almost fanatic on the subject of metal fatigue, and maintains the most rigid quality controls. Most of the Ferrari accidents can be traced to human error in one form or another: a missed shift, a tire that should have been changed, a bend entered 3 miles an hour too fast, and so on. If there is an overall explanation it is that Ferrari cars are very fast, and Ferrari drivers, being picked from among the world's best, are likely to be men who try very hard.

There are those who think they try too hard, and do so because the *Commendatore* is capable of imposing tremendous competitive pressures on them. Some critics have found this brutal, but to anyone who has ever watched, up close, a college football coach at work, Ferrari's methods do no seem so rough.

They have, in any case, served his purpose. No racing team in history has won so much prize money. The drivers' world championship has been won in his cars, the constructors' world championship, the championship of sports cars and of touring cars, again and again. This year two Americans are driving for him, Phil Hill and Richie Ginther, both Californians, with the ranking German driver, Wolfgang von Trips. Ginther is reserve driver

(Ferrari will usually run two cars) and Hill is the number-one. He is an intense, taut, fluent, and intelligent man, a theoretician who possesses a profound understanding of the behavior of race cars at high speed.

Ferrari is conservative, not quick to undertake major changes. He was not an early convert to disc brakes and fuel injection, for example, and the recent trend to ultralight rear-engine Grand Prix cars found him lagging. The British dominated 1960 with Cooper and Lotus and BRM rear-engine cars. Ferrari did put out a rear-engine car, but its production was hurried and it was no great threat to the English builders. This year sees a new international formula, specifying 1.5-liter engines to replace the old 2.5s, and a new team of blood-red Ferrari *monoposto* cars will come out of the shiny-clean shops at Maranello, through the green gate across from the tree-shaded courtyard of the inn, to campaign around the world again. They will certainly be very fast, reflective of Ferrari's intense pride and patriotism. His purpose, he has said, is "to build cars for champions to win championships in." He has won every race of major consequence except one, Indianapolis. Hastily set up Ferrari cars have appeared at Indianapolis, but they have not run successfully. For an Italian team to mount an Indianapolis campaign requires major effort, including absence from perhaps three potentially lucrative European races. Ferrari will eventually make the effort. Someone who knows him well has said, "To Ferrari, a race he hasn't won is a thrown gauntlet."

Meanwhile the lithe and lovely *gran turismo* machines will come from Maranello in ones and twos and threes, each of them an example of the purest expression man has yet been able to give to the age-old wish to move privately, speedily, and elegantly over the face of the earth.

—1964

Motoring's
Classic
Revival

Time was, say just after World War II, when $1500 would buy a Duesenberg double-cowl phaeton in fair shape. Coffin-nosed 810-812 Cords went for half that. *Before* the War, an example of the rarest of all U.S.-built automobiles, the T-head Mercer Raceabout, was sold for $50. Three hundred times that price might buy it today, and it might not. A good Model J Duesenberg can bring $10,000. An old story, to be sure. A few of the things man makes, even though the creations of craftsmen, not artists, are so happily conceived that they outlive their lifetimes. There are never enough of them to go around: George III thuja-wood cabinets, Bréguet watches, clocks by Thomas Tompion, silver by Paul Revere. When demand exceeds supply and prices become no matter, someone will take action and the result will be either a counterfeit or a replica. A replica, someone has said, is a forgery made by an honest man, like the replicas of the British sovereign minted a few years ago for sale to European hoarders. They were exact copies, but they weren't counterfeit because the British government no longer made the coin, it wasn't in circulation, and because the man who did make them saw to it that they had a bit more gold content than the British mint itself had used.

As far as I know,* no one has ever forged an automobile. But the notion of making replicas of desirable models is no new thing. In the 1930s Frazer-Nash made the Tourist Trophy Replica, a duplicate of a famous race-winning car. Again in the 1930s the Brewster company of New York used to buy Rolls-Royce limousines and town cars, discard the original bodies and mount two-seater roadsters on them, replicas of the standard, but always rare, Piccadilly model. An elegant carriage it was, too, transportation *de grande luxe* for two people, its tiny cabin atop the long wheelbase giving it something of the air of a Louis Quatorze sedan chair carried on poles long enough for four bearers fore and aft. I owned one, and regret selling it. I owned a T-head Mercer too, and a Packard double-cowl touring car, and I would like all of them back. It cannot be done. However, though there be small hope for me, there is hope for you, if you pine for a coffin-nosed Cord, or a Duesenberg, or the SSK Mercedes-Benz of the 1930s, for plans to make replicas of these cars, varying in precision from case to case, are afoot.

The Duesenberg project is the most ambitious, which is fitting, since the Duesenberg was among the most notable of American motorcars. The company's life was short, and few Duesenbergs were built, only about 470 of the Model J and SJ cars on which the legend is based. The car was expensive, from $14,750 to $25,000. It was big, and not by present standards an easy car to handle. Driving one now, one notices a "trucky" feeling at low speeds: The steering, the clutch, the brakes are heavier than custom today will tolerate, and the car seems very big indeed. All this fades away on the high side of 50 miles an hour, coming into what is after all the country in which the Duesenberg was meant to live. As a limousine it hadn't quite the degree of hushed mechanical refinement that marked the great Rolls-Royces that were its contemporaries, although the detail and luxury of its coachwork equaled anything on the road, and surpassed most. But the Duesenberg was two things, the Rolls-Royce only one: Both cars made elegant town carriages, but the Duesenberg was a tiger on the open road as well. Its builders proposed to throw it into competition with the best European makes, Rolls-Royce, Mercedes-Benz, Hispano-Suiza, Isotta-Fraschini, Minerva, Bentley (nothing American was then its peer) and they succeeded so handsomely that to this day most people believe the Duesenberg was made in Germany.

The name, of course, is German; Fred and August Duesenberg were born in Germany, and comparison of the Duesenberg, particularly the SJ model,

---

*A true statement when I wrote this article in 1965. It is emphatically not true today. —K.W.P.

with the 540K Mercedes-Benz, another fast, luxurious, 8-cylinder, super-charged automobile, is legitimate, but there the matter ends.

Fritz Duesenberg, August Duesenberg's son and Fred Duesenberg's nephew, is chairman of the board of the new Duesenberg company, and the first of the new cars will be in its owner's hands, if all goes well, one day in 1965, just short of thirty years after the last of the old ones was sold: November 1936. The two will look nothing like each other. The new body is by Virgil Exner, former Chrysler vice-president, a major figure in automobile styling, and his son Virgil Exner, Jr. Final decisions had not been made when this was written, but the body will be, the Exners intend, massively impressive, elegant, and carrying about it a slightly sporting air. Effort has been made to bring to it some design points, particularly in the front end, reminiscent of the classic car, but they are not many. (Exner has done this before; he showed a "modern" Mercer Raceabout at this year's Paris Salon.) A near copy would be difficult and impracticable in many ways. There was really no standard Duesenberg—bodies were made by many coachmakers: Rollston, Derham, Murphy, Willoughby, LeBaron, Judkins, Weymann, Walker, Holbrook, Brunn, Castagna, Hibbard & Darrin, Bohman & Schwartz, Dietrich, Locke, Fernandez. About 175 different bodies were built on the J chassis, and probably as many as 100 of them were unique —one of a kind.

Performance of the new Duesenberg must be surmised at the moment, since the essential factor, the power-to-weight ratio, hasn't been established. The car will weigh something around three tons and the engine will produce 400 to 500 horsepower. It will probably be a Lincoln engine, which is to say Ford, and 500 horsepower is well within reach. The old supercharged Duesenbergs, the SJ model—only thirty-eight were made—had 325 horse-power and were guaranteed at 104 miles an hour in second, 130 in third. Performance of the new one should be comparable. If aluminum or fiber glass were used for the body, it would be quicker, but the decision has been taken to do it in steel, and in Italy. Nowhere else in the world today are there coachmakers who could undertake the assignment at anything approaching a feasible cost. As it is the car will cost about $18,000, a startling figure at first glance, but reasonable in the present limited luxury-motorcar market: The standard Phantom V Rolls-Royce V-8 costs $26,000 in London; the bottom of the line, the Silver Cloud model, $15,445. The Ferrari 330 GT brings $17,000-odd in the same market, and the British dealer sold six of them off the floor at the last London show. The new Duesenberg company's hope to sell 300 units the first year thus appears rational. The car is coming in a boom time, as did the old one, regularly priced at $14,750 to $17,500 with a few to individual order at $20,000 and perhaps two at

$25,000. In 1935, $17,000 was a great deal more money than $18,000 is today.

Ettore Bugatti, a man who lived and thought on baronial levels, had a hotel near his plant in Molsheim in France for the convenience of customers who preferred to pick up their own cars rather than trust them even to factory delivery drivers. Duesenberg has adopted this notion and improved on it: there will be guesthouses on the factory grounds available to clients at no charge.

Certainly the Duesenberg will be unique in the American market. Owners need not expect to meet another one in a good many thousands of miles of driving. If the first model, the sedan, has the somewhat sedate air inherent in that kind of body, still it will be luxurious, beautifully finished, extraordinarily satisfying; and the convertible model expected to appear perhaps in 1966 should be as spectacular as any *décapotable* France or Italy ever knew.

No one has much doubt that an exciting body will come off Exner's drawing board, and the engine poses no problem. There are half a dozen V-8s in Detroit that would do nicely. Knowledgeable engineers do have some reservations about the chassis. The design of a chassis from scratch is not as simple as it sounds; it is not just a matter of riveting up a steel framework and hanging engine bearers and four wheels on it. Inevitably, hundreds of unpredictable little problems arise; the debugging of a new chassis design is a frustrating and time-consuming business. Still, experience and the weight of money counts and Fred McManis, Jr., president of the company, has said that there is $40 million of Texas money in the vaults, and more where that came from. Paul Farago, a Chrysler veteran, is in charge of production, and Dale Cosper, ex-Studebaker, is chief engineer.

Brooks Stevens of Milwaukee, among the best-known and most versatile industrial designers in the country (he has done everything from trains to eggbeaters), has taken an easier road with his Excalibur SS: he is using the standard Studebaker Daytona chassis, the Chevrolet 327 engine, and the Paxton supercharger, all time-proved components. His plans are less ambitious, too: he hopes to make sixteen cars a month to sell for $7000, with no intention of expanding production beyond that. Eight cars had been built, sold, and delivered last January, putting Stevens and his son William, whose particular baby the project has been, well ahead of the field. Stevens has a second replica, a Bugatti, on the stocks for 1966.

Unlike the Duesenberg people, who have said that they want nothing to do with automobile buffs, that they intend making only a limited appeal to nostalgia, that they are creating a new car on an old name, Stevens is taking dead aim on the fanatics who count four or five years well spent in the restoration of a classic car. Down to the great slab of leather hood strap, he and his son have tried their hardest to make the Excalibur SS look thirty-five years old.

"We want to make a *reliable* classic car," Stevens told me. "Our idea is that here's a classic that will take you where you want to go *and* bring you back."

He has something there. I've driven thousands of miles in classic motorcars, my own and other people's, and to tell the truth I was uncomfortable much of the time. One listens to the sound of the thing like a symphony conductor terrified that the first-chair oboe will goof in the middle of an eight-bar solo. One develops an absurd ability to distinguish among engine sounds—is that a loose bearing? is that piston slap? the supercharger gears didn't sound like that yesterday—and chassis and body noise. Things happen so suddenly. I was driving an Isotta-Fraschini town car on a dark country road one night when without a second's warning the entire electrical system quit—ignition and all the lights. Driving a Bugatti, a sudden tremendous rhythmic thumping began on the floor boards. I thought it was the drive shaft, running, on that model, at engine speed because the gearbox was on the back axle. I had visions of this big black steel column, about four inches in diameter, coming up through the one-inch wood floor and beating me to death. I shut everything off. It was a generator belt come loose, nothing, it took barely an hour and a half on my back in the gravel to put on the spare that a previous, and bright, owner had provided. I've had the chain come off a Morgan Three-Wheeler, wrap itself around the single rear wheel and lock it, at 40 miles an hour, tight as a bank vault, setting up a remarkable skid. And so it goes. Brooks and William Stevens may well be stoned to death some dark night by a posse from The Classic Car Club, but they've produced a car that looks, to all but the most discerning eye (fat tires, disc brakes, and so forth), as if it had been hand-assembled in 1930 but owns no screw or bolt that will mystify the smallest Chevrolet or Studebaker dealership in North Dakota. Except that I know that among all right-thinking folk the penalty for the usage is death by drawing and quartering, I would say it was a fun thing, the Excalibur SS.

It's extraordinarily seductive on first sight. Stevens set the engine well back in the frame, not only for better balance, but to give the machine the radiator-behind-axle look that characterized the original. (This design point appeared last on the British-built H.R.G., still available postwar, and I for one was sorry to see it go.) The radiator itself is a massive slab of chromium cut as near as no matter at all to the mold of the original SS and SSK Mercedes-Benz cars. The outside exhaust pipes come from the same German maker who supplied them to Mercedes. And the thing will *go.* I haven't driven it, since the first one has yet to come to England, but Stevens tells me his son has seen the high side of 150 miles an hour in the supercharged version, and that brings up another point. The temptation is great, in driving a classic car of notable performance, to use the performance, and this is not the course of wisdom. A competent and indisputably courageous racedriver once almost indignantly refused to drive my 1912 Mercer. "If you put that thing through a crack-test," he told me, "you wouldn't have the guts to *sit* in it, much less drive it." He was right.

No such inhibitions will mar the pleasure of driving an Excalibur SS. It can be fully extended in confidence that it is as likely to stay together as any other motorcar; further, it's remarkably roadable, and well endowed with the other two primary safety factors, tremendous acceleration and great braking power. It is meant to serve as a perfectly tractable high-performance road car, a *gran turismo* motorcar, but it has shown startlingly fast test times over standard sports-car road circuits. The Stevenses, father and son, expect to campaign an SS or two this summer.

The original S cars from which the Excalibur is derived were road cars, too, in basic origin, but they were campaigned in races all over the world. They were heavy, going nearly two tons, and hard to handle, but they would stick, they were quick, and they were built to last the distance. They took a lot of silverware back to Germany.

They were created by that genuinely great designer, Ferdinand Porsche, who has so many legendary motor vehicles to his credit, from the Prince Henry Austro-Daimler to the Tiger Tank of World War II, the Volkswagen before it, and the Porsche after it. There were four variants: S, SS, SSK, and SSKL—Sports, Super-Sports, Super-Sports-Kurtz (Short), and Super-Sports-Kurtz-Leicht (Light). First time out, in June 1927, with Rudolph Caracciola driving, an S won the race inaugurating the opening of the Nürburgring circuit in Germany. From then into the early 1930s the S cars did well, sometimes attracting more attention by their near misses than by their outright wins. For example, Caracciola came very near winning the 1929 Grand Prix de Monaco in an SSK. One would think the car ill-suited to the circuit, a true city-street course, with straights so short that even today's G.P. cars can't get over 120 miles an hour on the longest of them, and well studded with right-angle corners. Still, in a car with 110 mph top speed and an acceleration time of forty-five seconds from 0 to 90, Caracciola led the race for a time, and probably would have won except for a two-minute-plus pit stop for tires and gasoline. He came third to two Bugattis. Again, in the 1930 Le Mans, a race held to be the private property of the Bentleys, which had won it in 1927, 1928, and 1929, a single SSK, Caracciola again up, with Christian Werner codriving, led the field until the failure of a component—the generator—put its lights out around midnight. But Caracciola won the 1930 Irish Grand Prix in an SSK, and set a new course record doing it.

It was just at this time that one could see the watershed of design begin to move away from the heavy brute cars of racing's beginnings toward the tiny, feather-light Grand Prix cars of today, and Hans Nibel, who had succeeded Porsche in Daimler-Benz, attempted to lighten the SSK without basic change. Holes, big ones, were drilled all over the chassis, until the side members looked like Zeppelin framings; the camshaft profiles were changed and the valves enlarged and a bigger blower, stuffing the air in at twelve pounds per square inch instead of eight and one-half was fitted. The horse-power of the resulting SSKL was rated 300 and it won the 1931 Mille Miglia. But the Daimler-Benz engineers knew that Porsche's basic design had been taken as far as it would go. They tried one last thing; streamlining the stark, wind-grabbing chassis for the 1933 Eifelrennen on the Nürbur-gring, but Caracciola couldn't drive the car (brake failure had broken his thigh in practice at Monte Carlo; he had hit one of the stone walls that line the circuit almost from end to end). Otto Merz ran in his stead, lost the car on a rain-washed circuit, and was killed.

Stevens's Excalibur SS should be faster than Daimler-Benz's SSK, and more comfortable, but it will lack one characterisitic that endeared the old car to many. It was a characteristic of Mercedes supercharging that the pump blew air *through* the carburetors rather than sucking from them as is the usual practice. A hurricane of pressure air blasting through a three-inch carburetor throat past valves and venturis and whatnot set up a great racket, and the supercharger scream of the S cars, as well as the 540Ks that followed them, was a notable feature of the design, indeed one hard to miss noting, particularly since it was intermittent: use of the blower for longer than ten seconds at a time was not recommended, since it would raise the horsepower from, say, 120 to 180, imposing considerable stress. The total effect was as if, in a modern car, one dropped from fourth gear to third and simultaneously turned on a siren. No one sets up a supercharger to blow through the carburetor anymore; the Paxton that Stevens uses is almost silent. It might be suggested that he set up a little siren to fake it, but he would doubtless hear from the police if he did.

The new Cord will be supercharged, too, if the client pleases. It is using a proprietary engine, the Chevrolet Corvair, which comes with a super-charger option. The Cord departs even further than Brooks Stevens from the Duesenberg base idea of making no attempt at simulation of the origi-nal: it's a precise copy, to eight-tenths scale, of the Model 810-812 Cord of the 1930s, coffin nose, front-wheel drive, and all. Only the body material will be wholly different—a thermoplastic laminate called Expanded Roya-lite, made by U.S. Rubber. This is so remarkable a substance that one's inclined to the German word *Wunderstuff:* it's cheap, light, easily formed in heated dies; very rigid, resistant to weather, acid, salts, and so on, integrally colored, has high insulation properties, and is stronger than 18-gauge steel. One more: when someone puts a fist-size dent into it you pick up a commercial air gun, blow 500 degrees of heat on it, and the dent rises to the original surface.

Like the Duesenberg and the S Mercedes-Benz cars, the Cord is a venerated image, and with reason. The first one, the lanky-looking L-29 model, appeared in 1929, an interesting automobile, but no great success. It was too long, at very nearly 138 inches of wheelbase, and there was a serious design flaw buried in it: the engine had been set so far back in the chassis that insufficient weight bore on the front wheels. Running at a steep slippery hill, weight transfer on the L-29 would put so much on the rear wheels, which were slave, and so little on the front, which drove, that the car might refuse the slope. This annoyed the owner, particularly if mass-produced Detroit tin stampings at 25 percent of the Cord's cost were running on past it. The L-29s were very good-looking indeed, though, particularly the roadsters, and they were the first front-wheel-drive cars to go into series production in the United States.

The front-wheel-drive idea, at the moment in the ascendancy in the United States, is an old idea in Europe, where it originated. There's a choice of historical precedent: Nicholas Cugnot's steam tricycle of 1769 drove through the single front wheel. Latil of France built a proper front-wheel-drive vehicle in 1899, driving the steered wheels through universal joints. The American Walter Christie built a front-wheel-drive race car in 1904, and six more after it, and some New York City taxicabs after them. The race cars were fast, but brutes to handle and difficult to start. Christie mounted his engines sidewise in front, a notion held to be one of the preeminent signs of brilliance in the famous Mini-Minor by British designer Alec Issigonis. A million Mini-Minors have been turned out in the last few years and the design will certainly be imbedded in the history of the automobile. The French Citroën is probably the best-known front-wheel-drive car in the world, and is another classic design.

Advantages of the system are compactness, extra interior room due to the absence of the tunnel carrying the drive shaft to the rear wheels and the front-compartment hump housing the clutch—these and a positive superiority in traction on slippery surfaces. The number of times the world's most exacting rallies have been won in recent years by Minis and SAABs (a Swedish front-wheel-drive) clearly demonstrates that. This year's Monte Carlo rally was so brutal that of 237 cars starting, only thirty-five reached Monte Carlo at all, never mind reached it with a chance of winning. A Mini won it, a Porsche was second, a SAAB third. Granted the driver was the Finnish champion Timo Makinen, one of the finest snow-and-ice specialists of all time (second, Eugen Bohringer, the German champion; third, Pat

Moss-Carlsson for the highest placement a woman has ever made in the Monte), and granted that he was well supported by the British Motor Company factory with such niceties as eighty-six sets of tires for the 2600 miles, including five kinds of steel-studded covers, still it was another demonstration of the virtues of front-wheel drive on tricky surfaces. The heart of the matter is that when you turn the front wheels into a hard corner, and apply power to them, you get a better response, directionally, then you do if you apply power to the rear wheels, which are still a little way *out* of the corner, and tending to push the car straight on, and thus *out* of the corner. There are many funny little tricks an expert can do to demonstrate the agility peculiar to front-wheel drive; for example, he can run the car fast down a narrow road, put the wheel all the way over, accelerator hard on, lock the rear wheels for an instant with the hand brake, and whap! the thing has spun in its own length and is motoring rapidly back where it came from. An expert, I said. If you must try it, I suggest a supermarket parking lot on a Sunday. Incidentally, Makinen never takes his right foot off the accelerator, does all braking with his left.

The 810-812 Cords, the coffin-nosed cars, were born out of the Duesenberg. Fred Duesenberg had died, as a result of an accident in one of his own cars in the Pennsylvania mountains in July 1932, and the Duesenberg company, twelve months later, was beginning seriously to feel the loss. Harold Ames, the new president, asked Gordon Buehrig, then with General Motors, to come to Indianapolis and design a small, low-priced Duesenberg to be built on the Auburn chassis. The design was made and set aside and Buehrig was transferred to Auburn, where he did the boattail Auburn Speedster. In 1934 the Auburn company decided to revive the small Duesenberg program, with two changes: abandon the Auburn chassis for a new front-wheel-drive design, and call it not a Duesenberg but a Cord, after E. L. Cord, who controlled the company—he had originally backed the Duesenberg brothers. The new design was finished in the summer of 1934, and summarily dropped in December of that year. In July 1935, with the company in bad shape, the panic button down and locked, Buehrig, in Indianapolis, was given twenty-four hours in which to prepare, and deliver in Chicago for a board meeting, photographs of the quarter-scale design model of the Cord that had been on ice for six months. The pictures were made by an assistant of Buehrig's, Dale Cosper, whose name now appears on the new Duesenberg board of directors. They were done by 2 A.M. and the decision next day was to go, to make a new car, although there was less than a million dollars in the bank.

Gordon Buehrig, who's now with Ford, has always had full credit for the Cord design, and he has spent years trying to point out that he did only the body shape and the interior. Ted Allen, Herbert Snow, George Kublin,

Louis Schwitzer, George Ritts, Bart Cotter, Stanley Thomas, Stan Menton, and many other people worked on engine and chassis and production. Buehrig had three assistants besides Cosper—Vince Gardner, Paul Peter Renter von Lorenzen, and Richard Robinson. But while the Lycoming engine in the Cord was a good one, the chassis design sound, and the production of the car—on a bargain-basement, cut-rate system that would make a modern Detroit engineer whimper with fright—a miracle of enterprise, the primary factor in its success *was* the styling. A compliment Buehrig has treasured was, "The car looks as if it had been born on the road and grew up there."

The 810 Cord had a lot of things first; It was the first true four-passenger convertible, it had a true disappearing top, it was first to demonstrate the no-running-board thesis successfully, it had a step-down floor and such novelties as disappearing headlights, this minute being made much of by, for one, the Buick Riviera.

The Cord failed for two reasons: the six-month lag between design and decision to build gave insufficient time to produce cars for the arbitrary deadline—the New York Automobile Show of November 1935. Cars were produced, but they were largely mock-ups. There was not enough time for testing, and the first models delivered to customers had two bad faults: they overheated and they jumped out of gear. These were bugs easy to eradicate, but they hurt, and they furnished ammunition for rival companies' counterselling. (Counterselling is unselling, or propaganda, as when a salesman tells a prospect, "Of course, you know that the Blank V-10 has a tendency to put itself into first gear if you leave the engine running? Yeah, they lose a lot of people that way. Crushed to death against the garage doors.") For another thing, the Cord was expensive. It was a $2000–$3000 car, at a time when a Buick cost $885, a Studebaker President under $1000, and even a Lincoln-Zephyr only $1320. Those were the only things wrong with it, though. When the engineers had worked the bugs out, it was a fine, fast, roadable motorcar, and almost universally thought to be a beautiful one. It has stood the test: an as-new Cord is worth more today than it was in 1937, when production stopped. That is true of few automobiles.

The veneration in which the Cord is held was the primary thing that brought the new company into being. Glenn Pray, a former Tulsa high-school teacher, and Wayne McKinley, a Belleville, Illinois, auto dealer, thought of it, as others had, but they took action. They formed a company and bought what was left of the original Auburn-Cord-Duesenberg company. They got patterns, dies, blueprints, 600,000 pounds of spare parts, and had it all shipped to an abandoned cannery in Broken Arrow, Oklahoma. The production factory will be in Tulsa, and it's hoped that the first year will see 2000 cars made and sold at around $4000.

At least one group of overseas businessmen must be watching the new Cord operation with interest—the ones who own the original Cord body dies. Just before World War II, these dies, with the New York City Sixth Avenue Elevated and a lot of other scrap, were shipped to Japan. Most of the stuff was fired back at us, but someone in Yokohama thought the Cord dies were too nice to break up for bombs, so they're still there. I'm sure the Tulsa people intend theirs to be the first and last of the Cord replicas. Perhaps not.

But one thing we do know. If sales of the Cord, Duesenberg, and Excalibur SS equal or surpass expectations, we can look forward to all manner of rejuvenated makes and models, from exotic foreign vintage machinery down to—but maybe not including—the Edsel.

—1965

What Makes Men Race?

Emile Levassor Of France won the first automobile race, run over the 732 miles from Paris to Bordeaux and return, June 11 and 12, 1895. Levassor drove a car of his own design, the Panhard-Levassor (Panhards are still made today) and he drove the whole way himself, allowing his riding mechanic to have the tiller only when the car was running slowly uphill. He was on the road for fifty-three hours, and running for forty-eight hours forty-eight minutes. He came into Paris fresh and full of bounce, had a cup of soup, two poached eggs, two glasses of champagne, and gravely told reporters that no one should ever be allowed to run an automobile at such dangerous speeds at night —he had averaged 14.9 miles an hour, which doesn't sound like a blistering velocity until one thinks of doing it over pitch-black country roads on kerosene headlamps.

Ripping down the Mulsanne Straight in the Le Mans 24-Hour Race these days, cars touch 180 in the night and more. Last year, Richie Ginther's Ford GT was clocked at 200 along Mulsanne!

In the seventy years since Paris–Bordeaux–Paris it's probable that more people have watched automobile racing than any other sport man has devised.

During the decade before World War I, crowds as big as 500,000 saw the old Vanderbilt Cup races; 300,000 packed themselves into Indianapolis last year; and when the Mille Miglia was run in Italy as it used to be (it was abolished in 1957), over a thousand miles of open road from Brescia to Rome to Brescia, the total of spectators could only be estimated—and in millions. Six-figure crowds go to Le Mans in France every year, and to the Grand Prix of Germany at the Nürburgring.

The sight of a fast car screaming past brings an excitement boiling up from very deep within us. Why? Perhaps no one knows. There is this, that motor racing is one of the four primal sports, all of them distinct as a group from the lesser sports, the stick-and-ball games for example. These are mountain climbing (man against nature), bullfighting (man against beast), boxing and wrestling (man against man), and racing (man against time). All are basic to life; all have been part of man's existence since the dawn of humanity. Of the four, racing, which of course began as foot racing, has changed the most, and that, perhaps, accounts for its fascination. The compulsion of racing must, *per se,* be in proportion to the speed involved, and automobile racing is the fastest kind of racing we can watch. (Closed-circuit airplane racing, the only kind worth watching, is little seen today.)

I think motor racing pulls its millions to the world's tracks and circuits, big and little, because we want to be the men, vicariously, who are in the cars; we want to be that daring, that skilled, that far set apart from the mob —and after it all we want to wear the laurel wreath, drink the champagne from the silver bowl, take the money, and go home to race another day.

The drivers? Some men drive, as some men go deep-sea salvage diving, groping among the razor-sharp shards of broken ships in 150 feet of silt-solid water, for money pure and simple. There are not many of these, and they are never among the immortals of the game. Most do it, I am convinced, because they are obsessed; they have found an excitement that nothing else offers.

The most sensitive and articulate of the truly great drivers of our time was the Englishman Stirling Moss, who retired in 1962—not because he wanted to, but because a crash had so slowed his reflexes he felt he could not go on—and then only after he had set a record that may never be breached in our times: he ran in 466 competitions and won 41 percent of them. Moss said, "I think motor racing is the greatest of all sports, but also more than a sport; as a very few men can do it, it is an art form and related to ballet."

I think this a profound and penetrating observation. The art of ballet is the art of incredibly skilled, rigidly controlled movement, and that is the root of its fascination. Motor racing is incredibly skilled, rigidly controlled movement, but movement at the greatest overland speeds man can achieve, performed under the most brutal discipline conceivable.

An art form? In its highest expression, yes, but you must be lucky to see it. You must be in a corner, the right corner, at the right time, watching the right car, and you must know, too, that it is not the car, and not the engine, and not the wheels that matter; the driver's link with reality and with life is nothing so obvious; he controls the car, wins or loses, through his understanding of what is happening at the place in which all the forces that make up the terrible equation meet: in the four little oval places, as big as the palm of his hand, where the rubber meets the road. If he doesn't know what's happening there, he will be a veteran loser.

City-to-city racing, or roadracing, was the first racing, and it is still the purest and most demanding form. The great pioneer roadraces died with the Paris–Madrid of 1903, stopped at Bordeaux by the authorities on the ground that it was too dangerous to be allowed to continue. There had been an appalling number of crashes; drivers and spectators and soldiers guarding the 342-mile course had been killed. The winner, Gabriel, driving a Mors, had averaged 65 miles an hour, which meant that he had run at 80 and 90 for mile after mile on the dusty, primitive roads, lined with 3 million people.

Of the great city-to-city races, and in-town races ("round the houses" the British called them), two are left: the Targa Florio in Sicily, run since 1906, and the Grand Prix de Monaco in Monte Carlo. The Targa Florio circuit covers 44.7 miles of Sicilian mountain and countryside, ten laps, 447 miles, rising and falling as it goes through Cerda, Caltavuturo, Coltesano, Campofelice. Inhabitants of the towns are hopefully petitioned by the authorities to stay off the streets and keep their front doors closed as the cars scream through. Like the twenty-four-hour race at Le Mans, the Targa Florio is a sports-car race, which means that the cars must have certain amenities, (headlamps, for example) and must possess, at least technically, one passenger seat.

The Grand Prix of Monaco is a Formula I event—that is to say, a race for single-seat Grand Prix automobiles, the fastest on the circuits. It is traditionally the opening race of the year, run in May to begin a season that will end with the Grand Prix of South Africa in the winter. Run through the streets of Monte Carlo, the G.P. of Monaco is the last of the city races, and it is high on the list of the most glamorous sports events that we know. To sit on the terrace of the Hotel de Paris, vermouth-cassis in hand, and watch the pencil-thin howling cars rip through the right-angle corner past the Casino—or, better still, to lean over the rail of a balcony on the harbor side of the hotel and see the cars come up the hill from Ste. Devote, touching 120 miles an hour where 60 would frighten most of us—this is to see automobile racing at its positive peak. The air is warm and soft and bright, the streets are tree-lined, and there are flowers everywhere.

Monaco is a short circuit, 1.9 miles, but it runs uphill and down, through turns right-angle and tighter, including a 180-degree hairpin that can't be taken faster than 30 miles an hour. It runs through a tunnel, a tunnel set in a bend, so that the exit can't be seen from the entrance; it is 130 yards long, this tunnel, and the top-rank drivers do 115 miles an hour through it, to come out into the light again and make perhaps 120 on a 150-yard straight. More corners, an artificial barrier or *chicane,* a downhill run, then along the harbor wall at 110 mph to the start-finish line and up the hill to do it all over again.

Monaco and the Nürburgring, in Germany, are "drivers' courses," perhaps the two most demanding in the world. At Monaco, there is almost no room for error; if a driver loses control of his car, he will hit something solid and unyielding—a tree, a granite railing, a marble wall—or he will go into the water. Monaco makes more stringent physical demands than any other course, too: weight loss of five pounds or more is common and even veteran drivers have finished with badly blistered hands.

The Nürburgring is an artificial road-circuit in mountainous country, 14.1 miles to the lap, with about 175 bends and corners, rising and falling over hills as steep as 17 percent. It is a long circuit to memorize, and a driver *must* memorize every major bend and corner. The Nürburgring is so diabolically difficult that it can extend the most skilled drivers. It is significant that three of the greatest drivers who have lived, Tazio Nuvolari, Juan Manuel Fangio, and Stirling Moss, all drove the best single races of their careers on the Ring. Nuvolari and Moss both pulled off the same incredible *tour de force*: they won with cars that were demonstrably slower than the opposition.

The twenty-four-hour race at Le Mans is difficult and dangerous because, like the twelve-hour race at Sebring, Florida, part of it is run in darkness, and because, since it's a sports-car race, there is a tremendous speed differential between the fastest and the slowest cars—as much as 80 miles an hour. Passing, at 180 miles an hour in night and fog, a car that is doing only 100 is not an exercise for beginners.

There is such a bewildering variety of racing in the United States and Europe today that a man making a full-time effort couldn't hope to see more than a fraction of it. There are club races, hill-climbs, rallies, ice racing in Scandinavia, and the British specialty called "trials" in which cars designed for this task alone try to climb what look to be impossibly steep and muddy hillsides.

In the United States there is single-seat track racing in every variety from Indianapolis to half-mile dirt county-fair circuits. There is stock-car racing, which offers the spirited spectacle of a car that looks just like your own blue hardtop doing 175 miles an hour. There are the dragsters, now reaching *beyond* speeds of 200 miles an hour in the standing-start quarter-mile.

In addition, there is roadracing on the more than forty circuits built since the war from Connecticut to California. To European drivers and manufacturers, the two most important American races have been Sebring and Watkins Glen, in upper New York State. Watkins Glen is the venue of the Grand Prix of the United States, and counts toward the world championship, as each country's Grand Prix does. Indianapolis does not count, but since the appearance of the British driver, and former world champion, Jack Brabham, in a rear-engined car at the 1961 Indianapolis, and particularly since the genuinely stunning emergence of Ford as a primary factor (*nine* cars were Ford-powered in 1964, and not one suffered engine failure, an extraordinary accomplishment for a new engine), European drivers are paying more attention to it.

The appearance of the British world champion, Jimmy Clark, at Indy in 1963, when he ran second to Parnelli Jones in a controversial finish, and last year, when he was put out by a damaged tire after setting a qualifying record of a hair under 160 miles an hour, convinced American drivers that the Europeans after all were not rank beginners, and the success of drivers like A. J. Foyt, the top U.S. money winner this year, on road circuits, convinced the Europeans that the track specialists were not mere heavy-footed truck drivers. The American, Phil Hill, was champion of the world in 1961, the first American to hold the title, and Dan Gurney and Richie Ginther of California are on any list of the top dozen in the world.

The reemergence of the United States as a power in international racing after too long an absence is in major part due to Ford's decision to throw full weight into an international racing program.

For years now the Italians and the British have dominated sports-car, *gran turismo* (fast touring), and Grand Prix racing. In long-distance events, where stamina at top speed matters, Ferrari has set the world standard, with Porsche of Germany hard behind; an almost private contest among British drivers has settled the world championship: John Cooper and Colin Chapman of England, with the Cooper and Lotus Grand Prix cars, blew into oblivion the classic front-engine race car. But the Ford GT cars, one of which led fifty-four cars at Le Mans for the first hour and twenty minutes of the race this year . . . Carroll Shelby's *Cobras,* which took first, second, and third in the GT category at Sebring in 1964 . . . the Ford-engined Lotus cars that brought Jimmy Clark so near to winning Indianapolis in '63 and '64—these things are changing the balance. And in the Daytona 1250-mile Continental race in March of this year, a typical Ferrari driver's setup, Ford-engined cars took the first four places.

Not such a new thing, however; after all, Henry Ford himself set a world track record in the famous 999 in 1904: one mile in 39.1 seconds. Perhaps it's just a matter of the circle coming around again. We can hope so.

—1965

At
Ten-Tenths
of
Capacity...

Now and then an editorial writer in a far corner of the land calls baseball the "National Pastime," but the fact of the matter is that baseball is boring, as a major-league umpire not long ago said flatly in *True* magazine; and on the statistical evidence, much of the populace has abandoned its dubious attractions for a sport of more elementary excitement: racing. Horse racing attracts 40 million or so admissions a year because one can bet money on it. Foot racing, lumped with the other track and field sports, is a minority endeavor. But the biggest crowds ever assembled on the North American continent have come together to watch automobile racing, a sport on which hardly a dollar is bet from one year's end to another. If wagers on the horses were forbidden tomorrow, automobile racing would instantly become the world's first sport.

Why? No one is sure. In twenty years of watching motor racing and pondering its attractions, I have come to limited conclusions: everyone drives, has driven, or wants to drive an automobile, and therefore everyone can identify with the racedriver, who does this one thing so well. Furthermore, the risk of death is forever present in automobile racing. It is significant of the high rate of attrition of motor racing that the two oldest Grand Prix drivers who were active as this was written, the American, Masten Gregory, and the Frenchman, Maurice Trintignant, began their careers in 1956 and 1955.

It has long been held gospel that racegoers hope to see drivers killed. I do not believe this. I do believe that they want to see drivers go to the very edge of the precipice, to the rim of death, but they want them to come back. It is important that they come back, because the spectator so tightly identifies himself with the driver. He does not want to die; therefore he does not want the driver to die. But he does want the driver, as his alter ego, to demonstrate his bravery by hazarding death.

Finally, and probably most significantly, the racecourse shows us life and death in essence, in compression. Here a fortune is made or lost in three hours. A man makes an error in judgment and dies of it, not ten years later, but three seconds later; another, innocent as a lamb and watchful as a wolf, is struck dead in an instant, as though stabbed from behind in the night.

A fatal incident on a racecourse has an obviously depressing effect on most of the audience. A certain number of people will leave the course. A fractional minority will demonstrate a morbid and perverted interest. Most will say, sadly, "Terrible. Still, that's the way it is."

Drivers are quite unlike other men in such essentials of dangerous living as vision, motor reaction, ability to concentrate, and so on, and quite like other men in that some of them think about death a great deal and some, apparently, almost not at all.

The Marquis de Portago, killed in the Mille Miglia in 1957, a dedicated hedonist, often thought of the mortal hazards of Grand Prix driving, but not seriously in fear. A few weeks before he died, Portago said to me, "If I die tomorrow, still I have had twenty-eight wonderful years." In a note to a friend just before his last race he said that he thought he might die, that he did not like the car he was to drive. (To drive a car about which one has reservations is a serious mistake, but one that young drivers often feel forced to make. David McDonald, killed at Indianapolis in 1964, had told his father that he did not like the handling qualities of his car and suggested that it frightened him.)

Four of the greatest drivers, Tazio Nuvolari of Italy, Rudolf Caracciola of Germany, Juan Manuel Fangio of Argentina, and Stirling Moss of Great Britain, all lived to retire. Nuvolari had been terribly injured in many accidents, and several times was given up for dead; Caracciola had two severe crashes which undoubtedly hastened his death; Moss had only two bad accidents, but he was so battered in the last one, in May 1962, that he was paralyzed and in a coma for over a month; Fangio had only one bad accident and one serious injury in his career, a broken neck. All four might be excused a mild obsession with death, and it was clear that the thought of it was often in their minds.

The type of racing a man does seems to matter in this connection. The Europe-oriented Grand Prix driver is often a complex personality; he is likely to be sophisticated and introspective. He may drive in a dozen countries a year, including Australia and South Africa. He is probably as much at home in New York as in Rome. He is usually reserved and withdrawn: Jimmy Clark, a Scots landowner who is presently the champion of the world, pleasant, courteous, but unreachable in casual contact; Joachim Bonnier, a dark-bearded Swede who lives in Switzerland and runs an art gallery as a side endeavor; Olivier Gendebien, a wealthy Belgian aristocrat with a formidable record in the Underground during the Hitler war; Graham Hill, implausibly good-looking, almost a caricature of the Guards officer (which he is not), a lifelong devotee of the arduous sports, an oarsman, a former champion of the world; John Surtees, former motorcycle champion of the world; Phil Hill, the only American to be champion of the world, who keeps in his car a tape recorder stocked with classical music and is an authority on the player piano; Richie Ginther, chief driver for the Honda team of Japan, who likes best to get on a motorcycle and go rock-hunting in the California desert country; Maurice Trintignant, mayor of the town in France in which he grows wine.

The cars these men drive—they are built to an international standard called Formula 1—are improbably small, light, low. They weigh 1000 pounds or so, are driven by a small rear-mounted engine—only ninety inches cubic capacity (less than one-quarter as big as a Chevrolet)—and steered by a wheel only a foot in diameter. Most of them have no chassis as such but are built on a stressed-skin principle somewhat like an airplane. The fuel tanks are placed alongside the driver, under his seat, and over his knees; he is almost encased in gasoline, and he sits in a recumbent position, arms and legs straight out. Drivers lower themselves into the cars, wriggle down with their arms over their heads.

Two British designers, John Cooper and Colin Chapman, are responsible for the tiny rear-engined race car which has been a standard everywhere in the world except the United States since 1960. Their appearances at Indianapolis in the past few years—Jimmy Clark, in a Lotus-Ford, was second in 1963 and looked a certain winner in 1964 until tire failure put him out —have forced into obsolescence the standard American race car, particularly the Indianapolis roadster. This car has been something of a freak for years, since it could not run in regular competition anywhere else; indeed, was unsuitable for almost all other tracks.

Indianapolis cars are built with a left-side weight bias, which is of considerable use on that track but would make the car dangerous in a right-hand turn. Since 1934, with few exceptions, the heavy majority of cars running every year at Indianapolis have been basically identical. Three chassis, Kurtis, Watson, and Kuzuma, have dominated the track, and one engine, the famous Offenhauser-Meyer-Drake four-cylinder. Offenhauser-engined cars won all but three races from 1934 to 1964. The appearance of Jack Brabham in a Cooper in 1961 and the full-out entrance of the Ford Motor Company into racing radically changed the scene last year, with nine Ford engines in the race, all mounted in the rear. (Rear-mounted engines reduce the car's frontal area, which gives better penetration of the semisolid mass that is air at 125 mph and upward.) Estimates on the cost of the engines ran as high as $50,000 per unit, and Ford made them available without cost, stipulating only that Ford mechanics service them. Remarkably, not one case of engine failure was recorded among the Fords.

One of the antediluvian roadsters won the 1964 Indianapolis. The winning driver was A. J. Foyt of Texas, who had won in 1961. Foyt is a big, good-looking man, thirty years old. He is probably the best driver in the United States, and unlike most Indianapolis or "big-car" drivers, he wins in the smaller "sprint" cars as well, and in stock-car and sports-car races. He is in the business to make money, and he makes a good deal of it: the first-place man at Indianapolis these days expects to go home with $175,000 in cash, goods, and contracts. On the European Grand Prix circuits, first place may be worth $2000, with another $1000 in appearance money. Dead-last place is worth more than that at Indianapolis—$5750 this year. Foyt averaged 147 miles per hour, which meant that he was going through the turns (engineered in 1909 for 90 miles per hour) at 140, and reaching 190 or so on the straightaways.

Foyt and Parnelli Jones, who won in 1962, are perhaps typical of the American track driver: outdoor-bred, athletic, honorable, straightforward men, quick to anger, quick to fight, who tend to view racedriving as a more desperate endeavor than it may seem to the Europeans, since they see it primarily in economic terms. They are not much concerned with the esthetics of the sport, or its history. They have an eye on retirement, and they try to invest their money wisely. They are not colorful men, and they distrust those who are.

A decade ago, it was the fashion among U.S. track drivers to disparage the Europeans, call them "sporty-car" drivers, suggest they would not long survive in the fierce hub-to-hub competition of the dirt tracks which are the American school courses. Similar courtesies were extended by the Europeans. To a Grand Prix driver who had won on the Nürburgring in Germany, 14.1 miles to the lap, 175 corners, uphill and down 3000 feet, an Indianapolis driver was a trucker who knew no more than to stand on the accelerator and turn left. Listening to spokesmen for each camp, one marveled that such communication failure could occur.

The jet airplane changed all that, as it has so many other things. The jets made it possible, although still very difficult, for at least the wealthier of the European teams to compete at Indianapolis and still meet their contractual obligations on the Grand Prix circuit, which schedules a major race almost every Sunday in the season. European drivers discovered that Indianapolis, though it looked so simple, was nothing of the sort at the speeds required today, and the Americans were surprised to find that the Europeans were superlatively good drivers. Many Indianapolis veterans were amazed to see Jimmy Clark post the fastest qualifying time of the thirty-three starters last year, and take the lead immediately after the race began. They needn't have been. After all, he was the champion of the world. A local interviewer asked Clark if he was thrilled to be running in "the greatest race in the world" and was appalled when Clark replied, no, actually he had found the Grand Prix of South Africa more exciting.

Single-seat race cars are at the pinnacle of American automobile racing, but stock-car and sports-car and hot-rod racing make the base on which the structure rests. There is hardly a community of any size that does not support stock-car racing, and thousands of events are run off every year. It is easier by far for the spectator to identify with stock cars. They are standard sedans, at least in outward appearance. Since they will do 160 to 170 miles per hour, they are not quite the same inside as the Ford or Plymouth just off the showroom floor, but at 100 feet the differences are not obvious. A stock car is a sedan that has been stripped and rebuilt to precise tolerances by racing mechanics. The process is called "blueprinting," and it means that the vehicle has been brought up precisely and in every particular to the manufacturer's set standards. The chassis and running gear are strengthened by welding and bracing; the interior is gutted of everything flammable; the doors are permanently shut; the driver is surrounded by a cage of steel tubing to protect him in roll-over situations. Fatalities are rare in stock-car racing, and a good driver running good equipment can do well. He can make $40,000 a year and upward.

The hot-rod drivers not long ago were dedicated amateurs, most of them young, most of them on the West Coast, who built their own cars and ran them for pure sport. Hot rodding today is very highly organized, and there are drivers who make from $20,000 to $50,000 a year in the simplest, most stylized form of the sport: the endeavor to run an automobile from a standing start to maximum speed in one-quarter of a mile. The terminal velocities reached by cars in the fastest categories are hard to believe. As this was written, the record was 199.7 mph, and unofficially one driver had done 202! These speeds are reached in the seven- to eight-second range. For comparison, a standard passenger car that will reach 80 to 85 miles per hour in a standing-start quarter-mile, and do it within sixteen to seventeen seconds, is a fast car.

There is nothing in the world of sport more spectacular than the run of a big dragster, a "rail-job." It looks like no other automobile in the world. The design evolved from a "slingshot" built by the eminent Mickey Thompson in the middle 1950s, and so called because the driver sat in a little pod out behind the rear wheels, like a stone in the leather pouch of a slingshot. The driver still sits there in today's rail-jobs, behind or just beside two enormous tires, their flat treads a foot wide; in front of him is the engine, a big V-8, a General Motors diesel locomotive supercharger mounted on top of that. Somewhere up in front there is a shiny spun-metal fuel tank holding a couple of gallons of exotic fuel: nitromethane, methanol, benzene. The front of the car is supported on a couple of spidery-light motorcycle wheels. There is no radiator, no fan, no cooling arrangement except the water in the engine block.

Dragsters run in pairs. They are push-started by trucks, rumble down to the starting line the wrong way of the course, turn widely, so that the one on the left-hand side of the track now takes the right, inch up to the line, watching the starter, break a timing-light ray, and go. Clouds of rubber smoke wreathe the drivers as the big tires spin on the asphalt. Often the front of the car will rise three or four feet into the air under the brutal torque going through the rear wheels, and when this happens, of course the steering wheel ceases to furnish a useful function. The driver keeps his foot down and waits for gravity to put the front wheels where they belong. Presumably his expression is calm and inscrutable, but one cannot tell: he is lost in blue-white rubber smoke, and he is wearing an asbestos-and-aluminum-foil suit, gloves, and face mask, armor against flame.

The noise as he leaves the line is appalling. Spectators unashamedly clap palms over ears, but even so, the shock waves produced by the four big exhaust pipes on each side of the car batter at one's viscera: the engine may be pumping out 1000 horsepower. The two cars simply disappear; a quarter-mile down the track, and that is a very short distance indeed, a light pops on, left or right, showing which car has made it first to the finish, and simultaneously two big parachutes blossom from the rear of the cars— brakes alone wouldn't stop them. After a bit the cars come back along the side return road, dead silent, hustled along by push trucks. You can see the drivers now. They are usually young men, always slender (twenty-five pounds of extra weight in the driver's seat notably increases the car's tendency to lift, to do a wheel stand, a "wheelie," and this is undesirable), and one of them is smiling. He is the winner. He is happier than he was three or four minutes ago, and richer.

Sports-car drivers, on the other hand, must be content with more glory than cash, although limited professionalism is allowed. Sports-car racing began the postwar revival of automobile racing in this country with a race at Watkins Glen, New York, in 1948. Sports cars, like stocks, must have been built with the accommodation of at least one passenger in mind; a sports car is by definition a two-seater. It is never run on a track; its natural habitat is the road circuit, and sports-car people are proud of this adherence to the grand tradition: after all, automobile racing began on the road, and purists depose that it should never be done elsewhere.

In Europe, since the demise of the Mille Miglia and Ulster's Tourist Trophy, there is only the Targa Florio of Sicily and the Le Mans 24-Hour Race in France. Le Mans is the premier sports-car race of the world, bringing perhaps 250,000 spectators together every year. Like the Sebring 12-Hour Race in Florida, it offers the extraordinary excitement of motor racing under headlights—and the bigger Le Mans cars can touch 200 miles per hour.

In the United States the privately owned, specially constructed artificial road circuit is the rule, and some forty have been built since 1950. Bridgehampton on Long Island, Daytona in Florida, Lime Rock in Connecticut, Road America in Wisconsin, Riverside in California are busy and well used. There is a new circuit at Watkins Glen—the cars no longer roar through the streets a few feet from the watchers on the curbs as they did in the innocent old days—and it is over this circuit that the Formula 1 cars run in their single appearance on this side of the Atlantic, the Grand Prix of the United States, usually in October.

The new Watkins course was built after a car flicked into a crowd, killed one person, and injured a dozen others. There was some talk, then, of legislating the race out of existence. It came to nothing. When a Mercedes-Benz flew into a spectator enclosure at Le Mans in 1955 and killed at least eighty-five spectators, more pressure was mounted but the race went on. Efforts to outlaw the sport have been unremitting since about 1900, but I believe we will have motor racing as long as we have automobiles. The enjoyment of speed, the enjoyment of risk, is deep within us. The great drivers do not run for money, and they are not mad. Of those I know, Stirling Moss has made it plainest to me:

"To drive a really fine, balanced race car at ten-tenths of its absolute capacity, right on the edge, at the point at which one more mile an hour will send it rocketing off the road into the woods—this is the most splendid and most rewarding sensuous pleasure, save one, known to man. Once you have known this pleasure, believe me, it is hard to give it up. Remember, it is an intellectual exercise as well. If you cannot concentrate absolutely on this effort for three hours, and I mean *absolutely,* without a single extraneous thought, you will not long be with us."

As long as this excitement is to be found, men will drive, and other men, jealous of them but settling for second best, will watch.

—1965

The
Mercer

There are fewer than thirty Mercer Raceabouts in the world. The last "new" one to be discovered turned up in 1948. It had cost—fresh out of the factory in Trenton, Mercer County, New Jersey—$2500. It could be sold today, over the telephone, for $20,000, indeed perhaps for $30,000. Why? What is so intriguing about this spidery-looking, uncomfortable, primitive automobile? Why would many collectors be happy to trade, say, three Rolls-Royces for a good Mercer?

I remember my own, the last one ever found, the 1948 car. I had written an article about the Mercer in that year, and a man who had read it wrote to me:

". . . You speak of the Mercer Raceabout of before World War I. I thought it might be of interest to you to know that there is at least one still undiscovered, so to speak. I have it stored away near here. I bought this car in 1932. It is a 1912 model. The party who sold me that car told me that the mileage showing was all the actual mileage it had done: 14,413. Really it is a wonderful car to drive. It has a terrific burst of power and handles far nicer than any 1948 car, you can really see what you're doing and where you're going. The man I bought it from has a certificate that the car made 90 mph on a dirt track in California in 1913, I think it was Santa Monica. I had it to about 70 on a gravel highway, but that was all I felt like taking, the road being what it was . . ."

The letter was postmarked in the village of Delburne, in Alberta, Canada, and the car had stood in the open, in an apple orchard, through seven Canadian winters.

I wrote a reply to the owner, Mr. Don Brown, and after a few weeks, we agreed on a price. Mr. Brown took the car to the railhead and shipped it to me. Then he wrote me a letter:

". . . I got up at 5 A.M. and took the truck and my hired man and we went out and towed her in. We had it in the freight car by 7:45. Well, we had breakfast and then we went back and fastened it. You needn't worry about that. It isn't going to move an inch, and it wouldn't if it went to California and back. I wrapped both axles in burlap and chained them to bolts run through the freight-car floor and double-locked underneath. Then we built a cribbing of 4 × 4 timber around the Mercer. The car was sealed and no other goods will be put into it along the way . . ."

Three weeks later the freight car came into the yards at Norwalk, Connecticut, near where I lived, and after I had paid $540 in charges, it was mine.

I had not gone alone to pick it up, and that was a good thing. I had taken with me a friend, Mr. Conrad Lofink, one of the best old-car mechanics and restorers of our time. To me, the Mercer looked a total wreck. I wouldn't have given $50 for it. But Conrad Lofink looked at it happily and said, "I think this is the best Mercer I have ever seen. Take a pull on the handle, and see if I'm right."

I did, and wonder of wonders, the engine turned over easily and smoothly.

"It's beat up on the outside, though not half as bad as some I've seen, but as far as I can tell now it's never been left ungreased, and that's a plain miracle," Lofink said. "Let's get it on the truck and take it home."

We tore off a homemade leather windbreaker incorporating a Model T windshield. We threw away the head lamps, also Ford. The upholstery was hopeless, rotted and shredded. We ripped it off and left it lying in the freight yard. (None of this surprised me, I must say. Mr. Brown had sent me photographs of the car, and he had described it, and he had been absolutely honest and accurate. Still, to see the car itself was a jolt.

In Lofink's tiny workshop, we took the Mercer down: there was not a speck of rust on any working surface, from one end to the other! The pistons had been drilled out for lightness, the connecting rods had been machined down, and more than *twenty pounds* of steel had been skimmed off the giant flywheel! Why? It took a long time to find out: this Mercer had been raced by the great Berner Eli (Barney) Oldfield, and had been modified to his order. It was a unique and wonderful find, far faster than the standard Mercer Raceabout guaranteed to do 75 miles an hour as it came from the factory door.

Over the next six months, Connie Lofink stripped the car to the last nut and bolt. He tore it down to the point where two sawhorses were set up to receive the side frame-members, and he built it up from there. New hickory-spoked wheels came from a wheelwright in Pennsylvania; the curved after-body, with its tiny tool-holding cubbyhole, was rebuilt in steam-bent ash; a dashboard and sills (they cover the side chassis-members) were made of the best mahogany. Seats were made and upholstered in red Morocco leather. New 34" × 4" tires, a size not commercially available for twenty years, were bought from Firestone at $182.50 a set. We found the rare "Monocle" windshield, a circle of glass clamped to the steering post.

And then one day, when I got off the commuters' train from New York in the cold dusk, there in the station yard in Wilton was the Mercer—beautiful in brass, mahogany, red leather, and gold-striped maroon enamel—and Connie Lofink standing beside it. I had insisted I wanted a starter, which the Mercer never had, and Connie, with equal force, had said he would not put one on the car, because it was not original and thus would be fraudulent. It was an autumn day, a light wet mist in the air, when I went to the car and thanked Connie for the surprise. He pointed to the huge crank nestling in the leather-strapped pocket that kept it from swinging when the car was in motion.

"Start it," he said. "Put the crank in at seven o'clock and give it one hard pull-up."

I drove the Mercer home, and to this day I think of that ride as one of *the* excitements of my life.

I drove the car a good deal after that, on the road, every day, here and there. True, there were difficulties. On a parkway, it so excited ordinary motorists that they would come alongside, look, and almost forget to steer. It was noisy, if one used the cutout, a thing we no longer hear much about: a device that opened the exhaust to the air this side of the muffler, so that the car sounded like a battery of cannon firing at a regular rate.

It was a cold ride. The Mercer had no bodywork, and, worst of all, the accelerator pedal was outside the body; one rested one's instep on a brass stirrup, and the wind ran straight up one's trouser leg!

It was tricky, too, driving the car, because the brakes were almost nonexistent, and one had to look a long way ahead, to be safe. The foot brake was a joke: it squeezed a pliers-like arrangement around the drive shaft, and would not perceptibly slow the car at all; the hand brake, a great three-foot-long lever, operated on the rear wheels only, and would hardly slow them unless it were put on hard enough to make them skid.

Still, with all the difficulties, driving the Mercer was a delight that I have not had since, in driving perhaps a hundred other kinds of cars. It was easy, sitting there in the wind, to think of the great racedrivers who made their names on Mercers, and imagine oneself among them: Pullen, De Palma, Wishart, Knipper, Bigelow.

In May 1912, Ralph de Palma drove a Mercer Raceabout 150.5 miles in 130 minutes 43 seconds—an average of 69.54 miles per hour, on an ordinary road circuit, not a speedway! Men took Mercer Raceabouts straight from the showroom to the racetrack and won with them. In August of 1912, for example, a standard Type 35C Raceabout was taken from a Columbus, Ohio, showroom to a dirt track where it set up new records for distances from 75 to 200 miles. Such a feat is wholly beyond imagination today. No one can today go into a showroom in Indianapolis, let us say, buy a car, and take it to the Indianapolis 500 with the remotest chance of qualifying, never mind winning, the race. Truly, the Mercer was a great automobile.

Perhaps this was because it was the creation of men who were extraordinary themselves, indeed possibly great men. The Mercer firm was founded by a son-in-law of F. W. Roebling, of the Roebling family whose name is inextricably associated with the building of the Brooklyn Bridge (that monument to early engineering that still stands in New York, carrying more traffic than its designers ever dreamed of, safe and solid nonetheless). The engineer who designed the Mercer, Finley Robertson Porter, was one of the great originators of the industry. Happily, he lived to be a very old man; he lived to see his car the most esteemed of all; he lived to know that his name would be ranked with Ford, with Bugatti, with Royce, with Ferrari.

It is amusing to think that the Mercer engine produced only 20-odd horsepower, not as much as some outboard boat engines put out today. When we think of the racing-car engines of the golden period, the 1930s and 1940s—of the Mercedes-Benz cars, for example, that delivered 646 horsepower. . . ! The Mercer won races not on brute power, but on the purposefulness, the brilliance of its design. Like the Bugatti, the Mercer was a wonder and a marvel on the road. Even today, this minute, a 1912 Mercer, on a winding, twisty road, in the hands of a really good driver, can give a 1966 car a lot of trouble. It may not be comfortable, it may freeze you to death, blow your breath back down your throat, use up all of your strength in pushing down the heavy clutch, shifting gears, hauling back on the huge brake-lever, but—if you can stay with it—it will really go.

Most Mercer enthusiasts think of the years of the T-head, 1911–1915, as the golden years of the make. (T-head, because the engine combustion-area was shaped like a "T": the piston came up in the center, and on each side was a spark plug, the whole making a T-shape.) But there were other Mercers. In 1915 Finley Porter left the firm, and a new designer, Erik Delling, came aboard. The post-1915 Mercers were splendid motorcars, but they were not the rough and hairy manhandlers the early ones had been. Now Mercer made cars that would carry more than two people, and carry them in something approaching comfort, if not so fast. Mercer made touring cars, with full-width windshields and tops and side curtains. They were slower, and if they were not so exciting, they were much more comfortable. These were made into the mid-1920s, when the company had to give up, faced with the mass-production force of Detroit.

The Mercer Company never had more than 450 employees; no more than 500 cars were made in any one year; only 5000 were delivered in the whole history of the company and of these, of all models, only 105 are known to exist today.

—1966

The
Duesenberg

There is a short and superselect list of automobiles that will be remembered as long as our civilization lasts—names like Rolls-Royce, Ford, Mercer, Bugatti, Cadillac, Cord, Duesenberg, Jaguar, Alfa-Romeo, Mercedes-Benz. But one make, the Duesenberg, stands almost alone for many reasons and for one in particular: only 470 Duesenbergs of the great J and SJ models were made, yet today, thirty years after the last one left the factory, 240 of them still exist. Indeed, twenty-four Duesenbergs are right now owned by their original buyers. And a Duesenberg that cost $17,500 in 1932 is *still* worth $17,500, if not more.

Like the Silver Ghost Rolls-Royce and the Type 35 Bugatti, the Model J Duesenberg was so far ahead of the other motorcars of its time that none of them could reasonably be compared with it.

Legends and wild stories have been built up around every great automobile, and the Duesenberg is not an exception. For example, most people believe that it was a German car, as they believe that Henry Ford wouldn't make a Model T in any color but black, or that the Rolls-Royce factory used to lock the hood so that only a Rolls-Royce mechanic could work on the engine, or that the Tucker could not be made to back up. The Duesenberg was an American automobile and everything in it was American. Oddly, though, it wasn't made in Detroit, but, at various times in its history, and in various models, in Iowa, New Jersey, and Indiana. True enough, Fred Duesenberg, who with his brother August, was the creator, designer, and builder of the car, was born in Germany, but he came to the United States when he was eight years old. That was in 1885.

The Duesenberg family settled in Rockford, Iowa, and Fred Duesenberg, who was to see the day when a Detroit firm would offer him $50,000 a year as a designer, left school when he was seventeen. As engineer, designer, manufacturer, he was entirely self-taught. If a genius is one who knows something without quite knowing why or how he knows it (as Mozart could compose immortal music before he had ever heard of the laws of composition), then Fred Duesenberg was at least a near genius. Like Ettore Bugatti, he could merely glance at a part and say, "It won't work." Or he could listen to an engine running on a test stand and say to expert engineers, "Tear it down; it isn't right." (Henry Ford had this eerie ability, to a degree; so did Henry Royce, who could pick up a piece of round brass rod and file it by hand into a perfect square, measuring it by eye alone.

Farm machinery—reapers, binders, steam-tractors—these were the first bits of machinery Duesenberg worked upon. But because he was so strongly creative he went off on his own as soon as he could and began to make bicycles. He made good ones, particularly superior racing bicycles, and he rode them himself. In 1898 he set a world record for cycling two miles. From bicycles, logically, he went on to making motorbikes (he set a world three-mile record on one of them), and when, in 1900, the first garage in Des Moines was opened, he was on the payroll. Later he and August worked for the Rambler automobile company in Wisconsin, and in 1903 they opened a garage of their own in Iowa. In 1904, with the financial backing of a Des Moines lawyer named Mason, they built their first racing car. It was highly successful—and the Duesenberg brothers were still in their middle twenties.

Ability of the kind the Duesenbergs had cannot go long unrecognized, and in 1910 the Maytag washing-machine company bought them out. Fred and August continued to build cars under the Mason name, and in 1913 they set up their own company under their own name: The Duesenberg Motor Company in St. Paul, Minnesota. They began to make high-performance engines for racing cars and motorboats. (A Duesenberg-powered boat was first in the world to do 60 mph.) Racedrivers soon knew that the best engines were to be had in St. Paul, and the top drivers of the day began to run them, people like Barney Oldfield, Ralph Mulford, Eddie Rickenbacker. During World War I the Duesenbergs made military engines of all kinds, reaching a pinnacle with a 900-horsepower V-16 model that was the biggest the world had seen. But they thought of this work only as something that had to be done, a patriotic necessity; their hearts and hopes were set on a single goal: an automobile, and not just another automobile to compete with the commonplace vehicles then chugging around the country. The Duesenbergs intended to make the best automobile in the world.

One barrier stood in the way: money. It seems almost a law of nature that the genuinely creative person cares little for money and almost never keeps what comes his way. He wants money only to carry on his work, and beyond that usually he doesn't concern himself. Fred Duesenberg is said to have *given* an engine design to his friend Harry Stutz, and he didn't even bother to take out a patent on his invention of the hydraulic four-wheel brake system, which would certainly have made him a millionaire, probably many times a millionaire. At any rate, to raise money for their dream car, the Duesenbergs sold the factory in which they had built their engines during the war, they sold designs, they took a dollar where they could find it, and they moved to Indianapolis, where they began to build racing engines. They made only four of them that year, 1920, but three of them were in cars that ran in the Indianapolis 500-Mile Race that year, and they placed third, fourth, and sixth. Later that year they took the Land Speed Record: Tommy Milton did 156 mph on Daytona Beach in a car that had *two* 8-cylinder Duesenberg engines mounted side by side. The reputation of the firm was made, and the great legend had begun.

The first proper Duesenberg passenger car was called the Model A and it was made until 1926. It was a sound, solid automobile, but the body-styling trends of the time were against it, and the 500-odd that were sold never had the glamour of the mighty Model Js and SJs that were to follow. In a way, the Model A was a preparation, an exercise for what was to come. It was an expensive car—$6500, a tremendous price for the time, when $5000 less would buy, say, a Buick—and its owners found nothing to complain about.

They ware driving a car that had a famous racing name, and that, then as now, meant a great deal. They were running the same engines that were insisted upon by racing men like Peter de Paolo, Harry Hartz, Davis Lewis, Eddie O'Donnell, Jimmy Murphy. Tommy Milton had won the great 300-Mile Elgin Race in a Duesenberg; in 1921 Jimmy Murphy had taken the French Grand Prix in a Duesenberg, to this day the only time a European Grand Prix has been won by an American driver in an American automobile: there were eight Duesenbergs in the entry list for the Indianapolis 500 in 1922, and seven of them finished in the first ten. One Model A touring car ran 3155 miles on the Indianapolis track in April 1923, at an average speed of 62 mph, with the motor never stopping. (Gasoline and relief drivers were put aboard from another car running alongside at anything from 50 to 90 mph.)

The Duesenberg racing record is unique: Duesenbergs ran at Indianapolis twenty times; they ran in twenty-seven major races and placed in twenty-four of them; they held sixty-six records ranging from the standing kilometer to the greatest distance covered in twenty-four hours, taken on the Utah salt flats by Ab Jenkins for 3253 miles at an average of 135.47 mph, which meant that he was doing 160 much of the time.

It's an axiom among automobile manufacturers that racing is a splendid way to get publicity—splendid, and hideously expensive. (When Ford cars won the Le Mans 24-Hour Race in 1966, coming in first, second, and third, estimates of the cost, from the beginning of Ford's racing program five years previous, ran as high as $10 million.) To profit properly from racing, a manufacturer must sell a great many passenger cars, and certainly the Duesenbergs never made more than 650 Model As and probably not that many. The equation simply wasn't working out, and by 1926 the company was in trouble. It was never an organization of great size, and at its peak the Duesenberg company did not employ more than fifty people.

Salvation lay in disaster, in a way; the Duesenbergs were taken over by one of the genuine *virtuosi* of American business, Erret Lobban Cord. Cord might not have been able to tell a magneto from a manifold gasket, but he understood finance, he understood promotion, and he wholly sympathized with Fred Duesenberg's bitter-end determination to make the best car ever to stand on four wheels. He said the magic words: "Never mind what it costs—build it." The result *was* the best car of its day, lovingly put together by a few devoted craftsmen on the payroll of a company that never made a cent of profit during its whole corporate career. And what of it? The time of greatness had begun.

(Between the Model A and the J and SJ, there did appear a Model X, but only twelve were made, and none is known to exist today.)

One still hears occasionally, in 1967, and probably still will hear, in 1987, the expression, "It's a doozy!" meaning it's something superlatively good, top-drawer, the best. No one knows who said it first, but he said it in 1929, when the Model J Duesenberg appeared in 1929, and of course it was spelled, "It's a Duesie!" The car stunned those who first saw it—and it still does. In 1929 American motorcars ranged from very good-looking (Packard, Lincoln, Cadillac, for instance) to hideous, with the worst-looking high in the majority. But of all the Duesenbergs I have seen, in the metal and in photographs, I can think of only three that were ugly, and all of them had been extensively modified by misguided owners. Most Duesenbergs, thirty or thirty-five years old though they may be, are still lovely to see.

The great coachmakers of the world were commissioned to build bodies on the Duesenberg chassis. Many cut their metal to lines laid out by Gordon Buehrig, later to be assured of immortality in the métier as the stylist of the 810 Cord. One major authority on the make, Raymond A. Wolff, has listed nineteen firms of bespoke or custom coach builders whose bodies adorned Duesenberg chassis—names like Judkins and Willoughby, Murphy, Weymann, Derham, Rollston, D'Iteren, Van den Plas, Graber, Saoutchik, Letourneur and Marchand, Gurney Nutting. On this list only Derham of Pennsylvania and Graber of Switzerland still exist, for custom coachwork died with the first shots of World War II.

Of the few companies that will now design and build a car body to meet the purchaser's precise specification, most are in Italy, and they must charge prices in the range of $50,000. Their customers, therefore, are big corporations that want a single spectacular show car for exhibition, or they are companies, like Ferrari of Italy, that can order a run of 100 to 500 bodies.

In the 1920s, custom work was commonplace. Indeed, most Rolls-Royce chassis were delivered *as* chassis—that is to say, as bare running-gear, frame and engine. They went directly from factory to coach builder, who would have, for his customer, prepared detailed drawings, in color, showing what he proposed to do with the car. Line and upholstery aside, the drawings might well indicate that the driver's seat, for example, would be made to accommodate the owner's measurements—or his chauffeur's!

Looking for the first time at a Duesenberg chassis—the frame built like a bridge of the best molybdenum steel, braced with seven cross-members, parts of the engine polished until it shone like silver, parts enameled in Duesenberg's own bright apple-green enamel, the very dashboard engine-turned, like the inside of a Tiffany cigarette case—a coach builder who did not try to reach new heights would have been a sloth indeed. The big 8-cylinder in-line engine produced 265 horsepower, at a time when 110 was considered powerful, and the car would exceed 100 mph with ease. The Model SJ, which appeared in 1932, had a supercharger, a high-speed pump to force extra gasoline-and-air mixture into the cylinders for greater power, and it would do 130 mph, reaching 100 mph seventeen seconds after a standing start. Few cars will do that today; in 1932 it was almost unbelievable. This chassis, bare, cost $8500.

Who bought these Duesenbergs, and what orders did they give their coach builders? The people who bought them were people who could afford anything they liked. A famous series of Duesenberg advertisements—they are among the best-known of all automobile advertisements—give us an idea. They were simple advertisements, line drawings carrying only four words of text: "He (or she) Drives A Duesenberg." One showed a man at the wheel of a huge racing yacht, the kind that used to compete for the

America's Cup, the kind that carried a crew of, say, fifty men. Another showed a man sitting in a baronial hall, listening to a cathedral-sized organ being played; another showed a beautiful woman, talking to her gardener, looking over a lawn the size of a football field.

Millionaires, then, bought Duesenbergs, millionaires and the famous, the talented, the socialites of the day. One saw Duesenbergs most often on Park Avenue in New York, Michigan in Chicago, Wilshire Boulevard in Los Angeles. To own a Duesenberg was almost required of a film star who wanted to prove that he had reached the top. Duesenbergs were made in two standard chassis-lengths: 142½ and 153½ inches, but two very special short-chassis models at 125 inches were made, one for Clark Gable, one for Gary Cooper.

The interior of the car could be whatever struck the buyer's fancy. The woodwork could be in ebony, trimmed in silver; or teak, or rosewood, or walnut. The upholstery could be in any fabric the best British looms provided, or in leather: morocco, pigskin, ostrich, anything. It was usual, in sedans and limousines, to specify a cocktail cabinet, fitted with decanters and glasses; a radio; a vanity case, with mirrors and perhaps perfume atomizers. Many owners asked to have rear-mounted speedometers, so that they could tell their chauffeurs precisely how much faster, or slower, they wished to be driven. Some had compasses, perhaps so that they could tell, even with all the silk curtains drawn, that the car was still going straight home, northeast by east!

The driver himself was very well informed. No instrument panel more completely equipped has ever been built into an automobile. There was of course a speedometer, reading to 150 mph, and a tachometer, to tell how fast the engine was turning, and all the usual gauges for gasoline, oil pressure, battery-charge condition, and so on. A clock, yes, but no ordinary clock; this was a split-second stopwatch. An altimeter served also as a barometer, in case a storm was approaching, and a brake-line pressure gauge would warn of low hydraulic-fluid pressure. Colored lights came on at intervals to remind the driver to check the battery-acid level, to change the engine oil, and so on. The Duesenberg was not attended to with a grease gun, as were lesser cars; metered amounts of oil were automatically pumped to the necessary places on the chassis.

Was the Duesenberg the perfect motorcar? Certainly not. Nothing mechanical is perfect. But it was what Fred and August Duesenberg meant it to be: the most luxurious fast car, or the fastest luxury car, ever built in series production. It was a delight. It still is a delight. A Rolls-Royce is quieter. A Bugatti, even a big one, like a Type 50, gives a livelier, lighter sense of going. A V-16 Cadillac is smoother. But a Duesenberg is faster than a Rolls-Royce, more luxurious than a Bugatti, more impressive than a

16-cylinder Cadillac. And perhaps these things are not important. Comparisons are odious, after all, and the vital fact about a Duesenberg, finally, is that it has an absolute and unique aura of its own, it is stamped with the personalities and the iron wills of the three men who made it: the brothers Duesenberg and E. L. Cord. It is, without doubt, a doozy!

—1967

The
Grand
Prix

The Grand Prix car is the epitome of the automobile. A dragster will outaccelerate it. A land-speed-record car will run faster by hundreds of miles an hour. A sports car is more civilized. Any kind of sedan is moe comfortable. But the Grand Prix car is the ultimate expression of the purpose of the automobile: to run fast and controllably over ordinary road. It is all automobile, all function, weighing, usually, less than 1500 pounds, pushed up to 180 mph-plus by a rear-mounted engine of 400-odd horsepower, small, thin-skinned, fragile. The driver, half reclining, his shoulders tight against a wraparound plastic windshield, holds at arm's length an absurdly small, padded steering wheel. A gearshift lever two or three inches high lies close to one hand or the other, and the gasoline tanks are around, under, and sometimes over him. Fat foot-wide tires on small wheels take the power to the road. The car is built to a precise standard, or formula, internationally agreed upon, and usually laid down, whatever else may be claimed for it, to restrict the car's top speed by limiting something —engine size, fuel capacity, minimum weight. Despite this, race-car speeds rise year by year in percentages that can be predicted. The Grand Prix car is built to Formula I, which is changed every four or five years. Formula II and Formula III cars are smaller and slower, compete in their own classes. A Formula I car can cost $50,000, the engine alone, $15,000 to $25,000—and ideally each car should have two spares.

This, then, is the instrument with which men play the most dangerous, demanding, scientific, and expensive of all sports. Next to real tennis (court tennis), it is the most exclusive of sports as well. Eight firms make Grand Prix cars, there are eleven races for them, and about twenty men qualified to drive them. (Only the spectator count goes to the other end of the spectrum. Motor racing is the number-two spectator sport, topped only by the aggregate of the three kinds of football: soccer, rugby, and American.) The drivers thus make up a superelite among the world's athlete-performers. Probably because they know that their work is more dangerous than anything comparable, much riskier than, say, bullfighting, they have little in common with men who play lesser games. They have a marked tendency to keep their own company. Like the very rich, they are really comfortable only with one another, yet they avoid forming close friendships among themselves, as gladiators did, and for the same reason. They are men of marked personality and peculiar physical equipment. As nearly as we can tell, looking back, they always have been. They have been flamboyant, like the giant Vincenzo Lancia, one of the first great drivers, who upended a pint of champagne and tossed the bottle to the crowd as he started an early Vanderbilt Cup race. They have been bitterly competitive, like George Robertson, who told his riding mechanic to throw a wrench at the car ahead to make it move over, or pugnacious, like Wilbur Shaw, who was sitting exhausted after winning a 500-mile race, burned, bandaged, just out of the field hospital, and twelve pounds lighter than he'd been before the race, when he heard another driver say, "Shaw's a lucky so-and-so." Shaw hurtled over a barbed-wire-topped fence and punched the man in the face. They have been cold, colorless, and calculating to the point of fascination, like Ray Harroun, who decided that an average speed of 75 miles an hour would win the first Indianapolis race in 1911, ran the 500 miles at 74.6, and did win.

There are more Harrouns than Shaws driving today. It was plain in the late 1950s that a new breed of driver was in the making, and I think the terminal date in the sea change may have been August 4, 1964, when Carel de Beaufort was killed practicing for the Grand Prix of Germany. The Count de Beaufort of Holland was the last of the titled gentlemen amateurs. In the beginning, drivers titled or wealthy or both figured importantly in Grand Prix racing; they were still important in the 1920s and 1930s, but after World War II there were only the Marquis de Portago, killed in 1957, the German Count Von Trips, killed in 1961, and the Count de Beaufort. De Beaufort—Carel Pieter Anthonie Jan Hubertus Godin de Beaufort— owned his car, a Porsche, and ran it as often as he could. He was a big man, over six feet and 200 pounds, a tight fit for a Formula I machine. Like Portago, he was pleasant, amusing, cultured, multilingual, much traveled, at home everywhere. Both died pitifully young, at twenty-eight. Portago's closest friend, Harry Schell, an American who had lived all his life in France, was of the Beaufort-Portago pattern. Schell was adventurous, extroverted, uninhibited, curious about everything, a practical joker on an outrageous scale. He laughed a lot, drove as carefully as was consistent with staying in the game. He had a flat in Paris, a house in Deauville, a cabin cruiser and other useful amenities, and he intended living forever, as Portago had intended. No one expected Harry Schell to be killed in a race— he had been hurt badly only once—and he wasn't: he was killed in practice for the 1960 Tourist Trophy race in England. He went flat into a brick wall at something around 100 miles an hour, no one knows why. Steering failure or hydroplaning—the circuit was wet—are the best guesses.

Swingers like Schell, who was a tail gunner for the Finns in the Russo-Finnish War, or Portago, who once flattened a man for smoking a cigar on a New York nightclub dance floor, have no counterparts running today. A Formula I car can represent $100,000 and its owner wants at the wheel a man who has sieved out of himself all impetuosity and derring-do. He wants him to go fast, very fast, for speed is the only name of the game, but he wants him ice-cold, unflappable, computerized, his helmet cosseting a brain full of diodes and printed gold circuits, programed to stay out of trouble, all and any kind, inside the car or out of it. Jack Brabham's number-two driver is Denny Hulme, and when they are running in the same race, Hulme's orders are to finish behind the champion. It's not on record that he ever tried it the other way. That's not done today. In the 1930s, driving for Mercedes-Benz, Manfred von Brauchitsch, an explosive red-headed Prussian aristocrat, blew loose and started to contest first place with the number-one driver. He ignored slow-down signal boards. The Mercedes team manager, the iron-willed Alfred Neubauer, was reduced to running out on the circuit to shake his fist at Brauchitsch as he charged past. Some say he had a gun in the fist. No such colorful tableau will be seen in the 1967 season.

Stirling Moss was the first of the truly modern drivers, and Jimmy Clark is the ideal today; indeed, Clark couldn't be tighter fitted to the purpose if he were the product of a twenty-generation breeding program. Clark is physically right; he's small, light, and strong. He's cold, a planner to his toes, panic-proof, and patient. He indulges in no public display of feelings. He's competitive on the circuit and quiet away from it. His home is a sheep farm in Scotland, and he spends as much time there as he can. He smokes and drinks little. He flies his own plane, as Brabham and Graham Hill—both married, fathers, and nonsmokers—do. Brabham may drink a glass of wine or two. Hill, if he isn't working next day, will take a drop of what's going, but he would be classified a total abstainer by the ilk of Duncan Hamilton, who retired in 1959. Hamilton's career was studded with memorable incident. At a party in Milan with Fon Portago, Peter Collins, Mike Hawthorn, Luigi Musso, and Eugenio Castellotti—all of them swingers, and all of them killed at the wheel—Hamilton appropriated an airport bus and did a couple of fast laps around the big square near Milan Cathedral. The police put up a roadblock. When one of them jumped up on the step, Hamilton opened the door to consider his complaint, but when the officer pointed a revolver at him, Hamilton, a big and powerful type, slammed the door on his wrist and confiscated the gun. He took the cap from another policeman whom he caught trying to climb in a window. He then announced that the honor of his family had been irreparably breached, and he would have to shoot himself. By now the ranking policeman on the scene was a captain, who pleaded with Hamilton not to do anything so rash, and finally agreed to forgive and forget, if only Hamilton would not blow his head off. In his autobiography, Hamilton notes that he could still detect symptoms of hangover a full week later.

It was the style of some of the gentleman amateur drivers of the golden period of the 1920s and 1930s to ignore the mere mechanical aspects of racing. When the car stood ready, they drew on their capeskin-and-chamois gloves and got into it, presuming it to be perfectly prepared. Today's driver takes a different view. Often he is capable of discussing design on level terms with an engineer. Jack Brabham, John Surtees, Dan Gurney, Richie Ginther, Graham Hill, and Bruce McLaren are all very knowledgeable people, with a test-pilot attitude toward the vehicle. Mike Parkes, an Englishman, works for Ferrari in two capacities—as development engineer and as driver. There are still drivers whose orientation is less obsessively professional, younger men who have nonautomobilistic outside commercial interests, or private means, some who are not really dedicated, not sure that if they are able they'll be driving five years from now. One of these may take the championship this year, or next, but he can do it only by bulling his way through the little mob of eighteen-hour-a-day professionals at the top.

Almost as soon as the automobile ran at all, men began to race it. Exhibitions and demonstrations aside, the first genuine race was run over the 732 miles from Paris to Bordeaux to Paris in June 1895. Emile Levassor won in a Panhard, at an average speed of 15 miles an hour, and solemnly told reporters that no one should ever attempt such hideously dangerous speeds again. Many drivers were prepared to accept the risks, however and the Paris–Bordeaux was only the first of a series of great city-to-city races, running out, with Paris as a hub, to Marseilles, Amsterdam, Lyon, Toulouse, Berlin, Vienna, Madrid. The Paris–Madrid, in 1903, was the last of them; indeed, the cars never made it to Madrid. The French authorities, horrified at the accident rate, stopped the race at Bordeaux. Of the 175 cars that had started in Paris at 3:30 that morning, only about 100 got to Bordeaux. Most of the others broke down, but there were many accidents, and at least a dozen people—drivers, mechanics, and spectators—were killed. The roads were bone dry, and the great spidery high-riding cars ran through clouds of blinding dust, their drivers sometimes steering by the tops of the trees that bordered the road. Primitive as they were, some of the bigger cars would do 90 miles an hour and more, with brakes that would barely stop a bicycle. The winner *averaged* 65 miles an hour for 356 miles, a really astonishing rate.

In the year before, 1902, a closed circuit had been set up in Belgium, the Ardennes circuit, starting at Bastogne and running fifty-three miles through Longlier, Habay-La-Neuve, and Martelange back to Bastogne. Ardennes was the foundation stone under Grand Prix racing, the logical extension of city-to-city racing. Fifty-three miles of road could be policed, after a fashion, and spectators could see the cars pass more than once. The American newspaper publisher Gordon Bennett had in 1900 offered a cup for an international race, first run Paris–Lyon in 1900; in 1903 it was run over a 103-mile closed circuit in Ireland. In Sicily, Vincenzo Florio founded the Targa Florio still going today, past fifty runnings; and in the United States, W. K. Vanderbilt set up the Vanderbilt Cup series. The French Grand Prix of 1906, at Le Mans, was the first to use the term. The concept of true motor racing as a competition by fast cars over ordinary two-lane roadway had been established as the ideal. It still is.

Some courses, like Le Mans and Rheims in France, incorporate regular highway; one, Silverstone in England, is based on a World War II airport; Watkins Glen in the United States and the Nürburgring in Germany were designed and built for racing, and simulate roadway. The length of the course can be anything: Monte Carlo is 1.9 miles to the lap, the Nürburgring is 14.2. A race at Monte Carlo, or, properly, Monaco, is 100 laps. The Grand Prix of Germany at the Ring is fifteen. This year's eleven races (there were nine last year) will be run in France, Monaco, Holland, Germany, Belgium, England, Italy, South Africa, Canada, the United States, and Mexico. These are the races that count toward the world championship for drivers and the championship for constructors, the manufacturers of the cars, on a system of points for winning and placing. They are properly called *grandes épreuves*—the word means "test," or "trial"—and purists argue that only the old European races are *grandes épreuves*, excluding such social climbers as Mexico and the United States. That aside, a country can have a number of Grand Prix races, that is, races run to the standard set up by the world governing body of the sport, the *Fédération Internationale de l'Automobile,* but it can nominate only one as its *grande épreuve,* and this one is designated with the name of the country: the *Grand Prix de France,* and so on. The G. P. of the United States is run over the 2.3-mile course in Watkins Glen, the upstate New York village where American roadracing was reestablished in 1948.

The first 1967 Grand Prix was the South African, run January 2 at Kyalami. Pedro Rodriguez won in a Cooper-Maserati. Rodriguez had not won a G. P. before. His primary reputation, and it is a formidable one, is as a long-distance specialist. Pedro and his younger brother Ricardo began their careers on the Mexican motorcycle circuits. They moved to sports cars and Ricardo won a race at Riverside in California before he was old enough to have a license to drive on the road. He was killed in practice for the Grand Prix of Mexico in 1962*

The drivers' world-championship system was set up only recently, in 1950, and nine men have held the title since. One, Juan Manuel Fangio of Argentina, won it five times; Jack Brabham of Australia, the current holder, three times, and Jim Clark of Scotland and Alberto Ascari of Italy, twice each. One American has been champion: Phil Hill in 1961. Fangio won twenty-four Grand Prix races during his career. Clark, next highest ranked, has so far won twenty. British drivers have dominated the field for more than a decade.

It is usual, in American journalism, to qualify the champion's title, the ordinary form being "roadracing champion of the world." This is a gratuitous and egregious error. The fact is that the champion of the world is just that: the universal boss, properly ranked over the lesser talents who drive only stock cars, midgets, dirt-track cars, sports cars, Indianapolis cars, and so on. The Grand Prix driver's car, and the terrain over which he moves it, demand all of the separate skills of the other and lower categories, raised to the nth power. It is basic to an understanding of the fantastic level of skill required to drive a G. P. car flat-out to know that it has nothing whatever to do with driving a two-seater sports car at 100 miles an hour on a parkway; there is virtually no connection between the two things, save one so tenuous as to be analogous to that between a hand-cranked hurdy-gurdy and a cathedral organ. Thus, the really great Grand Prix driver can drive anything. He can outmatch the specialists in their own fields. Examples abound. Stirling Moss of England was as capable in sports cars as in Grand Prix. He won the most demanding of all sports-car races, the 1000-mile cross-country Mille Miglia, at the highest average speed ever recorded,

*Pedro was killed in Germany in 1971.

almost 100 miles an hour, which meant doing 175 on slippery two-lane roads, and going into cities at 150. He won the coveted Coupe des Alpes of the Alpine Rally, a stock-car event, three times in succession for not having lost a single point, a feat accomplished only once before. He drove land-speed-record cars and he drove karts.

When Jimmy Clark came to Indianapolis in 1963, moguls of the "500" establishment, parochial as Tibetans, unlettered and naïve, were merry at the prospect of a "sporty-car" driver pitted against the brutal reality of the "Brickyard" and the hairy men who ran on it. It was instantly obvious that as far as skill mattered, Clark could blow off any driver in the place when and where he pleased. Two years later, having sorted out problems of rules, rubber, and pit crews, he did just that. There were those who were astonished, because Indianapolis was the first big trackrace Clark had tried. They need not have been. Jack Brabham ran for years on Australian dirt tracks. It was valuable schooling, but he didn't learn how to drive, in the full sense of the word, until he went to Europe.

Of every 100 men who attempt a serious stab at Grand Prix racing, talented men with good backgrounds in other kinds of driving, two or three will, in the course of anything up to five years, make it: they will step into the ring of twenty or so drivers who are internationally ranked, which is to say, licensed to drive Grand Prix cars. Of this number, perhaps half will be good enough to be serious contenders for the world championship; one out of five of this group will almost certainly win it. In some years there may be one out of the top five—he will not necessarily be the champion— so incredibly skilled that he approaches the eerie. In its seventy-two years of existence, motor racing has produced six such: Tazio Nuvolari, Rudolf Caracciola, Juan Manuel Fangio, Stirling Moss, Jimmy Clark, and Jackie Stewart. All of them were clearly gifted far beyond common capacity, and all remarkable for obsessive single-mindedness and blinding concentration.

Concentration is the single most valuable attribute of a Grand Prix driver, assuming he has the ordinary armorarium of needed skills. It is easy to see why. Think of yourself in a car that will do 190 miles an hour, on the Bonneville salt flats, with a completely clear, billiard-table-level ten miles ahead, marked on the crystal surface by a six-inch-wide tar-black line. One mile from the end of the course, you have arranged for two bright-red flags to be stuck into the salt, so that you will have time to brake. You have only to crank the car up to 190, keep it reasonably close to the black line, and stop it gradually. For miles around, there's nothing you can run into. In this simple situation, so placid in the telling, you will find yourself concentrating until your head hurts, because once you have passed 125 miles an hour, a single coarse movement of the steering wheel, a bungled gearshift, a panic lunge at the brake is enough to start the car sliding, to roll it, and to kill you.

Now, put yourself in the situation of a Grand Prix driver running in the race that usually opens the season—the Grand Prix of Monaco. You are wearing flameproof underwear and flameproof overalls, leather gloves and the best helmet the aviation industry can produce and money can buy. Your goggles cover the top half of your face. For the rest, you tie on a mask of white flameproof cloth. You are now fireproof—for a maximum of thirty seconds. If you're not out of the burning car by then, all bets are off. You have lowered yourself into the vehicle by stretching your arms over your head and tucking them into the car afterward. You have just enough arm movement to turn the steering wheel through the limited arc it requires and to flip the gearshift lever through its four, five, or six slots. You are going to get tired of that, because you'll have to shift every three to five seconds for two hours and forty minutes: about 2500 times—and 2500 clutch-pedal movements. You'll put the brakes on as hard as you know how 600 times. The car has been set up, or chassis-tuned, to your precise requirements, which may have made it almost undrivable by another man. You may prefer that it understeer a bit in the corners, tending to go straight, or plow, where another driver would rather have the rear end swing out. Within reason, your mechanics will adjust the car to do anything you like, to help you in your basic problem, which is to make it go just as fast as it possibly can every foot of the way. This means holding it at a speed just a hair under the rate at which it will lose all tire adhesion and fly off the road into the scenery. If you go slower, everyone will pass you; faster, you'll be out of the race and probably into the hospital. Everything is complicated by the fact that you are going to race through city streets, nowhere more than two cars wide. Monte Carlo is a hilly city, and you are going to go steeply up and steeply down; you are going to go through right-angle corners, hairpins, fast bends; once a lap you are going through a tunnel (at about 120) so curved that you can't see the exit from the entrance, and will have to hope, 100 times, that no one is sliding crosswise in front of you. Out of the tunnel you will howl along an unfenced waterfront. High curbs, marble and granite buildings, plate-glass windows, trees, and water border the circuit. There is not a yard of ground in which a driver can make the slightest mistake and not pay for it, in lost time, damage to the car, or injury to himself.

No two circuits are alike. The Nürburgring has 176 bends, and rises and falls 3000 feet. Zandvoort, in Holland, lies in dune country. A strong wind blows off the sea and lays sand, nearly as slippery as oil at high speeds, on the corners. At Spa, in Belgium, it nearly always rains. Last year the weather was clear at the starting line, but halfway around the 8.7-mile circuit the whole field of cars, running about 140 mph, slammed into a wall of rain. Because he must constantly adjust to changes in his environment ranging from minor to startling (driving a G.P. car fast in traffic requires about five decisions a second), the driver must function at a high efficiency without interruption, and he must have unusual equipment to begin with. Most G.P. drivers are slightly but strongly built. (Big men are unusual.) They have notable endurance and they recuperate quickly from injury. They are rarely ill.

It's hard to think of one who is not physically compelling in one way or another, and since women are irresistibly attracted to men, no matter what they look like, who are conspicuously wealthy or conspicuously brave, racing drivers can move centered in shoals of good-looking women. The committed ones—wives, mistresses, friends—cluster around the pits, and the closer they are to the drivers the more likely they'll be actively helping, scoring, timekeeping, whatever. They want to be busy, they don't want to think about what it's like on the circuit, about what may happen out there. The others, most of them attached to men of lesser rank than drivers, men concerned with the sport in any capacity from team manager to spectator, float about looking madly glamorous in hip-huggers or golden-leather mini-skirts. The drivers are not more than momentarily diverted. The girls, they know, will be around forever, but this race, today, will never be run again.

A London psychologist, Berenice Krikler, made the only study of the G.P. driver I know, using as a sample five of the top rankers, including two world champions. She found that they were well above their national levels in intelligence; that their motor reaction times were, on average, no faster than those of a control group of nondrivers, but that they were capable, when motivated, of reaction times quite beyond those of the control group, and were particularly fast in foot reaction; that their concentration was superior, equal to that of college graduates of higher intelligence than theirs; that their mental speed was below average in relaxed circumstances but extraordinarily high when they were put under stress. (Most people, of course, react oppositely.) They were nonimpulsive, attentive to detail, patient, persistent, and very realistic in the goals they set for themselves. They felt somewhat detached from ordinary life, and took a great sense of exhilaration, power, and control out of driving, so much so as to indicate that retirement is probably harder for a racedriver than for any other comparable professional. The root fascination for the driver lies in his control over a vehicle that combines brute power and great delicacy, with high stakes riding on his maintenance of this control—wealth, fame, life, or death.

Wealth is probably the least of it. One or two drivers at the top of the tree may get into the $100,000-a-year bracket, sometimes perhaps quite a little way into it, but most are pleased to do $20,000 or $30,000 a year. On European circuits, first prize for a big race may be less than $3000, to be shared with the owner of the car. (First prize at Indianapolis in 1966 was worth over $150,000 to Graham Hill, the 1962 world champion who won.) The driver will take up to $1000 in "starting money," paid if he begins the race, regardless of where he finishes. A top-ranking driver will have contracts with manufacturers of everything from tires to toothpaste, and these can bring him $50,000 a year, or $1000, depending upon how well he did the season before. The percentages of owner-driver splits are tightly held secrets, but they are not often as good as 50-50. The driver's solution would seem to be to race his own car, but the cost is so nearly prohibitive that there are only three men trying. Joakim Bonnier, a Swede, and Guy Ligier, of France, are independently wealthy; Bob Anderson, an Englishman, actually makes racing support him, a feat for which he is held in awe.

Another factor militating against privateers is that the race-car manufacturers will not sell cars as good as those they propose to run themselves. The only private *patron* still trying to buck the factories is Rob Walker of the Johnny Walker Scotch whisky firm. Walker's financial resources are of course ample, but no amount of money will buy a duplicate of Enzo Ferrari's or Jack Brabham's number-one car. Walker has had his triumphs—one of Moss's greatest races was Monaco 1961 in a Walker-owned Lotus, the second time a Walker car had won that Grand Prix—and, in the old British sports tradition, he will probably go on as long as he has a chance of winning and as long as the tax people will let him; but when he finally steps aside, it's unlikely anyone will take up the torch.

The major firms currently building Formula I cars are Honda of Japan, Ferrari of Italy, All-American Racers of the United States, McLaren, Brabham, Lotus, Cooper, and BRM of Great Britain. Ferrari and Lotus sell passenger cars in limited numbers, as does Honda, which also has a broad supportive base in industry. Brabham manufactures race cars for sale and has sold 250 of them (Formula II, Formula III, Formula Junior), which makes him a General Motors–like giant in a field in which the sale of a dozen cars is a big deal. McLaren—a firm headed, like Brabham, and Dan Gurney's All-American Racers, by a driver, the New Zealander Bruce McLaren—makes Grand Prix cars. Cooper has a profitable backup in modifying passenger cars to go faster than standard. All-American Racers sells Indianapolis cars, Gurney-Weslake cylinder heads, and has had oil and tire sponsors.

In the beginning, race cars were fast versions of passenger cars by the same builders, and their costs were reasonably charged to advertising. In the 1930s, the Italian and German governments under Mussolini and Hitler subsidized Grand Prix teams as instruments of national propaganda, a gambit that reached its zenith in the monster Auto-Union and Mercedes-Benz cars running just before World War II. One of them, the W125 Mercedes-Benz of 1937, weighed less than 1650 pounds and produced 640 horsepower. The German cars were unbeatable, and they did serve a provably useful propaganda purpose. Today propaganda is still the root support behind motor racing, but it is commercial, nationalistic in purpose. An oil company may allocate $500,000 a year to racing, to be able to advertise that So-and-So won the G.P. of Whatzit on Blotz gasoline and oil. It was to make this support possible that exotic fuels based on alcohol were forbidden in Grand Prix racing a few years ago in favor of gasoline—aviation gas, to be sure, but gas just the same. The connection between the 130-octane fuel in a G.P. car and the regular in an MG in Birmingham is meaningless of course, but it sells gasoline. Only three companies make racing tires today —Firestone, Dunlop, Goodyear. The competition among them is fierce and on a twenty-four-hour-a-day basis. Spark-plug makers, battery companies, all manner of people lumped as accessory suppliers are willing to buy some of the publicity value of Grand Prix racing. For the builders of whole cars, it's a little tougher. A sports car or a *gran turismo* car can look a lot like a standard showroom sedan—thus the millions it cost Ford to win Le Mans were intelligently and usefully spent—but it's hard for the average motorist to relate his station wagon to a Lotus. A Grand Prix car is not a desirable consumer device.

Advocates of sports that are dull, dangerous, or immoral have always been resourceful in fostering and defending them. Boxing, as ugly an endeavor as has been sanctioned for public display in our time, is touted as character-building. Until it became totally absurd, the cliché traditionally supportive of horse racing was, "It improves the breed." Fleeter carriage horses, sturdier draft animals were available, our grandfathers were asked to believe, because of the Mendelian pressures built up on the tracks. The boredom of baseball was excused on the ground of patriotism, the game was held to be as American as apple pie—a European culinary invention, by the way. Motor racing has its own cliché: "The race car of today is the passenger car of tomorrow." This line is most often hustled by motoring journalists anxious to inflate the importance of the field they cover and by racetrack promoters. It is completely without substance. The late Laurence Pomeroy, the foremost world authority on Grand Prix automobiles, wrote, "Nearly all the worthwhile inventions of automobilism had been lodged in the Patent Office before the first Grand Prix of 1906, and the few remaining discoveries virtually coincided with the early period of Grand Prix racing. . . ." He goes on to list twelve basic inventions, all of which have repeatedly been claimed as originating in racing, and none of which did. He might have added two dozen other things, from the automatic transmission and power steering to the limited-slip differential, to disk brakes, all of which came to racing long after their use by civilians. I did believe for years that motor racing had contributed one thing to the general welfare—the rearview mirror. I believed and even, *mea culpa*, lay down on paper that Ray Harroun, who won the first Indianapolis 500 race, had devised the rearview

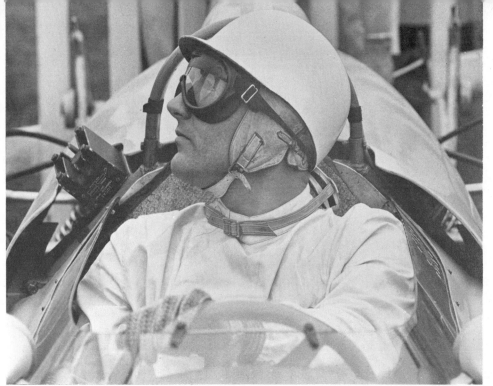

Top: Jesse L. Alexander; Lower Left and Right: Wide World Photos

Above: Stirling Moss just before the start of his 466th—and last—race, at Goodwood, England on Easter Monday, 1962. He was so severely injured in this race that he retired. At right, Alfonso, Marquis de Portago, pilot, jai alai player, steeplechaser, boulevardier, Grand Prix driver. He was killed in 1957. Below, happily still alive, still competing and still winning, Pat Moss Carlsson, former international horsewoman, a rally specialist in motor racing and probably the supreme woman driver of all time.

The V-16 Cadillac—this is a 1931 example—was a super-status symbol and an excellent piece of machinery to boot, smooth and powerful. The little door forward of the rear fender opened the golf-bag compartment.

A double-cowl phaeton on the Packard Super Eight model, 1933. This body-style was frequently erected on luxury chassis of the time. It was most elegant, true, but too windy to be practical at anything but modest speed.

A Type 57SC Bugatti convertible, an ultra-high-performance car of the 1930s equating with today's Ferrari, Maserati, Lamborghini. A coupe of this model was auctioned in 1971 for $59,000. The bidding lasted exactly six minutes.

Before the appearance in 1930 of the 8-litre Bentley, the "real" Bentley—made before Rolls-Royce absorbed the company—was a sports-racing car. The 8-litre (100 were made) was a luxury carriage, bare chassis, $9000.

Paintings by Jerome Biederman

Possibly the most costly—$12,600—model car in the world, a Ferrari 250 GT by Henri Baigent. Everything on the foot-long car is exactly as in the original, from the engine to the bird-seed-size instrument-panel lights.

Above: J. Barry O'Rourke

Right: Illustration by Dennis Luczak

Andy Granatelli's revolutionary turbine-powered Indianapolis car. Driven by Parnelli Jones in 1967, a minor bearing failure prevented its winning.

This Ford-engined Lotus, Jimmy Clark up, first seen at Indy in 1963, drove the standard U.S. race car into obsolescence. It finished second in 1963 and won easily, going away, in 1965.

Never a winner at Indianapolis, the Novi campaigned for years, beginning in 1941, running a supercharged V-8 engine. Ten years later it was fast enough to break the track qualifying record.

The Miller dominated track racing in the 1920s and 1930s. It was efficient, soundly designed and starkly beautiful. It could win anywhere, and did.

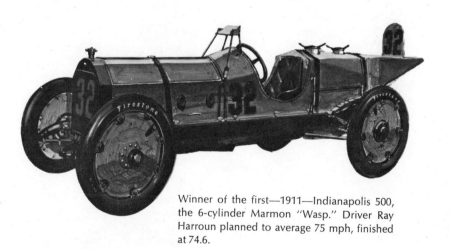

Winner of the first—1911—Indianapolis 500, the 6-cylinder Marmon "Wasp." Driver Ray Harroun planned to average 75 mph, finished at 74.6.

Illustrations by Dennis Luczak

One of the rocks on which the Jaguar empire was founded, the SS-100 roadster. It was fast enough (100 mph) and was visually most appealing.

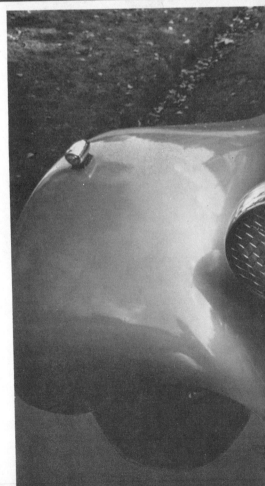

Top Left: Richard Fegley;
Lower Right: Michael Boys

The Playboy Stable of 1972, a gentleman's assemblage of fine motorcars of wide variety meant to suit any imaginable purpose, and ranging from a dune buggy to a 600 Mercedes.

Building replicas of famous cars is a persistent phenomenon. This 812 Cord is a slightly smaller treatment of the legendary 1937 original.

Another pair of replicas, on the left a close duplication of the supercharged Auburn speedster, outside exhaust pipes and all. Next to it a prototype Bentley replica which did not go into production. Both used U.S. engines.

The D-type Jaguar, 285 hp, the most successful of the company's competition cars. In the 1957 running of the Le Mans 24-Hour Race, it took the first four places.

Commercially the leader of the replicar parade has been Brook Stevens' SS Excalibur, modeled on the SS Mercedes-Benz. It's made in two- and four-seaters.

A 1967 Ferrari 330 GTC with body by Pininfarina: a 300 hp V-12 would take it to 165 mph. Not the best-looking Ferrari ever, its performance was worth $14,400.

Upper Left and Right: Larry Gordon; Center: J. Barry O'Rourke
Lower Left: Michael Boys; Lower Right: Marvin Koner

Mercedes-Benz has built passenger cars since the turn of the century and racers for nearly as long. This is a 1929 sports-racing SSK.

Only 470 Model J and SJ Duesenbergs were built. The car was a
legend in its own time, and is
now the most valuable of all U.S.
production automobiles.

One of the last of the front-
wheel-drive Cords, this 1937
phaeton shows the beauty of line
and mass that established its utter individuality.

Larry Gordon

The future will certainly see, because it must, the prohibition for city use of 20-foot-long cars carrying an average 1.2 passengers. The substitute may look like this, the roof hinged to swing open, steering and accelerator combined in a tiller-bar, a smogless engine rear-sited and removable.

Illustrations by Sydney Mead

The Iso Grifo was an Italian-American hybrid, body by Bertone, engine a Chevrolet Corvette. It would do 160 mph with the big (350) engine and sold for $13,000.

Marvin Koner

mirror because he proposed to run the race alone, without the usual riding mechanic to tell him what was going on astern. This jolly little fable was lately blown out of the water by one Thom Skeer of Woodbridge, Virginia. Writing to the magazine *Road and Track*, Mr. Skeer avers that the rearview was patented (No. 516,910) in 1894—for use on bicycles. He deserves a vote of thanks. It is enough that automobile racing has produced such nonutilitarian devices as seats made out of gas tanks and engines that will turn at the unlikely rate of 200 times a second. The rest is hypocrisy. One does not hear the Swiss argue that ropes developed for mountain climbing have meant stouter clotheslines for the housewife. The Spanish would deny that the *corrida de toros* has improved the breed of anything except the bulls, and that only to make them more nearly absolutely useless for anything except killing horses and men. Grand Prix racing similarly should be its own justification. There are few endeavors in which men voluntarily add life risk to the production of an esthetically moving spectacle. That is enough. More should not be asked.

—1967

The
Lady
or
the
Bugatti

"Peter!" Elisabeth Harmon whispered, muffling the
telephone, "It's for you—it's Dr. MacIntosh."

Slumped in the big chair in front of the fire, Peter
Harmon peered at his wife over the top of the newspaper.

"Who?" he said foggily.

"Dr. MacIntosh, idiot!" Elisabeth said. "The head-
master at Montford. Here!" She was holding the
phone at arm's length, as if it were radioactive. Peter
took it gingerly.

"Hello?" he said. The operator counseled patience,
and he covered the mouthpiece with his hand. "This
can mean only one thing," he said softly. "Billy has
slugged his physics master or something, and they're
sending him home in the morning."

"Let us pray," Elisabeth said.

"Dr. MacIntosh?" Peter said. "How are you, sir?
Fine, just fine . . . No, not at all, go right ahead.
. . . I see . . . Of course . . . Well, I must say I . . . Yes,
I understand . . . Naturally . . . Well, I must say I'm
surprised . . . Of course I will, be glad to . . . And I
do thank you . . . Not at all, sir, not at all . . .

Good-by." He dropped the phone into its cradle and sat peering dreamily into space.

"Well?" Elisabeth said. "What did Billy do? How bad is it?"

"Very flattering, I must say," Peter muttered. "What do you know," he said, "MacIntosh wants me to address the Parents' Day Assembly. How do you like *that*?"

"I *know* you're a great man," Elisabeth said, "wise, witty, charming and all that. I keep *telling* you so. What does MacIntosh want you to talk about, 'Merchandising the Modern Curriculum'?"

"He suggested 'Sportsmanship in a Changing World,'" Peter said loftily. "He is not concerned with my accomplishments, notable though they be, in the field of advertising."

"Well, you had to wait twelve years for it," Elisabeth said, "but catching that pass in the Minnesota game in '46 has finally paid off, hasn't it. Tell me, when is this gala?"

"Fifteenth of next month," Peter said.

Elisabeth counted on her fingers. "Darling," she said, "I think I'd better get a new coat. I can't go up there and expose myself to all those filthy-rich mothers in a ratty black karakul. Not when I'm the wife of the guest of honor. Out of the question."

"I suppose," Peter said. "What were you thinking of?"

"Mink, what else?" Elisabeth said. "A modest, conservative ranch mink. I really don't think wild mink is worth the difference, do you?"

Seeing that he was about to be trapped into taking a stand in favor of ranch mink instead of against mink in any form, Peter held his tongue.

"Besides," Elisabeth said, "we still have that $6000 from selling the Mercer Raceabout and the Morgan Three-Wheeler. It'll be a twist, don't you think, turning a couple of smelly antique automobiles into a mink coat?"

"Six thousand dollars?" Peter gasped. "You're going to blow $6000 on a *coat*?"

"Certainly not," she said. "I can do very nicely with $1500. And you ought to get a new suit, too. Get a good one; get one for $125 or so."

"Gee, thanks," Peter said. "Maybe I will." He reeled off toward the kitchen. "Is there any coffee left?" he said.

It was not just the coffee that kept Peter Harmon awake that night. He had another problem. He went to sleep finally, and dreamed that he was sitting in the precise center of the football field at Montford Academy, peering through the windshield of a hopelessly battered, smoking, lopsided 1955 station wagon, while all around, their head lamps sneering at him, were the Rolls-Royces, the Bentleys, and Eldorados of the other parents. He woke up with Elisabeth holding him in bed by main force.

"Peter!" she said. "You're having a nightmare."

" 'S nothing," he muttered. " 'S all right." He pulled the covers up to his ears and tried once more.

The next morning, pounding into New York on the 8:11, Peter contemplated the matter. He could rent something lush, of course, but it hardly seemed cricket for a man about to address the impressionable young on the worth of sportsmanship. He'd just call up old Potter and see what was stirring. He had his secretary put in the call as soon as he'd read the morning mail.

"Potter here," the voice said.

"Peter Harmon, Leonard," Peter said. "How are things at The Vintage Car Store?"

"Matter of fact, rather good," Potter said. "I sold that chain-gang Frazer-Nash yesterday; you know, the red one. Chap just left for Chicago. Very keen type. He wouldn't even put the hood up. And how can I make *you* happy, old boy?"

Peter stated the facts in the case.

I don't suppose you'd want an 8-liter Bentley?" Potter said. "It's as big as a bus, very impressive. Bit scruffy, though."

"No, I've got to have something clean *and* impressive," Peter said.

"You know, I've got just the thing for you," Potter said. "A Type 50 Bugatti, a three-passenger coupe by Million-Guiet. You know the Type 50, don't you: 5 liters, twin cam, double blower. It'll run all day at 40 miles an hour, no fuss of any kind; but when you put your foot down and the blower begins to puff, it will drive you right into the upholstery. Zero to 60 miles an hour in eight seconds, that sort of thing. Fantastic racket from the supercharger, a scream you can hear for blocks. Very impressive, all in all."

"Clean?"

"Very nearly mint," Potter said. "Dark red and black. There are only a dozen of them left in the world, you know."

"And money?"

"Oh, $4000 for a friend," Potter said.

Peter took a deep breath. "Well, I'll come look at it," he said.

Peter met his wife for cocktails, the day she bought the coat. It was a superior coat; he was struck with the beauty she lent to it and glad she owned it—really glad, he told himself, and not just because he was craftily using her buying it to excuse what he had done. They had a long dinner and a short movie; and when Elisabeth suggested they take a cab to Grand Central, he said he'd rather walk. He didn't even have to guide her; she stayed on the right side of Fifth Avenue, and she even convenienced him by pointing as they came abreast of it.

"What an odd-looking car," Elisabeth said.

"Oh, I don't know," Peter said. "I think it's rather handsome. Certainly unusual looking."

"You have a perverted taste in automobiles," she said. "It looks like a hot rod made by a backward child. Look at that squinchy windshield; how could you ever see out of it?"

"That's the whole point," Peter said. "In a car like that you have a little privacy. It's not a goldfish bowl for everybody to peer into."

Elisabeth walked over and looked at the big red lozenge on the radiator. "Bugatti," she said. "An Italian car."

"French," Peter said.

"French, schmench," Elisabeth said. She looked over her shoulder at her husband. "Come, little boy," she said. "Mustn't touch." He didn't move.

Peter opened the door. "May I drive you home, lady?" he said.

She stared, and the green orbs of her eyes burned into him and through him and way beyond him. "Oh, no!" she said. "Oh, not *again!* I couldn't *live* through it! First that horrible Mercer, and then that treacherous three-wheel beast, that Morgan, and now this? Just answer me, yes or no, did you buy that thing?"

"Yes," Peter said. "I certainly did." He tried to sound firm, but he was beginning to hear the faint, faraway tinklings of an alarm bell. In Peter Harmon's life Elisabeth was unique in two ways: she was the dearest girl he knew, and she had the most fantastic temper this side of the Cameroons.

She was standing stock-still now; he watched her in bemused fascination. He wasn't alone. A small knot of curious types was hovering around, pretending to look into store windows.

Elisabeth slammed her purse to the sidewalk. She slipped out of the mink coat like a magician, took two quick steps toward Peter and hurled it through the open door into the cavelike darkness of the Bugatti. Then she spun on her heel and marched down the avenue.

Peter pushed the big door shut, remembering, even in the stress of the moment, to be gentle—after all, this was not any old car—and ran after his wife. Twenty feet away he remembered: new mink coat, unlocked car. He dashed back, grabbed the coat, picked up the purse, and ran again.

"Elisabeth, please," he said. "Put your coat on, at least." Holding her with one hand, trying to throw the coat over her shoulders with the other was too much even for an All-American, and her purse slipped from under his elbow to the sidewalk. He let go of her, stooped to pick it up, put the strap in his mouth, gathered up the coat again, and once more ran for her and caught her wrist.

"Elithabeth," he said, "pleath!"

"Let go of me, you embezzler," she snapped. "Let go of me or I'll bite you to the bone."

A soft Irish voice sounded from the street. "Is he bothering you, lady?" it said.

"Mind your own dammed bithness," Peter said through the purse strap. He turned his head in time to see a policeman slide out of a squad car.

"All right," the cop said, an edge in his soft voice. "Time out. Let go of the lady, mister. And as for you, ma'am, kindly stick around for a minute." They stood there, glaring at each other like a pair of tied cats.

"Would it be easier for you to talk, Mac," the policeman said finally, "if you took that bag out of your mouth?"

Peter unclamped the death-grip lock of his jaws on the purse strap and handed it to Elisabeth. The policeman gently relieved him of the coat and held it while Elisabeth shrugged into it, like a schoolgirl.

"Now then," the officer said. "My partner and I are finishing a very rough tour, and we would just as soon not be bothered with you two unless you have serious business. Do you want to sign a complaint against this fella, Miss?"

"I'd adore to," Elisabeth said. "But I guess I won't. It wouldn't do any good to put him in jail. He's a hopeless case."

"You two are married?" the officer said. They admitted it. "Why don't you go on home, then," he went on. "And if you still feel like fighting, you can do it in peace and quiet." He stood looking at them for a few seconds, nodded, and left them. The green-and-white car moved off slowly.

"Great," Peter said. "You really fixed that one up."

Elisabeth tried to regard him in stony silence, but a grin trembled around the corner of her lips, and suddenly she had her hands over her mouth, helplessly trying to stuff the laughter back down her throat.

If I live to be 150," she said, "and I hope I do, I'll never, *never* forget the sight of you standing there with that purse in your mouth! But never!"

"You coming?" Peter said with what he conceived to be frigid formality.

"Sure, Rover," Elisabeth said. "I'm coming." She staggered after him, gagging with laughter.

The squad car was standing beside the Bugatti. The big policeman pulled his head and shoulders out of it and looked up at them.

"It's you again," he said dismally.

"It's my car," Peter said.

"Is it, now?" the policeman said. "You don't have a front license plate on it. Is it in the car, by any chance?"

"Well, no," Peter said. "You see, I just got the car, and . . ."

"Spare me the details," the officer said, hauling out the big black book. "Those are pretty big headlights," he said. "Would you mind just turning them on for me?"

The lights were 12-inch Marchals, and when Peter snapped them on, the officer recoiled as if from a blow. "Turn 'em off," he said quietly, "before you burn the paint off this fella in front of you. They'd do fine for a locomotive, but for a car they're illegal. In New York City, that is." He made another notation. "Does it have a working horn, I wonder?" he said.

Peter reached in and pressed the button. The twin-trumpet Cicca air horn bellowed briefly. "As illegal a horn as I ever heard," the officer said, "and me with a headache." He wrote busily, handed Peter the ticket, and said good-night.

He leaned out the window of the squad car. "I forgot something," he said, "but I'm not getting out of this car again, short of murder. Just do me a favor and let us get a couple of blocks down the street before you start the engine. I have no doubt your exhaust is 100 percent illegal." He nodded and rolled up the window.

"I guess *I* brought him down on your head," Elisabeth said. "I'm sorry." Peter didn't answer. He started the engine and cranked the car away from the curb. Forgetful of the big semiracing Bugatti engine under the bonnet, he tramped on the accelerator. A bestial scream rattled the windows on both sides of the street, and the car was flung ahead like a stone from a giant's slingshot. Peter barely stopped it for a red light.

"Oh, boy," Elisabeth said. "You've really got one *this* time! What a treasure!"

She might have spoken again on the hour's ride to Westchester, but Peter wouldn't have known unless she had shouted. He concentrated on driving the car. Potter had been right; it was a fantastic automobile.

In terms of 1958 money, it had cost $16,000 when it was new in 1934, and it went like a $16,000 automobile—brute power marvelously controllable. When it rumbled into the Harmon driveway, Peter felt fine, the gruesome episode on Fifth Avenue a long way behind him.

"An enchanting experience," Elisabeth said. "I may want another ride in it, say next year."

The baby-sitter wrenched her eyes away from the television set long enough to say, "A telegram came for you, Mr. Harmon. It's on the dining-room table."

Peter held the wire in his hand for a long time after he'd read it. Finally, Elisabeth took it from him.

"REGRET NECESSITY DEFERRING YOUR APPEARANCE," she read. "CHAIRMAN ALUMNI FUND-RAISING GROUP WISHES USE OCCASION ANNOUNCE SUBSTANTIAL NEW ENDOWMENT. ACCEPT MY APOLOGY AND URGENT INVITATION APPEAR SAME EVENT NEXT YEAR. MACINTOSH."

"I'm *so* sorry, darling," she said.
"Can't win all of 'em," Peter said.

"Why, this was a win all the way down the line, darling," Elisabeth said. "You've got the Bugatti, I've got the mink, and they'll both be just as good next year. See?" She kissed him hard.

"On your feet, Hilda," she said. "Mr. Harmon is going to ride you home in his nice new automobile." She paid the girl and saw them to the door. "Don't speed," she said, "but hurry back."

"I'll do that," Peter said.

—1959

Targa
Florio

Every year, in the hot spring, the Sicilians run the oldest automobile race in the world—the oldest, perhaps the most colorful, certainly the luckiest, and historically the last of the real long-distance over-the-road races—the Targa Florio.

The day of the Targa is virtually a national holiday in Sicily, and it would be almost impossible to estimate the number of people who watch it. They hang from rooftops or lean over balconies in the towns of Campofelice, Cerda, and Collesano. They cluster on the very edge of the sixteen-foot-wide road out in the countryside, and on the straights that run beside green meadows and farmers' fields. They bunch at the dusty hairpin turns in the mountains. Buildings everywhere are daubed with "VV" signs, the abbreviation for *Viva*, meaning "Long life to," or "Hurrah for," or whatever you like, followed by the names of cars or drivers: "*Viva* Ferrari," "*Viva* Vaccarella."

Going through the towns, favored drivers are showered with flowers from the balconies, and if they run into trouble out in the countryside, they can expect all kinds of enthusiastic assistance. If a car slides off the road—and many do—a small mob of men and boys will materialize instantly to pick it up and put it back, and the driver will probably be given a quick pull at a bottle of wine at the same time. The enthusiasm of the spectators is limitless, and they are most resourceful. A driver who thought a broken throttle cable had put him out of the running watched a guitarist whip a string off his instrument and do a repair good enough to get the car back to the pits. In most races, anyone aside from driver or mechanics who touches a competing car automatically disqualifies it, but in the Targa anything goes. The Targa ·has been run for half a century, and to watch it is almost to go back to the birth of the sport.

Some people, and not all of them Sicilians, think the Targa is the greatest race in the world. It has run fifty times since it was founded in 1906. They argue that this is what the automobile was meant to do, that this is the only true and meaningful test of the racing car: to run it hard and fast over open road, uphill and down, and the devil take the hindmost. Compared with this kind of racing, they say, the round-and-round of a track like Indianapolis is silly. The only course that comes close to the Targa Florio is the Nürburgring in Germany, but that is only fourteen miles around, and it's an artificial circuit, made as a public-works project in the 1930s. The road over which the Targa Florio goes is real road, and none too good in places, either.

The word *Targa* is Italian for plaque, and Florio is the name of the man, Don Vincenzo Florio, who originated the idea of the race, made it, and dominated it absolutely until his death in 1959, when he was seventy-six years old. Vincenzo Florio's father was one of the wealthiest men in Sicily. When Vincenzo was five, his older brother bought a De Dion motor tricycle. It excited Vincenzo as nothing else had ever done. His brother went to Paris and brought back a Peugeot. Next he had a Benz, then a Fiat . . . Vincenzo Florio began a passionate attachment for automobiles that was to govern all the rest of his life. By the time he was twenty, Florio was determined to become a racing driver and to organize races of his own. He began to stage private races, in which all the cars belonged to him, and in which everybody, including his chauffeur, was told to make every effort to beat him.

Florio himself didn't run in the first Targa, which got under way early in the morning of Sunday, May 6, 1906. There were ten entrants who were optimistic enough to face the ninety-mile circuit, rising and falling 4000 feet, about thirty miles from Palermo, Sicily's major city. Vincenzo Florio had spent money freely to make his race a success; not only was the prize a solid-gold plaque made by a Paris jeweler, but he had gone to much trouble to attract spectators. He had built grandstands on the fastest straightaway and he had advertised the race widely all over Sicily. The race was a long one: nine hours and thirty-two minutes, with the winning car, an Itala driven by a man named Cagno (of whom not much was heard again), averaging about 29 miles an hour.

Because the rate of speed had been so low, and because the race had been run so far from the population centers of Europe, the first Targa Florio roused no great interest, but Florio's promotion efforts never flagged, and when the cars came to the line for the second running, in 1907, there were fifty of them. Sometimes Florio entered himself. He did in 1909, and finished second, in a Fiat. But he wasn't a serious driver, nor even a very good one, and after he had crashed a Mercedes against a bridge in the 1912 running, he gave up. Until World War I, however, he saw to it that nothing interfered with the running of the Targa Florio every year, and by 1914 a driver who hadn't entered it couldn't very well claim to be in the first rank of his profession. In 1912–1914, and again in 1948–1950, the racecourse was one lap of the coast road running completely around Sicily. This was one of the three circuits that have been used. The first one was called "Big Madonie." The circuit in use since 1950 is called "Little Madonie" and is about forty-five miles in length. There are nine laps to the race.

It begins in the town of Cefalu and climbs up toward the Madonie Mountains into Cerda. It rises into the hills, circles, drops, climbs again, and comes back to the coast. The spring countryside is lovely: green meadows covered with yellow, red, blue wild flowers, growing corn, wheat, artichokes. (The Sicilians say of a driver who goes off the road, "He went into the artichokes.") The road has never been really good, and the surface breaks up easily under the pounding of the cars. Parts of it seem extraordinarily slippery, wet or dry; the natives say this is a result of having donkey manure ground into it for decades. The road slashes past stone bridges an elbow-length away, and some of the best views are from house balconies, looking almost straight down into the cars. There are between 893 and 1300 curves to the lap, depending upon who makes the survey, and the longest straight is about five miles—the Retilineo di Bonfornello—along the seacoast, good for 150 miles an hour.

The Targa Florio, at first sight, seems one of the most dangerous races imaginable, with spectators crowding everywhere, innumerable hazards, natural and manmade, for the drivers. Yet in the whole half-century of it, no spectator has been killed, and only one driver. He was Count Guilio Masetti, who won in 1920 and 1921, and was killed in 1926. Many drivers have had close calls. The great Antonio Ascari went off the road in 1919, and although not seriously injured, was pinned in his car, unable to move. He was not found for ten hours.

It has been commonplace for drivers to find themselves in desperate situations in the Targa, although sometimes they were not as badly off as they thought. In 1922 Henry Segrave broke down high in the mountains. By the time he and his mechanics got the car running again, it was pitch dark. Segrave tried to drive, but it was impossible; he couldn't see two feet in front of his wheels. He gave up, and went to the single farmhouse that was showing a light. Segrave had no money; neither he nor his mechanic spoke a word of Italian. Somehow he convinced the very dubious head of the household that he wanted only a lodging for the night. He and his mechanic slept on the floor, while his friends, back at the pits, certain that he had fallen victim to the dreaded Sicilian *banditti*, organized a search party. They found him next morning, vowing that he would never spend another night on a stone floor, no matter what the alternative.

Vincenzo Florio said that merely to finish the Targa, never mind win it, qualified one as a complete driver, and the statement was never disputed. Because the road is so narrow, the cars are started at thirty-second intervals. The Targa is man and car against nature, against the road itself. If a driver is to have a chance of finishing well up, he must keep his car on the very knife-edge of control loss all the time; that's to say, he must drive so fast that another mile or two an hour will put him off the road. Even the best *pilotos* will inevitably misjudge this margin now and again.

Stirling Moss, driving a Mercedes-Benz in the 1955 race, came through at the end of the first lap in the lead, and by the end of the third lap he had stretched this advantage to five minutes, with Eugenio Castellotti, on a Ferrari, second. But at the end of the fourth lap, when he was due to hand the car over to his codriver, Peter Collins, Moss was nine minutes *behind* Castellotti! He had gone into a bend too fast, the car had drifted off the road and dropped ten feet into a field full of rocks. Somehow Moss slammed it back onto the circuit, but he had to treat the car so brutally in the process, that he boiled away all his water and added extensively to the damage the Mercedes had already suffered. Collins jumped into it, and although he did not know if it was safe to drive at all, much less at top speed, he broke the lap record, and when he gave the car back to Moss, it was in the lead again. Moss, for his part, broke the lap record repeatedly again, and won the race by more than five minutes. He brought the $20,000 Mercedes-Benz across the line looking like a rolling piece of junk, but that didn't matter: Alfred Neubauer, the legendary Mercedes-Benz team manager, made his usual gesture of triumph; throwing his hat under the front wheel as the car crossed the line, laughing as it was crushed and spun aside.

Moss and Collins knew the circuit as well as a non-Sicilian could know it, of course. The Mercedes-Benz racing organization was famous for thorough preparation, which meant, among other things, as much practice as was humanly possible. If a driver doesn't know that the road goes sharply right at the bottom of a certain hill, and then sharply left, he cannot possibly drive as fast as he should. Competitors who haven't had time to learn every bend have sometimes gone to great trouble to paint private signals on stones, trees, fences, bridges, and the like. There's a danger in this, though. One year, when a French driver had privately sign-posted the whole circuit, he found nothing at all to guide him on the day of the race. One of his rivals had gone out the night before with a bucket of whitewash and a big brush!

For the most part, a driver in the Targa is trying to beat the field, *all* the other drivers, but there have been a few races in which two men drove as if they were alone. In 1921, for example, when Achille Varzi and Tazio Nuvolari were running, Varzi on a Bugatti, Nuvolari on an Alfa-Romeo. Nuvolari has been held by many authorities to have been the greatest driver who ever lived, and in his day Achille Varzi was almost as much esteemed. The two were deadly personal rivals; indeed, it was impossible for them to drive on the same team, since nothing would induce them to cooperate. In 1921 the circuit was wet, which meant heavy mud in many places. At the last minute the Alfa-Romeo team manager ordered mudguards put on Nuvolari's car, but Varzi had none, and before the first lap was over the spinning front wheels had soaked him to the waist in mud and water. He drove as fast as he had ever done, nevertheless, wiping off his goggles when he dared, and driving blind when he had to. At one point a fuel leak set the car on fire: Varzi screamed to his mechanic to climb on the hood and beat out the flames with a seat cushion. Varzi finished so exhausted that he had to be lifted out of the Bugatti—only to be told that Nuvolari had won.

Later, in the cool of the evening, under the bright Sicilian stars, Vincenzo Florio met Nuvolari, strolling alone, taking a little fresh air, as he said. Florio asked him if he was glad he'd won the race.

"Well," Nuvolari said, "at least I can say I'm glad I beat Varzi!"

It takes men like that to win the Targa Florio, and it takes a superb automobile. Only cars with great speed, the best possible brakes, leechlike road-holding, and endurance approaching indestructibility can win in Sicily —cars like Bugatti, Alfa-Romeo, Mercedes-Benz, Ferrari, Porsche. In recent years, Ferrari and Porsche have been the most successful, in the hands of drivers like Nino Vaccarella, a Palermo lawyer who won in 1965, or Willy Mairesse of Belgium, who won in 1966. Vaccarella has the great advantage of living in Sicily and thus knowing the circuit intimately, down to the last inch, and Mairesse is a famous "charger"—a driver who puts his foot flat down on the accelerator and leaves it there. Mairesse has crashed many times, he has been badly injured, but he still drives only one way— fast. To win the Targa Florio, nothing less for it will do.

—1967

Model
Cars

Would you pay $12,600 for a brand-new Ferrari coupe? Of course you would; a new Ferrari is a bargain at $12,600. Even one only a foot long? Yes, and it's still a bargain at the price. More than a bargain. It's cheap. The man who made the car, Henri Baigent of England, put three years and 11,000 hours of work into it, so he charged barely more than one dollar an hour.

Baigent is one of a group of great automobile model makers who have appeared in the years since World War II, a period that has seen the hobby of model-car collecting change from the casual pastime of a few people into a worldwide hobby of such proportions that it supports an industry. (Over an identical period of months, 2,500,000 real Citroëns were sold and 2,109,177 miniature models of the same car.) A custom model maker like Baigent or Michel Conti of Italy may spend months on a single car, but during that time one factory may produce 10 million models two to four inches long.

The range and variety of model cars available today is incredible: in cost, anything from 29 cents to $15,000; in size, one inch to a foot and a half; in detail, from a simple stamped-out wheels-and-body tin-toy cheapie to a gasoline-engined radio-controlled racer. The bible of the little-car world, *Model Cars of Today*, by Greilsamer and Azema, lists 7000 models by 174 manufacturers in 17 countries—and the authors say it was not their intention to attempt a complete catalog.

There are five basic categories of model cars, and many varieties in each category: (1) antiques; (2) finished cars made of plastic or metal; (3) do-it-yourself kit cars; (4) powered cars running gasoline engines or electric motors; (5) model cars made from "scratch," that is, from raw material.

The world saw a model car before it saw a car: The first vehicle recorded as moving under its own power was a wheeled toy about two feet long, built for the Chinese Emperor Kang-Hi by a Jesuit missionary, Father Ferdinand Verbiest, about 1678. It ran on a reaction engine, that is to say, a jet engine. Father Verbiest's car was simple—a wheeled platform on which was mounted a firebox. Over the firebox Father Verbiest put a rounded copper vessel or container, closed except for a spout pointing to the rear. When a container was filled with water and the fire lighted, steam shot out the spout, producing motion in accordance with the principle discovered by Newton —every action has an equal and opposite reaction.

Father Verbiest's miniature car moved for exactly the same reason that a blown-up balloon, released, will shoot across the room. This method of producing motion was discovered not by Father Verbiest, by the way, but by an ancient Greek named Hero of Alexander. Hero made a device called an aeolipile, a round vessel with several bent spouts coming out of it, all pointing in the same direction. The vessel was mounted on two upright posts in such a way that it could turn freely. When it was filled with water and a fire put under it, the steam squirted out the spouts and spun it. The aeolipile was the first engine that did not work by wind or waterpower.

There are, unhappily, no working models of steam-powered automobiles on the market today, but Stanley Steamer models aren't hard to find. Three big U.S. firms make them: Aurora, Revell, and Renwal. A French model manufacturer, Precisia, makes a model of the Cugnot steam tricycle of 1769, the first self-powered man-carrying vehicle in history.

Men have always been fascinated by tiny things. As soon as man made *anything*, he probably made a miniature of it, beginning with the caveman's first spear. And as manufactured devices became more complex, so the challenge to reproduce them in miniature became more compelling. The sailing ship enchanted model makers for centuries. Not all ship models were made for fun—300 years ago, big-ship builders, having no blueprints, instead used detailed models, exact to the last carefully fitted joint.

Fascinating as sailing ships and steamships may be, they don't have the mechanical complexity of the automobile, or its almost universal appeal.

The first commercially made car models appeared a bit more than forty years ago, under the American Tootsie Toy label. In 1934 Dinky Toys of Great Britain came on the market. Both these companies made metal models, but in 1950 a firm called Old-Timers offered do-it-yourself plastic kits, a tremendous step forward because of the ease with which the car could be assembled. A few years later slot racing came along, making car-to-car competition possible, and threatening, for awhile, to run the model-railroad business out of sight.

Car collecting has the fascination of all the great hobbies, the root of which is the simple fact that there is no limit to it, no end. It is doubtful that any collector, anywhere, ever said to himself: "I now have everything I want. My collection is complete, there's nothing I can add to it."

Suppose you decide to collect pre-1934 models, antiques. You can start in your own attic. Maybe that old trunk that belonged to your grandfather has a cast-iron Model T Ford buried under a moth-eaten sweater. (That's where I found mine.) Then you can move on to your friends' attics, cellars, closet shelves. If there's an antique store in your neighborhood, check it out. One of my friends found six old cars, including a rare wind-up Delage racer. They were in the drawer of a dresser standing in the back room of an antique shop, and he got them for a dollar each. In the course of an automobile trip you're sure to pass an antique shop or two; they're particularly thick in New England. Stop and look. When you have a few cars in your hand you can start repairing them, repainting, restoring, trading—and you may never stop.

Present-day models are easier to come by, because all you need is a catalog and some money. Two big mail-order houses are Autoworld, 701 North Keyser Ave., Scranton, Pa. 18508, and Sinclair's, 3416 West Lake Rd., Erie, Pa. 16505. If you live in a sizable town, there's almost sure to be a place handling U.S. and foreign-made models: a toy store, department store, stationery shop, even a drugstore or a newsstand. The bigger the store and the wider the range of stock, the more manufacturers represented. Among the manufacturers are Aurora Plastics, Fred Bronner, Reeves International, and Lynn International. Other companies are: Associated Hobby Manufacturers, Imai Kagaku Company, Ltd., Model Rectifier, Revell, Hubley, Tyco, Atlas, Bachman Brothers, A.M.T., Lindberg, Monogram, L. M. Cox, Strombecker, Deluxe Topper, and Jo-Han. On newsstands you'll find magazines devoted to model cars. *Car Model* is one such. A sample copy direct from the publisher is 50 cents: write to *Car Model,* 615 Ridge Rd., North Arlington, N.J. 07032.

Many collectors specialize. Even though most models are under six inches in length, there are so many available that it's almost necessary to specialize, unless you can turn one room of your house into a museum. You can concentrate on antique cars, models of full-size automobiles built before, say, 1914; or "classic" cars, dated roughly 1920–1939; sports cars; racing cars; standard passenger cars; hot rods and record-breakers; military vehicles; trucks of all kinds, or fire engines. Whatever category you choose, you'll find that your specimens show fantastic attention to detail: Opening hoods, doors, windows, trunks (with miniature suitcases) are common. You can have radio aerials, external mirrors, working suspension and steering, adjustable seats, detachable wheels. Would you believe a rear-seat television set, with a lighted picture on the screen?

The best models are the result of hundreds of hours of work before a single car comes off the production line. (When they do come, they come fast, as fast as 10,000 an hour.) The big manufacturers all work from full-scale factory plans, and in models as small as 1/43 scale (1/43rd the size of the real car) you'll find things like tiny simulated rivets on chassis and body parts. The master molds for plastic and metal models are made with as much care as Detroit master dies, and by artisans no less skilled. Incidentally, scale sizes run over a wide range. The smallest commercial model I know of is 1/87—which comes out to about 1¼-inch wheelbase —and the biggest is 1/8.

Whatever you buy in a finished model car, there are two things you should do as soon as you get it home: wax it, and wrap it in transparent plastic film. Any good wax will do. You'll need toothpicks covered with soft cloth to get into the tight places and you'll find that a complete waxing of a small model is a time-consuming job. But it's worth it. After the wax has dried and been polished, wrap the car completely in transparent plastic. If you want to know why, leave your model on a tabletop or a bookshelf for a couple of weeks and then see how much dust has settled on the wrapping. You'll be surprised. Dust that has drifted into the corners and crevices of a model car is very hard to get rid of, and as a rule a car that has become really dusty never looks right again. When the plastic itself turns dingy, throw it away and put on a new piece. A model treated in this way will look brand-new for years.

After you've been collecting finished models for a while, you'll begin to notice things you don't like—details that can be improved, poor paint jobs, and so on. For example, there's a Mercer Raceabout on the market, painted lavender. The full-size Mercer T-head Raceabout, one of the great cars of all time, was never finished in that color; so many collectors strip the model and repaint it, perhaps in a golden yellow, which was a standard factory color. While you're about it, you may want to add some authentic details: a starting crank, or an acetylene-light tank on the running-board. Once you've started, it's perfectly possible to spend six months on this little 3¼-inch Mercer, if you decide you'll get down to details like spark and throttle levers, a "Monocle" windshield, and scale instruments. (You'll have a valuable model, by the way, and, unless you choose to duplicate it, the only one of its kind in the world.)

Instead of modifying standard models—customizing is the word most car-hobbyists use—you may prefer to build your own. You can start with plastic kits at less than a dollar, cars that can be put together without so much as a drop of cement, and you can go on to the ultimate stage of producing original models by drawing your own plans, making your own parts out of raw materials—metal, wood, plastic, or leather. There's a vast amount of ground in between. Many plastic kits are fairly simple and will produce a good-looking car with a few hours of work. One of my own favorites is Monogram's 35B Bugatti, a Grand Prix car. This kit gives a beautiful, professional looking model. Another stage up, and harder to do, but not at all really difficult, is an all-metal job like Auto-Kit's SSKL Mercedes, a really stunning model. The top kit at the moment is certainly Pocher's F2 FIAT, which costs about $60. There are 823 parts in this kit, 173 in brass; 506 in steel, iron, copper, aluminum, leather, and cloth; 144 in plastic. Detail is remarkable (all parts were checked against a specimen of the car itself in an Italian museum) and the finished model measures seventeen inches long, seven inches wide, and weighs three and a half pounds. It can be bought fully assembled for $175, but what would be the fun in that?

Advanced model makers use kits as starting points only, modifying as they go. They may combine parts from different kits, or so alter a standard kit that the finished product is almost wholly an original creation.

Gasoline-engined models, fully assembled and ready to go, can be bought for $10 to $15. I think they're remarkable bargains at those prices. They need careful management, though, when they're running—usually on a circular track or a drag strip—because they go fast enough to hurt if they hit you at full bore. Radio-controlled cars cost from about $35 to $150, but they don't need mechanical restrictions, such as tethers. They run free, under control by a little black box in the operator's hands. The cheaper ones must be controlled in sequence: start, turn right, turn left, stop; the top-line radio cars can do anything a real car can do—and from 100 feet away.

Slot racing is the most popular form of competition, and deservedly: it's almost as exciting as the real thing in full-size race cars. Slot racing got its name from the track, a wood or composition surface carrying a narrow slot which guides the car on the course and feeds current, governed by a hand control, to the electric motor running it. The excitement and delight of slot racing come from the realistic behavior of the cars: take one of them into a bend too fast and it will spin off the circuit, just as a big car would. A good slot car will run at scale speeds of 300 + mph. You can buy a slot car, including motor, for under $5, and you can go up to $50 and more. Serious competitors build their own cars, starting with the chassis, sometimes even winding their own electric motors, finishing with a commercial lightweight body. Slot tracks come in all sizes from tabletop to the big commercial setups that may be eight slots wide and a couple of hundred feet long. If you live in a big town, or near one, you may be able to find one of these tracks. Anyone who sells model race cars can help you find it.

The first slot cars were strictly stock, off-the-shelf items. But the good ones now are not only wickedly fast—loaded witth such refinements as wide-track silicone-treated sponge-rubber rear tires for maximum adhesion and driving power—but beautifully detailed in bodywork: headlights for night racing, for example. The trend is toward absolute realism, even in working cars, and custom-built models are so good that photographs of them alone, showing no other objects with which they can be compared for size, will deceive all but experts.

I have a model of a Mercer Raceabout that will pass this test. It was made for me about fifteen years ago by a British master model builder, Harold Pratley, of London. It is 12¾ inches long, 5½ inches wide, five inches high. The model was made from scratch; there is not a commercial piece in it. Mr. Pratley started with the raw metal, wood, leather, and rubber, and made *everything*. And he had never seen a real Mercer! The car Mr. Pratley duplicated in miniature was my own Mercer, and he worked from hundreds of photographs and detailed measurements I sent to him. The car has working steering, adjustable suspension, moveable gearshift and brake levers, and each handmade bolt in the chassis has a handmade nut on the end of it. The word MERCER is engraved on each of the brass hubcaps, and in proper scale: big on the big rear ones, proportionally smaller in front. There was one flaw in a light mounting on the car when I photographed it for Mr. Pratley, and of course he faithfully duplicated that, too. (No, I'm not going to tell what it was!)

The wood wheels intrigue me more than anything else on the car; each has its twelve hand-carved spokes flawlessly fitted into wooden rims. Even today after more than a decade of steam-heated winters, wet springs, and blistering-hot summers, the wheels show not a trace of warping or checking. They might as well have been made of cast iron. Harold Pratley, by the way, worked in a shop in his house smaller than a respectable closet, and used only the simplest of tools.

Two other great English makers are Rex Hays and Cyril Posthumous. Posthumous has built for Queen Elizabeth, and the Montagu Museum has a collection of Rex Hays race-car models. (One of the most important automobile museums in Europe, the Montagu Museum is in Beaulieu Abbey, Brockenhurst, Hampshire, England.) Jacques Catti and Alain Petit of

France, Manuel Olive Sans of Spain, and Michel Conti of Italy are younger men of equal expertise.

No model maker, past or present, surpasses Henri Baigent in fidelity to the original and attention to detail. The Baigent Ferrari referred to at the beginning of this article is absolutely indistinguishable from the real thing in ordinary photographs, and as for detail . . . the tires and the upholstery are not only identical to the full-scale car's, they're made of the same rubber and leather. The clutch, the gearbox, and the differential all work; the radiator will hold hot water under pressure in its tiny tubes; the steering steers, the disk brakes brake, and the springs and shock absorbers function perfectly. There are thirty lights in the car, turned on and off by subminiature switches. The wire wheel spokes are *tapered,* thinner, finer at the rim ends than at the hubs, a detail I don't recall having seen in any other model. But that's nothing, really, when you consider that the windshield wipers can cope easily with a scale-size tropical rainstorm. Each wiper is driven by an electric motor almost too small to see. I admit that all these things amazed me, but the little thing—little, indeed—that reduced me to a state of mild shock was the speedometer, about a quarter-inch in diameter. The rear wheels are run by an electric motor, and the speedometer needle accurately indicates their speed! At the same time the matching tachometer shows the engine speed. And for night driving, naturally, these two instruments, like all the rest, are individually lighted and rheostat-controlled, from full-bright to dim.

One thing is missing: air conditioning. But that's not Henri Baigent's fault. When the car he copied was built, *Commendatore* Enzo Ferrari wasn't putting air conditioners into his cars. Just heaters. And the heater is there, set to keep the interior of the model at an even 75° F. Now, if Mr. Baigent could just find a Ferrari driver, about four inches tall . . .

—1968

Indy—
The
Golden
Brickyard

When the first Indianapolis 500-Mile Race was run in 1911, the speedway management thoughtfully provided 3000 hitching posts for horses and the house was priced 50 cents, $1, and $1.50. No provision is made for horse-borne trade today and the price spread is $5 to $35. What else is new? The track is still the same flattened oval laid out in 1909, two and a half miles around, the long straights five-eighths of a mile, the short ones one-eighth, the turns one-quarter, banked at nine degrees, twelve minutes, to be safe at 90 miles an hour—but if you don't go through them at 140 now, you're obstructing traffic. They still proudly call it the greatest race in the world, which it isn't, and never call it the oldest closed-circuit race in the world, which they proudly could; a big brass band still plays "Back Home Again in Indiana" before the start and a bugler sounds taps in memory of the forty-six lives the race has taken down the years. Quiet in their cars, thirty-three of the toughest professional athlete-performers alive, from lumpy-knuckled, short-fused veterans of the dirt tracks, happy at the pinnacle of their profession, to ice-cold Scots and Sassenachs jetted in from the Grand Prix other world, more at ease in the cream-and-gold, blood-and-fire ambiance of Monaco, here out of pride and for the loot, all wait to hear the courtly anachronistic command, "Gentlemen, start your engines!" The hundreds of balloons float up from the infield, the cars circle the track once under restraint, a noise like no other noise the world knows is turned on, and they go, hoping, each, to get through the crowded first five miles without signing on for a ten-car lash-up, with the biggest crowd that annually comes together for any purpose in America watching. Indianapolis seems to be indestructible. Here the chariots will always run. A.J. Foyt, a three-time winner, says, "I think of it in the same way I think of the Kentucky Derby: it's the only one. There are other tracks running, sure, and in the next few years there'll be more, and bigger, and better. But this one, this one is Indy." The place has survived wars, depression, neglect and, lately, such assaults as the Foreign Invasion, the Ford Revolution, and the Terrible People-Eating Turbine Car, and still it flourishes. Long live the great round-and-around and the sacred ten-pound bricks!

A bicycle racer started it all, Carl Fisher, a destiny's tot who quit school at twelve to sell papers and candy on the steamcars. He was one of those who, if dropped into Iceland carrying $2 and a box of matches, would come out a millionaire. He saved his pennies, started a bicycle-repair shop, then a store, sweet-talked a big manufacturer into giving him 120 bikes on the never-never, made money and, in the way of the gifted, smelled the horse-less-carriage revolution from afar. He owned the first one in town, went to New York for the 1900 auto show, went back, and started an agency. You raced to sell, in those days, and Fisher bought a big Winton and played the country fairs. His proposition was a flat $500 fee and his big stunt was a match race with a horse. Bring on the fastest horse in the county, he'd say, and we'll go for any distance you like, so long as it's over 200 yards. The horse always outgunned him on early acceleration, always got a good lead, always lost in the last few jumps.

Fisher came to be a pretty good chauffeur, he ran with the likes of Barney Oldfield and Louis Chevrolet, but he knew the money game, as they did not, dying broke for it, both of them.

Mike Todd and P. T. Barnum would have admired Carl Fisher. He knew his time for the way it was. When he wanted to introduce a new-model Stoddard-Dayton, in 1908, he had the car hooked to a big free balloon (he qualified for one of the first U.S. balloon-pilot tickets), put himself behind the wheel, the balloon captain in back, and for three hours drifted over Indianapolis at 1000 feet.

Fisher had been to Europe, he'd seen the fast French and German and Italian cars running; he knew racing was the way to go, but he'd watched Vanderbilt Cup races here, too, and he knew that roadracing wasn't for

America. For one thing, the embattled farmers wouldn't stand still for it; worse, you couldn't sell tickets for a race over fifteen miles of public highway. A track was the thing, and in Indianapolis, which then looked like the center of the industry: Marmon, National, American, Marion, Premier cars were all built there. Fisher pulled in Allison, they sold A. C. Newby and Frank H. Wheeler, and for $72,000 the four of them bought 320 acres of land northwest of town. They called in a New York engineer, P. T. Andrews, and told him to have the plant ready by June of 1909. Andrews signed on 450 men, 300 mules, 150 road scrapers, assorted six-ton and ten-ton rollers, and went to work. The idea was to lay down two inches of gravel, two of crushed limestone, stone dust, and thousands of gallons of liquefied tar.

On June 5, the Speedway ran a balloon race or, rather, the start of one: 3500 people paid to see it and 40,000 watched for free. Fisher flew in the race and got as far as Tennessee.

In August, automobiles ran at the speedway. Under the pounding of hard tires on 90 mph machines, the track surface crumbled like chalk. The back wheels threw stones at slingshot velocities into the plain-glass goggles of following drivers. Work-staggered mule teams were still pouring tar on the track three hours before the first event. Every race worsened the track—cracks, potholes, blinding dust. Charles Merz, driving a National, lost everything, left the course, spun into a crowd, killed two spectators and his mechanic, Claude Kellum—the first Indianapolis fatalities. The race was stopped and the four owners decided to pave. Bricks were best, Andrews told them. So they laid 3,200,000 ten-pound paving bricks in a bed of sand, level to within three-eighths of an inch in twelve feet. The hardhanded Indianapolis bricklayers worked fast: a shift was nine hours then; and in that time, 140,000 bricks would go down. The ace of the crews was timed at 250 an hour. His name, alas, has been lost. He is The Unknown Bricklayer. Finally it was done. A ceremonial "gold" brick (bronze and brass, carburetor-body alloy) was laid at two in the afternoon, Friday, December 17, 1909. James J. Jeffries, the former heavyweight champion of the world, had the first ride. They tried racing right away, in nine-degree weather, and drew 500 paying customers. When it got warmer, Fisher ran a race between an airplane and a propeller-driven car. The plane won. He put on another balloon race. He put on a Memorial Day program of forty-two short races. Then he decided that too much was too much, that there should be only one race a year and that one the longest the public would sit still for: 500 miles, he decided. Every Memorial Day. That was the law as Fisher laid it down, and his writ still runs.

The first real race was 1911's. Ray Harroun won it, an engineer for Marmon who had retired as a driver after he'd won the national A. A. A.

championship in 1910. He was a thoughtful, calculating man, Harroun. He designed the engine, modified the stock chassis into a single-seater (everybody carried a riding mechanic in those days to pump oil, change tires, watch for overtaking cars), and stipulated he'd drive the first 200 miles and the last, letting a relief driver handle the middle hundred. He slip-sticked a decision that a 75 mph average was the fastest he could run with reasonable tire wear. When he heard that other drivers were going to protest his lack of a mechanic, he got an eight-inch by three-inch mirror, welded it to the car with half-inch iron bars. It wasn't the first rearview mirror ever, but it may have been the first on an automobile. The morning of the race, the fuzz cleaned out 200 overnight gate crashers, let in a claimed 80,000 fans (Indy has never released a precise head count), and turned the cars loose. Harroun ran at 75, and when the chargers went by him, he let them go and passed them later in the pits, changing tires. He won by a full lap, at 74.6, and retired for good. He took $14,000. (First was worth $171,227 to A. J. Foyt last year.) The Marmon Wasp (it was first called "The Yellow-Jacket," but that was too much for the headline writers) was retired with him.

It was once fashionable among roadracing enthusiasts to knock Indianapolis as an endeavor requiring little skill, a libel in part built up by Indy people themselves. Bill Vukovich, winner in 1953 and 1954, killed in 1955, a man who lived in a steady slow burn, said, "All you have to do to win is stand on the gas and turn left." There is vastly more to it than that, although it's probably true that it's easier for a Grand Prix driver to do well at Indy, cars equal, than for an Indy driver to do well at, say, the Nürburgring, fourteen miles around, 3000 feet uphill and down, or Monaco, where even a minor mistake, like Bandini's last year at Monaco, can kill you. But the Brickyard seen from the watcher's point of view, not the driver's, has one great advantage over almost every other big-league course in the world: here you can *see* what's happening. How many saw Mike Hawthorn outbrake Fangio on the last corner of the Grand Prix of France in 1953? Who saw Stirling Moss, losing all his brakes at 130 miles an hour just before a bend in the 1957 Mille Miglia, make the corner, and stop the car with wheel and gears? At Indianapolis, almost everyone can see almost everything. In 1912, Ralph DePalma had the race won in the 195th lap, twelve and a half miles to go, when a connecting rod let go in his Mercedes, tore a hole in the crankcase and dumped his oil. He kept on, the car running slower and slower as the engine tightened up, down to 40 miles an hour; he toured around, waiting for it to seize solid—three and a half miles out. He and his mechanic pushed it all the way in, while Joe Dawson, who had been five laps behind when the con rod broke, went by them time after time, flat-out, to get there first. DePalma got $380.42 for that.

When Fisher founded Indianapolis one of his major selling lines was that the track should be a proving ground, a laboratory for "the industry," and this is still said.

The statement isn't true and it's too easy to refute to bother with. When a breakthrough has been made in some quiet laboratory, it is often so flamboyantly demonstrated on the track that it does seem to have been born there. Four-wheel brakes, hydraulic brakes, disk brakes are examples. The year 1913 saw such a breakthrough at Indianapolis. Jules Goux and Georges Boillot, drivers for the French Peugeot factory, and an Italian driver, Paolo Zuccarelli, worked out some ideas for a better racing engine. They took them to a Swiss draftsman, Ernest Henry, got the backing of the factory, and made a team of new cars in 1911. They won almost everywhere they ran. They were radical: small engines, hemispherical combustion chambers, double overhead camshafts, four valves per cylinder. American engines of the day were slow-turning and big—a 1912 Simplex went almost 600 cubic inches. Peugeot sent two cars to the 1913 Indy, and once their drivers, Goux and Zuccarelli, had accepted some local advice on tires and average speed, it was all over, bar the shouting: Goux won, running at 80 miles an hour most of the way, with an occasional spurt at 90. He had killed four bottles of champagne during his pit stops—it was a very hot day—and said afterward, *"Sans le bon vin, je n'aurais pas pu faire la victoire."* It was the last time the winning driver, not the engine, ran on alcohol, and it was the first Indy Revolution. After 1913, the big engines were dead.

The French came back in strength for 1914, Peugeot and Delage sharing the first four places; the first American, Berner Eli Oldfield in a Stutz, fifth, and 4 miles an hour off the pace. A Belgian Excelsior and a British Sunbeam chased him in, but foreign cars never did so well again. Quick to get the message once they'd really been shown, as they would again when the British invaded in 1963, the Americans came back. The Duesenberg brothers, Fred and August, to be, with Harry Miller, among the treetop legends of the golden 1920s, had run a car in 1914. Eddie Rickenbacker, who had appeared as a relief driver in 1911, drove it to tenth.

Engines were smaller in 1915 and, for the first time, starting position in the race proper was set on qualifying time. Ralph DePalma won. He broke another connecting rod, but only three laps from the end, and made it in. The next year, with few foreign entries because of the War, and the race cut to 300 miles, DePalma, irked at the serf-like stature of the drivers vis-à-vis the wealthy promoters, asked for appearance, or starting, money. Fisher was appalled at what looked to him the thin entering wedge of socialism and refused indignantly. Dario Resta took the race in a Peugeot. (The 1911 Peugeot was the most-copied design in automotive history: engineers took it apart, measured each part to the thousandth of an inch, and built duplicates for Vauxhall, Straker-Squire, Humber, Premier, Delage,

Opel, Nagant, Aquila Italiana, and the eminent authority Griffith Borgeson, author of *The Golden Age of the American Racing Car,* wrote "[the Peugeot] engine and chassis were the textbooks for Harry Miller and Fred Offenhauser.")

During World War I the track was used as a military aviation post and for farming.

Indiana patriots, still hot-blooded from the war to make the world safe for democracy, made noises about the irreverence of sports on Memorial Day, and the race was updated to May 31. (In 1922, the local American Legion stuffed a bill through the state legislature to the same effect; but the governor vetoed it.) A Peugeot owned by the track, Howdy Wilcox up, won in 1919 before an audience that included Eddie Rickenbacker, a great war hero now, the number-one U.S. fighter pilot, his unblinking 1000-yard stare ranging on things other than racedriving. (A few years later, he bought the place.) Three men were killed in 1919, and another, Elmer Shannon, nearly died in one of the freak accidents that racing produces every decade or so: running ahead of him, Louis Chevrolet lost a wheel and the bare spindle severed the timing wire on the bricks; one end of it whipped around and razored an artery in Shannon's throat. In the time it took him to get to his pit, he nearly bled to death.

The Mad Twenties may really have been, as they're so often called, the golden years of U. S. sport, days of titans—Dempsey, Ruth, Jones, Tilden. They were surely big years at the Brickyard. Gaston Chevrolet, one of the monumentally unlucky Chevrolet brothers, had a good day that day in May 1920, winning in a Monroe, a Louis Chevrolet project engineered by Cornelius van Ranst; but the best part of the decade was to belong to Fred and Augie Duesenberg and, most of all, to Harry Miller among the builders, and to drivers still as well remembered: Jimmy Murphy, Tommy Milton, Peter DePaolo, Harry Hartz, Ray Keech, Leon Duray, Lou Meyer, Lou Moore, and Frank Lockhart. Lockhart was the legend, a name as big as Jack Dempsey's, if over a far shorter time span.

Lockhart won the "500" the first time he drove it, in a car he didn't know, on a wet track. He was a dirt-track driver out of California, a tremendous natural talent, a near illiterate who never really learned to spell but almost certainly had genius, if genius is the obsessive drive to do superbly well something one has never been taught to do. Robert Millikan, Nobel Prize winner, told Lockhart's mother that her son was a born scientist who should at all costs be given a college education. Mrs. Lockhart, living by sewing, couldn't see how to make it. Lockhart had the real obsession: he never played with other children; instead, he took things apart and put them together again. When he was on his own, he had no time for anything but the machine. He married the only girl he ever dated. He had never heard the crushing dictum "If you won't sell your mother to buy paints, you are no true artist," but he believed it. He made his mother hock the family furniture to buy tires. He drove flat-out; sometimes he would kick the car into an entering slide yards before a corner. In the formal sense, his ignorance about engineering was profound, but he made many mechanical innovations in his cars; indeed, two 91-cubic-inch Millers that he set up were the most successful of even that exalted make. He won everywhere. He was so tense before a race that he usually vomited. He broke track and straight-line records all over the place. He wanted the Land Speed Record, held then by H. O. D. Segrave of England at 203 mph, and in February 1928 he went to Daytona with a car of his own basic design, two linked Miller engines stuffed into a chassis that was tiny, compared with the monsters the British used. The Stutz company put up most of the money, so the car was called the Stutz Black Hawk. At something around 225 mph he ran into rain, lost visibility for an instant, hit wet sand, and lost the car. It flipped end for end, rolled into the Atlantic, landed on its wheels. There was a fair surf up. Fred Moscovics of Stutz got to him first, held his head out of the water to save him from drowning until he could be lifted from the car. He wasn't really hurt, and in April he was back at Daytona. He wanted the L. S. R. not only for itself but for what it could bring him: money, muscle, room to move, leverage to shove himself upward. His mother, sick and penniless, wired him for $10. He wired back:

> "MA I HAVE THE WORLD BY THE HORNS. YOU'LL NEVER HAVE TO PUSH
> A NEEDLE AGAIN. I'LL NEVER HAVE TO WORK ANYMORE."

He blew a tire at about 220. His body landed at his wife's feet.

The pattern changed in the twenties. The accessory people, the spark plug, carburetor, nut-and-bolt makers, began to bring in money: $23,550 in prizes in 1920, as against $5275 the year before. Finding a potentially winning car wasn't any more a matter of cut-and-try: you needed a Duesenberg or a Miller or a Frontenac-Ford. During World War II, the supremacy of foreign cars had vanished. The Americans had evolved a specialist vehicle for round tracks, superbly conceived and fined down just for that. It was good for nothing else. Suspension was hopeless, and on the Indianapolis bricks, drivers took a fearful pounding, sometimes they and the mechanics taped themselves belly to shoulders; the brakes were good for three hard stops in succession at most, and what of it, they were only for coming into the pits; you couldn't downshift at speed. But the engines were marvels: when top-rank U.S. passenger engines put out .75 horsepower per cubic inch, a Miller would do 2.75! It was Miller who originated, or at any rate said loudest and most contemptuously, "Detroit Iron."

Racing people said of Harry Armenius Miller that he couldn't design a rattrap by himself, but they said, too, that he was an instinctive master who knew inside him how it should be done, who could see it there in his head, even if he couldn't do the mathematics. He was a carburetor man, a swinger who loved money but hated keeping it, a man who could attract talented people and bind them to him. Fred Offenhauser worked for Miller and Eddie Offutt, and there had been a day in the summer of 1919 when Leo Goossen had walked into Miller's little plant in Los Angeles. Leo Goossen, *the* American race-car designer, a world eminence, a quiet man, to the background born, whose hand was laid on every U.S. racing engine in the line that runs straight Miller-Offenhauser-Meyer/Drake-Ford. Goossen was a consultant on the Ford racing-engine project, and the Ford engines are assembled by Lou Meyer.

Miller's first success came with an engine built to the specifications of Tommy Milton and Ira Vail and drawing liberally in concept and detail from Duesenberg and Peugeot. (They took him blueprints and parts.) Jimmy Murphy won at Indy with it in 1922.

Miller shared an outstanding characteristic with Ettore Bugatti (who complimented him by plagiarism: Bugatti took his first overhead-camshaft design from Miller's layout). Like Bugatti, Miller demanded that his engines and his automobiles be esthetically beautiful as well as mechanically efficient. A Miller race car could be identified as far as it could be seen. It looked like nothing else on wheels, lean, airy, light, purposeful. Griffith Borgeson, who restored a Miller with his own hands in the 1950s, marveled at what he found: every part an exercise in metal sculpture. Miller would not waste weight even on a gearshift knob by crudely turning it from the solid. His were hollow, thin-walled castings! He sold his cars for oddly flat-rate prices: $5000 for an engine, $10,000 for a rear-wheel-drive car, $15,000 for a front-drive. He would see the day, in 1929, when two of his cars ran first and second at Indianapolis and were followed home by twenty-five others. Miller won Indy a dozen times. If he had lived, he'd have seen a day when every car of the thirty-three ran an Offenhauser, the Miller's direct descendant. But Miller couldn't make money as fast as he could spend it, and the Depression found him with no cushion. He went bankrupt. Fred Offenhauser took over the shop, and in time Lou Meyer and Dale Drake had it from Offenhauser, but it was really all the same engine, the Miller engine. It was all downhill from then until he died, in 1943, alone except for Eddie Offutt. He had forbidden his wife to live with him, because he couldn't bear her looking at him: he had cancer of the face. She had loved him, but she had been afraid of him, too, in a way: Harry Miller was clairvoyant and prescient. He could give her whole phrases she had been about to speak, he could predict death, and often did until, finally, spooked, she forbade him. Once he said to Leo Goossen, showing him one of his crude but startlingly pertinent drawings, "Leo, *I* don't do these things. I get help. Somebody is telling me what to do." Perhaps. But if they were reading him the future, they were holding out on him.

Louis Chevrolet was another wildly capable man and fatally flawed, too. He should have died a multimillionaire. He was gifted, full of drive, and he could work good workmen into the ground. He gave his name to the Chevrolet car—it was detail-designed by Etienne Planche—when W. C. Durant was running General Motors. Chevrolet was a big man, quiet and gentle, but he had a fierce temper and when he quarreled with Durant— who may have tempted him deliberately—he not only broke off the relationship, he sold Durant all his stock. When he fell out with his next sponsor, Albert Champion of the spark plugs, he beat him half to death. He was not only hot tempered—he even broke with his brother Arthur, finally—he was unlucky. Businessmen gulled him easily. His timing was terrible: he set up an aircraft-engine business with Glenn Martin, only to run into the Depression. He turned over his interest to Martin, who went on to glory. Chevrolet had been not only one of the great constructors of his time—Monroe, Frontenac, Chevrolet—he had been one of the topmost drivers, but he didn't know how to make use of himself. In 1933, he was working as a mechanic in a Chevrolet plant. He died in 1941, heartbroken.

Fred Duesenberg, born in Germany and brought up in Iowa, was a self-taught mechanic at seventeen and ran his own bicycle-manufacturing plant at twenty-one. (He raced his bikes, and held the two-mile and three-mile records.) He and his brother August fell naturally into automobiles and by 1907 were building a 2-cylinder car, called the Mason after the man who backed them. The brothers ran four Masons in the "500" race of 1913, one of them finishing ninth. The next year, Fred and August Duesenberg were on their own in their own plant in St. Paul, Minnesota. Their racing cars began to be noticed, and on the side they built excellent marine engines. They built aircraft engines, too. During World War I they were commissioned by the government to build the Bugatti 16-cylinder aero engine, a design failure. They built one of their own that produced a reliable 800 horsepower, but the war ended before it could go into production. By 1920, the straight-8-cylinder engine that was Fred Duesenberg's hallmark was ready to show in a passenger car, and the firm was solidly set up in Indianapolis. Duesenberg brought out a supercharged car in 1920, reintroducing a thoroughly all-American idea. The supercharger was invented by the Roots brothers of Connersville, Indiana, in 1859 and was used, in a modified form, on the Chadwick passenger car in 1906. Superchargers, or blowers, became standard wear on Duesenbergs and Millers. They have begun to show again: the eight Offenhausers that ran in 1967 had them and there will be supercharged Fords running this year.

Tommy Milton took the world Land Speed Record in a Duesenberg in 1920, at 156 miles an hour; and the next year, Jimmy Murphy won the French Grand Prix for Duesenberg, the first time an American car and driver had done it. (Murphy then bought the car from the Duesenbergs, stuffed a Miller engine into its chassis, and proceeded to outdistance the 1922 "500" field.) Duesenbergs won at Indy in 1924, 1925, and 1927. Those were the great years. But the Duesenbergs, like the Chevrolets, were poor businessmen in a trade in which even good businessmen fared poorly, and the company failed. The Duesenberg name and talents were bought by E. L. Cord (Auburn-Cord-Duesenberg), whose interests lay in passenger, not racing, cars. And it is for passenger cars that the Duesenbergs are best remembered now, although they made only a few more than 1000. Of the Model A Duesenberg, their first effort, 667 were built, and 470 of the great S and SJ models, priced at $14,750 to $20,000 and to this day among the most sought-after automobiles ever made in America. In 1930, the Duesenberg brothers went separate ways. Fred died after a crash in the Pennsylvania mountains in 1932. August stayed on with Auburn-Cord-Duesenberg. The great Mormon Meteors—record-breaking cars run on the Utah salt flats by Ab Jenkins—were from his hands. He died in 1955.

Racing broke some people like dry sticks, but some laughed and loved it, like Wilbur Shaw, or loved it without laughing much, like Eddie Rickenbacker, and made it pay like slot machines. Wilbur Shaw laughed, but for all that he was a charming and civilized man, it was just as well to laugh with him, not at him. He came to the Bricks in 1927 in a Miller, ran fourth. He went on to be a fixture. He won in 1937 and 1939 and 1940, the last two times in a Maserati, the first foreign car to come first at Indy since 1919. Shaw was a charger. In 1931, he ran a Duesenberg airborne over the wall on the northeast turn. He walked back into the Speedway and took over another Duesenberg, nearly flipped it, too. When his new riding mechanic flinched, Shaw yelled, "You think that was something, you should have been with me last time." Eddie Rickenbacker took over Indianapolis the year Shaw first ran, when Carl Fisher finally retired, keeping it as it was, keeping the staff, the legend-wrapped T. E. "Pop" Myers, who ran the place, Steve Hannagan, the press agent; and when Rickenbacker gave over, in 1945, to Anton Hulman, Jr., who still owns the plant, it was Shaw who set up the deal and served as president and general manager until 1954, when a private plane in which he and three others were flying from Detroit iced up and went in.

Shaw had seen a lot of it go by, he saw the Miller-Duesenberg era give over to the Offenhauser-powered roadsters. The year he went over the wall, a Cummins diesel ran the whole way without a stop on thirty-three gallons of furnace oil and finished thirteenth. He was second in 1933, when the iron-faced Rickenbacker put down another driver's rebellion. Five men died that year, two in 1934, four in 1935. Sometimes a car would come back, next year, and kill again. Sometimes a 50-cent bit would fall off a car and smash the driver; sometimes luck would spin around: in 1941, Shaw *knew* he'd win, but in putting out a big garage fire that year, firemen washed the chalked markings off his spare wheels and he couldn't pick out a bad one he knew was among the twelve, hadn't time to retest them. A wheel broke in the race, put him into the wall, and spilled fifty gallons of methanol all around him. For some reason, it didn't flash, a good thing, since Shaw had three vertebra fractures, was paralyzed from the waist down. By this time, the cars weren't going by their right names, they were Something Specials, whatever the men who put up the money wanted to call them.

World War II came and went, leaving the place weed-grown and ragged. Strange cars came up, like Lou Fageol's twin-engine, and the utterly unlucky but much-loved Novi cars, first run by Lew Welch of Novi, Michigan (tollgate Number 6 on the Grand River Plank Road out of Detroit). Mauri Rose, a careful, planning man, a superb driver, came up, won three times, and went away whole and with the money. The drivers tried to get 40 percent of the gate receipts, which other tracks were paying them, but Shaw said no and won in the end, as Fisher and Rickenbacker had. They started giving the pace car to the winner. Great ones died, like "Shorty" Cantlon and Ralph Hepburn. (Heat exhaustion killed a driver in 1953, Carl Scarborough.) New hard-try owners like J. C. Agajanian came up, drivers like Bill Vukovich appeared from nowhere and ran wild. Anton Hulman, who doesn't need to make money on Indy, plowed hundreds of thousands back, in new stands, tunnels under the track, asphalt paving on the whole circuit except for a ritual yard-wide strip at the finish. A. J. Foyt and Rodger Ward, and Parnelli Jones, who were really to take money out of Indy, showed from the minor leagues. Offenhauser made all the engines, Watson, Epperly, Kuzma, Kurtis, Lesovsky built the chassis. The form had been stabilized into the "roadster," beginning when George Salih, chief mechanic on Lee Wallard's winning car in 1951, modified an Offy engine to run lying on its side instead of straight up. This gave a lower center of gravity and smaller frontal area.

Came 1961, the golden anniversary year. The definitive history of the race was published, *500 Miles to Go,* by Al Bloemker. Jack Brabham, a Grand Prix driver out of England via Australia, shipped in a Cooper G. P. car running a rear-mounted Coventry Climax engine. When he tested, he had roadrace tires on and his engine was 85 cubic inches smaller than the Indy type. He lapped at a steady 145.144. The handwriting was up there, but few saw it. One who did was among the owners of the fleet of big standard Offy-engined roadsters, Art Lathrop. He said, "Gentlemen, you are looking at a million dollars' worth of junk." In the 1961 race, Brabham finished ninth. He wasn't bothered by the fact that his car hadn't been designed with a left-turn weight bias, like all the others. He could make ground easily on them in the turns, but on the straights, when the big 4-cylinder Offys started to put out, he just didn't have the power. The track itself gave him no problems. He'd come off the back-country dirt tracks of Australia, he'd driven the wickedly demanding Grand Prix courses in Europe. All a driver needed to beat the roadsters, he knew, was a Grand Prix chassis with enough engine stuffed into its rear end.

The same idea had come to someone else: Daniel Sexton Gurney, a young California driver who was uniquely equipped to take the large view. Gurney had started driving sports cars early in the 1950s, had got a good ride in a Ferrari in 1957, and the next year ran at LeMans. By 1961, Gurney's tall (6′2″) and rather startlingly good-looking presence was a fixture on the Grand Prix circuit, and not only there. Alone among Americans, he is equally facile with sports cars, Grand Prix, track cars and stocks. He could bridge the then tremendous gap between the Indy and the Grand Prix people. It really *was* a gap, and something more: hostility and disdain were the watchwords in each camp. The Grand Prix drivers felt that theirs was the classic form of the sport, the form in which it had been born, driving on *roads* or winding circuits formed like roads, a new and different one every week, usually in a different country, from South Africa around the world through Europe to Australia. The Grand Prix or Formula I car, they believed, demanded a skill the American track drivers knew nothing about. The Americans, for their part, thought the G.P. people a gaggle of esthetes in "sporty cars" who waved each other through the corners and would cave in the first time they came against hard-nosed wheel-to-wheel competition. Said the G.P. faction in riposte, "And these are drivers who run for the pits if there's a sprinkle of rain!" (Even a tropical cloudburst won't stop a G. P. race.) European drivers who had come to Indy down the years hadn't fared well: Rudolf Caracciola hit a bird; Alberto Ascari had a wheel collapse; Nino Farina and Juan Manuel Fangio tried with poor cars. A special race at Monza in 1957 that brought the two factions together for the first time did nothing to make them all buddies together. The race had been set up to make all concessions to the Americans: run on a banked track, counterclockwise, in heats to allow repair on the cars, called in case of rain, and so on. Needing nothing but straightline power, the Americans won as they pleased.

But in 1962, the British designer Colin Chapman, taking up the rear-engine design John Cooper had revived, built a monocoque Lotus, very light, very strong, incredibly handy, and full of sticking power. His number-one driver was Jimmy Clark, champion of the world and probably the greatest G. P. driver of all time—he has won twenty-five G.P. races, more than anyone else ever. But Chapman's Coventry Climax engines, built to the International Formula I, could not deliver the 400-odd horsepower of an Offy. The answer, Gurney thought, would be a Ford. Ford alone of U. S. makers was interested in racing. In 1962, Gurney brought Chapman together with Ford in the persons of Leo Beebe and Lee Iacocca, aggressive and forward-looking top-rankers in the executive echelon.

The Chapman-Gurney proposition was simple: the rear-engined car was now the world standard, whether the moguls of the Indianapolis establishment knew it or not (they didn't): the light, immensely strong Lotus, running on sophisticated G. P. suspension, could outstick any Indy roadster in the turns, and a 350-horsepower engine, running on gasoline, could beat the 400-hp Offys that burned methanol and nitromethane at a much higher miles-per-gallon rate. On this factor alone, the Lotus would save a good deal of time on pit stops. In the autumn of 1962, Clark won the Grand Prix of the United States at Watkins Glen and then took the car to Indianapolis for testing. Leo Levine quotes him in *The Dust and the Glory*, a remarkable history of Ford racing:

"Remember, the car had come straight from Watkins Glen so it was running on normal roadracing tires and was not set up for left-hand turns only and the banking. I did about 100 laps on that occasion and I remember thinking that it was all a bit dull. My fastest lap of 143 mph average made most people sit up and take notice but what made them even more interested was the speed at which I was taking the turns. The Indy cars rely on their acceleration between the bends to give them their high lap times and the fastest time an Indy car had recorded in the turns was something like 138 mph. Our Lotus was doing over 140 in the corners."

The project was put in hand at Ford. It was madly complicated, unbelievably difficult. Only the merest handful of the tens of thousands of Ford workers were concerned, and the priorities on the Indianapolis effort were not the highest. There were forty-eight-hour workdays, hopeless frustrations spiraling on endlessly, temper explosions. When they did get a Lotus to Indianapolis for testing, they had one engine for it and it wasn't complete, pieces had to be cannibalized from stock Ford Fairlanes to make it go. But it did go, 146 for Clark, who then had to jet back to Europe to meet a racing commitment, 150.501 for Gurney, the second-fastest average in speedway history. The establishment owners and drivers, fortunes in money, total careers tied up in the Offy-engined roadsters, were not happy. They didn't like anything about the car, including the color of it, green. Indianapolis people are superstitious, and green, like women in the pits or peanuts, was held to be deadly bad luck for one and all. You had to get killed if you drove a green car. Standing next to Parnelli Jones and A. J. Foyt, Jimmy Clark, small, slight, boyish, didn't even *look* like a driver. His soaring reputation everywhere else race cars run meant nothing.

When qualifying time came around in May 1963, there were 200,000 people watching. Clark qualified his Lotus, toylike beside the big roadsters, at 149.7 and Gurney did a hair less, then they ran for the jet to Europe and the G. P. of Monaco. Parnelli Jones and A. J. Foyt ran their roadsters faster, 151 and 150. Came the day. Jim Hurtubise, in a Novi, ran away at the start, but Parnelli Jones came up hard and took over. Fifty miles into the race he was twenty-two seconds ahead. Gurney and Clark were tenth and eleventh and apparently content to stay there, but after the sixty-seventh lap, when Jones and Roger McCluskey, who'd succeeded him on top, had made pit stops, Clark and Gurney were first and second. At lap ninety-three, Gurney had to come in for tires, an unlooked-for eventuality apparently due to a bad chassis setup. He was in the pits for a long forty-two seconds. Clark came in for fuel and another very long pit stop: thirty-three seconds, but he came out second to Jones. Gurney had dropped to ninth. Jones came in again for more fuel (the alcohol-burning Offys had to make three stops) and as he went out, an accident brought out the yellow caution flag, holding cars in position. The flags were out several times during the race and Clark was interpreting the Indianapolis rule literally: reduced speed and no passing *anywhere* on the track. (In Europe, yellow means caution only at the site of the accident or whatever has brought it out.) But Indy drivers habitually do pass other cars under the yellow if they're notably slower, and they do run fast down the backstretch where official observation isn't so tight. Jones made time under the yellow, but when he came out after his third and last fuel stop, Clark was only eleven seconds behind and charging. He got the interval down to 4.5 seconds on the 178th lap, with twenty-two still to go. Then The Great 1963 Oil Hassle started.

The drivers had been told that anyone dropping oil on the track would be summarily black-flagged, brought in, and when Jim Hurtubise's car had shown oil, it was done. Now Jones's roadster began to show a clear oil leak out of an outboard-mounted tank. Everyone saw it. Colin Chapman and J. C. Agajanian, Jones's sponsor, got to Harlan Fengler, chief steward, practically simultaneously, Chapman demanding the black flag, Agajanian denouncing the very idea. It was a rough spot for Fengler, the Ford Motor Company on one side and Indy's biggest, one of the mainstays of the establishment, on the other. Before he made up his mind, someone pointed out that Jones was no longer throwing oil, because the level in the tank had dropped below the end of the crack it was leaking through. They let him run on and he won by thirty-nine seconds. Clark was second and Gurney brought the other Ford in seventh, held down by his tire change and by long pit stops. Clark said afterward that he thought he had been beaten by the yellow flag and the oil. Chapman figured Clark had lost fifty-nine seconds under the yellow flag. "We should have lapped Parnelli," Clark said. Cries of "Foul!" rang through the land. The veteran Eddie Sachs, who felt that both he and Roger McCluskey had spun out on Jones's oil, called the winner a liar to his face and when, on Jones's request, he repeated it, Jones knocked him down. (Later, Sachs, a volatile and amusing man, obligingly posed for photographers flat on his back with a little black flag in his mouth.) But the point had been made. Rear engines were mandatory and the Offy roadsters were headed for the edge of oblivion's cliff. Jimmy Clark could drive with anybody and would take all but the topmost as he pleased. And a major American manufacturer was in big-league racing for the first time in decades.

A year isn't a long time as race-car building goes, but for the 1964 Indy, six rear-engined Offenhausers showed up, with eighteen of the old roadsters, three of the perennial Novis, and six Ford-powered cars. The Lotus entrants, of course, were Clark and Gurney; Ford engines had been made available as well to Bobby Marshman, Eddie Johnson, Dave MacDonald, and Eddie Sachs. (At first, the V8 engines cost $31,400 apiece to build; later, Ford got it down to $22,800.) They were flying: Clark and Marshman had qualified at 158 and 157 and had the two top places; Gurney was in the second row at 154 beside Foyt and Jones, who had chosen to stick with the roadsters, at 154 and 155.

When the flag fell, Clark, long known in Europe as the fastest starter in racing, grabbed a 100-yard lead, with Marshman behind him. The rest of the pack, coming through the turn at the head of the straight, was led by Dave MacDonald, driving his first Indianapolis race. He was trying too hard, he spun, hit the inside wall, burst into flame, rocketed back into the straight in front of Eddie Sachs, who had nowhere to go and probably never got his foot on the brake. Sachs's fuel tank went up in a yellow ball of flame and a black mushroom of smoke towered into the sky to be seen miles away. Eddie Sachs died instantly, MacDonald, burned over his entire body, lived an hour. His father said later that MacDonald hadn't liked the car's handling and hadn't wanted to drive it. Many mourned Sachs, too. He had lived for Indianapolis. One year, sitting in his car before the start, he was in tears. He wanted one win, then he'd quit. He had been second in 1961, third in 1962.

An hour and forty-five minutes later, the twenty-six cars that could still run started in the order they'd been in when MacDonald spun. Bobby Marshman, running at 156 mph, challenged Clark for the lead and Clark let him go. On the thirty-ninth lap, diving for the infield to avoid a car ahead, Marshman knocked the oil plug off his engine and that finished him. Clark stayed in the lead for eight laps, until one of his tires threw a tread, wrecking his rear suspension. Parnelli Jones took over and led until his car caught fire in a fuel stop, and A. J. Foyt, in what he called his antique roadster, ran on to take the money: $153,650. The unlucky Dan Gurney had been pulled in in fear that his tires, too, would let go.

Seventeen rear-engine Fords ran in 1965. Jimmy Clark and Colin Chapman and Ford now had everything sorted out. They were running on the right rubber, they knew the rules and every hairline local interpretation of them, they had hired the fastest pit crew in the world, the legendary Woods brothers off the Southern stock-car tracks, and they had even designed a fuel nozzle for the required gravity system that actually accelerated the stuff as it poured through. Clark, who had qualified at 160, went as he liked, almost cruising—he drove hard only twice, and then briefly—and won at 151. Parnelli Jones, swerving his car from side to side to pump the last drops of fuel to the engine from a nearly bone-dry tank, came second, and the remarkably talented Mario Andretti, running for the first time in the "500," was third.

All but nine cars in the field of thirty-three were Ford-engined in 1966, which saw a spectacular eleven-car pile-up on the first lap, with no one hurt but all eleven cars out of the race. After the restart, an hour and forty minutes later, Andretti led, then Clark, who hit oil and spun. Lloyd Ruby led in one of Dan Gurney's new All-American Racers until the 166th lap. The Scot Grand Prix driver Jackie Stewart ran in front until his car lost its oil pressure with ten laps remaining. Graham Hill, a former world champion, came in to win, with Clark second. There were five Fords in the first six places and the name was up forever beside Duesenberg, Miller, Offenhauser.

The year of the Fiery Dragon was 1967. Gas-turbine cars had come to Indianapolis before: John Zink in 1962, Norman Demler in 1966. Neither made the race. The turbine engine, invented by Air Commodore Frank Whittle of the Royal Air Force in 1940, put the piston engine out of business as far as high-speed aircraft use is concerned. Running at a constant speed, in high altitudes where it is most efficient, the turbine, in its jet form, is supreme. Compared with a piston engine, it's very simple: it takes air in at the front, compresses it with one water-wheel-like device, mixes fuel with the air, ignites the mixture, which blasts out the rear end with great force, using some energy on the way to spin a bladed wheel that drives the compressor wheel up front. Reaction moves the plane. A gas turbine works the same way, excepting that, to put it crudely, most of the power is used to spin the second turbine wheel, which can be hooked to a propeller, or to wheels, and the jet effect is negligible. As long ago as 1950, the Rover Company of England ran a gas-turbine automobile 150 miles an hour and even competed successfully at Le Mans. The United States Automobile

Club, anticipating the eventual appearance of turbines at the Brickyard, had laid down regulations for them, including the vital one of annulus, or effective air-inlet size, which governs the amount of power a gas turbine can produce. This was set at twenty-three square inches; and in 1967, Andy Granatelli, a former driver, speed-shop owner, and perennial Indianapolis sponsor, entered a gas-turbine single-seater under Studebaker STP sponsorship, with Parnelli Jones nominated to drive it. The engine was by Pratt & Whitney, the designer a British-trained engineer, Ken Wallis. At first, no one in the establishment was much impressed: previous turbine entries had done nothing and Granatelli had never had a winner. The fact that Jones was up to drive shook some people, though, since he could have almost any car he wanted. Then the word got around that his fee was a flat $100,000, win or lose, and so there were those who thought he was doing it for the money. But when qualifying time came around, everyone who could hold a watch *knew* why he was doing it: barring accident to the car or somebody shooting him as he sat in it, Jones was going to win. The STP had four-wheel drive, a modification of the British Ferguson system, so that the power went to the track from everywhere, not just the front or back wheels alone; it stuck in the curves as if it were nailed down, and Jones could pass anyone he liked anywhere he chose. And, the sad story ran, he was running at 65 percent of the available power.

The horsepower figure on the STP car—it was painted a Day-Glo orangey red that practically burned out the eyeballs—was cited as 550, nothing extraordinary and less than many other cars. But its torque, or effective twisting power, was 1000 foot-pounds, about three times that of the Ford and Offenhauser engines running against it. Further, while a piston engine has to be brought up to near-maximum revolutions per minute before it delivers its maximum torque, a gas-turbine engine of the free-turbine type can apply maximum torque from a standstill, within a second. There was nothing for the other drivers to do but hope the thing broke.

It went that way. Parnelli Jones jumped into the lead immediately, sitting comfortably alongside his big blowtorch, running almost in silence compared with the piston cars, and stayed there until the race was called for rain before it was well under way. For the first time ever, it wasn't restarted until the next day, when Jones ran in front monotonously, except for one little spin and two pit stops, straight to lap 197, when a $6 ball bearing in the transmission let go and sent it to the barn—probably forever. A. J. Foyt, riding a Ford rear-engined Coyote of his own and his father's making, was lying a canny second. He had a sure win, but he had a premonition, too: he was suddenly sure he was going to see another multicar pile-up. He backed off to a crawl, around 100 miles an hour, and when five cars piled up in front of him on the finishing straight, he threaded through them and went to get the $171,000.

Soon enough afterward, the U. S. A. C. announced a change in gas-turbine specifications: a reduction in the annulus area from twenty-three to fifteen square inches. Granatelli was outraged. No engine of that size exists, he said, and his own could not be modified and would not be competitive if it were. A scrapper and a persuasive man, Granatelli jumped for the rostrum and made The Case of the Outlawed Turbine into a cause celebre. It was, he said, a simple matter of the establishment banning what they knew they couldn't beat. But the U. S. A. C. wouldn't give him an inch, much less eight square inches, and he went to court. Win or lose, he says, he'll be back this Memorial Day with turbines. So will others. Probably most competitive will be a team of two turbines sponsored by Goodyear and Carroll Shelby and designed by Ken Wallis. They, too, will be four-wheel driven, and 1967 World Champion Dennis Hulme and Bruce McLaren have been nominated for the rides. If one of them runs as Parnelli Jones ran, someone will say, looking at the serried squadrons of rear-engined Fords, "Gentlemen, you are looking at a million dollars' worth of junk!" and the big wheel will start around one more time.

—1968

The Wonderful Chain-Gang Car

When I was living in England a couple of years ago I saw an advertisement in the "For Sale" section of one of the automobile magazines: "Chain-gang TT Rep. 'Nash, recently tuned Blackburne, B.R.G., concours. £1500 o.n.o. ALD 5693 after 6 P.M."

Reading this ad I became excited, because translated out of British sports-car shorthand, it offered for sale one of the rarest and most unusual automobiles in the world: "Five-chain drive Tourist Trophy Replica [a model named after the famous race in the Isle of Man] Frazer Nash two-seater sports car with a Blackburne engine [one of the best] in excellent mechanical condition, painted British Racing Green [the national race-car color, usually a dark bottle-green]. The car is in such good overall condition that it is capable of winning a *concours d'élégance* [a kind of automobile beauty contest in which entries are judged for originality, cleanliness, perfection of finish, woodwork, upholstery, and so on]. Price 1500 pounds [then $4200] or a near offer [the owner was willing to bargain a little]."

Promptly at six o'clock I dialed ALD 5693 and asked if the car were still available.

"Yes, it's unsold," said the man who answered. "However, three people have made appointments to see it this evening, and I daresay I shall have sold it by nine o'clock. The motorcar is under covenant, and since your accent tells me you are an American, I could not consider an offer from you. I'm sorry." He hung up.

I was not surprised. I had heard the same thing before. I could even sympathize with the thinking behind it. After all, in the whole period of its manufacture, from about 1924 to 1938, only 348 Frazer Nash cars were built. They were assembled virtually by hand, each to the buyer's specification, and they used a drive system no other car has had. The surviving cars, approximately 150 of them, are thought of as national treasures by British sports-car devotees. When a Frazer Nash changes hands, the new owner is nearly always asked to sign a covenant, or agreement, promising not to allow the car to leave the United Kingdom.

I was still determined to own a Frazer Nash. It was on the list of most-desirable cars I had made up years ago, with the Type 50 Bugatti, the Super-Sport Morgan Three-Wheeler, and the Mercer Raceabout. I kept on looking, making inquiries, reading advertisements, and I finally did find my Frazer Nash. It had been taken completely to pieces, stripped almost to the last nut and bolt, and then left for seven years in a damp, earth-floored garage. This basket case of a car (much of it actually *was* in baskets) came on the market only because the owner had killed himself (in despair over ever getting it together again, someone morbidly suggested). Bids had been invited and mine was highest. However, when I spoke to the estate executor on the telephone, instantly betraying my non-British origin, he asked if I would be good enough to step down in favor of the next-highest bidder, a Londoner. I refused. I was then told that, in that case, I would have to sign a covenant binding me never to take the Frazer Nash outside England, Ireland, Scotland, and Wales. I refused that, too, and there the matter stood. I owned a car I couldn't have. Finally the head of the Frazer Nash section of The Vintage Car Club, a good friend, came to my rescue, and the covenant was modified: I was not to remove the car "permanently" from the U.K. So far, I haven't removed it at all: it's in Bedfordshire, divided between a machine shop and a body shop. As this is written it's entering the third year of restoration! However, some day I'll have it, looking like new with its rosewood dashboard, red leather upholstery, black paint glistening with genuine ground-up fish scales. (My 'Nash was built in 1933, and that's how its "black pearl" paint was made!) Will I ever sell it? Absolutely not.

Why are Frazer Nash owners so obsessed with their cars? Sometimes they seem worse, even, than Bugatti owners. What makes a 'Nash so desirable?

At root, it's because Frazer Nash cars, like Bugattis, have definite, strongly marked personalities. They are *peculiar*. They don't feel or act like other automobiles. They behave oddly sometimes. Like a really good horse, a 'Nash demands skill and respect from the driver, and if these aren't given, the car may take control, go its own way. For example, because of the peculiarity of its drive system, if you go fast into a corner in a 'Nash and take your foot off the accelerator, the car may go straight off the road, showing a strong understeer condition in which the front wheels won't hold. But, properly handled, Frazer Nashes are rewarding, safe, and fast. They're handsome, too, most models having outside exhaust pipes, an outside gearshift lever, and hand brake. The 'Nash's squared-off hood may be held down by wide leather straps, it probably has two small racing windshields tucked behind the main one, and its steering wheel is big and businesslike. And the 'Nash is rare: I don't suppose there are a dozen in the United States.

This intriguing vehicle began as something called a cycle-car. Around 1900 there began in England and in France a vogue for a kind of small automobile, usually a roadster, or sometimes one-passenger only, with a very light body (wood-framed perhaps), propelled by a motorcycle engine driving the rear wheels (or one of them) by chain or belt. This device was called a cycle-car. It was impractical, but fun. One of the best was the G-N, for Godfrey-Nash—H. R. Godfrey and Archibald Frazer-Nash. (The man's name is hyphenated; the car's is not.) A good cycle-car, because it combined lots of power with little weight, had formidable acceleration, and racing G-Ns are still in use in England today. The G-N flourished until 1922, and on it was evolved the chain-drive system which was to make the Frazer Nash unique among full-size sports cars. It is worth looking into, and it works like this:

The drive is taken from the engine through a clutch in the ordinary way, but the usual gearbox just behind the clutch is missing. The drive shaft ends a little way short of the rear axle, where it is geared to a cross shaft carrying four sprocket wheels, like bicycle-drive sprockets (the big ones, with the pedals) but thicker and half the diameter. A heavy chain runs from each of these sprocket wheels to a sprocket on the rear axle, and these sprockets are of varying diameters to give first, second (and reverse), third, and fourth gears. All the chains run all the time, but only one set is working at a given time, its driving (small) sprocket having been locked to the spinning shaft by a simple in-and-out mechanism called a dog clutch, which is actuated by the gearshift lever in the driver's hand.

The "chain-gang" Frazer Nash system was attractive to competition drivers because it was so easy to change gear ratios with it. For example, on a racecourse that had long straight stretches, the 'Nash owner would simply take off his fourth-gear sprocket and put on a bigger one, for higher speed. For a hill climb, where acceleration was important and where he might never get into fourth gear at all, he would take off his third-gear sprocket, or his second, and substitute a smaller one. And because the car had no differential, the gearing—which in an ordinary automobile allows one rear wheel to turn faster than the other, say in going around a corner, and which also allows one wheel to spin helplessly in snow or mud while the other stands still—meant the Frazer Nash had superior traction and that, in turn, meant superior acceleration. This solid rear-axle effect also gave the car the unusual handling characteristics that endeared it to its owners: in every corner, the back wheels had to slip a bit, since they were turning at the same speed, although one of them was going the long way around the corner and the other the short way. To minimize this, Archie Frazer-Nash put the rear wheels closer together than the front, giving the car an odd crab-track look. But even so, the rear end behaved in a manner all its own, and it was easy for an experienced driver to take the car very fast around a corner by letting the rear wheels break loose and slide.

There are disadvantages, of course. Five chains running just behind the driver's seat make quite a lot of racket. Real 'Nash devotees find it soothing; others, irritating. The floor of the car and an underpan enclose the chains, and in theory seal them off, but oil is constantly being thrown around.

Probably no car ever built was produced in such a variety of models, in such a small total, as the Frazer Nash. The 348 examples had many model designations: Colmore, T.T. Replica, Byfleet, Nurburg, Exeter, Falcon, Shelsley, Boulogne, Ulster. They were all open cars, with a single exception —one sedan was made—and they were all two-seaters excepting the Colmore, which carried four. Various engines were used—Meadows, Blackburne, Anzani, Gough—some of them supercharged. (The Shelsley model had *two* superchargers!) Very few Frazer Nashes were built and put into a showroom to await a buyer. The car was ordered, and *then* built. This system was useful to the company because it didn't require tying up a lot of money in inventory; it was good for the buyer because he could have the paint color, upholstery, instruments, and gear ratios exactly as he liked them.

Around 1928 Captain Archie Frazer-Nash sold control of his company to W.H. and H.J. Aldington, and their garage and showroom in Isleworth, London, still carries the name. The first Tourist Trophy Replica, the most popular model (eighty-five of them were made) appeared in March 1932; and in November 1933, the magazine *Autocar* said of it: "A Frazer Nash, no matter which particular type it happens to be, cannot possibly be judged by ordinary standards, for it is a car that appeals to the enthusiastic driver on account of its sheer performance and for the way in which it can be handled. . . . By virtue of an excellent proportion of power to weight, and because of the special and very rapid gear change, the acceleration of the car is terrific . . . on a long journey it is an astonishing car . . ."

The "terrific acceleration" the magazine exulted over was actually a 0-to-60-mph time of eighteen seconds, but that was fast in 1933. A comparable 1968 sports car, say the Jaguar E-type, will do 0 to 60 in about eight seconds; so thirty-five years of progress have improved the Frazer Nash performance by only some ten seconds. Top speed was 85 to 90 miles an hour for the car as it was delivered, and the cost was £525, about $2625 then and perhaps $5500 today.

A few single-seat racing models were made, but sheer top speed (one specially tuned supercharged model did 120) was not the 'Nash's strong point. It did best in hill climbs and in such events as the brutally difficult Alpine Trials, when what mattered was maneuverability, ruggedness, and acceleration on snow-covered mountain roads. A typical six-day Alpine would run from Munich in Germany to Bern in Switzerland, via Innsbruck, St. Moritz, Turin, Nice, and Geneva. In the 1932–33–34 Alpine Trials, 'Nashes won seven prizes for an overall record that few comparable makes have approached.

The most successful Frazer Nash competition driver was a gifted young man named Alfred Fane Piers Fane, who could make the chain-drive car do things no one else could manage. Fane served the firm as a volunteer demonstrator, but there were those who felt that a ride with him, particularly on a wet road, could be so terrifying that the passenger never wanted to sit in a 'Nash again, much less buy one. An enthusiastic owner once told Fane of a piece of highway with a sharp bend which he could just get through at 55 miles an hour—after a great deal of practice, and if the road were absolutely dry. Never having seen the bend before, and in a pouring rain, Fane ran through it at 70.

After the war, a new Frazer Nash appeared, wholly different in design, using a German BMW (Bayerische Motoren Werke) engine and a conventional drive shaft. It did particularly well in such long-distance races as Le Mans and Sebring, but "chain-gang" owners refused to take it very seriously. For them, there is only one genuine 'Nash, and that's the one with the chains singing underneath the floorboards, the back wheels twitching around the corners in quick little slides, the short, rigid gearshift lever outdoors (if you don't like getting your arm wet in the rain, you can cut one sleeve off an old slicker and put a rubber band on each end). They believe that what a British writer said in 1937 was true then and is true now: "It is the only 'real' sports car of the old type left to us." Perhaps it is, at that.

—1968

Masten Gregory Lives!

Speed, in Aldous Huxley's opinion, provided the only genuinely modern pleasure. There have been men, sober, intelligent, expert, who went beyond Huxley, who maintained that speed is the penultimate sensuous delight available to humans. Two of these were automobile racing drivers of the topmost ranking, the legend figures Rudolf Caracciola and Stirling Moss. They were entitled to speak. The racedriver most acutely senses speed. The flier, except in landing and taking off, feels he is floating; the skier and the bobsledder cannot generate speed, but must beg it from gravity; the speedboat driver goes fast, but always over roughly the same course and because only a few square inches of his boat are wetted, he doesn't enjoy an essential—precise control. The racedriver can summon 220 miles per hour with his toe, using the power of a herd of 400 horses to move a vehicle weighing a little more than a thousand pounds, a vehicle as susceptible to his directional bidding—up to a point, up to a point—as an architect's pen and ruler. The courses on which he runs change with every race, today a flat oval a mile around, tomorrow a fourteen-mile mountain circuit, 3000 feet up, 3000 feet down, 178 curves. The delight of hazard, the sensuous wonder of straight-line sheer speed, the swinging rhythmic pleasure of hills and curves taken flat out, and the conviction of absolute environment control (a professional peculiarity that is always, ultimately, illusory), these combine to bind the racedriver so tightly to his trade that it is harder for him to abandon it, to retire, than for any other competitor, entertainer, athlete. "Racing is a vice, and as such extremely hard to give up," Alfonso de Portago wrote in 1957, a month before he was killed. The man who has driven long enough for the iron really to enter him, say five years, almost always quits only when he must, because there's no alternative; he has been hurt so he's incapacitated, or he's aging and slowing and no one will give him a good car. Sometimes pride will take him out. Stirling Moss was almost mortally hurt in a crash. He recovered, he was well enough to drive, but not to drive better than anyone else in the world, as he had been used to do, so he gave it up, in 1962. Some of his friends said on that day that he would never be able to stay out. He did run in an African rally several years ago, and last August there was a considerable stir in the European press when he entered a three-day endurance event at the Nürburgring in Germany. The Moss car, a Lancia (codrivers Ireland and Maglioli), was in first place in the twenty-sixth hour when the gearbox failed. Sometimes love: the Italian driver Piero Taruffi, a phenomenon who was still competing in major events at the incredible age of fifty, promised his wife, younger than he, that he would retire if he ever won the hardest of European long-distance races, the Mille Miglia. He hadn't won in twelve tries, but the thirteenth time he made it, and he quit. Sometimes sadness: Juan Manuel Fangio of Argentina, five times champion of the world, got out of the car, he said, because he had seen too many of his friends killed. But it was hard for all of them, and bitter for one at least, and when you see them now, at Monaco or Silverstone or the Nürburgring, you know you are not looking at happy men, although Moss, who has never betrayed the least emotion if he could help it, and he could, will fool you unless you have been watching him for a long time.

Masten Gregory of Kansas City and Rome ran against Fangio, Moss, Portago, Taruffi. He remembers them and many others: Peter Collins, Mike Hawthorn, Wolfgang von Trips, Jimmy Clark, Jean Behra, Lorenzo Bandini, Jimmy Bryan, Eddie Sachs, Ludovico Scarfiotti, Eugenio Castellotti, Mike Spence, Ken Wharton, Harry Schell . . . the dead alone make a long list. No one whom Masten Gregory knew as a driver when he began racing, in 1952, is still competing. Of that considerable company he is the only one left. Gregory has been driving for sixteen years, a span unremarkable in most professions, but extraordinarily prolonged in his. He ran first at Caddo Mills, Texas, in November 1952, and most recently in the 24-Hour Race at Le Mans, France.* He has lived through crashes that reduced the cars to junk, he has been burned and broken, three times he has simply stood up and bailed out of cars running more than 100 miles an hour, but nothing shows and at thirty-six he could pass for a student. His heavy black-rimmed glasses frame thick lenses; he walks stiffly, mechanically, as if someone had just wound him up and put him down and pointed him; he has lived in Europe for years, but he has a strong Missouri accent still: "Jesus Christ, Ah hate the sight of blood, specially mah own." His voice is a booming double-bass, and in a crowd people sometimes look past him, five feet eight, a hundred forty pounds, wondering where the rumbling noise is coming from. His manner is relaxed and polite, almost courtly. "A race in Palm Springs," another driver remembered, "some bloody amateur got in the way and Carroll Shelby ran right over him and of course wiped out his car, and afterward he came over to Shelby and said he was going to beat him to death. The man looked like he weighed two hundred fifty pounds, but before Shel could decide whether to belt him or not, Masten got between them and told the man, very politely, to get lost or he would personally do him. This monster looked down at old Masten, he got some kind of a message and he just went away."

Shelby, now a wealthy sports-car manufacturer (Cobra/Ford) and an eminence on the international racing scene, remembers the incident. "Masten is gentlemanly, soft-spoken," he said a few weeks ago, "but he says exactly what he thinks, you know where you stand with him. That's one of the reasons I like him so much. That, and the tremendous amount of guts he has."

Gregory doesn't drive as often now as he used to: so far this year only at Daytona, where he crashed at 180 mph, Indianapolis, where a weird sequence of misfortune kept him out of the starting field, and Le Mans. "I won't do it forever," he says, "because I can't, but I love it. I love the life. Motor racing is very pleasant, if you don't have too much fear, if you can *enjoy* what you're doing. If I couldn't go motor racing I'd have to do something else involving hazard, risk, because it's moments of risk that make the rest of life bearable, valuable, or delightful. I do think you have to be a bit strange, though." ("Only the ones who really have the monkey on their backs stay at it as long as Masten has," said another driver, long retired.)

Boris Said of Connecticut ran the European circuit with Gregory until he gave up motor racing for Olympic-class bobsledding. "Masten was wild," Said says. "He was a strange man. Still is. Look, Masten just won't take a challenge, any kind. I remember one day, Masten had a Thunderbird, we were on some narrow street and a Cadillac with four hoods in it cut him

*Gregory drove at Le Mans in 1971, too.

off. I was in the back with my girl, Masten was up front telling his girl some long mixed-up story, these jokers chopped us, and about half a block later Masten caught them, he got next to them, he laid that Thunderbird on them, he bounced them off a parked car and right up on the sidewalk, chug! They nearly went through a store, and the thing I liked, where I thought, you know, old Masten was showing the difference, he never stopped telling the story, he didn't miss a syllable, he just threw them off the road like snow off a shovel and kept right on going.

"Masten is deceptive. Nobody looks less competitive than he does, he doesn't look like a charger, which he is for sure, and God knows he's a survivor. I mean, you can see Parnelli Jones walking down the street and if you don't know he's a racedriver you do know he's a competitor at *something*, for sure. But you can be with Masten for a long time, and then there's a day he drops those beady eyes on you and suddenly you know he'll go. You remember, at Indianapolis two years ago he started thirty-first and in half an hour he was lying sixth. Anybody who blows off twenty-five Indy drivers in thirty minutes is *serious*, and he's not thinking much about what he's going to have for breakfast tomorrow, either."

"Bobby Said calling anybody else 'wild,' that's fairly quaint," Gregory said. "Boris has done more wild things in his sleep than most people have when they were drunk. I think he went bobsledding sort of for recreation after he gave up motor racing, and last winter he had a little shunt at St. Moritz, the sled dragged him down the chute, beating him on the ice, I understand they put a hundred eight stitches into his face. I don't think I've got 108 stitches in my whole body."

Masten Gregory is the last of an almost extinct breed, the sportsmen drivers, talented, individualistic to an extreme if not eccentric, sometimes wealthy, titled, or both, who decorated and sometimes dominated Grand Prix and sports-car racing in the years before and after World War II. They've gone for good, they'll never be back.

"When I started, racedrivers had an attitude completely different from today's; there wasn't nearly as much money involved, and we were racing the way that gentlemen amateurs played polo. Nobody thought a lot about money. I inherited some money in 1951, and the first two years I went racing I must have spent $75,000 more than I took in. Today it's an industry, everybody has accountants and managers and tax people, the top drivers all have businesses on the side. People like Portago, and Taffy von Trips, Peter Collins, Mike Hawthorn, Carel de Beaufort, if they were still alive I don't know how they'd fit in. They were all hedonists, they were doing it for fun first and money second, if at all. They were men who made their own rules."

So they did. Portago, at a Paris street crossing, thought a Citroën had come too close to his girl. He flicked a cigarette after the man driving it, hit him in the face with it. When the man got out of the car Portago knocked him down twice. He acted as his own attorney in the consequent assault case, defending on the ground that he, a Spaniard, had been upholding the traditional French posture of gallantry toward women. He lost.

De Beaufort. Driving to Watkins Glen, he met a friend on the road; they changed cars, a Porsche for a Mercedes-Benz. It was raining heavily. De Beaufort led, and after giving the other man ten miles in which to get used to the Mercedes-Benz, he began to go fast. His friend was shortly well beyond his own limits, but, knowing the Mercedes would stick to the road at least as well as the Porsche, he decided that if he ran precisely at De Beaufort's speed, and in his exact line, clearly marked on the wet road, through the corners, he would not kill himself, and they ran a long way like that, and came downhill into the town in the rain at 120 miles an hour. "They wouldn't just fine us for that, Carel," the man said, "they'd put us inside." "You, perhaps," De Beaufort said, laughing. "Me, I have diplomatic immunity." He was a Netherlands count, a big man, six four or so, gentle and good, twenty-eight when he was killed practicing for a race in Germany in 1964.

Harry Schell, an American who lived in France, signed on with the Finnish Air Force as a tail gunner in the winter war with the Russians, out of a sense of outrage, and for kicks. Duncan Hamilton, an English driver, was caught by a policeman, after a race in Germany, tearing down the national flag. The officer ordered him to come down. "Very well," Hamilton said, and let go of the pole. He weighed nearly 200 pounds, and the policeman didn't get out from under.

The swingers are all gone, killed at the wheel, almost to a man, but Jimmy Clark of Scotland is dead, too, smashed against a tree in Germany last April; he was as cold and systematized and computerized as a man could be, eerily competent, no swinger he, and twice champion of the world. In his eleven years of racing, Clark had not had a serious accident. He was thought bulletproof and his death stunned and frightened people who had not been much affected by the deaths of others. Drivers usually know why accidents happen. "He was *tired*. He was missing shifts. You could see it was going to happen two laps before it did." Or, "The engine was misfiring. It cut out cold just as he went into the bend, and with nothing to put on the road naturally he spun out." But Clark's crash, like Moss's six years ago, is a mystery. He made no mistake. As nearly as an inch-by-inch examination of the car could show, nothing broke on it, it simply drifted off the road and into the trees, starting, some people think, a spooky kind of chain reaction among top-line drivers: April 7, Clark killed at Hockenheim; May 7, Mike Spence killed at Indianapolis; June 8, Ludovico Scarfiotti near Mount Rossfeld; July 7, Jo Schlesser at Rouen.

"I was about thirty-two or thirty-three," Masten Gregory said, "when it came to me that in all my earlier life I had never really believed I would live to be thirty. I hadn't made any *plans*. I didn't think it was worthwhile, it wasn't going to happen that I'd live to be thirty. It wasn't only my own opinion. Stirling Moss told me flatly that I was going to kill myself. At the beginning of my career, everybody thought I'd kill myself, and looking back, I'm surprised that I didn't. I was driving mainly on reflexes, I didn't *know* anything about driving, I just had quite a lot of natural ability. Actually I didn't have many crashes, but I was in a delicate condition, right on the edge, most of the time. I had a ridiculous, stupid lack of fear, and I had cars in ridiculous attitudes. I just cannot understand how I could have had them that far out of shape and still kept them on the road. Of course, sometimes I didn't.

"The first real shunt I had was at Pebble Beach in California in 1954. I had just bought a 4.5 Ferrari and I didn't know the car, I didn't know it at all. I accelerated too hard and the back end got away from me and I overcorrected and it went the other way and hit a tree and the tree cut off the whole back end of the car right behind the seat. It happened so fast I didn't have any time to think about it. First I was out of control and next the accident was over. I don't remember being frightened at all, but I must have been, and if you're frightened in a crash situation you can't *do* anything, your mind goes solid. Of course, in 1954 I didn't know *how* to do anything, either.

"Now my last crash—I hope it was my last one—at Daytona last month was interesting because it showed how it is when you've had a few shunts, so that you don't get terribly frightened, and when you do know, technically, how to cope. A wonderful thing happens. Time slows down to a crawl, or else your mind runs like a computer, you know everything that's going on, and you can just sit there and consider the alternatives that will get you out of it. Anybody who's been driving for a long time can do that, like Moss when his left rear wheel came off at Spa, in Belgium. He sat there and planned out the whole accident in the fat part of a second and a half. Portago used to say, when he was steeplechasing, 'When you fall at a jump, the thing to do is to look around for a horse to hide behind. There always seems to be lots of time.'

"And there is. At Daytona, I came by the pits in the middle of the night, flat-out, that's about 180 mph in the car I was driving, a Ferrari, and just before I got to the braking point I saw sparks and smoke, and some kind of shape, on the road in front of me, it was a car that was rolling over, although I couldn't be sure of that in the dark. I banged the brakes on. And then instantly I hit a patch of oil the car in front of me had dumped, and *I* went sideways; then a Porsche I'd just passed hit me and tipped me over and my car started rolling down the track. I thought, well, this is fairly dismal, the major danger here is fire, upside-down, ruptured tanks, all that. There was no point in trying to steer, so I just let go of the wheel, and there was no point in worrying about hitting something, the fence, another car, because there was nothing I could do about it, I had no control. On the second roll, the car hit the road very hard, and my head hit the roof, so I pulled my head down, tucked my chin into my chest, in case the roof came in. Then I half undid the latch on the seat belt—it was a combined double-shoulder-and-lap harness—to be sure it wouldn't jam, so I could get out if the thing burned, but I held the two parts together with my hand, because I was still rolling and I needed it. I was convinced there'd be a fire, because every time the car rolled right-side up it bottomed somehow and a tremendous sheet of sparks flew up between my legs. Finally it stopped rolling— landed on its feet—and the windshield had popped and was long gone, so I looked out and I thought, well, right, it's down to about 20 miles an hour, which is a great improvement on 180, I slipped the buckle, rolled out onto the bonnet and just stepped off the thing and walked into the infield.

"The crash is inherent in racing, it's bound to happen, because the whole point of the exercise is to run the car so fast it's just skimming the edge of control-loss all the time, and if you live through your first couple of emergency situations, that's likely to be pure luck, but afterward you can think, you can sort out the alternatives, I've thought of as many as seven or eight things to do, that's not extraordinary, so have a lot of people. Years ago I went off the road at Silverstone in England at about 135. I was passing a car, he pulled over on me, I had to go on the grass, it was wet with rain, and when I turned the wheel to get back on the circuit, the car didn't respond, it was in a full understeer attitude and it was heading straight for an embankment. Well, I thought, this is a poor situation, and I tried dabbing the brake pedal, sort of interval braking, you know, you try to hit it ten times a second, that was no good; I put the clutch in so the rear wheels wouldn't lock up under engine compression; I turned the wheel a bit back toward the embankment, to see if I could get some bite, no; I turned it violently, full lock the other way, nothing, and finally I said to myself, if this car hits that embankment going at this rate, there's going to be one hell of a wreck, it's going to *destroy* the automobile, I'd be better off out of it. So I stood up on the seat and stepped over the side. The car hit the bank and wiped itself out. I landed on the grass, I hurt my shoulder, it was paralyzed for a while, but relatively little happened to me really. Afterward I started thinking about it, I wondered if I had done the intelligent thing. Actually, of course, I had certainly done the right thing, because I was alive.

"Another time I let an emotional factor get into the equation, and I got hurt. This was in England too, and the steering broke in a bend, the car shot off the road, I knew what had happened, and I thought, I had better get the hell out of this, but then I thought how embarrassing that would be, because I had jumped out of two cars before that belonged to this same man, I thought, poor David, I'm going to wreck another one of his cars, and so I stayed in it for a while and tried some things, and nothing worked, I didn't really think they would, I'd already thought about them and rejected them, and I started out, but too late, I was only halfway when it hit, my legs caught momentarily under the dash and I broke mostly everything on my left side. The car broke in two under the seat, the headrest jammed up against the steering wheel, leaving about two inches where I would have been, and the entire ensemble burst into flames. That was the last time I jumped. If anybody'd ever told me I'd leap out of a car doing 135 miles an hour . . . but there can be times when it seems pretty sensible.

"I had five fairly thorough crashes, the kind that totally destroy the automobile, in the years 1958 and '59, and a British writer, Peter Miller, made a list of ten drivers, all of them my contemporaries, who had been killed in shunts no worse than mine. He was suggesting, I guess, that I was lucky, and I must have been, because lots of it has to be pure chance, but I was doing what I could to help myself, too, I was thinking. I don't count on much outside assistance in life. You are wiser to help yourself. And you have to plan it in advance. It's fundamental to survival to get out of a crashed or crashing automobile as fast as you can. You have to make it an instinct, almost. When Moss had his bad accident at Goodwood, and was pinned in the car, he was totally unconscious, then and for a month afterward, but his body was moving and struggling to get out. In 1954 in Buenos Aires I saw Forrest Green flip his car and lie under it for a long time, and then as he was crawling out it burst into flames, he caught fire, he leapt out from under, he ran around for a while on fire until some firemen caught him and put him out, but he died later. I often think, why didn't he get out immediately, because in all probability since he got out of it eventually he could have got out of it immediately, with a little resolution. I suspect he hadn't thought enough about it.

"People are fascinated by crashes, and it's not that important. If you go fast long enough you'll lose the car occasionally, but it's going fast that matters. That's the name of the game, after all. Not many people understand that the idea is to go as fast as the automobile *will* go. If the engine ought to turn 9000 revs a minute and it does only 8600, that's depressing. You want to go so fast that you can tell the difference between thirty-five pounds of air in the tires and forty, you can feel the weight of ten gallons of fuel slowing you down. I remember when I was nineteen, I was running in a street drag race one night in Kansas City, my girl was with me, I made her get out and sit on the curb, I wouldn't take a chance, hell, she weighed a hundred pounds. She was sore. We were married that year, though, 1951."

("I'd rather not talk about it," he said. "We were married, we had four children, we were divorced. When we lived in Italy, I used to come home from work, like the commuter getting off the train, home to the family, and the children would run at me, yelling, 'Who won, Daddy, Stirling?' And we'd all laugh.")

Last February Gregory drove up from New Jersey to meet me in Connecticut. He was in the United States to do some weeks of testing on a mile track in Phoenix, Arizona, he was staying in New Jersey with George Bryant, the owner of his Indianapolis car. We went to The Elms in Ridgefield for lunch. The car was a Cadillac. He drove with his left hand lying in his lap, thumb and two fingers on the wheel, but he never turned his head or took his eyes off the road. Most professionals drive civilian cars like that, handling the controls carelessly and indifferently because at 40 miles an hour along a village street nothing is happening; still, without seeming to look, they see everything in a 180° arc around them, having come to believe, years past, that this is a way to stay alive, like breathing. They usually have good 20/20 vision, although in racing as in boxing and some of the stick-and-ball games extraordinary vision seems a requirement for absolute eminence: of the five greatest drivers who have lived, three were demonstrably optical freaks and I believe the other two surely must have been. Corrected vision, like Gregory's (he wears London-made prescription goggles), is rare, indeed almost unheard of.

We left the Cadillac on the street in front of the inn. It had New Jersey tags. It belonged to George Bryant. Gregory doesn't even own an automobile.

"It's a matter of priorities," he said. "I've had a lot of money and I've had very little, and in between, and I know money isn't worth everything. I used to spend it as if I were printing it; now I'm selective. I don't see the point in owning a car, I don't use a car that much; when I want one I rent it. But I do like to go skiing for six weeks in the winter, and if it costs me as much as a Fiat would, all right. When I travel I don't want to stay in any but the best hotels, or eat in any but the best restaurants. Food is important. When I went to France in 1954 I was a hamburger-and-malted-milk devotee—I still think the really good hamburger and the really heavy malted are great culinary contributions—but I weighed only a hundred and twenty-five pounds. I was in a race at Montlhery, Jean Behra won it in a Gordini, I was second in a Ferrari, and everybody thought that was pretty remarkable for a new boy, but I knew the only reason Behra had beat me was that I absolutely ran out of strength. So I went on a 3500-calorie diet, and I started going to the very best restaurants because in a mediocre restaurant I wouldn't eat. And so I got interested in food. One of the reasons I like France is that you can't get a bad meal in France unless you're an idiot, and even then it's hard; you can get an ordinary average meal, but not a bad one, and if you go to any trouble you'll always get a superb meal. I want a dinner I can spend three hours over."

The Elms is a superior restaurant and we had a good lunch, a chunky pâté, capon, salad, a bottle of Latour-Martillac. I had sherry before lunch; Gregory smoked a pipe, as he had been doing all morning. It was new to him: he burned matches.

"I gave up cigarettes, but one of the reasons I smoke a pipe is that I don't like the way food tastes if I'm not smoking at all. For example, if I'm not smoking, I can taste every ingredient in a sauce and it spoils it for me, I can taste the fish stock and the cream and the sherry and the pepper and whatnot all separately and it's no good. If I smoke, everything blends in properly. On the other hand, wine tastes better if I don't smoke, but wine isn't as important to me as food is. Good restaurants always have some pleasant inexpensive wines on the card; I drink them, I don't have to have a great Romanée-Conti or whatever.

"I don't often drink spirits . . . in this country it's a hanging offense if a driver drinks even twenty-four hours before a race . . . at Bari in 1955, it was a night race, the start was at ten, a Le Mans start at that, everybody waiting to sprint across the track to the cars, and there was an ice-cold wind howling in off the Adriatic, Jesus Christ, it was cold, and a fellow from Shell Oil came down the line with a tray of glasses of cognac. Marvelous! What a scene! Think of that at Indianapolis: thirty-three guys standing at attention beside their cars, the biggest brass band in the world playing "Back Home Again in Indiana," and somebody comes hustling along with big shots of bourbon. There would be a Congressional investigation."

In May I saw Gregory at Indianapolis, the day before the 500-mile race, raining, as it had for something like twenty-three days of the month. He was stalking along the garage area in tan slacks and a thick, ribby, olive turtleneck sweater. He needed a haircut, and he looked, as he often does, as if he had just finished telling himself a secret joke, and was on the point of smiling. What had he been doing? Mostly playing gin with Jochen Rindt, the Austrian driver with whom he'd won Le Mans in 1965, and trying to find the other good restaurant in Indianapolis. He hadn't qualified, he wouldn't be in the race. The Bryant car wouldn't go, he couldn't get it past 176 mph on the straights, a rate at which it couldn't possibly qualify as one of the thirty-three fastest automobiles trying.

"I was offered a couple of other rides, but I didn't like them, then Jochen suggested to Jack Brabham that he give me his other car, and that was a car that could win, I was happy about that. Jack took it around to check it out, shake it down for me, and somebody had forgotten to take out the warm-up spark plugs and the engine blew. They had to phone Jack's shop in Australia for another engine. They shipped it right away, but the airlines people lost it in Los Angeles for two days. Then the L. A. customs wouldn't clear it, but Brabham found out he could get it cleared in New York, so they flew it to New York to get it into the country, technically, and then back to Indianapolis. They worked on the car for two days. There was one day of qualifying left. It rained. I had ten laps of practice in the car. Rindt's car was identical, he could get 212 mph on the straights; mine was 700 rpm down on what it should have been, but it was still very nice. There was time enough to give me one chance to qualify. We put in the qualifying fuel, the nitro, I went out, the plugs fouled immediately, I couldn't get an average over 145 and that was that."

The study of racing drivers has been a minor vogue among psychologists in the past fifteen years, and the conclusions at the end of the paper nearly always note the drivers' ability to maintain at least external equilibrium and calm in the face of absurd and needless frustration, together with their other oddities: *faster* reaction times, instead of the normal slower, when put under stress; 180 pulse rate while driving; independence; need for dominance; minimal awareness of the emotional requirements of others; and so on. Gregory stayed to watch the race and then flew home to Rome.

"I find Indianapolis very exciting, which is not fashionable. I think it's possibly the greatest motor race in the world, as a race, although I don't think much of the track. It certainly isn't an interesting track, but it's bloody difficult. An Indianapolis corner, in my opinion, is per se more difficult than any other one corner anywhere because you are in it for such a long time, you're rushing around it between 140 and 155, and you're in it for about five seconds, that's a long time to be going that quickly in a corner, and you've got to come out of it at 170 and miss a concrete wall by a foot or so. It's a boring race, in a way, but technically difficult.

"There used to be a lot of hostility between American drivers, Indy drivers, and the Europeans (I think of myself as a European driver, most of the time). We lacked respect for them because we felt that all they could do was drive in a circle to the left, and they thought all we could do was take out a sporty car and drive what they thought was a relatively safe kind of motor racing. Time, and getting together, has changed that. Jimmy Clark shook up some people when he came over here and won Indianapolis, and A.J. Foyt did the same thing when he and Dan Gurney won Le Mans. Foyt is very good. Parnelli Jones, I think, is the best I've seen run on the tracks here, a superb driver, a classic driver. I do think the American oval driver puts a greater premium on sheer bravery and what bravery is worth . . . some of them stand around the pits and talk about how brave they are and how tough it is out there with everybody pushing and shoving, but it's all nonsense because you're doing 200 down the straight at Indy and at the very

least 140 in the bends, and all those people know very well that if you touch
a wheel at those speeds, the least shunt, one car against another, you're both
most likely dead right then. It doesn't happen. They're trying to psych you.

"I'm not interested in proving that I'm brave, if I'm brave. I couldn't
possibly care less. What difference does it make? If you're balanced, not
altogether neurotic, if you have some serenity, I think you're afraid only of
what you don't know, and it can be something quite silly and inconsequen-
tial. You remember when Bobby Said had that wild, swinging menage in
Pound Ridge, his wife always had cats around. Remember the puma? He
was quite small, but there was a cheetah that was as big as a bloody Great
Dane. I was sitting in a chair one day, the cheetah came into the room and
walked over and looked me right in the eye, he was that big. That cat had
me psyched from then on. He knew it, and he used to follow me around.
I wouldn't hear him, he'd just *be* there. He followed me into a bathroom
one day, I turned around and he was standing in the doorway, watching
me. I was too scared of him to go over and try to bluff him out of the door.
I yelled for Boris. Yet a cheetah isn't much, as big cats go, they have a small
mouth, and nonretractable claws, like a dog's. I shouldn't have been scared
of him, but I didn't know about cats, and so I was.

"I think there've been a few drivers who were afraid of driving—afraid
until they got into the car, that is, then they were all right. And there have
been drivers who haven't liked certain races, like Le Mans or the Mille
Miglia. Le Mans bugs some people because they're spooked by running 180
mph at night when there can be fog around, and knowing they'll come up
on cars running 100 mph slower. Of all races, I'd rather have won the Mille
Miglia than any other, but they stopped it when Portago killed himself and
those other fourteen people. That was a pity, he was a most interesting and
unusual man, intelligent, dashing, brave, lovely, and moody in a nice way.
The first time I met him, we were flying to Buenos Aires, Phil Hill, Carroll
Shelby, Bob Said, and I, in 1954, and here was this dandy-looking guy with
this gorgeous girl, the Marquis de Portago and Dorian Leigh. That was his
first race, he couldn't drive worth a damn then, but he was a very good
driver finally . . . They're talking about starting the Mille Miglia again, I
hope they do, a thousand miles down one side of Italy and up the other,
people doing 200 on ordinary two-lane roads. Of the real roadraces that are
left, the Targa Florio in Sicily is, I suppose, the greatest race*course.* Monte
Carlo is fantastic, a Grand Prix race run over a circuit that is 100 percent
city streets, it's hard to believe when you first see it."

The battery in Gregory's C-Jaguar went flat at Buenos Aires, but he was
still working on the money he'd inherited in 1951 then, and he bought the
winning Ferrari on the spot for $12,000. He took it to Europe and began
to campaign in earnest. He shared a villa in Italy with John Fitch, the first

227

American to be offered a place on a Mercedes-Benz team. It was a considerable household: Fitch too had brought his wife and children. Gregory looked so young that the other drivers protested him on sight when he went out to practice for his first race, at Rheims. He came in fourth, and got out of the automobile to find he had made an instant reputation. He ran in the Portuguese G.P. at Lisbon, broke the hill-climb record at Prescott in England, was second at Goodwood and Montlhery, first at Aintree, first at Nassau.

By 1957 he had tied for fifth place in the world championship, a remarkable accomplishment for a driver a bare five years from his first ride, and extraordinary in that he was running his own car, a three-year-old Maserati at that. It's axiom that no factory will sell a private owner an automobile as fast as those allocated to its own team. In 1955 the Mercedes-Benz 300SLR sports cars, Moss, Fangio, and Kling driving, were held invincible. That was the year Moss won the Mille Miglia in a 300SLR at an average speed of nearly 100 mph, something that seemed incredible at the time and still does. Running his own Ferrari in the 500-kilometer race at Nürburgring that year, Gregory came in third, behind Moss and Fangio, ahead of Kling's Mercedes-Benz and Farina in a factory Ferrari. At the prize-giving dinner, he was invited to sit at the Mercedes-Benz table, as befitting the only private owner who had ever beaten a Mercedes team car.

"I had a long talk with Stirling Moss that night; he was saying, man, these Mercedes people are terrific, nobody ever built a race car the way they do, and nobody ever ran one the way they do. I agreed they were very good —after all, the oldest racing organization in the world—but, I said, if the Americans ever get serious about racing, watch out, and of course Stirling said I was bloody nationalistic. I wasn't at all, I said, supposing General Motors or Ford went into racing, it would just be a matter of buying the engineers, buying the talent . . . and of course in time it came out that way, with Ford.

"I drove a Ford at Le Mans in 1964 with Richie Ginther. Richie drove the first two hours and was leading, but then we had a long pit stop. When I went out we were in second place and the gearbox broke. Three of them broke that year, I believe. Anyway, later on in England, the team manager said I'd been driving over my head, and I'd broken the box. It's the only time I remember being really sore all the way through at a team manager. I told him he was out of his mind, and I said to myself, I'm coming back next year and I'm going to blow you off, boy. I got a Ferrari from Luigi Chinetti, North American Racing Team, and that year, '65, was the year Rindt and I did win.

"I think it's odd that one can be selectively competitive. I have little sense of competition in business, for example—although much more now than formerly—but if I'm skiing, say, I don't want anyone in front of me, if I have to play seven sets of tennis to beat you, or nine if it comes to that, okay, I'll play nine, and in racing, if I don't pass a car it's because for some reason I don't want to, or I *can't.* Either my car won't go fast enough, or the other driver is outdriving me or outthinking me, psyching me. Moss was the master at that, at psyching you. You were psyched before you got into the car, with him. He never ran out of things to do to you. Fangio psyched you too, but differently, he came on like a tired kind of fat man, a very nice man who was sorry he was going to have to run away from you, but that was the way it was . . . it was inevitable, too bad. But you might be running behind Moss on a wet course and you'd notice he was sliding a lot in a certain place, he seemed to be almost losing the car, and you'd think, if *he's* having trouble, I had better watch it, so you'd back off, and next time around you'd wonder where he was, and maybe then you'd realize he'd been throwing the rear end out just for you. He could do that only to a new boy, of course, but he had something for everybody. Say in practice, by going absolutely flat-out, ten-tenths all the way, taking every known chance, you'd do, let's say, a lap in three minutes fifteen seconds. And you'd come in and find out Stirling had done 3.12. So, if you were on the same team, maybe he'd offer to switch cars. And he'd do 3.12 in your car and you'd do 3.15 in his. That was how he convinced you. That was why he had you psyched.

"I tried for years to beat Moss, and never did. There were times I pushed him hard, and times I passed him, but I never beat him. I had him beaten once, at Havana in 1958, but he got away. I had a 4.9 Ferrari, just back from the factory, the ideal car for the course. Stirling had a 4.4 and Fangio had my 4.7 Maserati. In practice I did the fastest lap by about a tenth of a second, Stirling was second fastest, and Fangio was third, but the day before the race Fidel Castro's people came out of the hills and kidnapped Fangio, so he was out; Maurice Trintignant was put into the car, but he'd had no time to practice, so he didn't count. When the race started Stirling went into the lead immediately, and I was right behind him. We had a bunch of bad cars in the race, old Masers leaking oil and so on, the course got terribly slick, we were doing about 190 on the Malecón by the sea wall, sliding and slipping all over the place, and Stirling must have decided this is idiotic, I'm going to let Gregory go first and find the slippery places for me. Besides that, the word around Havana was that the Castro people who had kidnapped Fangio were going to shoot the leading driver, so really nobody wanted to lead the damned race. Anyway, Stirling waved me by in a corner. We came to a hairpin, there was only one line through it that was safe, it was perfectly dry and the rest of it was so oily you couldn't get traction. Naturally, Stirling wanted to drop in behind me, and I wouldn't let him; when he'd slow down I'd slow down and keep him beside me. We went through there about as slow as you could run, I made him stay in the oil, I dropped into bottom gear, and picked up about 200 yards on him immediately. The next corner was a third-gear corner, and I came flying into it, and there were people all over the place, nothing but people in the road. A Cuban we had been about ready to lap had lost it and gone off the road and killed five people. The crowd panicked and ran into the road, a marshal was standing there waving a red flag. Obviously they were going to stop the race, so I slowed right down, Stirling caught up to me and we went through the people at about 15 mph. We were just through the mob, just before the finish line, when Stirling dropped into bottom, accelerated by me and took another red flag at the finish line. I was still in third gear and by the time I got into bottom he was miles ahead of me. They gave him the race, and I couldn't believe it. I was upset, I'd been trying so hard for so many years to beat him. It wasn't an important race at all, but I wanted it, and I went up to Stirling and told him I thought he was stealing it. He said, don't be bloody silly, Gregory, you ought to read the rules, boy, the only place you can get a red flag is at the start-finish line, it doesn't count anywhere else. He was dead right, of course, you could always count on Stirling knowing the regs, backward and forward, but I still wouldn't hold still for it and I said I'm going to protest you. Stirling said, look, Masten, Castro will be in power in another month—he was always clued up on all that sort of thing—Batista will be out, Castro will be in, if you protest the money will be put into escrow and neither of us will ever see it. I told him I didn't give a damn, I was going to protest him anyway. I said, Stirling, I've tried for too many years to beat you. He said, all right, Masten, look, it's $10,000 first-place money and $7000 second, we'll pool it and split it. So I said, all right, and we sorted it out that way. Some people say that was the only time anybody ever came out ahead on a money deal with Moss, but I never did beat him. Never in any of the races we ran together.

"I've won, I think, twenty-five or thirty races, all over the place, Portugal, England, France, Germany, Italy, the United States, Sweden, Canada. I don't know how many times I've run, it would have to be in the hundreds, but I do have one race in my memory that was perfect. That was, of all places, Omaha, Nebraska, July 1953, a Sports Car Club of America race, no big deal, although all the best people in this country were there. I won it in a C-Jaguar. Two hundred and fifty miles. That day, I went into every corner as deeply as I could get, I braked at the absolute maximum . . . perfect, every single lap and every corner was as good as I could make it. I didn't make one mistake, it was all smooth and lovely. Every other race I've done, every one, no exception, I've made a mistake, or two or three, or at least there was a bend I could have taken half a mile an hour faster, or a straight where I could have braked half a second later, or I braked half a second late and got out of shape . . . something, but I do have that one time, that one at Omaha, when it all went right, like magic.

"I should have kept the Omaha trophy. Usually I don't keep them, I give them away, most often to whomever owns the car. If I get a particularly nice silver tray, if it has some utility, I can serve drinks on it, I'll keep that, but I've given the cups and things away. I just don't want them. Another thing about trophies, if you keep them around, people will come in and want to talk about them, and about racing, and all that, and I'm not interested in that kind of conversation. I don't want to talk about racing except with professionals, and even with them I'd rather talk about something else. I don't keep a scrapbook, as so many drivers do, it's surprising how many people have saved everything, right back to sitting on Dad's lap in the family Ford, age three. I don't like to think about things in the past, things that have happened. It isn't that it makes me feel old or anything, I'm just not interested, the past has little meaning for me. Although I like *things* out of the past, I prefer antique furniture to any other kind, I like tapestries, I like old-master paintings, my cut-off point is about 1910, I think, anything painted after that loses me. I'd rather go to an opera than a discotheque, I don't want all that noise, drinking too much, a cellar full of solid smoke. . . . I like a ballet, left with an evening to myself I'd rather see Fonteyn and Nureyev dance than anything else. I enjoy ballet, but technically I don't know anything about it, I don't know the difference between an *entrechat* and a *jeté*. I just enjoy the movement, the music, the organization, the beauty. I'd rather play chess than gin. I play chess quite well, but I don't agree with the common notion that playing chess well has anything to do with intelligence. It has to do with the ability to concentrate, and concentration is automatic with a racedriver. If you haven't got at least as much ability to concentrate as, say, a college student on an M.A. level, if you can't concentrate absolutely for three hours, you'll kill yourself. I'm convinced that many drivers have died because they let go just for a second or two.

"No, if you look back, you'll regret things, and that's futile. Living in the past has never appealed to me. For example, I would like to have won the championship of the world. I never did, and it's unrealistic to think I will now, but I don't let it spoil things. I've had some great drives, but what a bore it would be to sit around thinking about them. I notice that people who look back tend to be passive, they hang around waiting for fate to deal them four aces or something. I don't believe in fate, I believe one can control 97 percent of one's life. The three percent is just luck, uncontrollable. Today is what counts, today is where the action is, and I believe you can control most of what happens to you today, every day. A belief in control produces a certain amount of serenity, too. Hell, there's no serenity, and no dignity, in being just another pebble in some big cement mixer, letting somebody else run your life. I was offered a pretty good ride at Indy last year, but the owner said I'd have to cut my hair short, I looked too much like a beatnik to drive for him, I'd louse up his image. I laughed. I wouldn't have gotten into his car if it's been the fastest thing in the country."

At the end of August, Gregory wrote to me from Rome:

". . . I enjoy life tremendously, and right now I'm very happy, but there've been times, even long times, when I didn't have a life that was really a tremendously happy one, but I always *thought* of it as tremendously happy. I appreciate what I do have, I appreciate it terrifically. I try to think about the good things. One doesn't have to have *much*. . . . I don't have many friends because most people, I'm afraid, just don't interest me, but I do like the ones I have, I do appreciate them. Probably it's unfortunate, but I don't have, in Rome, Paris, London, and New York, as many as fifteen or twenty people I like to be with, but I do have a few, and I look forward to seeing them. I no doubt miss knowing many very rewarding people, but I don't want the bother of sorting them out. It's like this, that I know seven or eight excellent restaurants in New York. Now, I might be able to find fifty very good restaurants in New York, after all there are more than 10,000 to choose from, but I'd have to go to two or 300 to find them, and I just don't want to eat that much bad food, and I don't want to be that much bored, with people.

"You wrote an article one time, you quoted Karl Wallenda explaining why he went back up on the high wire after that terrible fall in Detroit that practically destroyed the Wallenda family, he said that to be on the wire was life, the rest was waiting. That's right. I like to go motor racing, and I like to do the waiting in a quiet and civilized fashion. I stay in Rome most of the time. My house in Rome is an interim place, it has a view over the city and a garden, but it's not particularly interesting. On a weekend I may get a car and drive up to one of the lake towns, have lunch at an old castle, find a garden or a villa that's new to me, things like that. Or I may drive up to the mountains of the ' bruzzi to see some new ski resorts. When I'm at home I read a good deal. I listen to records, I have a good hi-fi system, most of it I made myself. I watch television. I like Italian TV. The Italians don't interrupt programs with commercials, you know, they run them all together. I play tennis. I swim every day. I became engaged a while back. I'm constantly with my fiancée. I share everything with her." At the end of the letter, he wrote, "I think now I probably won't be killed in an accident. I still find that a strange thought."

—1969

232

Classic
Car
Collecting

Automobile collecting passed out of the string-saving category some time ago. The international auction house of Parke-Bernet, a legend-draped eminence in the art world, now regularly conducts automobile sales; in a recent one, a Mercer brought $45,000. There are seventy-nine major automobile collections in Europe, including one in the Soviet Union and one in Israel; many of these are museums exhibiting only the automobile and artifacts related to it. The Montagu Motor Museum in England and the Museo dell'Automobile Carlo Biscaretti di Ruffia in Italy are two such, and world famous. In this country, the Harrah, Clark, and Cunningham collections, in Reno, Southampton, and Costa Mesa, California, are housed in museums. The automobile's standing as an object of art, formally attested in 1951 in the famous Museum of Modern Art show in New York (and again in 1953, 1966, and 1969), is firm today, and critics disposed to argue the point on esthetic grounds must concede instantly on the other standard by which, like it or not, art has always been assayed: value appreciation. Some automobiles are worth twenty times their original value and, while every indicator suggests that prices will continue to rise, it is still possible to assemble a worthwhile personal collection. Money governs: it can be a collection of established classics, or of less valuable specialties, or of near-current models shrewdly chosen as possible rarities tomorrow.

For a small classic collection—each car compellingly interesting itself, created by men of taste and talent and individuality, certain to increase in value year after year—I would choose ten cars. Incidentally, but importantly, each would be thoroughly enjoyable to drive. This condition would exclude many historically notable vehicles, simply because they're slow or unwieldy or unreliable. I think everything should run, and reasonably quickly, too. In this, if not in all else, I am a partisan of the British discipline in collecting, which holds it offensive to keep an old motorcar, even a valuable one, squirreled away and not run it. British sportsmen run racing cars of the 1920s, 1930s, and earlier in earnest competitions, accepting the risk of wiping out an uninsured $15,000 antique in a race for a $5 silver mug. A leader of this short-fused pack is a charming eccentric, Hamish Moffatt, who runs a 1926 Grand Prix Bugatti in flat-out races on *original*, narrow-section, hard-rubber tires, and in the rain. He wins, too.

To begin arbitrarily with a pair of two-seater sports cars: a Frazer Nash and a Morgan. These also have in common that they are chain-driven, British, distinguished in competition history, delightful to drive, and cult objects. The Frazer Nash was designed by Captain Archibald Frazer-Nash initially and built from 1924 to 1938. Not many were made: probably 348. I have seen only three in this country. The British regard the surviving 'Nash cars—there are about 150 of them—on the level of national treasure, and the Frazer Nash section of the Vintage Sports Car Club effectively controls their disposition. Perhaps half a dozen chain-driven Frazer Nashes appear on the British market in a given year, and it's usual to find their sale conditional on a promise not to export, although this can sometimes be overcome. I think the Frazer Nash is heavily underpriced in the current market at around $5000 and I expect to see it pulling $10,000 or so within the next few years.

A good 'Nash is recognizable as a thing worth owning at first sight: like the TC MG, which it somewhat resembles, it's a fortunate design, a happy one, everything falling properly together. The front axle is bare, well out ahead of the stone-guarded radiator, with its quick-release cam-type cap; hood length is right, body length right, nothing out in back but a saddlebag gas tank; leather hold-down strap on the hood, outside exhaust pipes, strap-held spare, outside gearshift, brake and spark lever, fold-down windshield, double aeroscreens behind it, walnut and leather—nothing extra, nothing missing.

Most numerous of Frazer Nashes are Tourist Trophy Replicas, named after a now defunct roadrace on the Isle of Man. There are many other model designations: Byfleet, Nürburg, Colmore, Exeter, Shelsley, Falcon, Ulster, Boulogne. The Colmore is the only four-passenger the company made; the Shelsley is supercharged—by *two* superchargers. Four proprietary engines were used—Anzani, Blackburne, Gough, and Meadows.

The Morgan Three-Wheeler, often called a Mog, or a Morgan Trike, is chain-driven, but in a simpler fashion: it has one wheel in the rear, and a single fat chain drives it. The Trike and the four-wheeler that is still being made were the creations of one H. F. S. Morgan, an Englishman of notable eccentricity and purpose. A whimsy of British tax law that fell with most force on the poor man encouraged the Three-Wheeler: tricycles, described as chain-driven vehicles of 896 pounds running on three wheels were taxed a straight rate annually, whereas automobiles paid a much higher rate, figured on horsepower. This law, pre-Morgan, restricted the working classes pretty much to bikes, until H. F. S. thought to make a three-wheel chain-driven car, in 1911. From then until 1952, 40,000 came out of the tiny Morgan works in Malvern Link.

The desirable Mogs are those of the prewar period, particularly Super-Sport and Aeros powered by big 2-cylinder motorcycle engines by Matchless, J. A. Prestwich, Anzani and Blackburne, which hung out in front of the radiator. They were brisk on getaway. A good sports-model Mog would do 85 as it came from the store; they were peculiarly susceptible to tuning and magic wasn't needed to work them up to 100 mph or better. They were brutes to drive; but once tamed, the characteristics that made them difficult changed them to challenging. The steering was heavy but very quick, the suspension rock-hard, the brakes negligible; yet, Trike experts could make them go very fast in what looked to be comparative safety. An English-woman, Gwenda Stewart, drove one at 72 mph for twelve consecutive hours, and took the three-wheel world speed record at 116 and a fraction, a figure that stood for many years. It took a hot factory-run BMW motorcycle sidecar rig to lift it, finally.

The Morgan had its little eccentricities: no doors were cut into the stark, open body, but it did carry a hood and side curtains, so that in a fall of rain or snow, the inhabitants were sealed up like a tank crew. This was acceptable, and even pleasant, unless the engine stalled, as high-output 2-cylinder engines sometimes do, because it had to be cranked, which meant unbuttoning everything in order to get out, an annoyance if ten cars behind were blowing their horns. It was for a long time held to be gospel that a starter wouldn't work on a 2-cylinder Morgan: the engine would kick back and tear things up. This isn't true, although the starter does need to be a sturdy one. Another Morgan oddity is the accelerator, a lever working off one of the steering-wheel spokes. It has no return spring; if the driver shoves it to wide open, it stays there until it is pulled back; and when the wheel is turned, it is important to remember, since the gas lever turns with it, that down is now on and up is now off, instead of the other way around. There are two other levers on the wheel, one for spark, one for mixture control.

An early Morgan looks decidedly flimsy, and when, at around 70 mph, running on anything but plate glass, it begins to buck and leap about, lifting the inside front wheel in the corners, it feels hazardous. A sense of some security comes in time, bred of the high power-to-weight ratio and the very quick steering, but it's true that the Morgan is nothing for crashing. The chassis is basically a couple of pieces of pipe, the floor is wood, and the gasoline tank is hung in the scuttle over your knees. To exit on the driver's side is something of an exercise, even when the car is standing still, and hot exhaust pipes run along both sides of the body, just under elbow height. Tire failure in the rear single wheel usually means at least a spin-out.

In the 1930s, Morgan began propelling the tricycles with softer and more civilized engines, 4-cylinder British Fords, tucked out of sight in the standard fashion, as an alternative to the big motorcycle twins; and after the war, they were standard. Cut-off date for the Ford Three-Wheelers is usually stated as 1951, but a few were made in 1952, and perhaps later, as favors for friends. The Morgan factory, a complex of seven small buildings, was run on an informal basis when the founder was in charge, and still is under his son, Peter. It is strictly a limited-production operation. A legend that is apparently immortal holds that one man paints all Morgans, with a brush. Not true; but there have been times when one man would have sufficed, periods when a production rate of one car a day or so was held to be ample. In 1965, for example, the ninety-four people on the Morgan payroll were turning out nine cars a week, all sold in advance, of course. The rule is the same today—everything presold.

Ford-engined Mogs can be found occasionally in England for $750 and up and for around $1200 here. The twins run higher and a fine one in original shape, or restored, can go to $2500. They are good buys now at any reasonable figure. A Morgan is easily broken up; their engines were always in demand. Two world wars and a serious depression junked many of them in England. Morgan Trikes will always be in short supply and their prices can go upward only.

I mentioned earlier that the last purchase of a T-head Mercer Raceabout had been at the Parke-Bernet sale in Brookline, at $45,000. It reflects the rarity of this model of Mercer (there are fewer than thirty known to be in existence) and its undisputed place at the top of the list of desirable American-built cars. The last "new" Mercer was found twenty years ago. It turned up in a tiny Canadian village as a result of an article I had written, and I bought it, completely unrestored, for $1250, a reasonable price at the time.

It's now in the Josiah K. Lilly collection in Massachusetts.

There are cars much sought-after today that didn't amount to a great deal in their own time, but the Mercer was exciting from the beginning. It was nearly unique in its triple-use capability: a good passenger, sports, and racing car. The Mercer Raceabout was sturdy, reliable, and unfussy; on the road, it would outperform almost anything else of its time, 1911–1914, and you could buy one, take it straight to a racetrack and win with it. It was a lot of automobile for $2500.

The Roebling family (the same people who built the Brooklyn Bridge) was behind the Mercer and the factory was in Trenton (Mercer County), New Jersey. Finlay Robertson Porter designed the T-head (so called because of the configuration of the cylinder head). Like the Frazer Nash, the Mercer is excellently proportioned; and although there's nothing much to it—hood, gas tank, fenders, two little seats, and a steering post sticking up out of a bare floor—it looks light, lithe, and lively. Its famous rival, the original Stutz Bearcat, seems pushy and out of balance beside it.

A factory guarantee of 75 mph came with the Mercer, and a modest amount of tuning would take it well over that. Mercers ran up a big racing record: in 1913, a good year, fifteen first places, twelve seconds, and six thirds. In ordinary use, the car is fun to drive, the big 4-cylinder engine always running slowly (2000 rpm at 75 mph!), the steering fast, if very heavy, and the suspension taut. Beginning in 1915, the company built a somewhat more conventional car designed by Erik Delling around a softer engine. These, also designated Raceabouts, are called L-heads. There were touring cars, too.

Any Mercer, dated 1911 to the year the company gave up, 1925, is valuable; but, of course, the T-head is the prize, and Mr. Harry Reznick, who took the $45,000 car, was probably well advised. Barring catastrophe, I see no reason not to believe his car will be worth, in the year 2000, twice its present value. It's a rule of collecting that really sound merchandise appreciates steadily up through the years, come hell or high water, war or deflation.

Certainly as rock-solid in value as the Mercer is the Silver Ghost Rolls-Royce. The Ghost was the first long-run-production car of the Derby-based firm; indeed, it had one of the longest model runs of all time—nineteen years, from 1906 to 1925—and, consequently, is on a lower rarity level than the Mercer. It was a better and a costlier car to begin with, however, and is now under such stringent demand that a totally unrestored 1911 brought $20,800 in a recent British auction, even though it was wearing a fussy and ungainly looking landaulet body. To extrapolate from that figure, a fine, pre-World War I Silver Ghost touring car would have made $35,000 at the same sale, or ten times its worth twenty years ago. The highest known price for Rolls-Royce is the $65,000 paid a few months ago for a 4-cylinder of 1905 vintage.

Frederick Henry Royce made his first car in 1903 and ran the company with an iron hand until his death three decades later. His partnership with C. S. Rolls began in 1904 and ended with Rolls's death in an airplane accident in 1910. It was Royce, a born mechanic and a man obsessed with unattainable perfection, who created the car; and the British Empire, gratefully, knighted him for it. The combination of elegance, silence, speed, and longevity achieved in the Silver Ghost Rolls-Royce has probably never been equaled. From the beginning, the car was guaranteed for three years unconditionally: parts and labor free. In some particulars, its design was less than genius-struck, but the quality of the material that went into it and the care its builders lavished upon it had not been seen before and probably have been equaled since only in the Mercedes-Benz shops.

If you can't find a Ghost within the extreme range of your bank account, there are valuable successor models. The Phantom I is a splendid car and the only Rolls-Royce besides the Silver Ghost made in the United States (in Springfield, Massachusetts, briefly) as well as in England. The P-II Continental, a rarity—fewer than 325 were made—and commensurately costly, is one of the dozen most capable fast touring motorcars that ever ran. The smaller Royces, the 20-horsepower, the 20–25, and 25–30, low on most autophilists' want lists up to the present, have been good buys for some time as the available stock of the bigger cars was drained away into permanent possession in collections and museums. A *coupe de ville* on a 20-horsepower chassis makes a lovely miniature.

England has known automobiles of reputation so puissant that one would be justified in thinking they'd been built in thousands. The Marendaz comes to mind, and the Leyland Eight and the Invicta, all cars famous in the connoisseur's memory and all made in very short runs. The most extraordinary of the lot may be the Squire, a potent sports car first dated 1934. Every reference book on high-performance cars lists the Squire, and many who've known all about the car for years have been staggered to learn, finally, that the total production was seven units. True, though. Only a dozen cars had been planned, and when the company, out of money, closed down in 1936, it had built twelve chassis and seven complete cars. The extra chassis and parts were bought up by the owner of one of the original eight, a Val Zethrin, and in the next three years, he slowly built three units, properly called Squire-Zethrin types.

Gregor Grant's *British Sports Cars* says of the Squire: "The late A. M. Squire was by way of being a genius, and there is no doubt that the 1½-liter Squire was one of the most attractive sports cars ever built . . . one of the most talked-about cars of the time. It bristled with interesting features developed from racing practice. . . ."

Adrian Squire, designer and builder, was a short, intense-looking man, dapper, wearing a big R.A.F. mustache. He was a draftsman and engineer at the MG factory, and long remembered as a good one. His purpose in the Squire was straightforward: he wanted to build the best possible sports car, cost no object. He consequently had to price the vehicle at $7500, a stiff figure at any time and seriously high in a period of economic spin like the 1930s. In two years, he did push the price down to $4000, still a lot, when MGs were going for less than $1000. Of course, the Squire offered a firmer base for the mechanical one-upmanship that has always marked sports-car people: a supercharged double-overhead-cam Anzani engine with a finned oil cooler out in front of the radiator, a Wilson preselector gearbox—and a signed statement that the car had lapped the Brooklands track at 100-plus mph.

When he saw he couldn't keep the company afloat any longer, Adrian Squire went back to the drafting table, this time for an aircraft firm. He was killed in a 1940 air raid. I know of three Squires in this country. Although it is very rare, indeed, the Squire has almost none of the glamorous history —competition or civilian—that attends some other low-production makes, and the car's worth is accordingly lower. I would think $10,000 a fair figure for a Squire in good to fine condition. Fair is one thing, though, and persuading a reluctant owner to give one up is something else. Still, one ought never to go over the market. A collector I know who has almost unlimited resources abides rigorously by a self-fixed rule never to go over the market, by which he means his own appraisal of the car's worth, weighted in the second place, and I think slightly, by what it's worth to him for any special reason. For the patient, prices often come down. Oppositely, there's the con man's dictum: "A sucker can't wait."

The Chevrolet Corvette Stingray, as hot a vehicle as Detroit offers today, will get to 100 mph from a standstill in 14.7 seconds. Thirty-five years ago, a Model SJ Duesenberg would do the same thing in only 2.3 seconds more, which is one measure of the esteem in which the car is still held. It was a low-production item, by American standards, 470 units, J and SJ, of which more than half are still in existence, an extremely high survival rate.

Most of the motorcars that are worth having and worth remembering were created by single men, individuals—Bugatti, Birkigt, Ford, Packard, Bentley, Royce, Lanchester—but two brothers, the German-born Frederick and August Duesenberg, made the Duesenberg. Granted, most credit goes to the dominant brother, Frederick, the older. Settled in Iowa farming country as children, they were bicycle mechanics, moved on to motorcycles and then to automobiles. Their first-built car was a Mason, named after the man who financed it: there wasn't a Duesenberg company until 1913. The first model was tagged A, and it was a superior, if unexciting car, the first in the world to have four-wheel hydraulic brakes. Of the 650 A's that were made, only about fifty survive. The Duesenbergs made engines for the government during the 1914–1918 war, but came into the peacetime boom market in thin financial shape. Money-making was never a primary interest for either of them; and although by 1922 their name was a sports byword (a Duesenberg, in 1921, won the first Grand Prix race ever for an American car, and seven of the first ten places at the 1922 Indianapolis 500 were filled by Duesenbergs), they were in money trouble two years later. Erret Lobban Cord (Auburn-Cord-Duesenberg) set them up again and work on the new satisfying project, which was to culminate in the model SJ, began in 1926. The first customers got cars in the spring of 1929.

The Model J Duesenberg of 1929 and the companion SJ, which appeared in 1932, sold in a basic price range from $14,750 to $17,750, with occasional flights to around $25,000, because they were by all means the best thing on the domestic market at the time; some of them are worth today twice what they cost new, because, with the exception of a very few badly bodied aberrations, they are stunningly good-looking, capable of blistering performances even by 1969 standards, and wreathed in an incomparable glamor. An unrestored sedan that was fairly scruffy-looking in my view changed hands for $35,000 not too many months ago. I remarked to a man who had dropped out of the bidding at $25,000 that I thought he'd been right, that the car was overpriced. He was not comforted. "I'd have gone $40,000 if I'd had it," he said. "After all, it's a Duesenberg, and it's *original!*"

In the span of the present car boom, Duesenberg prices have climbed like something by Picasso. The entire subject of classic pricing is one I find painful (I remember selling a very decent sedanca on a P-I Royce for $150), but I will bring myself to dwell on it long enough to state that D. Cameron Peck of Chicago, the most formidable of U.S. autophilists in the 1940s and 1950s, once offered a seven-passenger J Duesenberg sedan for $375. That was in the autumn of 1949; and while Peck's cataloging was not ecstatic ("A boxcar on wheels as far as body is concerned, but a good chassis"), still $375 did take the car; I wonder if $13,750 would today.

Duesenbergs more desirable than Peck thought his was—roadsters, say, and touring cars and phaetons—more often found pricings around $1500 twenty years ago. I remember being unable to persuade a man who said he was in the market even to go look at a Model J offered for $2000, because it was bodied by Saoutchik, a French coachmaker whose metal-beating ran to the bizarre. If it had been by Derham, Rollston, or Hibbard & Darrin, he said, it might be worth a look.

The Duesenberg factory originated no bodies, but delivered chassis to bespoke coachmakers, in the ancient tradition, to be finished to customer order; or, more usually, the factory bought bodies itself. Fourteen such firms furnished the factory at Indianapolis with some 380 bodies down the years. Murphy of California did most, about 125 bodies. Others were Le Baron, Judkins, Weymann, Walker, Brunn, Dietrich, Holbrook, Bohman & Schwartz, Locke, and La Grande. Foreign coachbuilders who raised bodies on Duesenberg chassis included Castagna, Letourneur & Marchand, Figoni, Franay, Van den Plas, D'Iteren Frères, Graber, Barker, and Gurney Nutting. A Duesenberg could draw attention even in a palace courtyard; and coachbuilders, looking at the bare chassis ($9500 for a J, $11,750 for an SJ), made up their minds not to stint on material. Today, Murphy roadsters and double-cowled phaetons by various American makers are most sought after.*

The Duesenberg could not compete with the Rolls-Royce in the silence of its going; there was too much engine for that—265 to 320 horsepower —but nothing was spared to mask the brute force under the hood, including a mercury-filled vibration damper on the crankshaft, and it ran very smoothly. For the period, the Duesenberg handled well and the brakes were adequate. Most buyers never used half its performance; it was a status symbol beyond compare, something that would, if it appeared today, drop a Cadillac into Volkswagen standing. In fact, two attempts were made to revive the Duesenberg, the last in 1966, but both collapsed against economic reality. Built as the Duesenberg brothers did it, an SJ Duesenberg bodied by, say, Hibbard & Darrin, would have to cost $100,000 today. Frederick Duesenberg died in 1932 as the result of a crash in the Pennsylvania mountains, driving one of his own cars, and his brother, August, in 1955, of a heart attack.

As unlike Duesenberg as anything on four wheels could be, but equally admirable as artifact and infinitely more blessed with originality, is the Lanchester in its early, tiller-steered form. There were heretical Englishmen who, practically laying their heads on the block, argued that the Lanchester was decidedly a better car than the Rolls-Royce. Perhaps not; although in the 1900s, there were known connoisseurs, including people in the royal household, who did prefer Lanchesters to "The Best Car in the World." In any case, it was an extraordinary vehicle; even today, a Lanchester is most pleasant to drive—quiet, nimble, and vibration-free; in its own time, it must have seemed a miracle. Like the Duesenberg, it was born of a brother act: there were three Lanchesters, Frederick, George, and Frank, with Frederick dominant. Frederick Lanchester was a kind of Renaissance man, universally accomplished. A practical engineer of the highest order, an inventor and innovator, he was a musician as well, a poet, a physicist, an aeronautical researcher. Builder, in 1895, of one of the earliest fine motorcars, he was publishing papers, four decades later, on jet propulsion and relativity. He

*In 1971, an offer of $60,000 for a phaeton was refused.

241

was probably a genius, and like many geniuses, he lived a long time, to be seventy-eight and laden with many honors, but fewer than he deserved. Similarly, his brother George: because the first Lanchester car had been destroyed in a German air raid at Coventry, George Lanchester, at eighty-three, and from memory, built a museum-quality model of it.

The Lanchester was so far ahead of its time that much of it was reinvented, years and years later, and credited to other names. First use of the disk brake is usually, and wholly erroneously, assigned to race cars and more correctly to airplanes, but indisputably, F. W. Lanchester had caliper-type disk brakes on his cars before race-car designers knew how to stop their front wheels and long before pilots could see any point in brakes at all.

Elegant was the word for the Lanchester. The first ones had 2-cylinder engines. As a rule, an automobile powered by a 2-cylinder engine can be seen vibrating half a city block away, but Lanchester's ran like a sewing machine: through a *tour de force* of sheer intellect, he had harnessed the cylinders into a system of six connecting rods and two crankshafts, instead of the two rods and one crank that were usual. The result was a canceling out and containment of the violent out-of-phase poundings inherent in the engine. Originality and intelligence shone through the design everywhere: for instance, Lanchester dimensioned the car to place the driver's eyes at what would be the average level for a walking man, so that movement and direction would not seem strange. His tiller rose at the driver's right side, the horizontal bar curved to fit the body, weighted, dynamically balanced, making steering into a driveway as natural as pointing the hand at it. Drivers who became well used to Lanchester tiller steering much preferred it to the wheel system. Lanchester never came up with a Scotch-tape-and-string solution to a problem, he worked in basics. When the owners of the ordinary car expected to grind the valves every couple of hundred miles, Lanchester's beautifully simple cooling system would let his go for 4000; the spark plugs could be adjusted with the engine running; oiling was automatic; his wick-system carburetor was indifferent to the dirty or mixed-strength gasoline of the day; the engine housing was between the two front seats, with all the hand controls mounted on a console over it, an arrangement that gave good balance to the car, and hung no weight out beyond the axles; the chassis frame was rigid and the suspension flexible—putting one wheel on a foot-high block had no effect on the other three—with the resultant superb ride; the entire body could be removed in five minutes without tools, and so on and on.

Lanchesters had a remarkably squared and balanced look, seeming always to be firmly placed on the road, particularly seen head on, when the radiator, in the water-cooled models, looked almost exactly twice as wide as it was high. (There was no need to unscrew the cap and peer into the hole to see if the water was up, by the way: Lanchesters had round glass-framed ports cut through the radiator shell for that purpose.) The cars were as stable as they looked, and because of this sure-footed way of going, and the quick steering available through the tiller system, they were easy to manage in the dreaded sideslip, or skid. English roads in the 1900s, often of stone or wood block and, of course, often wet and well dressed with horse manure, were wickedly slippery, and the versatile Dr. F. W. Lanchester included in the owner's manual that came with the car instructions on how to handle a skid, how to induce one for practice, and even how to do a 180-degree spin in the width of an ordinary road, a useful maneuver that is not easy in most modern cars—small front-wheel-drive types excepted.

Like most men of their turn of mind, the Lanchester brothers were not brilliant in business and they soon found themselves harnessed to play-it-safe boards of directors who were frightened by originality and believed that the proven way was always the profitable way. In the Lanchesters' private table of organization, Frederick was designer; George, assistant designer and production man; Frank, business manager. But the company had been insufficiently funded at the beginning, was chronically in a short cash position, despite an excellent product and devoted customers, and in 1904, it went through a forced reorganization, in the course of which most of the Lanchesters' financial leverage was taken from them. The firm later gave its stockholders substantial profits, little of which Frederick Lanchester or his brothers saw.

Around 1914, the Lanchester began to look more like other motorcars, with the engine out in front and wheel steering. (The tiller had been optional since 1907 and was dropped in 1909; it was great for a light car but didn't have enough leverage for a big one.) The 1919 model, a remarkably lithe-looking sedan, was a notable success and the most expensive car in the London auto show of that year, at about $15,000 (partially because the interior walls and the ceiling were of burr walnut, with an elaborate leaf-and-flower pattern inlaid in lighter woods). This was on the 40-horsepower long-wheelbase chassis, also the base for a really startling motorcar built to the order of the Maharaja of Alwar. The driving seat was completely open —no doors, roof, windshield, body sides, nothing; behind it was an open landau coach body, looking exactly as if it had been taken from a horse-drawn carriage, and suspended on fully exposed, curved, sled-runner springs, just as early coaches were. Upholstery was in blue silk and hardware in gold.

The last of the "real" Lanchesters came through the factory doors in 1928; after that, and another reorganization, the Lanchester name was tacked onto a cheap Daimler.

The 2-cylinder Lanchester remains an authentic marvel and a bench mark in the history of the automobile. It was a true original, owing practically nothing to anything that had gone before it.

Lanchesters rarely appear on the market today. The biggest collection is in the hands of a Briton, the primary authority on the make, Francis Hutton-Stott. One major American collector told me he would cheerfully pay $15,000 for a tiller-steered Lanchester in good to fine order.

A couple of years after the last Lanchester appeared, another talented and unlucky Englishman, W. O. Bentley, announced his version of the very fast luxury touring automobile. The 8-liter Bentley chassis alone cost $9000, the complete car could go over £3000, or something like $30,000 in today's money. It would seem that, with the 1930–1931 Depression in full crunch, Bentley could not possibly have chosen a worse time, but 100 8-liters were made and sold without extraordinary difficulty. Most of them still exist— huge brooding monsters from another age, a period that seems as remote as the Jurassic.

Ettore Bugatti, who thought himself a figure of elegance, and was, and a wit, and wasn't, said of Bentley, "He builds the fastest trucks in the world." Others said, small wonder some parts of Bentley's cars looked like castings for a locomotive, since he'd begun his working life as an apprentice in a roundhouse and did a full year as a fireman the old way, the hard way, balancing with the big shovel in the open lurching cab, left hand covered with a cloth against the firebox heat. (For supper, he wrote long afterward, the thing was to rub the coal dust off the shovel and grill lamb chops on it.)

Bentley left the railroads after six years (as soon as he found he could never hope to own and drive his own locomotive, his friends said). He took the agency for some French cars, one of which, a tourer called Doriet Flandrin et Parant, he modified so effectively that he began to win sports-car races in it. During World War I, he developed a superior aluminum piston for aircraft engines and designed two thoroughly good engines, the Bentley Rotary I and II. The British government ordered 30,000 of these engines; but, since Bentley was unhappily signed on with the Royal Naval Air Service, he profited only insignificantly.

With next to no money of his own, and the help of friends no better off, Bentley, like hordes of ex-Forces people, set up a motorcar-manufacturing company in 1919. Unlike most of the others, he produced a car, due to be known, in the fulness of time, as the immortal 3-liter, and began selling it in 1921. Getting the Bentley into actual production was a feat of mind over matter; the company didn't have a machine shop or a foundry or even a drafting room in the real sense of the word. Outside suppliers made the Bentley components and the Bentley work force put it together. It was a good car, very sturdy, dependable, run by a high-speed overhead-cam engine that was essentially a race-car engine made reliable. A 3-liter won the Le Mans 24-Hour Race in 1924, the first of five times the make was to do it.

There were 1639 3-liter Bentleys built, and 300-odd survive. The 3-liter begat the 4½-liter, which begat the Blower Bentley, which begat the Standard Six, which begat the Speed Six, which begat the 4-liter, which begat the 8-liter. They were all remarkable cars, big, high-riding, some of them hairy in the extreme, all of them fast and trustworthy, except the fifty Blower Bentleys, supercharged 4½-liters, which looked and sounded wonderful but never won anything. (Sir Henry Birkin, one of the legend-wreathed "Bentley Boys"—gentleman-amateur drivers, most of them, who campaigned the cars for the great fun of it—did come second to a Type 35 Bugatti in the 1930 French Grand Prix. This was a considerable feat, the Bentley being a big and heavy road car, after all, and the Pau circuit on which the race was run that year a twisty one.) The supercharger, mounted in front of the radiator, was huge and produced 110 extra horsepower, of which it needed 35 to run itself. W. O. Bentley didn't like it, and properly so, but it did make the blown 4½ the sexiest-looking car in the line, and a fine one today is certainly worth $15,000.

Largely because of their record at Le Mans, unparalleled until the Jaguars came along in the 1950s, the Bentleys grabbed the British as no car except the Rolls-Royce has ever done. The firm made motorcars for only ten years, at an average rate of about one a day (3061 in all); but the name is immortal, nevertheless. Financially, the company never recovered from its initial underfunding; and for five years, it was kept afloat by one man, who pumped probably $750,000 into it: Woolf Barnato, heir to a huge share of the Kimberley diamond mines. Barnato was a Bentley team driver. Even he gave up finally, and Rolls-Royce bought everything.

The 8-liter, if it had come earlier, might have saved Bentley. It was a most impressive motorcar, silent, by the standards of the time, at 100 miles an hour, and putting out so much torque that it would run in high gear from 6 to 104 mph. W. O. Bentley said, "By the late 1930s, I think we could have made it into a very good car, with a speed of at least 115 to 120 miles an hour, with silence and safety. It would have been interesting to carry out this work, and I am sorry I was not allowed to." As it was, the 8-liter was so strong that it didn't really matter what kind of coachwork was put on it. Light fabric bodies by Weymann were stylish at the time, and an 8-liter would fly with one of them, but it could move a seven-passenger limousine almost as fast.

W. O. Bentley has lived to see his car become a cult object and more, one in the line of artifacts locked into the history of the Empire: the longbow, the kilt, Big Ben, the Spitfire, the cricket bat, the pub, and the London bobby's hard hat. His last work, the 8-liter, was handsome, I think, as a short-bodied four-passenger coupe with a blind rear quarter, and I would look for one of those if I were to begin looking today. Found, I think it would take $15,000 to move it, and that might not move it far. Incidentally, Bentley models were to be told apart, among other indications, by the color of the enamel in the radiator badge, which might be green, red, black, or blue, except for the Speed Six model, normally green, but optionally anything the customer wanted. A Bentley was thus usually known as a Red Label or a Blue Label or whatever, although the factory intensely disliked the use of the word "label" instead of "badge." In any case, a proper 8-liter carries green enamel around the big black B.

You had to make a really big fast car if you were to count in the major leagues in the 1930s, and Ettore Bugatti, as was his wont, topped everybody with a thing that might have been called a 15-liter Bugatti if he hadn't chosen to call it a Type 41, or the Bugatti Royale. It was The End in almost every dimension and every particular—sheer bigness (seven feet from radiator to windshield, for example), price ($20,000 for the bare chassis), guarantee (for life), and so on. Ettore Bugatti was a superlatively skillful image projector, and the Type 41, the Golden Bug, as the British called it, was probably his master stroke. Hugh Conway, a primary Bugatti authority, thinks it possibly *the* most fantastic automobile ever. Only six were built.

Shortly after the war, an English *Bugattiste* who had a 41 with a sedan body asked me if I could sell it for him. I circularized the entire membership of the Sports Car Club of America without finding anyone who would get up $5000 for it. That car is certainly worth $50,000 today, but I doubt that an offer of twice that would move it. [In June 1971 Parke-Bernet auctioned a Type 575C Bugatti for $59,000.] Because the number of 41s built is positively known, there's no chance that a "lost" Royale will turn up; the six are all held in permanent collections here and abroad (Harrah's Automobile Collection in Reno, the biggest and best in the world, has two), and so it seems hardly fair to include the car in a suggested collection, however hypothetical. It *could* happen, but it's a 100-to-1 shot at the moment. That doesn't mean that a new collector can't aspire to a Bugatti. M. Bugatti did make between 6000 and 7500 automobiles, and at least 1500 of them still exist. They exist in wide variety—some fifty models—because their creator was a restless, volatile, experimenting kind of man. Ettore Bugatti had designed and built cars before he was twenty-one; and by 1910, he had a factory in Alsace-Lorraine. He built five automobiles that year, and it can truly be said that except for a very short period in the 1940s, the Bugatti has been in demand from that day to this. Bugatti's racing cars, his Grand Prix cars, were originals and, in some ways, the greatest of their time; his sports cars set standards that other makes were years in equaling. He was eclectic in design: tiny battery-driven child's cars, 110-mph open four-seaters, little leather-bodied coupes, big touring limousines, race cars, town cars—all carried the 3½-inch red-and-white Bugatti radiator badge. He made other things, too: boats, trains, airplane engines.

Another avenue of assault on the big, fast luxury car was Abner Doble's —steam. Doble reminds one of Bugatti; he was imperious, arrogant, aristocratic, obsessed with the attainment of unattainable perfection, and, like Bugatti, he had first intended being an artist, a concert pianist. There is a fixed law at work here; almost every automobile that is rated today as an imperishable classic, supreme in beauty or function or both, was created by a man of notable intelligence, sophistication, eccentricity, and civility, who was not motivated by money-making.

After he had abandoned pianism and the ambition that succeeded it, surgery, and had been schooled in engineering at the Massachusetts Institute of Technology, Doble raised $500,000 and set up shop in Waltham, Massachusetts. He built good steam automobiles, about eighty of them, but they were really only design exercises for his masterwork, the Models E and F Doble he built in California after his return there (he was born in San Francisco) in 1920. Between then, when he set up a new company with his brothers John, Warren, and William, and 1932, Doble made twenty-four steamers. These were the best steam automobiles we have so far seen. Earlier steamers had been dragged down by nuisance problems. It took thirty minutes of long, involved procedure and a blowtorch to start some of them. To shorten getaway time, it was usual to leave a pilot light burning under the boiler; this annoyed garage proprietors and ferryboat captains, and in some jurisdictions there were laws against it. The steam automobile engine could boil away twenty-five gallons of water surprisingly quickly, and it was usual to carry a length of garden hose, in case there was nothing handier than a pond or a horse trough when the tank went dry. Steamers like the famous Stanley would go very quickly, indeed, but only for a short distance, because the boilers couldn't make enough steam fast enough.

Standing outdoors in the dead of a Minneapolis winter, a Doble would start and move away twenty-two seconds after the switch had been flipped; most 1969s won't do a lot better. The Doble carried a steam condenser where the gasoline car had its radiator; enough of the water that went through the boiler was recovered to make thirty gallons last for 750 miles. It was fast enough: 95-plus mph. Like all steamcars, the Doble was nearly silent, had ferocious acceleration (a steam engine delivers maximum torque the instant the throttle is opened), and would climb the side of a house, if the wheels didn't slip. Writer Griffith Borgeson, who lived near the Doble factory in Emeryville, California, recalls a hill favored by the firm's test drivers. It was two miles long and steep: rising one foot in four. Gasoline cars had to rush it flat-out and even then might not see the top; the Dobles could start at the bottom from a standstill and whistle on up, accelerating to the point of wheelspin, if they felt like it.

Specifying material, components, and workmanship for his car, Doble named nothing but the best. He used chrome-nickel steel for chassis members, his machining was to the highest standards, and he liked steering wheels of ebony and nickel silver. Doble's standards and his limited production necessarily imposed high prices: $8000 and up—up to $11,200. There are fifteen E Dobles known at the moment; prices as high as $15,000 have been asked for unrestored, modified examples carrying nonoriginal parts.

Doble Steam Motors went under in the 1932 Depression, but Doble was concerned with steam almost to his death in 1961. Ten years before that, the McCulloch company (chain saws, superchargers) had mounted a serious and heavily financed approach to the steam automobile, with Doble leading, but it was abandoned far short of production.

So much for a collection restricted to ten automobiles, with the brutal omissions consequential to such limitation: the Alfa-Romeo 1750 Zagato, the Mercedes-Benz SSK, the Hispano-Suiza Boulogne are classics that come instantly to mind. But if they would add luster, they would add dollars, too: the Alfa, with two-seater body by Zagato, first seen in 1932, brings around $10,000 today. (A modern-engined factory-built replica offered a couple of years ago failed on the market.) The SSK Mercedes was a Ferdinand Porsche design built by the oldest and one of the most successful automobile constructor firms; it was much used by Rudolf Caracciola when he drove for the factory to win the Mille Miglia, the Tourist Trophy, the European hill-climb championship. SSKs were costly new and are in the $10,000–$15,000 area today. Hispano-Suizas run higher: $18,000–$25,000, justifiable in a car some authorities call truly the best car in the world; that's to say, better than the contemporary Rolls-Royce. The Hisso began as a collaboration between the Swiss designer Marc Birkigt, one of the immortals of automobilism, and Spanish financiers. Early cars were made in Spain, but Birkigt's final triumphs, such as the 12-cylinder Type 68, came out of France.

As the classics disappear into permanent museum custody, autophilists look in new directions and specialist collections spring up: child-size toy collections, for example. The best-known toy is the miniature Grand Prix car Ettore Bugatti built first for his son Roland and later for limited commercial sale. It was cataloged at the factory as Type 52. A 1928 model of this car brought $3000 at a recent British auction. Many others were made around that time and they are still being made; I have seen Ferrari, Mustang, GT40 Fords, and Aston Martin toys recently. These cars are usually about two-fifths size, battery-driven. The finest collection of drivable toys belongs to Francis Mortarini of Paris. He has about thirty. Toy-size cars attract many collectors. In the 1920s, some toys were elaborately detailed and up to twenty inches in length. Adam Pellicot of Stockholm has probably the biggest collection of toy automobiles—2500 of them.

Miniature road cars haven't caught on yet, but they will. Bugatti's *Bébé* Peugeot, the first practical small-automobile small automobile, would be the foundation of a miniature collection, with his Types 13 and 22, the Austin Seven, Bullnose Morris, American Bantam, Crosley Hotshot, Fiat Topolino, and so on. Almost every automobile-producing country made a miniature.

Cleverest will be the new collectors who buy in 1969 the cars that will be crowding Parke-Bernet's catalogs for the spring sale in the year 2000. If I knew what those cars would be, I'd have a barn stuffed with them standing on end. The best advice remains the art collector's rule: buy what you *like*. Most crystal balls are clouded. For example, on the ground of rarity, the Tucker ought to be a good buy, but it seems to lack basic appeal. The Edsel will be a rarity in 2000, but there may be little interest in it because it was a failure, and nobody loves a loser. The Tatra, a rear-engine V8 made in Czechoslovakia, is an interesting car; but while it's rare on this side of the water, there are thousands of them in central Europe. The Mercedes-Benz 300SL ought to be a classic, it was a breakthrough car and a success; enough were built to scatter the car around the world but not enough to make it common; it is good-looking and has an interesting history. I think the Ferrari will always be good, and racing Ferraris, because there are so few of them, very good. But the best guideline remains one's own taste—and it can't hurt to watch the quotations in the Sunday *New York Times* and magazines such as *Road and Track*.

How many cars make a collection? I think that three does it, if a viable association—historical, mechanical, personal, whatever—links them. Three at least as minimum and, as maximum, whatever your interest and your bankroll will reach. The ceiling at the moment is the 1,469 cars in Harrah's Automobile Collection.

—1969

Pat
Moss
Carlsson

Pat Moss Carlsson lives in a Buckinghamshire ham-
let, Ickford, two or three miles off the London–
Oxford road, down a one-wagon-wide lane strung
with blind, hedged corners and ancient, hump-backed
bridges. The house is new and modern, and half of one
wall of the living room is solid with trophies in silver,
ceramic, glass, and ivory, the best and the best-looking of the 1500 such objects Mrs. Carlsson has won
in international competition as horsewoman and motorist. She is one of the premier woman athletes of all
time and indisputably the best woman driver of fast
automobiles. Most of the competitors in her special-
ity, long-distance rallydriving, are men, and they take
her seriously. Even her husband, Erik Carlsson, a
legend-wreathed Swede, several times champion of
Europe, takes her seriously, since he has seen the day
when he finished sixteenth to his wife's third. It never
happened again, but still. . . .
  Rallydriving is what is left of the first significant
automotive competitions, the open-road city-to-city
races that began with the birth of the automobile in
the late nineteenth century and ended, for all practical
purposes, with the Paris–Madrid of 1903, a rolling

catastrophe in which so many drivers and spectators died that the authorities stopped it at the Spanish frontier. (One open-road event survives, the Targa Florio, in Sicily, run since 1906.) A rally is technically not a race but the distinction is fine. Best known is probably the Monte Carlo, run every year in January to insure that the trans-Alpine roads will be properly snow-clad or iced. Monte Carlo competitors, driving passenger automobiles, usually high-performance sports types, may start from various points in Europe, say Lisbon, London, Oslo, Warsaw, Athens, Frankfurt, Reims, or Monte Carlo itself. All routes are laid out for equal distances. Competitors must maintain precise speeds, to the second, or be penalized. The demanded average may be 37 miles an hour, which doesn't sound like much until one tries it, even on well-known roads in bright daylight. After the cars arrive in Monte Carlo, there is a mountain circuit of around 400 miles to do, all of it at night. And within every rally there are sections called special stages, ten, twenty, or thirty of them, and these are flat-out races over difficult roads, often at night.

It all adds up to driving of the highest professional level, and no one can hope to do well who cannot drive at 100 miles an hour on sheer ice at night in the mountains, with a rock-face on one side and a precipice on the other. A driver does nothing but drive: the other front seat is held down by an iron-nerved navigator who runs the clocks and reads the maps and the pace-notes. Pace-notes are precise, almost yard-by-yard directions over critical places assembled in days, sometimes weeks of "recce" (reconnaissance). The driver of a car doing 95 or 100 miles an hour over a curving hilly road at night must know, coming to a right-hand bend, that it is followed by a left-hander, or another right-hander, or a straight, before he reaches it. By the time he sees which way the road is going it may be too late. Even if he does make the corner safely, he will probably do something untidy and time-consuming.

In the golden 1920s and 1930s, rallydriving was an amateur sportsman's game, but it's been a long time now since an amateur has won a major event. Professionals, running factory-owned and factory-supported cars, win today. The factories, pushing for publicity (victory in a big rally will sell a lot of automobiles), provide the cars, mechanics, depots of spare parts along the route, which are notable for stacks of spare tires. Speeds are so high, and adhesion of rubber to road so near the limit, that a varied selection of sophisticated treads and compounds and steel studs is vital. Under some conditions, a car may take on a different set of tires every 100 miles or so. Rallydrivers are highly paid specialists, a separate breed. There have been Grand Prix and sports-car drivers, superb in their own fields, who loathed rallydriving: some admitted it terrified them. The best in recent years have been Scandinavians; Swedes, Finns, Norwegians. The Danes aside (Pat

Moss Carlsson ranks them with the Belgians and the Swiss as the worst drivers in the world), the Scandinavians have an abundance of snow and ice to make their roads interesting, and even in summer they are challenging, since loose gravel is a common surface.

Erik Carlsson, Pat's husband, was the first of the great Scandinavians, an innovator whose style on the Swedish front-wheel-drive SAAB was spectacular. Finding himself going flat-out down the wrong road, for example, he would make a 180-degree reversal of direction without taking his foot off the accelerator: steering wheel hard over, a quick on-off of the hand brake to lock the rear wheels and pivot the car on them and zap—running back in his own tracks. Spectators also thought it worthwhile to watch Carlsson get into the tiny SAAB. They wondered where he would put himself, at six feet four inches and 220-plus pounds.

Down the years, Carlsson has won nearly everything worth winning, and he retired in 1968. Mrs. Carlsson, driving now for the Lancia factory of Italy, hasn't yet thought of stopping. She's thirty-four. The idea neither burdens nor much impresses her, but she is maintaining a tradition and a famous name. Her father was a racing driver, her mother was Woman Champion of Europe (as Pat has been), and her brother is Stirling Moss. Like him, she began competition with horses, at six, and she was picked for the British International Team when she was seventeen. About 1000 of her trophies (she keeps most of them in a vault in her father's home) she won in the ring. In many years of jumping, she was hurt only once. She spooked a pony by taking off her jacket in the saddle; he bolted out from under her, and she broke an ankle.

The crash is inevitable in rallying as it is in all forms of competitive driving, and Mrs. Carlsson has had ten serious shunts and walked away from all of them. Minor crunchings and bumpings, fenders smashed in, bumpers ripped off, she doesn't count. On a running of the East African Safari, a brutal rally that has been enlivened by restless emerging nationalists who dig elephant pits for the cars or toss six-inch rocks through the windshields, she remembers hitting a deer only because the animal smashed the fan-belt pully on her SAAB, and Erik, running a few minutes behind her, had a spare in his pocket, the only time in his life he had ever carried one. His wife thinks this was perhaps fated.

Carlsson is a gentle bear type, a pleasant man, but he has a formidable temper and a tendency to be direct, and he is impatient of restraint and convention. When he first began to drive in competition, the Swedes called him something that might translate as "Erik-on-his-head" because his automobile seemed to be upside-down, sliding on its roof, a good deal of the time. Pat knew him as a competitor but they didn't meet until one bitterly cold night in the Swedish Midnight Sun Rally, Pat and her navigator were sitting in the car at a checkpoint when the window on her side darkened and something drummed on the roof. She cranked down the window. A large hand entered, bearing gifts, and a voice came out of the snow, "You like orange?" It was, she knew, a declaration of true love. They were married two years later. Erik Carlsson was deeply devoted to good food, but fried sausage represented the outer range of his wife's repertoire. She is now, he says, one of the world's great cooks, at home in the British, French, and Swedish cuisines. "I bought books," she says. "I went into the kitchen and I learned, that's all. I just kept at it."

The true competitive instinct is a rarity and is, like genius or beauty, fascinating. Most athletes are not really competitors. Even in racedriving, the most dangerous of all sports, there are men who are not last-ditch, lay-it-all-on-the-line competitors. Stirling Moss once remarked to me that his sister had the skill and the endurance of a Grand Prix driver but, like all women, lacked the essential competitive urge. A few days later I watched her in a sedan race at the Brand's Hatch Circuit near London. Running uphill, the driver next to her, a formidable Irish Internationalist, Paddy Hopkirk, moved in to try to bluff her out of line, and in doing so, touched her car. Instantly, with a booming as of a brass drum, she hit him with the whole side of her automobile, like a child swinging a toy. He hit her back and she hit him back and they went up the hill that way, in a series of merry crunches. I reminded her of the incident. She is a big woman but her voice is light and her English is precise and graceful. "I remember," she said. "Paddy Hopkirk. We were laying on each other."

She laughed. "I know Stirling thinks women are competitive only against the clock, but I know I'm much more competitive against other drivers, when it's a matter of looking over at someone and saying to oneself, 'Oh no, my boy, oh no you don't.' But I don't want to drive Grand Prix cars. The idea of running around and around a circuit bores me. A rally, when one's running over 2000 or 3000 miles of road, is something else. And I don't think I'm competent to drive 200-miles-per-hour motorcars. I think 120 is quick, and I've frightened myself at 130. Stirling once asked me if I wanted to go around the Silverstone Circuit with him in a new Lotus. I said, all right, if he wasn't going to go fast. He went off at a fantastic rate. He broke the lap record, with a passenger in the car. I never saw the road, I closed my eyes."

Pat Moss Carlsson has run in more than 150 international rallies. She drives 50,000 miles a year in competition and practice. (She didn't like driving as a teenager, failed her first test, and persisted only because she wanted to be able to haul her horses around from show to show.) In a six-month period last year she competed in France, Italy, Africa, Greece, Sicily and was at home for just three weeks. She thrives on this regimen.

She has an incredible energy-level, a family characteristic. In 1960 she ran in the Marathon de la Route, a flat-out blind through Belgium and Italy via Yugoslavia, August 31 to September 4, five days with no stops for food or rest. Strong men, their eyes glazed with fatigue, ran off the road, but Mrs. Carlsson won her class, the Ladies' Cup, and the whole rally overall and outright. That year she and her codriver, Ann Wisdom, were jointly awarded the Guild of Motoring Writers' "Driver of the Year" award, an honor which has most often gone to eminences of the Grand Prix circuit.

"I like rallying," she says. "After all, if one enjoys one thing that one can do well—that's what it's all about, isn't it? And it's how I met Erik."

—1969

The
Day
They
Dug
Up
Babs

Today's race cars are fragile, spidery-looking things, built for one race, rebuilt for the next. At season's end they often disappear as entities, cannibalized for new models. No more the sturdy, year-after-year campaigners of the past; many of them even now, decades beyond their prime, still running in amateur races. It's been a long time since one has known of a racing car that was personally named, or affectionately called "she." ("The old girl's timing seems badly off, Nigel.")

Past doubt, the British took this subphase of anthropomorphism farthest. In August 1926 an Englishman, R.B. Howey, was killed driving a Ballot racing car in Boulogne. Howey's body and the wrecked automobile were put aboard a trans-Channel steamer for England. Halfway across the ship's engines were rung down and the battered Ballot—it had hit a tree—was, with grace and ceremony, pushed over the side into the deep. The custodian of the car was a heavy-shouldered, broody-looking Welshman, John Godfrey Parry Thomas, an automotive engineer and gentleman amateur racedriver.

He was usually named Parry Thomas in print, but

his friends called him Tommy, his family, Godfrey. He was a bachelor, he had private means, he was rather withdrawn and distant, indifferent to notice and common opinion. In photographs he seems always to be wearing an old Fair Isle sweater, sometimes under a bagged tweed jacket. Few pictures I have seen show him smiling. One notices the girth of his upper arms. He was a strong man. His front teeth stuck out in what some thought a menacing way. He liked children, animals, and good-looking women.

As chief of engineering for the significant Leyland Company, his major work was a passenger automobile, the Leyland Eight, made during the years 1920–1923. It raised a sensation: the most powerful and most expensive British car then on the market. It was designed on a no-expense-barred basis, made with the "intention to produce the most perfect car it is possible to design and manufacture." It could be compared, Thomas felt, only with the Rolls-Royce. Some fourteen or eighteen units were built (authorities differ) and three of a modification called the Leyland-Thomas, one of which exists today and has shown 200 horsepower, a stunning figure for the early 1920s. That the Leyland should still have considerable renown, based on miniscule production, is not extraordinary in British motoring history; of a famous, almost legendary sports car of the 1930s, the Squire, only ten units ever lived.

On Easter Monday 1922, Parry Thomas entered a factory-prepared Leyland Eight in a race at the Brooklands circuit in Surrey, motor racing's Ascot ("The right crowd and no crowding," was the unofficial motto of the place) in illustrious company—Malcolm Campbell, Count Louis Zborowski, Kaye Don, Louis Coatalen, Major H.O.D. Segrave, all to become minor immortals. Thomas didn't distinguish himself that day, but he raced fairly steadily from then on, mostly at Brooklands, almost the only place in the British Isles where one *could* race. The track had been laid down in 1906, 200,000 tons of concrete spread to make a squashed oval three and a quarter miles long, two of them level, the rest banked as steeply as 1:30. Parry Thomas spent so much time at Brooklands that he thought it best to live there in a rented cottage inside the grounds.

He campaigned persistently the next few years. He was a good driver, unflappable, and advantaged in that as an engineer he knew what was going on beneath him. He won a good many races and wasn't often worse than third, but his interest gradually narrowed to high-speed record-breaking. On June 16, 1922, he took six international Class G records for the flying-start half-mile to ten miles. (By 1924 he had *all* the Brooklands Class G records, for engines not over 7.7 liters in size, or a little smaller than a Cadillac Eldorado.) By the end of July 1922 he had his first world record, for ten miles at 114.74 mph.

The ultimate in straight-line speed is of course the Land Speed Record, and in October 1925 Parry Thomas went to the Pendine Sands in Wales, a seven-mile stretch generally considered the best long straightaway in the United Kingdom. The weather was bad, but he came back in April with the same car, a monster that had been called the Higham Special when he bought it to rebuild. It was thereafter called "Babs," the contemporary diminutive for Barbara, but after what or which Barbara, Thomas never cared to say. Babs's engine was a war-surplus Liberty aero developing 500–600 horsepower and driving the two rear wheels through heavy chains running from sprockets beside and below the driver's seat in the manner of the day. Thomas pushed this behemoth—it was a hard car to handle—to 172-odd miles an hour and took the Land Speed Record from Sir Malcolm Campbell by more than 18 mph.

In February 1927 Campbell came back with a top of 179 for record averages of 174.8 for the kilometer and 174.2 for the mile. A month later, on March 1, Thomas returned to Pendine. He had flu, he was forty-one and looked rather older. The beach was wet and windy, impossible, and he spent a good deal of time, that day and the next, in bed. On the third the sky cleared and a try seemed reasonable. He ran the big car to the sand–it was strange and ungainly looking with a sloped carapacelike tail–and tried a run down the course and back for the required two-way average speed. Babs smoked and didn't go seriously quickly. They changed the plugs and reset the carburetors and Thomas roared off again. Running flat-out, he left the measured mile, a point at which he would normally lift his foot a bit off the accelerator; the car swerved, then somersaulted, landed on its feet, swerved the other way, made a half-circle, and stopped, not badly damaged except for the collapsed right rear wheel. But the right-side driving chain had killed Parry Thomas. Reid Railton, an engineer-designer and a Thomas associate, believed that the chain had snatched or jerked as Thomas decelerated, putting an insupportable stress on the wire-spoked wheel, which broke, causing the chain to part. The free end, coming around with terrible force, flailed, catching Thomas as the upper part of his body leaned out of the car, tipping because it had no support on the right rear corner.

Thomas was buried in the graveyard of Byfleet church, near Brooklands:

JOHN GODFREY PARRY THOMAS, BORN 6TH APRIL 1885. ACCIDENTALLY KILLED ON PENDINE SANDS WHEN ATTEMPTING THE WORLD'S MOTOR SPEED RECORD 3RD MARCH 1927. LIFE IS ETERNAL AND LOVE IS IMMORTAL AND DEATH WHICH IS ONLY THE HORIZON IS NOTHING SAVE THE LIMIT OF OUR SIGHT.

A wreath of violets, anonymously sent, carried the legend, RIDE ON, RIDE ON, IN MAJESTY.

Thomas's friends, whether in anger with Babs for having behaved badly, or in sorrow, decided that she must never run again. It was proposed, but voted down, that she be sunk at sea, as Parry Thomas had sunk Howey's Ballot. The final decision was to bury her on the beach.* A grave about seven feet deep was dug and a tractor pushed her in. To discourage souvenir hunters and ambitious but impecunious drivers, the story was spread that the car had been broken up with sledgehammers and that even Thomas's leather racing jacket, buried with Babs, had been slashed to ribbons, but in fact no such sacrilege was committed. A few years later the land came into the ownership of the Ministry of Supply and a police station was built over the grave. "Babs," wrote Thomas's biographer, Hugh Tours, "will never be disturbed."

Not quite so. Last year, one Owen Wyn Owen, an engineering teacher at a Welsh college, began to wonder if the big car oughtn't to be exhumed and exhibited, providing that more than forty years in wet sand hadn't put it beyond salvation. Matters of this kind are not quickly resolved in Britain and it took Owen more than a year and a short ton of paperwork to get permission. The police-station floor turned out to be substantial, nine inches of best concrete, but the last of it came away finally, the sand was shoveled off, and there was Babs, encrusted but whole. There was only one wheel on the car, but its racing Dunlop tire was sound, and held air. Excepting a cylinder-block break and the smashed hub, nothing seemed to be broken. Owen Wyn Owen announced that he would restore the car, to running order if possible, and make it a permanent exhibit in Pendine Village.

The exhibit will surely be a popular one. But Mr. Owen need not expect any heartfelt expressions of gratitude from Thomas's present-day peers or the motoring establishment, the bellwether publications of which were quick to indicate a dim and distant view. No one has called Owen Wyn Owen a ghoul, but no one has proposed him for the O.B.E. either.

Rumors that hard-hat divers have been seen over Howey's broken Ballot, full five fathoms deep on the course Boulogne–Dover, are not at present being taken seriously.

—1970

*A devoted member of the Bugatti Club Nederland has stipulated in his will that his Bugatti touring car be drenched in gasoline and burned—on his grave, one presumes.

The Mercedes-Benz C-111— Wundercar!

In the present life-style of the horse, we can descry the future of the automobile. The horse population of the United States is booming. In 1959, when we supported 4,500,000 horses, who would have guessed that 1969's total would be 7,000,000? At the turn of the century, with gasoline, steam, and electric automobiles proliferating, the extinction of the horse was widely mooted, and indeed did appear, to the penetrating mind, to be as obviously fated as the disappearance of the phonograph was to seem, a few years later, on the advent of radio. The survival of the phonograph lies outside the boundaries of the present inquiry, but the horse has lived on as an instrument of sport, and so will the automobile when its mass-transport function has been taken from it.

The *rate* of change is accelerating (Kitty Hawk to moon flight, sixty-six years!) and the multipassenger internal-combustion-engined motorcar may be shunted into the museums sooner than we think, replaced by public transport systems and by small, automated, tracked two-passenger vehicles. We can't afford the automobile's pollution now, and if we are not appalled at using 300 horsepower and a gallon of gasoline to push one man and five empty seats ten miles, our children will be. So we'll see a day when great seven-passenger Rolls-Royce limousines are taken off their blocks only to run a few miles in nostalgic review, as Brewster coach-and-four rigs are shown today in the enclaves of the very rich.

On that day, race cars will be running everywhere, as thoroughbreds do now, and more sports cars will be at large than there are now, their function, with the saddle horse, pure enjoyment, and transportation over the ground quite incidental. I don't know what these sports cars will be like, except that of course they must grow out of the most advanced current types. I do know where the peak is today: it's in the Mercedes-Benz C-111, a forty-four-inch-high, gull-winged-doored, Wankel-engined, 160-mph coupe that will be, the instant its production is announced, the most sought-after motorcar in the market. Blank checks will clutter dealers' mail. When? Not tomorrow, but in something like a year, I should think. This is my own surmise; Daimler-Benz officials insist that no plans for production exist, that the car is merely a *versuchswagen*—an experiment, a device intended for the working out of problems. Rudolf Uhlenhaut told me, when I saw the first C-111 at Stuttgart, how the problem had been stated: to build a fast two-seater sports car, roadable and comfortable. Uhlenhaut did not say "very comfortable" or "more comfortable than present sports cars," or anything of the sort; he used the single word. He speaks flawless Oxonian English and his meanings are precise. Fast. Roadable. Comfortable. The C-111 reaches 60 mph in 4.9 seconds and does 160-plus mph at 7000 engine revolutions a minute, but the engine, Uhlenhaut told me, will turn to 11,000. It is small—3.6 liters as against the Cadillac Eldorado's 8 liters—and midmounted in the present vogue for very fast sports cars, that is, ahead of the rear axle. Roadable, yes: the car swings from flat track to *vertical* banking at 100-plus mph as if it were running in a groove lined with ball bearings. And comfortable: the seats will be infinitely adjustable, air-conditioning will be standard, *und so weiter.* And no nonsense about 2 + 2 configuration, which usually means a tight fit in back for a couple of stunted children. The C-111 will accommodate two persons and a week's luggage in civilized style, and that's all.

It has been the custom of Daimler-Benz in the years the firm's names have been on automobiles (since 1886, making the Stuttgart house senior to all others) to bring out new models on no fixed schedule, much less on an annual basis. The engineering department, not the sales manager, determines release dates, and years may pass between models. The 1901 touring car, designed by Maybach, made by Daimler, and named Mercedes after the daughter of the man who sponsored it, Emil Jellinek, was the first automobile to depart wholly from the concept of the horse-drawn carriage with an engine stuck into it. The 1901 Mercedes drove the rear wheels from a front-mounted engine, had a pressed-steel frame, gate-type gearshift, honeycomb radiator, mechanically operated valves, steering by wheel, and so on. It was an original, and since then Daimler-Benz has produced, at spaced intervals, other originals: the S, SS, and SSK/SSKL models of the 1920s, designed by Ferdinand Porsche, passenger cars that could and did win races. And after them the heavy and overbearing supercharged 540Ks of the 1930s and the almost unbeatable Grand Prix machines of the same period—one of these, the W125, produced 646 horsepower out of an engine rather smaller than, say, a Pontiac's. After World War II, in 1952, the 300SL (300 for engine size, 3 liters or 300 cubic centimeters, S for Super, L for *Leicht*, light), appeared as a competition car. Two years later it was put on the market as the fastest (147 mph) production car in the world. In the beginning it was priced at around cost—$6820 and only 3258 300SL's were made until it was discontinued in 1962. The vehicle was a sensation in its own time and remains, seventeen years later, a desirable property at more than original cost.

A projected parallel between the 300SL and the C-111 is striking and despite announced company policy to the contrary, I think it valid. In the fullness of time the C-111 will be cataloged, under a more insinuating name, I hope, and in a limited edition at a reasonable figure. *Gran turismo* motorcars than can do 150 mph without strain tend to cost $20,000 or so and most of them fail somewhere: harsh ride, poor visibility, limited room, excessive noise, high maintenance-demand, spotty workmanship, low-grade or trouble-prone instruments and hardware—all difficulties little known to Mercedes-Benz clients and atypical of German production overall. The C-111 looks and feels rock-solid; it gave me, first as passenger and then as driver, an impression of beguiling security. Badly made automobiles betray that they are made up of thousands of bits and sections, many of which seem on the point of falling off; a well-made car, put together by earnest professionals, suggests that it is all one piece. Mr. Uhlenhaut obviously has confidence in the vehicle: he has commonly driven it 150–160 mph on the open road, in traffic.

The C-111 is not the first automobile to use the radical and sophisticated Wankel engine, but it is the first to offer it in an ultrahigh-performance car, and the Wankel's appearance in a Daimler-Benz vehicle, after more than ten years of research and development, puts a cachet on it, a seal of approval, and suggests that problems that had seemed likely to hold the Wankel down have been solved. The Wankel engine in the Mercedes C-111 is smaller than the transmission it drives. Looking into the engine compartment for the first time, someone said, only half-joking, "Where is it?" Small size is one of the Wankel's advantages. Another is ease of manufacture: there are only ten main working parts in the Wankel.

The Wankel is the newest prime mover we have, but the principle on which it works probably originated with the Pappenheim water pump in 1636, and was known to the inventor of our oldest engine, the steam engine, James Watts. Watts patented a rotary engine in 1769. His idea was perfectly sound, but the technology of his time couldn't accommodate it. Some competent authorities suspected that even present technology wouldn't be equal to the Wankel engine which appears to be simplicity itself but in fact is wickedly complex; its creation was an intellectual triumph. In a standard internal-combustion engine, a piston descending in a cylinder bore sucks in a charge of gasoline vapor, then ascends in the bore, compressing the charge, descends again, forcibly, as the charge is burned with near-explosive power, ascends again to push the used gases out of the bore. This sequence of events is called the Otto cycle after Nicholas August Otto, who demonstrated it in 1862. It is basic to the working of every internal-combustion engine, even those called two-stroke, which accomplish the same end with half the moves. The standard internal-combustion engine has been developed down the decades into a very good thing for driving vehicles despite the inherent disadvantage that the up-and-down of its pistons is violent, creates all kinds of shakings and vibrations, and must be converted to rotary motion before it can turn a wheel. How much better, men have thought for years, if it could be rotary to begin with.

Dozens, scores of rotary internal-combustion engines have been attempted. Only the Wankel has really succeeded. Why? Because although its creation was complicated, its working is simple and effective. A triangular piston revolves in an epitrochoid chamber. An epitrochoid looks like a circle that has been slightly flattened and slightly dented top and bottom, and within an epitrochoid a triangle of the correct size can revolve while maintaining its apexes, its corners, in constant contact with the walls of the chamber. At first glance it appears to be impossible, but it isn't.

As it spins, the Wankel triangular piston, which has rounded sides, sucks a charge of fuel into one of the chambers it makes in its turning, compresses and fires it, accepts power from it, and exhausts it. There are three power strokes per revolution, all three sides of the piston are working all the time, and its rotary motion can run straight into a gearbox, or transmission, without the further processing required by the standard engine: a piston driving a connecting rod which must turn a crank which in turn feeds into a gearbox.

Wankel ran his first engine, a small one, on February 1, 1957. It was the fruit of about thirty years of thought. Happily, he profited from his work. He sold his patent to the NSU company of Neckarsulm in Germany, which was responsible for much of the development work on the engine. Some 150 engineers worked to overcome the Wankel's early problems: heavy oil consumption, overheating, short spark plug life, "dirty" exhaust. More than 1,000 piston/chamber configurations were explored without finding one superior to the original's. NSU licensed other manufacturers around the world and by 1964 two Wankel-powered cars were running, the NSU Prinz in Germany and the Toyo Kogyo Mazda in Japan. To increase the capacity of a Wankel engine the method of choice is to add whole rotor units, and succeeding models, the Mazda Cosmo and the NSU Ro80 carried two-rotor engines. The Mercedes-Benz C-111 has a three-motor Wankel and is by far the most advanced and sophisticated of this type in existence.

–1969

Like
a
Collapsed
Balloon

Someone once showed me a twelve-inch-long model of a Nantucket whaler. It had been built in perfect detail: the keel was laid, ribs fitted and planked, decking put down. The ship was astonishing in its minutiae: it was copper-bottomed, covered with scale-sized plates fastened to the hull with 1200 scale-sized, handmade nails; the boats carried perfect oars and sharp-pointed harpoons; the tryworks on deck were of red bricks, hand formed, fired, and laid in mortar. A Revolutionary brig from the hands of the same master model-maker, I was told, carried cannon half an inch long, complete to microscopic touchholes, handcast cannonballs stacked beside them that precisely fitted the bores. I was anxious to meet the man who had built these ships. Particularly I wanted to see the hands that could fashion such incredibly perfect tiny things.

He must have weighed 190 pounds. His hands were truly huge, a ditchdigger's hands, sausage-fingered, and calloused. He laughed when he caught me staring at them.

"A man who's really good at something never looks the part," he said. "The best architect in this state is a client of mine. He's cross-eyed and his hands shake." He laughed again, picked up a piece of threadlike anchor cable, and with one hand tied four knots equidistant from each other.

Well, all generalizations are false, including this one, but still . . . I was inevitably reminded of his remark recently when I talked with the present world champion racing driver, Jackie Stewart of Scotland: John Young Stewart, who doesn't weigh 150 pounds, dresses in mad mod fashion, wears his hair shoulder length and, in all, looks as if he ought to be the fifth Beatle. And he goes about doing his thing, the most dangerous sport man knows, with all the dash and derring-do of a church usher. There *have* been racedrivers who would shake off half a dozen girls, vault into a car, and blast off in a cloud of rubber smoke. Not Jackie Stewart. Starting from cold it takes him some little time to be ready to punch the starter button, beginning with heavy thermal fire-resistant underwear and ending with a six-point seatbelt harness made to his order by an aircraft supply company. He takes every precaution known to his profession and some that are original with himself: for example, a set of steering-wheel-removal wrenches fastened to the side of the cockpit, painted Day-Glo orange, and carrying instructions for their use in the language of whatever country he's racing in on a given day, just in case an accident knocks him out and he has to rely on spectators to get him out of the car before it burns. But, once he's armed and armored, Steward cheerfully goes in harm's way and very, very fast. He's particularly quick in pouring rain, a circumstance that has been known to discourage some notably brave men. He sees no paradox in any of this.

"Sometimes you think if a man had any imagination he wouldn't be a racing driver," Stewart says, "because if he had a vivid imagination he'd say, 'For God's sake what am I doing here?' Certain things he had seen, certain images, images of certain accidents, he'd never get out of his head, but it's because I do have imagination that I have this big thing about safety. I *know* I'll have accidents from time to time. I *know* that somewhere along the road I'm going to have the odd knock. Now, if I can't be serious enough to know that when that knock comes I should be really well prepared for it, then I'm irresponsible, and I ought to be in some other line of trade."

A knock that Stewart recalls with some feeling came to him in 1966 at the Spa circuit in Belgium. This course is more than eight miles long, in a part of Belgium, near Francorchamps, noted for unpredictable weather. In 1966 the field of cars started the race in clear if cloudy weather, and halfway around ran into a rainstorm of cloudburst proportions. Water lay in sheets on the road; the cars began to aquaplane, a phenomenon in which a wedge of water actually lifts the wheels off the road, completely negating steering and braking effects. One car spun *nine* times on the two-lane road and went on safely. Another did a half-spin and vanished into the spray at 100 mph

—backward. Stewart, doing about 150, spun off the road, hit various solid objects including a house, and stopped with the car body wedged firmly around him. He had broken a collarbone and some ribs, dislocated a shoulder, and was concussed. But his primary difficulty was that thirty-five gallons of high-test gasoline had filled the cockpit like a bathtub and he was sitting in the stuff up to his waist. The dashboard had been wiped out, so he could not cut the ignition and the electric pumps were clicking away. Two other drivers, Graham Hill and Bob Bondurant, wrecked but unhurt, got Stewart out, but it took them thirty-five minutes because they had to loot spectators' cars for tools. The steering wheel was the main obstacle. Raw gasoline is caustic, and before he was discharged from St. Thomas's Hospital in London—unless he's totally unconscious, an injured British driver always demands to be taken instantly to St. Thomas's—Stewart had lost all the skin on his body from the waist down: "It all came off, Christ, the whole lot came off!"

It was after this incident that Stewart began to think of ways and means of shortening the odds. He was the first driver in Europe to use seat belts and the now universal face mask of fire-retardant fabric. He quickly followed the American driver, Dan Gurney, in using the "space hat," a helmet that covers the whole head and face, save the plexiglass viewing slit, with a sledgehammer-proof plastic. Everything he wears, gloves to shoes, is fire-retardant. Most of his colleagues have followed him, and if he's unhurt a driver can now count on an uncomfortable but safe thirty to sixty seconds in which to get out of a burning car. That's not too long, for exiting a 1970 Grand Prix car is a bit of a project at any time. To reduce frontal area, designers have lowered the driver into a semireclining position, almost as if he were in a hammock; there is no seat as such, just a thin padding on a sloped floor. The steering wheel isn't as big as a dinner plate, and the driver reaches it by stretching his arms straight out. There is no room for a bent elbow: a driver slightly too big for a new car found he couldn't move the gear lever at all with his right arm. There just wasn't enough space.

Stewart, a Scotsman living in Switzerland, drives a French car, a Matra, which uses a British-American engine, for a British team owner, Ken Tyrrell. Matra, primarily concerned with missiles and space technology, makes a small sports car in addition to race cars. The company furnishes the cars to Tyrrell gratis, writing off the cost against publicity. He runs two, his second driver being Jean-Pierre Beltoise. He buys his own Cosworth-Ford engines at $18,000 apiece (usually keeping eight of them on hand) and has useful sponsorship contracts with Dunlop tires and ELF, a French gasoline company. Running in the sky-blue which is France's racing color, strange to the world's circuits since the great days of the pre-World War II Bugatti, Stewart drove a Matra to first place six times in the 1969 Grand

Prix season, March 1 to October 19: South Africa, Spain, Holland, France, Great Britain, Italy. Only one other driver, Jimmy Clark, killed in a race in Germany in 1968, had won more than six *grandes épreuves* in a season, and then only one more.

Stewart lives in a handsome, formal-looking house on six acres of land overlooking Lake Geneva, for the reason usual to people whose incomes run well into six figures in dollars. "I couldn't live in the United Kingdom," he says. "If I tried to collect some capital for my family and live a reasonable life at the same time, I'd have no future for my children or my wife, never mind me." (British taxation falls heavily on unaffiliated or free-lance earners of all kinds. The sculptor Henry Moore is said to keep around $20,000 from his yearly $600,000 income.)

As a Swiss resident Stewart can spend no more than ninety days a year in the U.K. But ninety days are quite a lot if you operate cleverly. "I never arrive in London before midnight. I come in a few minutes after twelve, even if I have to stay in the transit lounge. If I'm out the next night I've spent only the one day in England. And besides the tax situation, Switzerland is a super place to live, from my point of view the only place. My children will grow up at least bilingual and perhaps trilingual, and the climate is far nicer for them than Scotland's. I travel like an idiot, and I'm fifteen minutes from the airport, hail, rain, or snow, and my house is not on the flight path. I can go anywhere in Europe in an hour and twenty minutes. Switzerland is one of the stablest countries in the world, and it's the heart of Europe. It's the only place for a racing driver to be."

A racing driver. If all the racing drivers alive elected to move to Switzerland, the Swiss would never notice an additional factor of population pressure in their tiny country. In any given year there are never more than thirty-odd men ranked by the world governing body, the *Fédération Internationale de l'Automobile,* as drivers of the first class, and no one can remember a year which saw more than six men of Stewart's ability practicing their profession. Motor racing is hideously difficult. It is separate from other sports, fenced off from them by many qualifications. It has as much to do with driving 80 miles an hour on a parkway as dancing a Viennese waltz has to do with tightrope walking. One thinks of bullfighting as dangerous, but few major *toreros* have been killed in the ring since 1946, and in that time scores of drivers have died, and died roughly: speared to death on their steering posts, decapitated, burned to the bone before 10,000 people while a TV-carrying helicopter recorded the scene from forty feet above, its big blades fanning the flames the while. If a baseball player strikes out, well, he will be at bat again, and in football a pass receiver who drops one may suffer nothing worse than a booing from the crowd. But the penalty for a mistake in racedriving can be six months in a hospital, or death. It has been truly said, any man who gets into a racing car intent upon going fast, merely resolved to go fast, is certifiably a very brave man indeed.

Race cars are fiber glass shells light enough for a child to lift, sloshing with high-octane gasoline, rolling on fat, doughnut-shaped tires on the ends of outriggers that snap like toothpicks in collision, an engine screaming under incredible stress inches behind the driver, the whole fiendish package capable of speeds up to 200 miles an hour. Their pilots live on fantastic skills, usually, I think, inborn, plus trust: the knowledge that the professional running a couple of feet alongside will behave predictably, coldly, properly. No driver will run hard against an untried man. The risk is too great. Reading 150 miles an hour with another car two feet in front, a driver must believe with all his heart that the man ahead of him will behave like his Siamese twin, accelerate when he should, brake when he should, take a predictable line through a corner, and he must feel that his own unspoken contract with the man just behind *him* carries the same terms, lest the three of them die.

Laced with electronic readout devices like those taped to an astronaut, an experienced racing driver in excellent health, with a normal pulse rate of seventy-two beats to the minute, may show a rate of 160 just before the start, and a rate of 140 for long periods during the race proper.

"Ah, now, I know that's true," Jackie Stewart says. "We tend to be excited. But I try very hard to overcome it. I try to run down my emotions to a point of lowest ebb, until I'm a soft rubber ball, a child's balloon you might say, that's had a pin stuck into it. I'm sitting in the car completely collapsed emotionally, literally with no emotion in me. I'm in neutral, at zero, I'm nowhere. Then, you know, whoever's sitting there alongside me, in the car next to me, I don't feel I have to outbrake him in the first corner, run deeper, you know, because I am sure he's excited, I am sure he's in the grip of emotion, and if he is that, then he'll make a mistake. He'll make a mistake, being in the grip of his emotions, and I, I hope, being purged of emotion, I will not make a mistake, and I will profit from his mistake, and pass him. I must be calm. Everything must be routine.

"And nowadays, you know, it is not so easy to pass another car on most circuits. In the old days, what am I saying, I haven't been around that long, after all I began driving seriously in 1962, but even as recently as 1965, say, the cars weren't so wide, you could have a scrape and a shove, and with the little tires we were using you were sliding all over the place, it was a lovely, languorous motion, and you slid inside each other, but now with these big ones, these great lumps of rubber, you're using all the road . . . these cars, they don't leave a lot of room for friends in there. You pass by using other people's mistakes and by sort of outfumbling, by conveniently embarrassing them. On the usual circuit, a two-lane road really, nothing more than that, there just isn't room for pushing and shoving, for charging up the inside and having them off. What you want to do, you want to make a good start, you want to have a few hot early laps to quieten the enthusiasm of the opposition, you want to approach the whole thing calmly, calmly. There must be no feeling of anything extraordinary. There must be no feeling of occasion. That's the essence of it, that there be no sense of occasion.

"The cars are so sensitive now, they're so highly bred, the car is literally alive with you, the car can change its personality in a second, like that! like a woman, and although you feel you had it doing all the nice things for you and coaxing and pleasing it, the next minute it changes its personality, turns vicious, and you either have an accident or you become real bad friends. Then you have to give it a good thrashing, as much for its sake as for yours, to come to terms with it because if you are tense and vibrant in the car it tends to be the same way, it is too responsive, too nervous, and while the nervous racing car we've had always with us, this thing we drive now is so inbred, it's been taken to such a pinnacle of precision . . . it really is alive, it must be mastered."

How long can one go on, mastering these lethal and always changing devices? It's a matter of submitting to the discipline required. Stewart doesn't smoke, doesn't drink, won't take a pill to sleep or an aspirin for a little pain. He won't look back on incidents like Indianapolis 1966, his first time there, when, leading by two laps with fifteen miles out of 500 to go, his engine lost its oil pressure, knocking him out of $125,000 or so and the sweetness of a win over people who had thought him a European sporty-car driver incapable of competing on level terms with the big rough Americans.

"From when I was fifteen to when I was twenty-three," Stewart says, "I was a trap shooter in international and Olympic competition. I was immersed in it, really giving it more dedication, more devotion than I've ever given to motor racing. Then I went sick on it. Suddenly, I never wanted to do it again. I thought, you must be mad, day after day, week after week, month after month, breaking clay saucers . . . I would love it if that could happen again with motor racing . . . that I could know life on that plateau was over, and another life had begun, and I could have a new interest and environment . . . but. . . . It's not in my own hands."

—1970

269

The
Germans
are
Coming!

If anyone invented the automobile, the Germans did. True enough that Homer thought of it; so did Erasmus and Roger Bacon and Darwin; Leonardo da Vinci sketched it, Ferdinand Verbiest made a self-propelled steam toy in 1668 and the list of later pioneers is long: Christian Huygens, Nicolas Joseph Cugnot, Nicholas August Otto, Alphonse Beau de Rochas, Etienne Lenoir, and Siegfried Marcus. But the automobiles made by Carl Benz in 1885 and Gottlieb Daimler in 1886 were cast essentially in the same form we know today, were technically sound and eminently workable; and, unlike most of their predecessors, *Herren* Daimler and Benz persisted and went on to improve their originals. The Daimler-Benz company, maker of the Mercedes-Benz, is the oldest motorcar manufactory in the world.

The German automobile industry is flourishing now, in a year that finds U. S. makers cutting back production, the Italians seriously hurt by strikes, and the British in deep trouble. Only Japan's prosperity compares with Germany's.

It's a cliché among people professionally concerned that some German cars are better than others but that the Germans simply do not make a really bad car. There are eight major German producers and three of them turn out motorcars that are world-standard setters: BMW (Bayerische Motoren Werke), Mercedes-Benz, and Porsche. The others, Audi, NSU, Opel, Ford, and VW, all have individual points of distinction, too: Audi for a superior small front-wheel-drive sedan, NSU for its pioneering of the Wankel engine, Opel for the sexy miniature GT, Ford for the strikingly successful Capri, and VW for the second Model T, the world-girdling Beetle. Incidentally, Audi, NSU, Porsche, and VW are all corporately intertwined, a matter of academic interest insofar as the present inquiry is concerned.

The root reason for the excellence of the German motorcar probably lies in the fact that the Germans take the automobile, as they take most things, very seriously. The factor of individual pride, the quality that was called craftsmanship when it was more nearly universally available for study, is probably stronger, in a higher percentage of workers, in Germany than anywhere else in the world. In mid- to top-range German cars, everything from bearing tolerances to the fit of doors, bonnets, and trunk lids—a precisely even gap all the way around—reflects the worker's determination to do it right, plus the implacability of the final inspectors.

Too, the German, like the Hollander and the Swiss, tends to be a compulsive worker. He appears to *like* working and, whether or not the impression reflects a valid motivation, he does work a flat-out sixty-minute hour. To come to a big German production line direct from a major British, French, or Italian factory is to see a fairly startling change. The difference in cleanliness, efficiency both mechanical and human and, most of all, intensity of effort, is striking. When I remarked on the generally sloppy and lackadaisical image being projected by the workers on the final assembly line of a first-rank British car, an official conceded the point and said there was nothing that could be done about it. "We try to make up for it," he said, "by very stiff inspection, and I think we do, but of course that's time-consuming and expensive. If we go on about it too much, we'll have a strike. Remember, we deal with thirteen separate unions."

Because German executives know how much of the credit for their high output of quality product belongs to individual native workers, from floor cleaners to test drivers, they prize them and are distressed when the country's labor shortage forces them to use imported workers. They say that while a Yugoslav or Spanish mechanic may be earnest and determined, he does not, even when thoroughly schooled, produce the amount and quality of work that is the German norm.

Intensive research is another weapon in the German armorarium. British, French, and Italian research tends to be empirical. If something new works fairly well, try making it thicker, thinner, lighter, or slightly differently cast.

The German is a science lover. The archetypal German engineer won't believe today is Tuesday unless you show him the calendar; after he has convinced himself that the calendar isn't, perchance, a forgery, he is inclined to check it out to be sure it's Gregorian and not Mayan or whatever. He sleeps with his slide rule. If he is anywhere near the first rank, he speaks another language, perhaps two. Rudolf Uhlenhaut, a lengendary Mercedes-Benz racing- and high-performance-car specialist, speaks an English so flawless in pronunciation that it's hard to duplicate in today's England. Uhlenhaut is empirical as well as theoretical: he is probably the only design engineer in the world who can fully extend any car with which he's concerned, from 200-mph Grand Prix machines downward. Some years ago, trying to discover why a driver was dissatisfied with a car, Uhlenhaut took it flat-out over the Nürburgring, the most difficult road course in the world (fourteen miles to the lap, hills rising as steeply as one foot in five, and full of fast bends and violent corners), at such a rate that he was embarrassed when he saw the clock—he had been under the team driver's best practice time.

German research tends to isolate specific problems and then concentrate, applying maximum weight of manpower and matériel until a solution appears. Mercedes-Benz's research and development on the Wankel engine, which has culminated in the fantastic C-111 sports car, is a case in point. It runs on the rotary internal-combustion Wankel engine, a power plant many engineers believed had a most limited future, or none at all, when it first appeared. Problems involving internal wear, lubrication, and combustion-chamber sealing seemed almost insurmountable. One respected authority predicted flatly, and in print, that the Wankel would never be heard of again. But at the moment, the Mercedes-Benz four-rotor version produces 400 horsepower for a total weight of 397 pounds, just about one-half the weight of a comparable standard engine. One serious problem, exhaust emission, which was not a problem when Mercedes-Benz research began over ten years ago, remains; it is presently the sole concern of a battalion of engineers and will probably be cracked within the year.

Specialization is another ingredient in the unique German mix. It's enough for a man to be able to do one thing only, if he does that one thing superbly and knows everything there is to be known about it. Just before World War II, one of a team of Mercedes-Benz Grand Prix cars practicing for a race in England developed a radiator leak. Alfred Neubauer, the team manager—he originated and perfected that function—had a specialist flown from Germany. The man soldered the leak in ten minutes' working time and was flown straight back to Stuttgart.

Research in essentials—Germans spend little time in merely cosmetic bodywork, for example, which is why their coachwork tends to be rather staid, more practical than striking—plus obsessive attention to detail and quality control by everyone from top to bottom of the work force: that is the basic German formula. There are other things, too. Continuity is one of them. The Germans have a big book: their industry is an old one and they remember everything that has been tried in the past. If an engineer thinks he needs to know the tire pressures used on the rear wheels of the race cars that won the French Grand Prix in 1914, it's only a matter of a few minutes to find out. And the market: there are no speed limits on German autobahns and the Germans are ferocious drivers. They expect a good car to run all day at 100 miles an hour and they expect it to last under that treatment. If it doesn't, they won't buy another one like it for a long time, perhaps never.

Expert opinion all over the world inclines to the view that the best automobile purchasable today—not the sexiest looking, not the fastest, not the most economical but the all-round *best*, judged by every applicable standard—is either the BMW 2800 or the Mercedes-Benz 300SEL 6.3.

The BMW 2800 CS is the top of a line that includes four other models, ranging upward in engine size and price—the 1600, 2002, 2500, and 2800 at bases of $2899, $3159, $5637, and $6663. The CS with automatic transmission tops the list at $8337. If you want to go for the full list of options, you can boost it to over $9000. For this you're getting a 6-cylinder, four-passenger, two-door coupe on a 103-inch wheelbase. If it seems a lot, looking at the car on the showroom floor, you had best take it out and run it fifty miles or so, preferably over the most varied roadways you can find, from straight and level parkway to a really atrocious, frost-heaved, winding up-and-down-hill country lane. You may never be the same.

First off, the BMW 2800 CS will run 0–60 mph in 8.3 seconds, which means you will not be hopelessly humiliated at the stop lights. It will show a top speed of 128–130 mph. But this is the bare beginning, significant only in letting you know you aren't riding in any mouse-powered economy wagon merely because it weighs only 3000 pounds. (It will deliver twenty miles to the gallon, though.)

Almost anything that has wheels and something to steer them with looks good in straight-line level running. roads that are crooked, and preferably rough and crooked, are the great winnowers. At 110 mph on a parkway, an engineer who had always owned domestic automobiles and had never ridden in a BMW guessed we were doing 80. He is a relaxed and stout-hearted type who enjoys riding number two or number three in four-man Olympic-class bobsledding, which certainly classifies him as a rugged passenger; but he had both feet well into the rug when he saw I intended taking a hard bend at 95 and petitioned for a lesser rate of speed by saying, "O.K.,

O.K., I'll buy it!" The car went through without so much as a whisper of tire squeal.

The braking power of the BMW will come as a stunning revelation to anyone used to even the best Detroit all-drum or disk-and-drum systems. The 2800 will stop well inside any American car, and in a dead-straight line, and ten times in a row. The Mercedes-Benz 600SEL 6.3 has the best brakes on any passenger car I know, and the BMW's are within a hair of being as good. In addition to stopping the car as if it had run into a wall of sponge rubber, they are so exquisitely balanced that neither the front wheels nor the rear wheels alone will lock up; in a hard stop, the car will normally shut down all four simultaneously.

The handwrought image the BMW projects on every surface and edge is evident in everything from the rubber bumpers, which ought to be Federally mandated, to the dashboard—hand-polished cabinet-grade veneer bonded to rock-hard multilayer plywood that simply cannot warp, crack, or shift a millimeter in any direction ever. This is a luxury motorcar by absolute definition: incredibly comfortable, fast, stable, quiet, and with every foreseeable contingency anticipated and provided for. Owners of lesser vehicles, much more likely to need tools, have to content themselves with a jack and a wheel brace; the trunk lid of the BMW carries a dropdown tray with nesting fuses, bulbs, spark plugs, and a set of tools including everything but gear pullers.

The BMW engine, to get to the heart of the matter last, pulls 192 horsepower and makes one wonder what point there can be in more. It produces the *spinning* sensation—the sensation that it is friction-free and connected to nothing at all—that is the hallmark of the true high-performance engine. It reminded me of the supercharged engine in a Grand Prix Bugatti I used to own, hand assembled, roller-bearinged, and running on hot castor oil.

I think manual shifting is pointless, but if you prefer it to automatic, the BMW's is as good as any in the world, smooth, precise, short-throw.

Dropping down the line, the smaller models diminish in performance (118 mph for the 2500, 102 for the 2002) as well as price, but the impression of absolute engineering efficiency—and honesty—remains a constant.

The long history of Daimler-Benz shows an expertise in public relations unique in the industry. For fifty years, at least, the Stuttgart firm has masterfully exploited the product, inducing newspapers and magazines to allot acres more of free white space to Mercedes-Benz cars in a month than their competitors could command in a year. The system is simple, foolproof, and expensive. The basic premise under which it operates is that no major exploitation will be attempted on anything but a genuinely newsworthy accomplishment (winning an important race or rally, for example) or strikingly new vehicle (the gull-wing 300SL coupe). Exploitation that is mere noisemaking is strictly *verboten*. Second, the technicians in charge of exploitation shall not be of a level of expertise lower than the standard prevailing in every other department.

As this is written, Mercedes-Benz is performing its classic publicity blitz, making an experimental prototype two-seater coupe the most photographed, most written-about automobile of the year, despite the grim handicap of a model designation of minus-zero exploitation value: the C-111. No one is being conned in this operation; the C-111 is a breakthrough vehicle of notable significance, indeed—an ultrahigh-performance automobile powered by the revolutionary Wankel engine. Even the announcement of its existence was instantly recognized all over the world as a bench mark in automobile history.

The Wankel engine is small and has few moving parts. Essentially, it is a combustion-chamber of an epitrochoidal shape (a circle slightly mashed top and bottom), in which a triangular piston (with slightly convex sides) spins on a shaft, the other end of which delivers the power wherever it's wanted. As the piston spins, with nothing but its points, or apexes, touching the combustion-chamber wall, it forms constantly changing sealed-off spaces. It takes these spaces through the classic Otto cycle of the four-stroke internal-combustion engine. Gasoline vapor is drawn or injected into one space, compressed as it's carried around to a spark plug, burned, pushing against the side of the triangular piston to make power, carried to an exhaust port, and ejected. Simple. Rotary motion in an internal-combustion engine. They said he couldn't do it. They laughed as he sat down with his slide rule.

The secret is in mating the shapes of triangle and squashed circle. In a cutaway view of a Wankel engine, it seems quite clear that the triangle cannot revolve while keeping all three apexes in airtight contact with the chamber wall all the way around, which, of course, it must do if it's to function; and which it does do. Wankel worked out the configurations mathematically and the first time he cut metal and made one, it worked. He conveyed the rights to NSU of Neckarsulm, a small but progressive motorbike and car maker; and by 1964, a Wankel-engined automobile, the NSU Prinz, was on the road. I remember going to Germany to drive it and being amazed at the size of the engine, about as big as a teakettle.

More than a dozen firms bought Wankel licenses from NSU: Citroën, Alfa-Romeo, Curtiss-Wright, Mercedes-Benz, Toyo Kogyo, Perkins, and others.

NSU stuck with it—the first Wankel-engined import, NSU's R80, has been certified for U. S. sale—and so did Toyo Kogyo of Japan, now turning out 1000 Mazda R 100s and R 130s a month. But while they were obviously successful automobiles—the R 100 also meets U. S. emission standards—the maximum horsepower figure, 126, was not impressive.

Then, late last summer, Mercedes-Benz ran out the C–111, billed as a *versuchswagen* only, a research and experimental vehicle not for production or sale. It would get to 60 mph from a standing start in 4.9 seconds, or half what most people think is quick, and would do 160–plus mph at a modest 7000 engine revolutions per minute. When I drove it I was tempted to think of it as the Ultimate Automobile: blindingly fast, comfortable, even comparatively *quiet*, and sure-footed past what seemed reasonable for something running on wheels.

Since that time, the C–111 has been refined and the new Geneva model is probably the final design. Busily returning blank checks drawn on banks from Addis Ababa to Zwickau, Mercedes officials still deny that the C–111 will be put into production for sale. I believe that it will be, although perhaps on a basis as limited as fifty cars for the entire world market.

Easier to come by are the sixteen other models of the Mercedes-Benz available in this country at figures from $4961 to $28,343, which is to say from the basic 220 sedan delivered on the East Coast, to the West Coast price of the monster 600 Pullman seven-passenger limousine.

The newest Mercedes is the 3.5 V8, just now becoming available. Until it went to a V8 for the big 600-series cars, Mercedes-Benz had been stuck on in-line engines, 4-, 6-, and 8-cylinder.

The 600 series is powered by a 6.3-liter V8 and it is an almost half-size version of that engine that runs the new 300SEL 3.5, the chassis/body similar to the 280SEL sedan. This is a fuel-injected 230-horsepower engine, light (less than 500 pounds) and characteristically quieter than the 6-cylinder it replaces. It's not blindingly quick (0-60 mph in eleven–plus seconds), but it's smooth and forceful and will take the car to 127 mph (100 in twenty-eight seconds), good enough for most U.S. motoring, even in Nevada. The engine is also used in the 280S coupe and convertible. The 280SEEL sedan remains in production, of course, and at $7657 is a most attractive and useful possession.

If I were to expose myself to its massive charms, I think the 600 Pullman would be my favorite in the Mercedes line, but I have forbidden myself the experience, lest the temporary lack of the 28,000-odd dollars required to engineer its purchase drop me into trauma. But the simple little 300SEL 6.3 sedan at $15,122 I *have* sampled, and extensively; and if I am ever so blessed by fortune as to save the squire's daughter from a runaway stallion and he asks me how possibly he can reward me, I shall quote Clarence Darrow's timeless epigram: "Ever since the Phoenicians invented it, money has been the most nearly perfect expression of gratitude," and, clutching his $16,000 (a round sum is most easily managed) in my hot little hand, I shall run, not walk, to the nearest Mercedes-Benz store.

The 6.3 of choice is black with black leather upholstery, because in that costume, it looks like nothing much, just a smallish sedan—112-inch wheelbase—of no startling profile, wholly lacking in sheet-metal overhang fore and aft, stolid and four-footed on the pavement. The chairs (one cannot call them mere seats) are clad in thick hide cunningly stretched over forms designed not by stylists but by orthopedic surgeons, and they hold one—grasp one, really—lightly but firmly, belted or not.

Short of the far-ranging 6.3 sedan, the Mercedes-Benz 280SEL is the instrument of choice; again, a perfectly balanced motorcar (oddly, because it looks smaller, the 280SEL has more usable room than a Cadillac), capable of extension far past its class. A candid-camera overview of a shopper in a Mercedes-Benz showroom will inevitably show him running a questing finger over the genuine tree-wood dashboard, trying to discover a microscopic flaw in the finish. Most unlikely: the iron-hard varnish has been burnished with a felt pad sodden in water and pumice or rottenstone. A quick rubdown now and then with a paste carnauba wax will keep it glistening for a decade. Which raises a point: a run-through of the classified ads in an automobile-buff book *(Road & Track,* for example*)* will turn up listings of Mercedes-Benz automobiles of vintage 1955 *et seq.* at prices that may alarm you. A brand-new Mercedes is an instant classic, due to the company's policy of changing body style slowly, slightly, sensitively; a decade-old Mercedes looks almost new and, if it has been decently driven, feels so.

Porsche, too. Oddly, because this is a *new* motorcar. The first automobile to wear the name off the production line—to use the term most loosely, because there really wasn't a line at all—Easter Monday, 1950. It took the factory four years to make 5000 cars; and even now, twenty years later, each day of production sees only eighty-six Porches produced in a plant employing 3700 people.

Factories making refrigerators, stoves, lawn mowers, and electric fans, never mind automobiles, are noisy past belief. Automobile factories are high on the double-decibel list; most automobile factories, that is. But Ferrari, Maserati, Aston Martin, and Porsche—no. In 1960, when I first entered the Porsche factory in Stuttgart, I was bemused by the comparative velvet silence of the place. The usual *brang-brang, choing-choing* of a motorcar manufactory was missing. Dead silence there was not: after all, things were being made; but the light clink of hammer on steel was the loudest sound to be heard. The reason was plain: rank on rank, mechanics were assembling engines, cradled in viselike holders, but they were filing, pushing, trying, trying again, filing once more. There were days, at the beginning, when each Porsche engine was die-stamped with the initials of the man who had assembled it. The practice was abandoned, finally, when the painters and

the upholsterers argued that they, too, had equal right to sign their work
—but where?

Porsche owners are cultists: Passing on the road, they almost invariably
flick their lights, trying to time it, trying not to do it first nor last but in
unison. It was a common salute between foreign-car owners in the old days
—1948, 1949—when a TC MG Midget stood for absolute sophistication;
but time and uncounted freighters full of VWs, Jaguars, Austins, and Hill-
mans diluted and destroyed it for all but the Porsches.

The Porsche that is Porsche to most of us is the Model 356, which ran,
in designations 356, 345A, 356A, 356C, and 356SC, from 1950 to 1964.
Rounded off, short wheelbased, high waisted, it is fast, agile, and—espe-
cially—reliable. The Achilles' heel of the high-performance car is reliability.
The woods are full of cars that will do 125 mph faultlessly—for a few
thousand miles. Then, straight down the two-lane into Disastersville, and
your friendly local foreign-car mechanic, six weeks from first phone call to
the final bill, 180 hours at $9.50 an hour. One of the endearing qualities of
the Porsche is its persistent effort to tell you that there is a message in those
all-lined-up-together screw slots: this thing will stick together. It does.

Early Porsches oversteered. That is to say, going into a bend, the rear end,
heavily freighted with engine and each wheel riding on its own short shaft,
independent of its mate, tended to move beyond the classic ellipse. All
rear-engined cars try to do this. In the first thirty minutes of my Porsche
ownership, I lost the thing completely twice, once in a hard descending
right-hand bend, once in avoiding a towed cruiser.

Long past, with Porsche, is all that—oversteer, understeer, *und so weiter.*
The 1970 Porsche is a neutral-steer car; which is to say, go into the corner
and drive the thing around, flat-out.

The going range of Porsches is extensive, although there are only three
basic models, the 914, the 914/6, and the 911, priced from $3595 to $9450.
The 914 is Porsche's answer to galloping inflation, the first Porsche ever
offered at a bargain-basement price, possible because it carries the Volkswagen engine, driving through a five-speed manual or Porsche's semiauto-
matic system. It will do a respectable 110 mph. As for carriagework, the
body can be described as a demiconvertible, in that the roof is detachable
—easily and quickly, too—and can be neatly tucked away in the rear
luggage area. A built-in roll bar lives under what would be, in a longer car,
a blind rear quarter—a device Porsche introduced some time ago in the
Targa model. The 914 is midengined, stashed just behind the seats (no, it
isn't particularly noisy), which allows luggage compartments in both nose
and tail. One can stuff an extraordinary amount of gear into a 914, probably
more than anything else its size can accept.

The 914/6 is the same body with the standard 125-horsepower Porsche engine. It's faster, quicker, and costs a basic $6000 with the five-speed manual. There's a little more chrome and wider wheels wearing fatter tires; otherwise, it's not easy to tell the two apart.

Standard, in a body style pretty much unchanged since 1966, is the Porsche 911, available at $6430 to $9450 in three models designated T, E, and S. The differences are primarily in the degree of tuning of the flat-six engine, the cars variously turning out 142, 175, and 200 horsepower. Since the car weighs only 2250 pounds, all three models can be said to be more than adequately powered and they have top-speed capabilities of 128, 137, and 144 mph. Reasonably driven, they will deliver twenty-three to twenty-six miles to the gallon—extraordinary figures for genuine high-performance motorcars. The S, the competition version, has been almost unbeatable in its class in Sports Car Club of America racing and Porsche is the present holder of the World Manufacturers' Championship.

I have owned Porsches since the early fifties, and I'm convinced that the Stuttgart company—one of the last family-owned manufactories, by the way—makes the best small car. They are superbly comfortable, fabulous performers, and really well made. A Porsche never appears to be trying hard.

Porsche no longer markets its own cars in this country, a new and larger dealer network having been set up by Porsche Audi; all to the good, because a machine as good as the Porsche deserves care by mechanics trained on it. The car will soak up an appalling amount of neglect and abuse, but it shouldn't have to.

The Audi marketed through the same dealerships is a medium-priced— $2995 to $3895—front-wheel-drive sedan. Audi is an old firm, founded in 1909 by August Horch, who also produced a massive luxury motorcar under his own name. Horch's was one of the four firms that combined to make the Auto Union, a 16-cylinder, rear-engined Grand Prix car, one of the two makes—Mercedes-Benz, the other—that completely dominated international racing in the 1930s.

There are two models of the Audi sedan, both 4-cylindered—the Super 90 and the 100 LS, 100–115 horsepower. Both will run just past 100 mph and, oddly, they show identical gasoline consumption: 26.4 miles to the gallon. The advantages of front-wheel drive have become well known in the United States in the past few years—Citroën, Oldsmobile Toronado, SAAB —a flat floor, due to the missing long drive shaft, and good traction, because the engine weight is on the powered wheels. The Audis have been popular in Germany, a good indicator.

Buick dealers handle the Opel GT in this country—a miniature *gran turismo* vehicle, sexy looking, and striking, one of the few automobiles that look good in bright orange, a color much commoner in Europe than it is here, for a reason that escapes me. The top engine is a 102-horsepower, 4-cylinder, providing 0-60 in ten seconds and 113 mph top speed.

Opel is another old-line German firm, famous for competition cars in the years before World War I and remembered by collectors of oddball facts for the first rocket-powered car, which ran in 1928, and quickly, too—125 mph—with Fritz von Opel himself at the wheel.

The NSU company makes a medium sedan, the R80, powered by a two-rotor Wankel engine. (To increase Wankel capacity, the method of choice is not to make the rotor bigger but to add another unit, as one does cylinders in a reciprocating engine.) NSU is about to start selling the R80 in this country, now that it has satisfied federal emission standards. NSU currently markets a three-model range of small sedans, the 1000C, 1200C, and 1200TT. They are rear-engined, 4 cylinders, transversely mounted. Modestly priced—at around $2000 to $2500—they are sturdy and attractive motorcars.

Another new face in this market is the 4-cylinder Capri by Ford of Europe, being sold by Lincoln-Mercury dealers at around $2300. A hotter version of the Capri available in Europe houses that comparative rarity, a V6, and it's rated at 144 horsepower, which obviously suffices, since the Capri has a 0–60 time of 9.2 seconds. It weighs only 2380 pounds. The engine has a potential well past 145 horsepower, and Europeans who use the car in competition have taken 200 horsepower from it with special carburetors and cylinder heads. And a German accessory firm sells a turbo-supercharger for the Capri. You won't be able to get this useful and entertaining device from your friendly local L.-M. dealer, but if you know anyone who's going to Germany this summer. . .

And in the beginning was the Beetle, the car that nobody, practically, ever believed in. Well, Ferdinand Porsche must have, since he designed it. But there have been some highly placed wrong guessers: the British expert, for example, who advised his government not to bother taking the VW as part of war reparations, because the thing obviously hadn't a shred of future. The elves of Wolfsburg knew something no one else knew.

The 1970 bug—you can tell it from the others by extra cooling slots in the engine lid—has 4 more horsepower—57. You can push it along at 81 mph now and no longer in peril of the dreaded final oversteer, which has long since been got rid of. Presumably, everyone knows that the VW now has an optional automatic transmission, as does the luxury version, the Karmann Ghia. The squareback and fastback models are longer and roomier than last year's. The great square-rigged VW bus has a more comfortable suspension system and all of them come with four neat little coupons good for trouble-shooting examinations in the car's first 24,000 miles. The diagnosing, involving ninety-six tests, is done by a system of electronic wonder gadgets (no more "It sounds to me like you need a valve job, mister") and each of the 1100 VW dealers in the country has one.

The eight major firms that form the German passenger-automobile industry make in all only about sixty models, but the range is the world's widest, running as it does from the Volkswagen, certainly *the* universal economy automobile, through the most technically advanced high-performance machines to the supreme motor carriage *de grand luxe,* the 600 Pullman Mercedes-Benz. If you can't find a German car that meets your needs, you're in the market for a horse.

—1970

A
Guy
Named
Gurney

Winning is what sports are about. But there are ways to make mere winning harder if your mind runs in that direction or you tend to be a little more competitive than most. You can always give the club champion five strokes if you want to beat him and really make it stick. There's a little extra kick to winning a transatlantic single-hand race in a boat of your own building.

Automobile racing began in Europe in the late 1800s, and excepting the Indianapolis 500, the great classic races are still run there: the Le Mans 24-Hour Race, Targa Florio, Grand Prix de Monaco. In 1921 an American, Jimmy Murphy, won the French Grand Prix in an American-built car, a Duesenberg. Since then, three Americans have tried earnestly to duplicate Murphy's feat the hard way by winning a major European race driving a U.S. car of their own manufacture. Two of the three—Briggs Cunningham and Lance Reventlow—were millionaires. Neither of them made it, although Cunningham, who spent millions in the effort over a period of years in the 1950s, came very close. The one who did make it, forty-six years after Murphy, was Daniel Sexton Gurney of

California, a nonmillionaire who did it in high style by winning the 1967 Grand Prix of Belgium in an All-American Racers' Eagle out of his own shop in Santa Ana. In achieving this feat, he broke the course record over one of the most difficult circuits in the world, and posted the fastest average speed ever for a Grand Prix race—148.85 mph.

When another American, Henry Ford, decided to go flat-out to win at Le Mans with an American car—and did—in 1966, Gurney was on the team. Again in 1967 he was one of the winning drivers and A. J. Foyt of Texas, the other. The Ford that won Le Mans in 1968 was fitted with Gurney-Eagle cylinder heads. In the same year, Gurney-built Eagles won two U.S. National Championships, plus the Indianapolis 500, and Gurney himself won three major races.

Gurney is the most versatile driver working today. He drives Grand Prix cars, Indianapolis cars, sports cars, and stock cars with equal competence. Which is rare. He builds cars and engines for himself and for sale; he runs a couple of related businesses on the side; he writes a column for *Popular Mechanics* and when he has an off moment, he may try to dispute the notion (widely held wherever automobiles run against each other) that he is the unluckiest driver of his time and—who knows?—perhaps of all time. Since their fortunes can hinge on such imponderables as a flawed seven-cent bolt, five pounds too little air in one tire, or the swooping path of a low-flying bird, all racedrivers expect bad luck now and then. The thing that distinguishes Gurney's bad luck from the ordinary kind is that *his* strikes when it really matters. In 1964 he was winning the Belgian G.P. in a British car, a Brabham, when he ran out of gas less than a lap from the finish line. At Sebring in 1966, his engine wouldn't start until ninety seconds after everyone else had howled away. He passed fifty-four cars in the next nine laps. Twelve hours and nearly 1200 miles later he was leading the race and was within half a mile of the end of it when the engine quit cold. At Riverside in California a few months ago, he was leading the Rex Mays 300 (he won it in 1967 and 1968) and leading it by one minute, fifty seconds—a stunning margin as those things go today. For all intents and purposes, he was over the hill, long gone and out of sight. Then the differential failed and he started getting power to one wheel only. He finished third.

Gurney says he doesn't believe in bad luck. Or the other kind. What Gurney does believe in all the way are the pioneer virtues—patriotism, clean living, honesty, and the real hard try. He's had his name linked with mom and apple pie so many times it's a marvel he hasn't turned into some kind of antimatriarchal, strudel-stomping playboy. It isn't so much that he's six foot two, weighs 190, blond but not too, and is well built, without bulging. He is improbably nice-looking, and those are truth-rays shimmering off his shiny white teeth. Gurney is a genuinely nice man. Motor racing is a combination of risky sport and exotic show business; overdeveloped competitive instincts and swollen egos are as common as five-fingered hands among its practitioners, but I have never heard of anyone denigrating Gurney. Only an abnormal mind could do that. One fellow once said to me of an eminent driver, "You must remember that beneath that unpleasant exterior there is a really nasty man." And of another, "The son of a bitch is so inept, he couldn't stir cooky dough for the Girl Scouts." Yet this same fellow said nothing worse of Dan Gurney than that he didn't think Gurney would be elected President that year. The magazine *Car and Driver* had instituted the campaign spontaneously, and "Dan Gurney For President" bumper stickers were frequently seen on imported machinery and Detroit muscle-cars, less often on Cadillacs and Lincolns. A cabal of some sort prevented the total of Gurney's write-in vote from being known, but it was probably formidable; perhaps as many as 7000 nationwide. However, things will be different in 1972, no doubt. I once suggested that Goldsworthy Gurney, one of the most notable of the pioneers who ran intercity steam-coaches in England around 1830, might be one of his antecedents, but Dan had never heard that Goldsworthy was in the family tree. His own father was a bass baritone for many years with the Metropolitan Opera Company. Dan Gurney was born in New York, grew up in Manhasset, went to college (B.A.) in California, then volunteered for army duty in Korea with an antiaircraft gun outfit. For three years following his army tour, he did engineering research and development work on aluminum continuous-casting machines. He came to think that if he didn't find out if he could make it doing what he had always liked to do best—drive fast—the neglect would haunt him.

In 1955 he began driving in amateur sports-car races. He was fast from the beginning—third in his first race. He drove Triumphs, Porsches, and Lancias, then in 1957 he got his hands on a big going automobile, a 4.9-liter Ferrari, and began to win races. He ran a Ferrari at Le Mans in 1958. In 1959, deciding to go for broke, he went to Europe to drive Grand Prix, or Formula 1 cars, for the all-conquering Enzo Ferrari. Drivers were almost willing to pay Ferrari for a ride then, and the deal was $160 a month plus percentage of starting and prize monies. Gurney did three races, and created a stir by finishing second, third, and fourth. The next year was thin, but in 1961 he ran in eight races, finished second three times, and was tied for third place in the world championship. Since then he has competed steadily all over the world. He has started in 241 races and finished 136 of them, more times in first—thirty-four—than in any other position. Last September Gurney dropped Grand Prix racing. He was facing the hard reality that the big money and the mass exposure—live and TV—are on this side of the water. Too, the amount of travel involved in a U.S.–Europe schedule can be absurd. In one six-week period a couple of years ago he crossed the Atlantic eight times. He runs Indianapolis sports, and stock cars out of his modern and immaculate All-American Racers headquarters in Santa Ana where the staff is headed by a longtime associate, Max Muhleman. At the same time, he has gone into a new business—Dan Gurney's Checkpoint America, a nationwide network of deluxe retail and service centers for sports and high-performance cars of all kinds. He switched his long-standing liaison with Ford to Plymouth, because he feels that Plymouth is less rigid and more receptive to new ideas. Racing is hideously expensive. An Indianapolis engine alone can cost $35,000, and a two-car team needs a minimum of four. Corporate sponsors are thus a necessity. A successful and energetic competitor like Gurney will pile up a lot of them in the changing circumstances of a few years. Goodyear, Mobil, Olsonite, Bardahl, Castrol, Hertz, Yamaha, Lincoln-Mercury, and similar companies have backed his efforts at one time or another.

Gurney is the legitimate father of the Indianapolis Revolution of 1963, a coup that showed the American track-car people, who had boasted for years that theirs were the best race cars in the world, that they were talking about stuff that was almost as out-of-date as the high-wheel bicycle.

In the late 1940s the British designer John Cooper had revived the old idea (evident in the 1923 Benz and 1934 Auto Union, both German) of mounting a race car's engine behind the driver for better rear-wheel traction and a smaller frontal area. The driver could be made to lie down, his legs stuffed into the place where the engine used to be. By 1961 the setup was standard in European Grand Prix cars. For years before this, Gurney had been thinking that G.P. cars, given bigger engines, would be certain Indianapolis winners, and when in 1961 a standard Cooper, undersized engine and all, showed up at Indy and finished ninth, he knew he was right. He invited Colin Chapman, the British designer of the great Lotus G.P. car, to the 1962 Indy—the first one Gurney ran in—and later took him to Detroit for a meeting with Ford executives. Gurney was so effective a catalyst that a Chapman-Ford racing project was immediately put in train. A dark-green Ford-engined Lotus, driven by Jimmy Clark of Scotland, world champion that year, appeared for the 1963 Indianapolis running and stunned the establishment by coming in an easy second. Given a better pit crew and better understanding of Indy rules, Clark would probably have won. As it was, his performance laid the front-engine single-seat car stone-cold dead in the market and made the Ford racing engine a world standard.

Gurney doesn't know how much longer he'll drive. He'd like to win at Indianapolis—he was second in 1968 and 1969—he'd like to go back to the Grand Prix circuits (there are three in this hemisphere—Canada, U.S., and Mexico). He's thirty-nine and perhaps not at his peak yet. He is very fast indeed in any kind of car, and he doesn't break the machinery. At Le Mans, Ford mechanics said that some drivers were chewing up gearboxes in a couple of hours of practice, but that Gurney's always looked like new. He's brutally competitive, a quite different personality in the car than out of it. Gurney and the formidable A. J. Foyt ran lap after lap in the 1968 Indianapolis race side by side, feet and inches from each other, 200 mph down the straights, 153 mph in the corners, flat-out, until Foyt's engine blew. No one who saw this *mano a mano* will ever forget it.

"It's a hostile environment out there," Gurney says. "I don't mean the drivers, for they have set up certain ethical boundaries and they observe them. I mean the cars themselves. They're hot and rough. I lost twelve pounds in one race, and in another, I saw guys come in after only an hour with their hands bleeding. The very idea of going that fast staggers your mind. It's also difficult to maintain precise vision with the wind buffetting your helmet and goggles.

"What you're doing is controlled fury. Every really good driver has a mean streak; everybody who's truly competitive has a mean edge on him."

Gurney takes a rational view of a risky business and does what he can to lower the odds—painstaking car preparation, physical condition, fireproof clothing, a lot of life insurance (at $15–$20 extra premium per $1000) —and then forgets about it. Driving at nine-tenths or ten-tenths—as fast as the individual man and machine can go and still stay on the road—is so demanding in concentration and skill and so rewarding in sheer kicks that it leaves small room for extraneous contemplation.

Still, I suspect that there are times, like the moment the differential let go at Riverside, when even Dan Gurney, an optimist all the way, can be excused for thinking there must be easier things to do. Like running for president, maybe.

—1970

A
Semester
at
Old
Superdriver
U

Stirling Moss once said to me that in years of traveling all over the world, he had met only one man who would admit that he was not a superb driver and a great lover.

"In those two areas," Moss said, "every male seems to be under a real compulsion to believe he's great. As for bed, who knows; but as for driving, most people haven't got the corner of a beginning of a clue."

It's an attitude well known to Bob Bondurant, former Grand Prix driver who is head of the Bob Bondurant School of High Performance Driving at California's Ontario Motor Speedway.

"Sometimes we have to spend most of the first day of the course changing people's minds," Bondurant said. "The typical attitude is, 'Well, I'm sure you can give me a few fine points—but I'm a pretty hot driver right now.' So we have to show him that he really isn't all that good and maybe he doesn't even know how to hold a steering wheel. After that, he may be ready to start to learn."

The high-speed, high-performance driving school is an old idea in Europe and some of the European schools, such as the Slotemaker Skid School in Holland, are well known. Probably because millions of Americans begin to drive at sixteen and believe they're polished performers at eighteen, the expert-school concept has been slow to root in this country. Most Europeans learn later in life, so feel more need for instruction. Too, they drive on varied terrain: *autobahnen*, Alpine passes, Swedish gravel roads, and, much of the time, under no speed limit. It's a sobering experience to be doing 100 miles an hour on a French *route nationale*, be passed by someone doing 140, and realize that even if your car can do 140, you cannot.

But there are other reasons for learning to drive really well and they are overriding in importance. Anything done well is enjoyable. If driving bores you, you'd think it a pleasure if you had learned to do it well; if you like driving, you'd enjoy it twice as much if you did it well. Driving an automobile is one of the twentieth century's required basic skills, as fencing was in the sixteenth century and riding in the seventeenth. The twentieth-century sophisticate ought to be a superior driver; indeed, it is almost obligatory that he be.

And skill is not only useful in a hazardous pursuit, it is almost an imperative need. Driving today *is* a hazardous pursuit, with the fatality rate running around 55,000 annually. For males in the eighteen-to-twenty-five age group, it is particularly hazardous. It is the primary cause of death, with more men between the ages of eighteen and twenty-five dying in automobiles than in Vietnam.

Three days after I had finished the Bondurant course, I was driving pretty briskly on 57th Street, a main crosstown artery in New York City, when one of the 20,000 potholes New York has as a souvenir of the past winter appeared just in front of me as the car ahead straddled it. The hole was three feet square, looked at least a foot deep and my right front wheel was headed straight for it. In the ordinary way of things, I would probably have braked hard, hoping to slow enough to get in and out of the hole without blowing a tire, breaking up the front suspension, or being thrown into the double line of oncoming traffic. It wouldn't have worked, because there wasn't time. I didn't even think about braking. I didn't think about anything. I turned hard left, straightened the car—a Pontiac Grand Prix—to run parallel with the traffic, passed three cars with nothing to spare, accelerating as I did, and didn't touch the hole.

The important aspect of this little exercise was that I did it instantly, in a blink, and that I couldn't have done it two weeks earlier. Bondurant had taught me to do it, using a fascinating device he calls the Accident Simulator, something that ought to be standard equipment in every driver-education school in the country.

The Accident Simulator is Bondurant's modification of a teaching aid developed by Paul O'Shea, a champion sports car driver of the 1950s. It's simple: at the end of a straightaway, three standard red-yellow-green traffic lights are hung over the entrances to three curving paths marked out by rubber pylons. The paths are little more than a car wide. Exactly eighty-eight feet before the entrances, an electronic eye runs across the straight-away, connected to a control box in the instructor's hands. As the student's car starts down the straight, all lights are green; but when his front wheels hit the electronic beam, the lights snap to a pattern preset by the instructor, say, from left to right, red-red-green. It's now up to the student to get into the green lane, without touching the brake, without hitting a pylon, and accelerate through and out of it. The situation being simulated is a crash just ahead, a stationary or violently slowing car or other emergency. The runs are made at 30, 35, 40, 45, and 50 miles an hour. For most people, 50 is the outer limit. Fifty-five is just barely possible for an extremely skillful driver who happens to be sharp that day. Over 55, it can't be done: the driver will not see the lights in time to do anything at all.

At 30, it's easy, if you're reasonably quick. At 35, it begins to be interest-ing. At 40, after perhaps six runs at the lower speeds, most people will brake, take out a pylon or two, or miss the lane altogether. If the setup shows three red lights, meaning stop dead before the lanes, you'll almost certainly lock the wheels and go in sideways. At 45, you see the lights almost subliminally, out of a top corner of the eyes. At 50, everything is hectic. One quick look to be sure the speedometer is dead on 50 mph (the instructor will spot cheating at 47–48), aim for the center lane and wait for your hands to do the rest, because your brain will give you the impression that it is out to lunch. If you try to *think* about what you're going to do, you'll probably spend the next five minutes setting up pylons, one or two of which will have managed to become wedged underneath the car.

It's most illuminating: after thirty or thirty-five runs through the lights, a driver will be so quick he can't believe it, he will be diving into a slot between pylons—narrower and narrower as the speed goes up—with what seems absurd ease. He won't be tempted to touch the brake, nearly always a formula for disaster if the car is not on a straight line; he will find it easy to do what at first seemed altogether wrong—*accelerate* past the emergency —and he will feel a sense of control of destiny that he never knew before. All in all, this transformation will have taken perhaps a long morning's work. And it *is* a transformation. When I was running the lights, a new Lotus Europa came onto the circuit and the driver, who was perhaps twenty-two or twenty-three, remarked that I seemed slow in reacting. I was coming into the lanes at 50 and making it clean about three times out of five. Bondurant suggested that the exercise might be harder than it looked and invited the Lotus driver to try it. He missed at 40, missed badly several times at 45, and declined even to try at 50.

The Bob Bondurant School of High Performance Driving is the only one of its kind presently in this country. The Sports Car Club of America, working through its 105 regions, runs weekend sessions of group instruction open to any member who is over twenty-one and can pass the physical. There are about eighty of the sessions a year, attendance running between twenty-one and 100 students. Those who satisfactorily complete two sessions or "schools" are given SCCA novice competition licenses. The Jim Russell School in Rosamond, California, is strictly a racing school, using single-seat cars from the beginning of instruction. The essential difference between the Bondurant curriculum and the others is that it carries more classroom-and-blackboard work (about 30 percent) and is designed to produce drivers very skilled at regular highway driving, who can then, if they like, go on to racing instruction. Bondurant's basic thrust is toward competence in high-speed driving. For example, the instructors of the Los Angeles Police Department who teach pursuit driving and car handling to the Los Angeles police force are graduates of the Bondurant school.*

His own racing career began in 1959, when he was the top U.S. Corvette driver. In 1963, he joined Carroll Shelby's Cobra team and drove for the Ford Shelby team in Europe. He was responsible for eight of the ten wins that gave Shelby the 1965 World Manufacturing Championship, the first time ever for an American builder. The same year, he began driving Formula I single-seat cars, BRMs, American Eagles, and Ferraris. He drove at Le Mans, too; but in June 1967, a steering arm failed at 150 mph at Watkins Glen ("I flipped from six to ten times, according to who was counting") and he came out of it with multiple compound fractures of both feet. He was hospitalized for months and, for a long time afterward, couldn't stand for more than an hour or so. Now he runs in an occasional long-distance race and is thinking about more of the same in the future.

Bondurant is a gifted teacher, patient and able to convey complicated ideas quickly and simply. He taught James Garner and Yves Montand to drive single-seat cars for the film *Grand Prix,* and Paul Newman and Robert Wagner for *Winning.* And they were really driving. Garner could have gone racing in Europe after *Grand Prix;* and Newman, after Bondurant passed him, was running the Indianapolis track fast enough to have won not many years before.

Competition drivers without extended experience have been his best instructors, probably because they're willing to adapt to his methods. His chief instructors now are Wilbur Shaw, Jr., twenty-four, son of the legendary Indianapolis winner, and Max Mizejewski, a twenty-five-year-old ex-

---

*Ambulance-driver students take a mandatory fast ride strapped to the stretcher. They drive considerably more smoothly afterward!

helicopter pilot out of Vietnam. Like Bondurant, they are patient, understanding, courteous, and with a certain amount of iron in them.

Unknowingly, students bare themselves to the instructors. Halfway through his third day in the Bondurant competition course, a student has made a chart on himself: his motor reactions are somewhere between quick and slow; he is reasonably courageous or wholly cowardly or something between; he is intent on learning to drive well, in order really to drive well or in order to convince someone, honestly or not, that he drives well; and so on.

Typically: a student on his last day is running the road course. His instruction is to run as fast as he can within the limits of consistency and safety and his own ability. Mizejewski is timing him and Bondurant comes by to watch.

Mizejewski says, "This is very interesting. He's chicken, you see. He'll improve his lap time by a couple of seconds for four or five laps, then, when he has cut one about as fast as he can, he'll scare himself and back off. Watch."

And so it turns out. The clock drops two seconds a lap and then rises. As the student comes by, he's pointing to the engine. Something is wrong, he's saying. But nobody believes him. The record of people who have gone through the school shows that the lap times of 100 students will vary by three to four seconds—no more. It's no use trying to fool the clock and drama doesn't count.

Enjoyment in driving is based, above all, on smoothness, the easy flow of the vehicle along the road, gently swinging through the curves, accelerating and braking almost imperceptibly. This sense of secure passage, similar to a steel ball rolling in a glass chute, is the hallmark of the expert. The driver may be going quickly or slowly, but a perceptive passenger will feel that he could hold a bowl of goldfish on his lap.

Smoothness is the obsession of the Bondurant school. I'm not sure it's possible to do an entire lap of a twisting road circuit, fast, with Bondurant and be told that the whole lap, all nine turns of it, was perfectly smooth, but it's exhilarating and rewarding to try.

For smoothness, control is essential; and for control, the driver must be sitting upright, buttocks hard against the back of the seat, hands at nine and three o'clock, with each thumb over a spoke, the knees not held upright but allowed to fall naturally to each side, this for relaxation and to clear the bottom of the steering wheel in a tight turn. (The hand position is particularly important: all other grips are faulty, up to, or down to, the American standard freeway stance, the right wrist draped over the top of the wheel, the left idle.) No other grip will enable the driver to hold the wheel in the case of a front-tire blowout or to make an instantaneous change in direction.

The beginning student's first exercise is to drive around an oval course perhaps 150 yards in length, around and around, in second gear, the car a Datsun 1600 sedan or a Porsche 914, trying to follow the correct line through the wide hairpin bends at each end, in close down the straight, out in a gentle arc that will just touch the apex of the curve, which is nearly always two-thirds of the way through, and gently in again. That there *is* a correct line through every corner, and a different one for almost every corner, comes as a revelation to most students, long used to going in, cranking the wheel around, feeding gas, and getting out somehow. On the mathematically pure line, the car will go around almost by itself; when a car is correctly taken through a constant-radius bend, the wheel can be set at the entrance and not moved again, even fractionally, until the exit. You can spend all morning learning to take a little sedan smoothly around Bondurant's oval—and you're still not concerned with anything but steering; there is no distraction. It's at this point that the fascination of the exercise begins to flicker in the mind: nothing could be easier than driving through a simple curve; yet it begins to appear that one can't do it perfectly three times in succession. The line may be wrong by only six inches, but it's wrong, nevertheless. At 35 mph, it mars the effort only esthetically; but at 70, it could kill you.

Now try it going to third gear on the straight, shifting to second just before the corner. Brake with the ball of the foot, lightly; roll the side of the foot onto the accelerator with just enough pressure to raise the engine speed to accommodate second gear; in clutch, out clutch, roll the foot off the accelerator, the brake pedal has been down all the time, put a very little more weight on it, off it, lightly on the accelerator, harder, all the way down coming out of the turn, pick up third gear, gently, just wishing the gear lever through, and start over again. Meanwhile, watch the line, don't go into the corner early or late, just clip the apex, let the car run out to the edge of the straight; if you move the wheel, you've done something wrong—and Bondurant will tell you so.

"That's pretty good, except at the last minute, you jerked the wheel, you caught yourself off the line. . . . You're coming in too early, you're in, you should be outside, brings you too wide here. . . . You're off the brake too early and on the throttle too soon, which pushes it down out the bottom of the turn. . . . You're braking too hard . . . light, *light* braking, what you're doing with the brakes, you want to balance the chassis on the wheels, set it up, get a nice patch of rubber on each wheel. Brake too hard, you'll pitch the chassis forward, unload the rear wheels, you'll have oversteer, the rear end will try to come around on you. Accelerate too hard coming out, you'll unload the front wheels, you'll get understeer. . . . Now you're braking too soon. . . . Pick up the throttle earlier, because the throttle has to steer you around the corner. . . . That was *nice,* that was very good, didn't that feel good to you? Light braking, *light,* just drag the calipers across the disks, don't stab it. . . . Man, you blew that one, you were two feet off the apex, what happened to you? . . . You weren't thinking. . . . All right, now, here, go; anyway, your upshifts are very nice, practically perfect, and I like the way you get right on the throttle coming out, that's right, good, stand on it, lot of people won't do that on this short straight, they're afraid the car will go off. . . . Beautiful, beautiful, keep it going, that was very nice. . . . See how good that felt, everything balanced. . . . Nice, good clean line through that one, too, you came in a hair too early, but you cleaned it up; you had to crank in a little more wheel, but you came out okay. . . . You've got one thing going for you, you're quick, you have quick reactions and good control; like back there, a lot of people, correcting that turn, they'd have cranked on just that little bit *too* much wheel. . . . Now you're braking too hard again, maybe you're going a little too fast, you let the clutch out before you'd fully picked up the throttle, you're blipping it instead of just picking it up lightly; Jesus, you still had the brake on coming *out* there, did you know that? Back off a little; here we go again, stay on the throttle just to the tree, off, brake, light, second, brake, let it run out. . . ."

Years of manhandling cars and their controls and years of driving without really thinking about it are the two heaviest handicaps students carry into the Bondurant school. And these are not new boys: nearly every student is better than average on a national standard and many have done some competitive driving. Still, it may be a day before they can shift gears properly, never grabbing the stick but pushing it lightly with the ball of the hand, pulling it gently with the fingertips, braking lightly, and progressively, and all the rest of it.

As for concentration—Bondurant has a short road course, under a mile, with nine turns, all different, and two short straights. To run on it fast, the driver must memorize aiming points for each curve and shutoff points; otherwise, running fast, they'll come up too quickly. The aiming point for one bend at the end of a straight is a tree. Just coming into this straight, Bondurant, sitting beside me, said something. Apparently, I hadn't been concentrating, because the remark distracted me and, suddenly, for what seemed a long time and was probably a second, I couldn't find the tree, I couldn't pick it out from the others. I went into the corner off the line, braked late, and blew the next turn as well. Another time, I was alone, in one of the competition Datsuns, going about as fast as I could make it go, with Bondurant following me. When he signaled me in, he said, "You started to get tired two laps back and your concentration fell off. Right?"

Right. As I had known, objectively, for a long time, that one *must* concentrate in driving, I had also known that the inept selection of the wrong line going into one corner would, absolutely, inevitably, put car and driver hopelessly into the wrong line not only on the *next* corner but on the one after that. But I did not truly understand this simple maxim until I ran a few times through the four-bend chicane on Bondurant's course. If you're six inches off the mathematically correct line on the first bend, you're off a foot on the second, three on the third, and as for the fourth—forget it.

The Bondurant curriculum is elastic, to say the least. There's a one-day course designed to show a pretty well unclued driver how to manage on the streets and the freeways. A two-day defensive-driving course takes this farther, into hard stops, spins, and skids. The high-performance course is meant to teach competence in high-speed road driving in 125-plus-mph automobiles; and the five-day competition course turns out drivers who can begin racing on the amateur-club level. Cost is $100 a day basic and $800 for the competition course, using school cars. The garage count varies. On a recent day, there were three Datsuns, three Formula Fords, two Formula Vees, two Porsche 914s, two Audi sedans, a Lola T 70 Group 7 sports car, and a Ford GT 40.

Considering that he teaches such advanced techniques as correcting a skid by spinning the car 180 degrees in its own width and then steering it straight backward (a maneuver requiring such fast wheel handling that the school cars have red-and-green taped identifiers on the left and right spokes), Bondurant's curriculum sounds a bit hairy; but in the two years the school has been running, no one has been hurt. The cars are rigorously maintained, heavily roll-barred; students wear shoulder belts and Bell helmets. Most of them graduate. The occasional washouts are casualties of the competition course. Shaw or Mizejewski will decide that a man will never make a competent racedriver; Bondurant will check him out; if he agrees, the student gets a prorata fee refund and is bade to go and sin no more.

The others go home happy, for the most part, impressed with their new skills or even overimpressed. Returning to his East Coast home at midnight, a recent graduate amused the lady who opened the door for him: he was wearing the school's Day-Glo orange helmet, complete with visor. "I'm going to wear it all the time," he said. He got the laugh he was trying for, but he was really only half joking.

—1970

The
Body
Beautiful

The Reuter Coach Works is a small, grimy building on the Boston Post Road in the north Bronx. The windows have not recently been washed. Within, a clutter of tools, tins of paint, thinner, varnish, automobile parts, exotic woods, leather, and categorically undefinable odds and ends that have been accumulating since the firm's founding in 1930. There are two rooms, one a little bigger than an ordinary suburban two-car garage, the other less than half that size. The bigger room, the main workshop, will accept four automobiles with walkspace around them. This unlikely looking *atelier* is staffed by four people, Gustave Reuter, forty-eight, his sons Richard, twenty-three, and Robert, twenty-one, and Reuter's mother, eighty-three, who lives in an apartment over the shop, observes through a wall window, and serves as telephone operator. ("When my mother turned eighty," Reuter says, "I finally had to tell her, no more coming down after quitting time, when we'd all left the shop, and cleaning the place up and sweeping out. During the war, when you couldn't get help, and I was in the army, she used to work with my father, she could block-sand all day long.") These four people run what many qualified to hold the opinion believe to be the best automobile body-restoration shop in the United States.* Reuter body painting, upholstery, and woodwork is so sought after by owners of antique and classic automobiles that if Gus Reuter accepts a commission today and enters it in what he calls the book, the owner of the car may not anticipate being asked to bring it in the next day, there's a waiting list. The cost will be $3500–$4000 and up. Engine polishing and chassis painting aside, no mechanical work whatever will have been done. Reuter expects all mechanical work will be done before the car comes into his shop lest, later, someone drop a wrench on a fender.

"I can't change a spark plug anyway," Reuter says. "I wouldn't know how."

There are other good restoration shops scattered around the country, in New York, New Jersey, Ohio, California, but connoisseurs maintain that they can tell a car that has been out-shopped, as Lucius Beebe used to say, by Reuter, on sight. There's nothing *outré* or peculiarly characterizing about a Reuter restoration, except that it's flawless. The best available materials will have gone into it, the procedures will be the classic procedures, and the expenditure of painstaking care and plain hard work will have been prodigious: the body may have had ten man-days of hand rubbing with sandpaper and soapy water, for example. The paint surface will be lustrous, glass-smooth, with no trace of the "orange-peel effect" that mars ordinary work. Leather and carpeting will fit to a millimeter and woodwork will show the subdued glow of hand-done French polishing or fine varnish cut back with rottenstone and water on felt blocks. Brass or nickel will have the gleam of burnished gold or silver. The car can go directly from Reuter's to exhibition or to competition in a *concours d'élégance*.

The Long Island Automotive Museum owned by Henry Austin Clark, Jr. is one of the oldest and best in the country. Clark says, "If I had to take out of my collection all the Reuter-restored cars I'd be in bad shape: we're showing about seventy-five vehicles at the moment and Gus Reuter did at least forty of them."

Dr. Samuel L. Scher of New York, a notably discerning American collector, a Reuter client for more than twenty-five years, says, "I've had dozens of national first-prize-winning cars [the highest category] and Gus Reuter's hands had been on every one of them."

Not all Reuter clients exhibit or compete their cars. Many maintain them for their own pleasure, treasuring them as irreplaceable artifacts, most of the time shrouded under tailored cloth covers against the errant fleck of

---

*Since this was written, Reuter has moved to a new and much bigger shop in Ridgefield, Connecticut. His mother, reluctantly, has retired.

dust, taken to the open road only in bright weather and then driven with great care. The antique or classic automobile is valuable. The market worth of particularly desirable items has passed $75,000 and is reaching for $100,-000 and authorities of established qualification believe that within five years auctions at houses like Parke-Bernet will show taking bids of $150,000 for single cars. A fee of $5000 to bring a possession of that potential to perfection is not excessive and a shop that can perform the pertinent services is obviously to be cherished.

"Of course everything is relative," Reuter says. "We did a Maxwell for Austy Clark in 1946, bodywork, wood, paint, upholstery, a drop curtain, a new running-board, and so on, for $375; today we'd have to have, for exactly the same job, say $3700–$4000.

"Even our customers don't always understand what the work amounts to. You have to strip the old paint, take off every microscopic trace of it. Then the metal-prep, clean it right down to the pores of the metal all over, glaze it smooth, put on the primer, sand, put on some color, sand, wet block-sanding I'm talking about, more color, more sanding, it goes on forever, and the painting itself is nothing. Lots of people can run an airbrush, lay on paint without running it or puddling it and so forth, that's nothing. It's what goes before that counts."

I was reminded of a Type 50 Bugatti coupe that Reuter restored for me fifteen years ago. He painted the right-hand door panel three times—because the first two tries had not produced an optically correct surface; squatting in front of the door, he could not see an undistorted mirror image of himself.

"When I started to work here," Reuter says, "when I was a kid, there were six men on the payroll, and they were all bosses. I mean by that, each one was a specialist. They had all worked with my father before, after he came from Germany, and before he thought of going out on his own, and they were all foremen. So it was a tough league. It wasn't easy to do work that would satisfy these men. And they were taking home maybe twelve dollars a week, and that was the way it was. My brothers were with us then, too—it was a real family operation. Walter, the oldest of us, died many years ago, and Eddie retired. My cousin, Oskar did all the wood and leather work for seventeen years.

"We weren't doing any jobs, then, for ourselves. We did the coachwork for Zumbach in New York. Zumbach was then the number-one foreign car shop. This was the original Zumbach Motors to which the present Zumbach's is the successor. They would send us the work, we would do it, Zumbach's man would come and pick up the car, and after a while we'd get paid.

"One day Zumbach's driver forgot to take our bill out of the glove compartment. The car was a Hispano-Suiza boattail and it belonged to a man who was a very early collector, now I'm talking about the time right after World War II. When he saw the bill he realized that Zumbach was charging him exactly twice as much as we were charging Zumbach, so he said to himself, I suppose, 'Well, now, how about that?' or something of the sort, and he came up to see us. And after that he sent us his cars direct. That was Alec Ulmann. He knew Jimmy Melton, he knew Austin Clark, and he sent them around, too. And that was when it really began—but with a disaster.

"Melton brought us a Pierce 66. It was our first big independent job, and we really tried, and it was gorgeous, beautiful. And right after Melton picked up the Pierce he sent us his 1907 Silver Ghost Rolls-Royce touring car, one of the great Rolls-Royces then running, and you can still say the same thing about it, it's in the Rockefeller collection in Arkansas now. And we did that one for him. And that summer the Pierce came apart, the whole finish crazed, cracked and broke up, it was terrible. What had happened, those Pierce-Arrow 66's had cast-aluminum bodies a quarter-inch thick and we had painted it in the winter and at that time we used coal stoves and it was too damned cold in the shop. So, in the heat of the summer the metal expanded and cracked the paint. Trouble was, we had wanted to do the best job in the world and we just put on too much material, too much glaze, too much paint, too much everything, and when the metal expanded the finish couldn't stretch enough and it all broke up. Naturally we asked Melton to bring the car back, we took it down to the bare metal and did it all over. We lost any amount of money on the job, but it was the right thing to do, and from there on, everything was downhill, we had cars from Melton and Clark and Ulmann and Dowling. When he opened his museum in Connecticut Jimmy Melton had maybe 150 cars and we had done, I would guess, 100 of them. And that was early, you know, when you could buy Duesenberg double-cowl phaetons for $1500 and Phantom I Rolls-Royces for $1000 and so on.

"There were fortunes to be made in those days and nobody, or almost nobody, knew it. My father-in-law had a junkyard near here, and he broke up, I will bet you, you think I'm exaggerating but I'm not, I will bet you he broke up $10 million worth of antique and classic automobiles. I'm talking about things like Pierce 66's and Silver Ghost Royces. Before the war you could buy a T-head Mercer for $50 and now they're $50,000 except that nobody will sell one, and they were breaking up these cars every day. There goes a Springfield Rolls-Royce touring car, there goes a Peerless, they used *sledgehammers*, they broke up whole cars, then bits and pieces, brass, lamps that you couldn't touch today for $250 apiece, anything they could destroy they destroyed. One strong guy, in a morning, would break up a car that would bring $50,000–$75,000 today."

Reuter drives a Ford. "I've never been able to afford a car I restored," he says. "And anyway I don't have the collectors' mentality. Collectors are strange people."

The singer James Melton was an early Reuter client. He was a perfectionist and a demanding customer but a faithful one. The body restoration on most of his cars was done by Reuter Coach Works and the mechanical work by Conrad Lofink, an eccentric master mechanic who worked out of a tiny one-car garage in Wilton, Connecticut.

"Jimmy had a car he wanted done in red," Reuter says, "and he didn't like any red I had in the place, there wasn't a chip in any book I had he would look at. So I told him I'd mix one up for him, and I did, while he watched. I threw in some of this and some of that, and it was a very fortunate combination: it showed as a deep, dark maroon in shade, and a bright red, really brilliant, in sunlight. I called it Reuter Red, but Jimmy maintained it was his personal color and nobody could use it without his permission. You remember, we did your Bugatti in Reuter Red and Jimmy said it was O.K. only because you were a friend of his, and at that it was a big favor.

"One day Dr. Scher was in the shop, and so was Jimmy, and the doctor wanted me to do a Phantom I Rolls-Royce, a double-cowl phaeton, in Reuter Red. Jimmy said absolutely not, he wouldn't let Doc have his red, no way, we had to take a red out of the book.

"The collector tends to be a jealous man. I'll have a car in here, and somebody will come in and look at it, and he'll say, 'Don't tell me, I know who owns that thing, it looks just like him, flashy, that's got to be Blank's, and he *would* paint it white, I'm surprised he didn't ask you to put pink fenders on it.' "

Gus Reuter would not, of course, put pink fenders on a car for anyone. His tendency is to tell the customer he's going to do the car in such-and-such color, with so-and-so trim and this-or-that leather. One good customer, outraged at what he considered to be Reuter's high-handedness in refusing to accept his color choice, twice insisted on it, and both times, once he had seen the cars in sunlight, asked Reuter to repaint them to his own first judgment.

"Of course," Reuter told me, "I wouldn't want you to use his name, but the man is just a little bit color-blind, always has been. He has a lot of trouble with yellows and browns, particularly."

"I wouldn't say so to Gus," the man he was talking about told me, "but he is definitely a little color-blind. It's amazing—Gus is an absolutely great painter, and he's just a bit color-blind."

"So help me," Gus Reuter says, "out of all the hundreds of cars we've done, I've never seen two that presented identical problems. They're all different, and it's just fascinating. I had a Duesenberg brought to me one time in a truck that was full of boxes and baskets, there weren't two parts of that automobile that were stuck together, and nobody knew what it had looked like, no plans, nothing. It was a fantastic challenge. And then there are the really odd ones. We had a Rolls-Royce touring car that had a single seat in back, and heavy leather padding all around it. This thing had belonged to an Indian maharajah, he used it for hunting, and he used to ride back there all alone, and stand up to shoot while the car was running, that was of course the reason for the padding. The fenders were a mess, unbelievable, dented and pounded down. I couldn't imagine what had done this to them until I was told. That was how the maharajah used to carry his dead tigers, draped over the fenders of his Rolls-Royce."

—1970

The
Mini
Revolution

Rattlesnake Raceway is a private road circuit, six miles from Midland, Texas, on Route 349, once the legend-strewn Pecos Trail. It was not called Rattlesnake Raceway out of whimsy: the flat, arid countryside around it—sparsely covered with coarse grasses, tumbleweed, mesquite—supports a formidable population of *Crotalus atrox*. The snakes come out of the bush to sun themselves on the warm concrete of the track and drivers now and then run over one; sometimes they go back and stone it to death. Out past the perimeter of the property there are groves of pecan trees, white-dotted cotton fields, and, fallow, the warm red Texas earth. This is oil country: there are 58,000-odd people in Midland, and an oil-company headquarters for every eighty of them.

Rattlesnake Raceway is the test track for the building-and-racing firm of Chaparral Cars, Inc., and it is the most sophisticated circuit in private hands. One must go to General Motors to find anything comparable. The radio-telemetry equipment at Rattlesnake enables Chaparral technicians to produce as many as eight simultaneous remote readouts on a moving car up to five miles away: speed, lateral *g* force, engine revolutions per minute, the time in second-fractions required to shift from third to fourth gear, deceleration rate, and so on. Photoelectric cells rim the track and it can be wetted down from beginning to end. Until it was made available to PLAYBOY, the circuit had not been open to any publication for extended testing. It was the ideal setup for us in assaying fourteen subcompact automobiles that were likely to demonstrate only slight differences in many categories—differences that would be impossible to establish by seat-of-the-pants evaluation.

Another advantage was multiple testing of the cars by experts: the three Chaparral technicians assigned to the project: Don Gates, chief vehicle engineer, formerly chief of the Product Performance Engineering Group at Chevrolet Research and Development; Wesley Sweet and Harold Gafford, race mechanics; Jim Hall, founder of Chaparral and one of the legendary figures, both as driver and builder, in U.S. roadracing; and Chaparral executive vice-president Cameron R. Argetsinger, who created Watkins Glen, oldest of American roadraces. We all drove the cars (Austin America, Capri, Colt, Cricket, Datsun 510, Fiat 850, Gremlin, Opel 1900, Pinto, Renault R10, SAAB 99E, Toyota Corona, Vega GT, Volkswagen Super Beetle) many miles on the circuit and on the road.

Jim Hall is particularly sensitive to a vehicle's performance on Rattlesnake, because in the development of his own cars, which have been fabulously successful here and in Europe, he has driven more laps on it than he can remember, certainly high in the thousands. For a two-mile course, it has a lot of variety: a double 90-degree corner, a long straight with a fast bend in the middle, a hard corner that tightens up wickedly the farther one gets into it, and an uphill blind bend. Then there's a skid pad of a 150-foot radius that runs around the building housing the radio and recording equipment. It was on this circuit and in the shops down the lane from it that Hall and his partner Hap Sharp developed the innovative Chaparral racing cars (first to use airfoils for increased rear-wheel adhesion, for example), and it was on Rattlesnake Raceway that the almost incredible Chaparral 2-J—the "vacuum-cleaner" car designed for Hall by a team of ten men led by Don Gates—first ran.

The new small cars come to the U.S. market under the force of compelling logic: the Volkswagen showed the way twenty years ago, and when the sales of VWs, Renaults, Fiats, and the like began to round 10 percent of the U.S. total, Detroit policy setters had to concede that somebody out there wanted them besides car snobs, budgeteers, and eccentrics. The returns are in now, and they affirm what many experts in various fields have felt for some time: we cannot indefinitely justify 3000-pound, 300-horsepower, nine-miles-per-gallon vehicles for the transportation of one or two people.

It's likely that in twenty-five years the four-car family will be commonplace and that all four autos will fit comfortably into today's two-car garages still standing.

The equation contains factors beyond the obvious ones of economy, ecology, historical imperative, Ralph Nader's stunning appearance on the national scene in the role of David against the industry's Goliath, and federal intervention. One of those factors is the postwar travel and recreation boom. People came home from their first European trips planning their second. If the price of two weeks in London and Paris was the difference between a Chrysler and a Volkswagen, then the local VW dealer was about to see a new face in his showroom. People didn't *need* another trip to Europe, but they *wanted* one more than they wanted another mighty juggernaut from Detroit. Rather suddenly, the American consumer found that he had a lot of new wants: a boat, a snowmobile, a weekend or summer house—and a smaller car, so that he could swing them. Once this phenomenon was big enough to see with the naked eye, Detroit's response was predictable. David E. Davis, Jr., of Campbell-Ewald, the Chevrolet advertising agency, has said that the Vega comes closer to meeting consumer want than any car General Motors has built since World War II, and perhaps even World War I. He may have something: Chevrolet sold 43 percent of its available stocks in less than three days after the Vega went on sale, smashing all industry records.

In choosing the cars for the test, PLAYBOY made no attempt at a Consumers Union dead-level standard, beyond shooting roughly for a $2000 base price. Because of model availability at the time (in the case of one make, there were only three cars in the country), it was impossible to specify options. We might not have done so in any event, because what we wanted above all was a group of cars that might have been picked at random on the street. One car, the SAAB 99E, a $3300 item, was included because we were curious to see what $1000-odd added to the $2000 standard would bring, and also because we suspected that some $2000 cars would arrive in Midland loaded with $1000 or more worth of extras, and we wanted to offset that by including a car that *began* at $3000. We took the SAAB instead of the equally attractive Swedish Volvo only because we wanted another front-wheel drive. Two cars did show up with $3000 stickers: the Gremlin, at $3180.70 on a $1999 base, and the Vega at $2945/$2197.

Mildly startling is the fact that of the fourteen cars, only one, the Gremlin, is totally American. The Capri is built by Ford of Germany, engined by Ford of Great Britain. The Dodge Colt is made 100 percent by Mitsubishi of Japan, the Plymouth Cricket by Chrysler United Kingdom, Ltd., sold in the U.K. as the Avenger. The Pinto's basic engine (1600 cc) is British and the optional one (2000 cc) is German, as is the optional automatic

CHART OF SMALL CAR PERFORMANCE I

MAKE AND MODEL	Top Speed mph	0-60 mph sec.	Miles Per Gallon @60 mph for 52 Miles	Stopping Distance 60-0 mph* ft.	Gs**	Noise Level in Decibels @15 mph	Noise Level in Decibels @60 mph	Speedometer Error @60 mph	Odometer Error @10 Miles	Drag @60 mph† lbs.	Drag @200 mph†† lbs.
AUSTIN AMERICA	77	22.1	32.8	148	.81	68	80	61.5	9.54	122.6	907.2
CAPRI SPORT COUPE	99	15.8	27.4	132	.91	67	75	59	9.64	134.6	977.8
COLT 2-DOOR	91	13	32	158	.77	62	76	58	9.72	125	867.3
CRICKET	85	16.6	29.8	133	.90	66	76	64	9.22	143.8	846.1
DATSUN 510 2-DOOR	90	18.6	30.6	145	.83	60	78	60.5	9.54	122.5	976.5
FIAT 850 SPORT COUPE	91	17.2	44.5	139	.87	69	80	59.9	9.55	105.7	590.1
GREMLIN	99	14.3	25.6	183	.66	66	78	59.9	9.96	154.4	1229.3
OPEL 1900 SPORT COUPE	97	13.8	29.1	132	.91	68	79	59.5	9.53	130.4	918.3
PINTO	81	20	30.3	162	.74	69	82	60	9.55	149	1011.2
RENAULT R10	83	17.6	36.2	149	.81	66	78	61.5	9.53	121.6	876.3
SAAB 99E 4-DOOR	93	15.9	29.4	151	.80	61	72	61.5	10.1	133.1	1041.7
TOYOTA CORONA 4-DOOR	91	15.5	29.9	147	.82	67	78	61.5	9.56	144.7	948.3
VEGA GT	95	12.8	30.8	127	.95	71	79	59	9.95	141.8	976.9
VOLKSWAGEN SUPER BEETLE	78	19	32.6	132	.91	64	79	63	9.16	122.4	976.7

*A hard application, just short of locking the wheels.

**The force that is trying to move the car sideways and is being resisted by the car's adhesion to the ground.

†The combination of all the forces that cause the car to decelerate: friction resistance, rolling resistance, air resistance—the higher the figure, the greater the drag.

CHART OF SMALL CAR PERFORMANCE II

MAKE AND MODEL	Horsepower @60 mph	Horsepower @200 mph††	Over-All Length	Wheelbase	Engine (cu. in.-cyl.)	Max. BHP @rpm	Max. Torque lbs.-ft. @rpm	Base Price‡
AUSTIN AMERICA	19.6	483.6	146.75 in.	93.5 in.	77.9-4	58@5250	69@3000	$1815
CAPRI SPORT COUPE	21.5	521.2	167.8	100.8	97.6-4	71@5000	91@2800	2395
COLT 2-DOOR	20	462.3	160.6	95.3	97.5-4	100@6300	101@4000	1924
CRICKET	23	451	162	98	91.4-4	70@5000	83@3000	2000‡‡
DATSUN 510 2-DOOR	19.6	520.6	162.4	95.3	97.5-4	96@5600	100@3600	1990
FIAT 850 SPORT COUPE	16.9	314.6	142	79.5	55.1-4	58@6400	47.7@4000	2111
GREMLIN	24.7	655.3	161.25	96	232-6	135@4000	215@1600	1999
OPEL 1900 SPORT COUPE	20.8	489.5	171	95.7	115.8-4	90@5200	111@3400	2326
PINTO	23.8	539.1	163	94	97.6-4	75@5000	96@3000	1919
RENAULT R10	19.4	467.1	167	89	78.6-4	56@4600	70@2300	1799
SAAB 99E 4-DOOR	21.3	555.4	171	97	104.3-4	95@5500	97.7@3000	3315
TOYOTA CORONA 4-DOOR	23.1	505.5	166.9	95.7	113.4-4	108@5500	117@3600	2281
VEGA GT	22.5	520.8	169.7	97	140-4	110@4800	138@3200	2546
VOLKSWAGEN SUPER BEETLE	19.5	515.9	161.8	95.3	96.7-4	60@4400	81.7@3000	1985

††Projected figures.
‡Base prices will vary according to locality, dealer and, for imports, proximity to port of entry.
‡‡Preintroduction estimate.

305

transmission. The Gremlin comes out of American Motors' parts bins and the Vega was newly designed from the ground up, though using the Opel transmissions. Otherwise, Detroit appears to have elected to use imports in phase one of its fight against imports.

All fourteen cars were thoroughly run in, whether they came to Midland truck-borne or under their own power. In an undertaking of this kind, it's safe to assume that the vehicles have been well prepared, but the degree of tune depends upon chance and the enterprise of the supplier. We suspected one car to be a cheater—deciding finally that it was not, only that it had been supertuned by the knowing hands of experts.

The tests required a week and were meticulously done to the highest standards of scientific discipline. Some of the equipment used—the remote pickup registering speed, acceleration, and deceleration, for example—was designed by Don Gates, made in the Chaparral machine shop, and is unique. Watching the recorder spew out feet of paper as the pens inked in a car's behavior was an almost eerie experience. "He's doing 62 in third gear, you see," Gates would say, "and that little jiggle means he's about 100 yards past the bend . . . there's a rough place on the circuit there . . . he'll brake about here in two seconds."

Space limitations and complexity have prevented the charts on pages 304 and 305 from fully reflecting the extent of the testing. The drag and horsepower figures are an example. Data fed into the computer for this test included the weight of the car and the driver, the rate of deceleration of the vehicle coasting with power off, and the density of the air. The figures were taken at 30 and 60 miles per hour and computer extrapolated to 100, 150, and 200. We have used only the 60 and 200 mph figures. Since the Fiat Coupe showed the lowest drag figure, 105.7 pounds at 60 mph, and would require only 314.6 horsepower to propel it at 200 mph, it was obvious that it would also show the lowest fuel consumption, and it did—44.5 miles to the gallon at 60 mph. Incidentally, this reading was so low that we repeated the whole test, with identical results.

To demonstrate understeer and oversteer, the cars were run clockwise and counterclockwise on a precise line around the 150-foot skid pad at speeds applying increasing side force to them. Understeer and oversteer are functions of front-and-rear-wheel adhesion: an understeering car tends to go through a corner at a less acute angle than the position of the front wheels would seem to indicate; an oversteering car takes a greater angle. Put another way, an understeering car driven past the limit of adhesion will plow off the road front end first; an oversteerer will spin off rear end first. Understeer is considered safer for passenger vehicles and the graphs made on each of the test cars showed the curves typical of understeer, with one exception: the Renault R10 showed some initial understeer, changing quickly to oversteer. The Renault was the only car we damaged: one of the Chaparral technicians had taken it to .58 *g* of side force, when it switched from under to oversteer, dug in the outside rear wheel to the rim, and gently turned on its side. Interestingly, detailed examination of the data subsequently showed that it had gone past the point of no return *before* the wheel rim reached the concrete. The driver unfastened his safety belt and climbed unhurt out the top door. Damage to the car was slight.

In appearance and performance, the fourteen cars moved all of us variously, but in the end we—Messrs. Gates, Hall, Argetsinger, Sweet, Gafford, and I—came to near unanimity. It's important to know that we had in mind the urban car, not the transcontinental grand touring machine, and that we were not attempting oracular infallibility. It was not our intent to say buy this, do not buy that, but rather to suggest, to point, to establish facts as a basis for individual judgment.

AUSTIN AMERICA.   This boxy little car derives in direct line from one of the bench-mark automobiles of our time, the Morris Mini, by the notably original-minded British designer Alexander Issigonis. There were three essentials in Issigonis's concept: for stability and full utilization of space, a wheel at each corner and minimum overhang; front-wheel drive by a front-mounted engine set transversely; suspension by hydraulic fluid interacting between front and rear: when a front wheel hits a bump, its rise instantly puts counteracting pressure on the corresponding rear wheel, thus lifting the rear of the body to the level already reached by the front. This concept, in various modulations, has been very successful and usually produces a superior ride. In fact, the Austin America has been compared with the Citroën, which uses a hydraulic system of much greater complexity. Front-wheel drive, by eliminating transmission hump and drive-shaft tunnel, gives a space bonus; the Austin is remarkably roomy for a 147-inch automobile. Steering is rack and pinion, brakes are disk and drum, with a limiting valve to prevent rear-wheel lockup, and the transmission can be either four-speed manual or seven-position automatic.

The makers claim a top speed of 85 mph for the Austin, but the fastest we could make it go was 77, and it had the longest 0–60 mph acceleration time, 22.1 seconds, of the fourteen cars. Braking was good and it showed a hair better gas mileage than the Volkswagen. Jim Hall thought the ride spongy—which may reflect the racedriver's preference for fairly taut springing—and objected to the car's tendency to "hook in"; that is, go to oversteer when the throttle was lifted in a corner. The Austin was not really stable on a straightaway. I thought the amount of engine noise and vibration excessive, and final data did show that only three of the cars were louder at low speed. For urban use, these flaws are not critical and will, for some, be overweighted by the excellent boulevard ride, good mileage, ample load space, and low price. I liked the car well enough, driving it around Midland streets, but I didn't enjoy pushing it hard on Rattlesnake, because performance was inadequate for that kind of work. The test car had a manual transmission. If I were buying, I would take the automatic, simply on the principle that in anything but a genuine high-performance motorcar, manual is a bore.

CAPRI SPORT COUPE.   A heavy swath through the European market has been cut by the Capri and it will do well on this side of the water. For some tastes, the Capri has a flamboyant air: fat bulge on the engine-compartment lid, thick crease along the sides, simulated brake-cooling scoops aft the doors, high-mounted race-type gas-filler cap. However, our consensus was that it's a sharp, good-looking motorcar. It was one of two fastest of the lot at 99 miles per hour and in the top group in acceleration: 15.8 seconds to 60 mph. Only one car, the Vega, outstopped it, and only two, the Opel and VW, equaled it at .91 g and 132 feet from 60 mph to standstill. This was an automatic, working off a well-placed T-bar lever, and if handled with reasonable regard for the workings of the device, it offered the sought-after turbinelike gear progression. The Capri had a number of insignificant but beguiling details—clock mounted conveniently on the shift console, for example, and a genuine, made-in-England gooseneck Butler map lamp. Performance considered, 27.4 miles to the gallon of gasoline is commendable.

We all liked the Capri and no one entered a heavy criticism of it. The 2000-cc engine would be my choice, and the automatic, but Jim Hall opted for the four-speed. He particularly liked the handling, flat ride, competent suspension and good straight-line stopping, and was not put off by the slightly excessive understeer that we all noticed.

DODGE COLT.   Mitsubishi has been selling the Colt in the home islands for a while and began peeling off 3000 to 4000 units a month for us at the first of the year. Good things are made by Mitsubishi, the Nikon camera for one, and the house is the biggest corporate entity in Japan, where antimonopoly regulations are not very anti: Mitsubishi is in ships, oil, airplanes, financing, insurance. One would expect the Colt to be a good, well-worked-out kind of automobile, and it is. Two of the figures we charted on it were exemplary —it squeezed the Volkswagen hard on mileage, at thirty-two, and only the bigger-engined Vega could outaccelerate it, and that not by much.

There are four body styles: two-door hardtop and four-door sedan, station wagon and two-door coupe, all running a 1600-cc engine, small but strong, single overhead cam, hemispheric combustion chambers, and five-bearing crankshaft. Devices usually thought of as optional are standard here: adjustable steering wheel, tilt-back seats (except in the coupe), two-speed windshield wipers, a good closed-window ventilation system. There *are* extras: air conditioning and automatic transmission. The interior is remarkably handsome, except for the trunk, and doesn't look at all "economy."

The Colt is fast all the way through the range—too fast, I felt, for its handling traits. Braking was poor, with front-wheel lockup and rear-axle hop easy to come by, plus oversteer in hard corners. The variable-ratio steering is pleasant for ordinary use. The Colt is a handsome little motorcar and I'd have liked it a good deal had it given me more of a sense of security.

PLYMOUTH CRICKET.   At first sight, the name plate and flower identifier on the side of the Cricket strike one as the cheapest-looking notion since fake-wood station wagons, but, bearing in mind the number of flower-power VWs cruising around, Plymouth may know something we don't. At any rate, here we have the Avenger, a brisk mover on the British market, its 70-horsepower 4-cylinder engine pushing one body style, the four-door sedan. Detroit publicists are seasoned experts in double-think semantics and a fine example of the art comes with the Cricket press material: "Designers attribute the distinctive styling of the Cricket to the fact that the car was conceived solely as a four-door sedan, not as an adaptation of a design for a hardtop. Thus, the styling is free of the compromises that are necessary when the same basic body shell is used for different configurations." Well, one body style anyway, pleasing to the eye and capable of transporting four humans in reasonable comfort.

The interior is not an unalloyed delight; there is a good deal of molded plastic and rubber matting in view. Controls are handy, except for what Plymouth calls "distinctively designed pods on the sides of the steering column" for lights, washers and wipers, and so on. These, and the ignition-steering lock, are perhaps not really bafflers, they just take a few hours of learning with the owner's manual on your lap. Getting in and out of strange automobiles all day does tend to build an understanding of the short fuse that is the outstanding characteristic of parking-lot attendants. Not being mnemonists, none of us even tried to remember on which car the transmission had to be in reverse before the key would stop squealing or which one mandated the key out, not in, to unlock the steering. As for safety-harness-fastening methods—no hope. A logical mind new to the problem might wonder why we cannot have standardization of these gimmicks, plus uniform dashboard instrumentation and shift patterns, but you and I know that permanent world peace will be easier to come by.

The Cricket's braking power impressed all of us as extraordinary. Jim Hall remarked it first, with the caveat that the fronts (power disks) were a bit *too* strong. I was surprised, when we had the data, to see that the Capri, VW, and Opel were better, if only by a little, at .91 g, and the Vega considerably better at .95—the Cricket had somehow felt stronger. Our car had a banshee howl in the differential, which I choose to believe was atypical, and a most alarming groan, with accompanying stiffness in the steering column, plus a reluctance to find center and stay there. Otherwise, the handling was exemplary and we all enjoyed driving it. I thought the Cricket's roadability fabulous when I noticed that I was going into the Mexican at 86 mph. Disillusionment came later, when the speedometer proved to be the wildest of all: it showed 87 for a true 80. Still, if that's the worst thing that can be said about the car. . .

DATSUN 510.   The Japanese automobile industry is the youngest in the world, and, next to the American, the strongest: Since 1956, production has doubled every three years! The Datsun is produced by the Nissan Motor Company, part of a huge complex of vehicle makers.

Nissan turned out 1,375,000 Datsuns last year, so the make, while fairly new to us, has been thoroughly debugged. In 1969, the Japanese exported only 14 percent of production and they are turning cars out so fast, to meet a steadily increasing home demand, that their own doom-criers point to 1974, when they'll be putting 3,300,000 cars a year on a wholly inadequate road network, as the year of saturation. Thus, as in so many other things, the Japanese will get there—in this case, a nationwide bumper-to-bumper traffic jam—before anyone else. (Presumably, Tokyo will have before that time made a new breakthrough in pollution control: even now, city traffic policemen take pure oxygen at regular intervals.) This farsighted view, plus the work obsession of the average Japanese, who makes even Germans look like dedicated loafers, accounts for the Japanese export drive, so formidable that it has struck fear into as sturdy a type as Henry Ford II. Incidentally, Nissan has been reported as intending to build a passenger car using the steam-powered engine—it cooks Freon instead of water—developed by Wallace Minto of Sarasota.

The sophistication of the Datsun 510 is reflected in items such as its expensive double-universal independent rear suspension that, unlike the basic swing-axle layout, keeps both wheels vertical relative to the ground over any road surface, and in interior noise level: in the low-speed range, it was the quietest car we had, only four points louder than the comparison Cadillac. It has a really working flow-through ventilation system and three adults can ride in back without unseemly intimacy. Handling is good if not extraordinary under stress and the normal ride is excellent.

FIAT 850 SPORT COUPE.   If this motorcar had a Made-in-Patagonia plate screwed to the fire wall, you would still know instantly that it's Italian. Perhaps not from the outside, but once the door is shut and you're looking through the pierced-spoke steering wheel at the saucer-sized tachometer and speedometer dials, once you hear the 4-cylinder engine, all 903 cc's of it, muttering away behind you, then it has to be. The body is deceptive; there's nothing extraordinary-looking about it, save the extreme rear chop, but, as the chart clearly shows, a lot of wind-tunnel hours have gone into it. The Fiat is a rarity: you can put your foot flat on the floor, and leave it there all day, without feeling you're throwing away gasoline. (When you do fill it, eight gallons is overflow.) The seats are comfortable and bucketed, but it's tight behind the wheel for a big man: Jim Hall, considerably over six feet, couldn't really find the combination. There's a lot of pedal offset to the right, which takes getting used to, so much so that several times, going into a corner, I caught myself looking down to be sure I wouldn't put both feet on the clutch and nothing on the brake. Like most rear-engined cars, it will show straight-line instability in a crosswind, but not enough to be a nuisance, and final oversteer if it's really pushed in a corner. The car is low enough to suggest, for the first fifty miles or so, that you're sitting on the road, but after that, you forget about it, probably because you're marveling at the amount of push coming out of 58 horsepower. Italian engineers have never worried a lot about noise, and the Fiat was one of the three loudest, level with the Pinto at 15 mph, and only a couple of points quieter than the Vega.

In a sense, the vehicle was outside our pattern, being oriented more toward touring than urban use. When I had a chance to run on the open road for fun, with fourteen cars to choose from, I usually took the Fiat, but when I went home at night, I drove something else.

GREMLIN.   On first sight, I liked the Gremlin better than anything else. I was in good company: the Gremlin was Don Gates's favorite, too. Cameron Argetsinger, who had said from the beginning that the Vega was number one, called us both daft. I still think the Gremlin a splendid-looking car; the rear-end treatment, I insist, is stunning; and I will not back off on dandy little touches such as the inset steps that make the roof rack an easy reach and the big dash-mounted lock for the glove compartment. (The test car carried every option but radar.) Once it's under way, however, the Gremlin is less enchanting. For example, the power steering is pure overkill, all power and no feel whatsoever. At Midland, we had the three-speed manual transmission, an archaic arrangement without synchromesh on first or reverse. To say the Gremlin won't stop is an exaggeration, but 183 feet from 60 mph is a long time to wait and wonder if you're going to hit the wall or not. In right-hand corners, the engine invariably cut out, presumably due to fuel starvation. Pulling 135 horsepower out of its 6 cylinders, it took the Gremlin pretty quickly out of the hole—14.3 seconds to 60 mph—and it was faster on top than anything save the Capri. The inevitable trade-off for this performance was in fuel consumption, 25.6 miles to the gallon, not really bad in the overall scheme of things, but lowest of the cars we had on hand.

I still like the way the rear window opens to take luggage. Granted, I might not enjoy that long lift over the sill, but it certainly does look dandy, rising lightly on its countersprings.

OPEL 1900 SPORT COUPE. Opel is one of the monument names. There've been Opels on the road since 1898 and, by 1912, the firm had made 10,000 cars; in 1935, it was the biggest producer in Europe. It's in the General Motors family now. The make has for years been thought rather staid and stodgy, but Opel used to swing, and when Gary Gabelich did 622 mph in a natural-gas rocket car last autumn, long memories recalled Fritz von Opel, who pushed a rocket car to 125 mph in the late twenties. The "doctor's-car" image is changing now: the Opel GT has had good acceptance here.

The Opel 1900 was one of my Midland favorites. I liked it so much that I drove it more than I should have. It had a solid, well-built feeling and it conveyed the impression that it would last. Oddly, though the body looks aerodynamically right, the sloping roof line being particularly attractive, it churned up quite a lot of wind noise, 79 decibels at 60 mph, ranking it even with Vega and Volkswagen. The engine, not itself notably quiet, was well insulated. Braking was superior, at 132 feet and .91 g, and it stopped dead straight. Extremely sensitive in the seat of his pants, like all racedrivers, Jim Hall was more or less critical of the ride quality on thirteen of the fourteen cars, the Opel being the only one he would say was "very good." It was quick—13.8 seconds to 60 and a top speed of 97—but still gave 29.1 miles to the gallon. All around, a good car.

PINTO. The automotive-mechanic population of the United States is about 40,000 short. In some communities, it's almost impossible to find a mechanic who'll come to start a stalled car: like doctors, auto mechanics don't make many house calls anymore. The do-it-yourself alternative collapses when you first look seriously under the hood of a standard V8. Change the spark plugs? On some engines, you can barely *see* them, and only a special jointed wrench, rubber-collared to hold the plug tight when it's loose, will bring it to daylight. Ford has a better idea: the Pinto is about as simple a vehicle as the market will accept and, with it, you get a 129-page illustrated home-service manual. It's loaded with labeled drawings and photographs and it starts at ground level: Figure 241, for instance, is captioned "Adjustable Wrench" and the one working part is clearly labeled "Adjustable Screw." Figure 243 is captioned "Hand Cleaner." (The stuff is called "GOOP"; it contains lanolin and other good things.) If your capacities are overtaxed by doing two things at once, such as reading and using a screw driver, you can get a recording. The Model T is back and there is hope for all of us.

Pinto, son of Maverick, is the line that leaps to mind—it has the same long hood and short deck. The car looks bigger than it is, and with reason: in one dimension, width, it's almost nine inches past the VW, a statistic reflected in interior room and not much roll in corners. The engine is the Capri's, with the usual transmission choices on the 2000-cc engine only. The smaller engine is available only with the manual. It's noisy—82 decibels at 60 mph, the highest figure we recorded—and a lot of vibrations come through. Road shock also is heavy through the body and particularly the steering wheel, a big one by today's standard. In braking—all drums—the Pinto compares badly with its primary rival, the Vega—162 feet against 127, and .74 g against .95. It was almost uncontrollable in panic stops from maximum speed. I thought it very good in corners and reasonably stable on the straights. The test car, running the small engine, did 81 mph; the 2000-cc version should add ten to that. There's a surprising amount of room in back—limited travel on the driver's seat, and none at all on the front passenger's—but you wouldn't want to live there. There is an extended option list and you can build a deluxe version of the Pinto if you like. But it still is going to be difficult to stop.

This observation suggests that the self-appointed car tester takes rather a lot upon himself—maybe too much. Usually, he's assaying only a single example, and the danger of condemning 50,000 automobiles for the flaws of one is ever-present. There are, however, two safeguards: if the car is bought anonymously off the dealership floor, that's one thing, but when the maker knows in advance, and can select the vehicle, one must assume it's a good one. Second, it's often possible to consult other testers. In the matter of the brakes on the basic Pinto, not many huzzahs are heard in the land.

RENAULT R10. Renault has been selling automobiles to Americans for sixty-five years, and the subcompact model R10 is, from a moneysaving point of view, king of the castle. Low in initial cost, at $1799, it's also a super gas miser: the test car did 36.2 miles to the gallon at a steady 60 mph, a reading not seriously threatened by any of the other cars and exceeded only by the phenomenal Fiat 850. It was by no means the slowest on pickup at 17.6 seconds and the actual top speed, 83 mph, was close enough to the maker's 85 mph claimed. It has disk brakes on all four wheels, good rack-and-pinion steering (the most positive system, a gear wheel on the end of the steering column meshes with mating teeth on a straight bar that turns the front wheels), and it can be stuffed into minimum parking space. In other words, good for city use. But for long over-the-road trips, not so good.

The R10 uses swing axles in the rear: two drive shafts universally jointed to the differential. The swing axle was one of the early solutions to the independent-rear-suspension problem, and it works: the bump the right-hand wheel hits has no effect on the left-hand wheel. This system has been used by some notably good automobiles, Porsche and Mercedes-Benz among them. Swing axles have a compensatory disadvantage, however, which is that the combination of short wheelbase, rear-engine weight, and swing axle makes a car relatively unstable in sidewinds and tricky in hard corners and sudden severe direction changing. If a swing-axle car is pushed hard enough, the outside rear wheel, which is taking most of the side force, will tuck under and begin to move the rear of the car independently of the front, setting up a violent oversteer. A driver who knows the phenomenon can cope with it if he's sharp, but he must be quick, because it's a right-now kind of happening. Sometimes, even an expert, like the Chaparral technician who was driving the Renault on the Rattlesnake skid pad when it dumped, will miss—even though he knows he's asking for it by pushing the car hard.

The Renault was not everybody's darling at Midland, the objections most often cited being the offset pedals and the odd gearshift positioning, the lever having to be stuffed into the seat cushion to get reverse, bringing it just about under your leg. The brakes were good, as would be expected of four-wheel disks on such a light automobile. But it was rough in sidewinds. In the Fiat, I followed Harold Gafford along Route 349 when he was running the Renault's mileage tests. A strong wind, gusting to 25 mph, was blowing across the road and Gafford had to work hard to hold the car dead straight and maintain a precise 60 miles per hour. I had gone for miles at rates up to 90 and, while the Fiat let me know it was windy out there, I wasn't in anything like Gafford's trouble. Jim Hall's reaction to the Renault's road behavior was definitive if brutal: he said that taking it hard into corners gave him the positive conviction that he was going to come out facing the other way. I can't believe that the good old swing axle will show up on many Renaults in the future.

SAAB 99E. I've been a SAAB admirer since 1959, when a factory-team driver took me for a flat-out ride on the gravel roads around Linköping in Sweden, and a week with the new fuel-injection 99E model did nothing to diminish my regard for the make. Beautiful it's not. The shape is chunky and boxy to the point of being positively antiesthetic. (But you can see the ground eleven feet ahead of the bumper.) Still, looks and heavy steering at slow speeds are all I can cite against the automobile. This is a vehicle that has been screwed together to stay. To peer into the engine compartment is a pleasure; it looks as if it had been put together by aircraft mechanics. The SAAB seethrough headrests are the most sensible made. The interior is luxurious and the high-speed sound level was the lowest of the fourteen. The Opel had better acceleration and top speed, but I was faster around Rattle-snake in the SAAB—attributable, perhaps, to front-wheel drive or, more likely, absolute confidence. But, as I said earlier, the 99E was running out of its class and it would have been surprising if it had not looked good. Still, it did do well, and it should have—price does matter.

TOYOTA CORONA. The Toyota Motor Company is the fifteenth-largest corporation in the world outside the United States, has been making cars since 1936, reached an output rate of 100,000 cars a month two years ago, and is now the world's number-five producer. With little advertising and an exploitation budget that Detroit would be ashamed to allocate to a new horn button, Toyota sold 208,112 cars here last year, second only to honorable number-one import. If you think all this happened by chance, return to square one. It was brought about by bright people, who had the inestimable advantage of knowing that they didn't have all the answers, or even all the questions. So they boarded JAL jets in large numbers, tried out cars all over the world, found out, and went back to tell the folks manning the drawing boards. The Toyota Corona isn't the most exciting thing on wheels since the curved-dash Oldsmobile, but it is a good automobile homing in tightly on its target.

The Corona four-door sedan has disk/drum brakes, a comfortable ride —which would be improved by bigger tires—and a well-thought-out, well-put-together interior of practically solid plastic that is so good you may not notice it. As with other industrial materials, the Japanese have certainly found out about synthetics in the past couple of decades. My notes on the Toyota begin with a remark about value for money: it carries as standard a lot of other makers' options—power brakes, adjustable seat backs, tinted glass, and whitewalls, for openers. And thirty miles to the gallon from a solid new engine taking 108 horsepower out of an overhead-cam, five-main-bearing configuration. Since the engine is 1860 cc, or 116 cubic inches, that's almost 1 horsepower to the inch. Another edge the Corona has is the four-door setup. Nobody really likes to climb into a car, particularly a small one, over a bent front-seat back, and Toyota proved the point by selling over 80,000 four-doors here in 1970.

VEGA GT. The Vega was, overall, the best in the corral at Midland, reflecting a clean success, one might almost say a triumph, in meeting conflicting objectives. For example, the Vega is certainly a subcompact—our test car, running the big engine and optioned to the roof, pumped out almost thirty-one miles to the gallon—but it looked and felt bigger than any of the others, a circumstance that endeared it to some of the testers on sight. Fear not, the long-conditioned American love for the big barge is not going to disappear overnight. The Vega outaccelerated everything else, outbraked all the others with room to spare, and even showed an almost-honest odometer, at 9.95 miles for 10, true. Negatively, it had the highest interior low-speed noise level, and the brakes, while they would put out .95 g, needed a lot of leg. When I first took it fast into a corner, I had a second or so of deep thought, and even Hall, used to standing on brake pedals, complained about the effort required. Handling seemed to be just about impeccable, the car completely controllable at all speeds and in all attitudes. The Vega was designed for an objective rarely achieved: absolute neutral steer with no loss of straight-line stability, even in wind. Theoretically, a perfectly neutral car, pushed past the limit, will go off the road all in one piece; in fact, when given enough throttle, the Vega will finally go to oversteer, but it will stick for a long time first.

The 2300-cc engine is unique. It has a die-cast aluminum block—the dies weigh 75,000 pounds—a high silicon content in the alloy making the usual inset iron cylinder liners unnecessary. The valves move on a single overhead camshaft driven by a cog belt that runs the fan and water pump as well. The engine is a strange-looking device, but accessible it certainly is—indeed, it looks lost in the space one usually expects to find crammed to the top with wires and plumbing. Like the Pinto, the Vega comes with owner's fix-it book, not as detailed and explicit, but adequate. Visibility is good, four people can be packaged in reasonable contentment, and the seats, while much too soft for my taste, will please short-trip riders.

The enthusiasm I'm reflecting for the Vega GT must be tempered by the observation that this was a top-line model, the second-heaviest-optioned car we had. It was the only one of the fourteen running on wide rims and fat tires, for example, and, while its handling was obviously inherently superior, the amount of rubber it was putting on the road had to be an advantage. It was a splendid motorcar, but it carried a $2944.75 sticker. The basic $2091 Vega 2-door sedan, with the 90-horsepower engine instead of the 170, cannot be expected to run with it or feel like it. This may be why Chevrolet has allocated only 20 percent of production to the sedan, while the coupe is down for 50 percent.

VOLKSWAGEN SUPER BEETLE. In line with carefully maintained tradition, the new Volks looks much like the old one on the road, except for a noticeably bulgier trunk lid. Inside, it's different: eighty-nine ways different, the factory says. The new engine delivers 60 horsepower and much of the suspension and chassis system, front and rear, is new—diagonal trailing arms in back and MacPherson struts in front, working on a track three inches wider. This change has finally fixed the handling problem that gave the old Bugs a deserved reputation as lethal oversteerers. (I once saw one spin across a four-lane freeway coming out of an underpass into a cross-wind.) Front-strut suspension takes less room, so a great deal more can be piled into the trunk. The heating system now delivers through seven outlets and there's a two-speed blower on the flow-through. The floor is fully carpeted and, all in all, there's not much left of the old bare-bones look. The interior detail is superb, with first-cabin German-quality workmanship showing everywhere. I suspect the Super Bug will be in heavy demand. The Midland test car certainly was: we took it off a dealer's floor, it was the only one he had, and, as it went out the door, an irate customer was still waving a wet check over his head and demanding that we bring it back.

The VW stopped inside everything but the Vega, Capri, and Opel, and it was surprisingly quiet once you'd slammed the doors. And with the windows closed, they take slamming, because the Bug is still all but airtight. What surprised us was the handling: The Super Bug really sticks in there, it was a revelation on the skid pad and you can belt it into a corner now without any of the old "oh-oh, here it goes" sensation. The VW, they say, is about to be shot down. I'll wait until I see the flames.

The subcompact is, perhaps, the wavelet of the future. An eminence of Detroit has suggested that when our children come of age, anything bigger than today's intermediates will be tagged deluxe. Possibly. If that's the case, the assaying we have attempted here may have some significance.

None of the fourteen Midland cars perfectly mated with the mold into which we were trying to fit it: a motorcar exactly suited to urban use, quick and sure-footed on the highway, esthetically delightful in form, and sophisticated in accommodation. Some cars were well sized for the city but esthetically unsatisfying. Others were fast over the road but flawed for urban use by individual traits such as high fuel consumption or heavy steering. The ideal doesn't exist. We must hope that it, or a reasonable facsimile, is on a drawing board somewhere.

And so, as the setting sun reddens the plains of Texas, we leave old Rattlesnake Raceway, slightly saddlesore and, maybe, a little wiser.

—1971

317

French
Show
With
Italian
Go

When André Citroën ran the company he founded in 1919, his cars carried no identifying name plates. A Citroën automobile was a Citroën because it looked like one and, if that wasn't enough, it mounted the double-chevron/herringbone emblem (⋀) suggesting, if only to those who knew, the gear-cutting business on which Citroën's fortunes—he was not a one-fortune man—were founded. André Citroën had little in common with a 1971 chairman of the board, who is vulnerable, wary, ever in danger of finding himself unfleeced under the steely stare of a Congressional committee chairman forensically armed to the teeth by Nader's Raiders. Citroën was an old-style tycoon. Bucking the odds at roulette in the legendary Deauville casino, he blew $500,000 in ten hours without a blink. He was of the original company of movers and shakers—Ford, Austin, Opel, Agnelli—who loosed the automobile on the planet, grew great, and passed on, full of years and honors, their ears innocent of the doom word "ecology." Citroën was not a wealthy man when he died, but he had run a merry course, and it may be that the path of ultimate wisdom is to live rich and die poor.

It's unlikely that Citroën, forward-peering as he certainly was, could have imagined the shape of the current top of the company's line, a simple little $11,482 four-place coupe called the SM—S for Sport, M for Maserati—an Italian-French amalgam combining a chassis that may be light-years ahead of its contemporaries with a four-cam V6 engine. It's probable, though, that Citroën would have scribbled his permissive initials on the plans, because he did like to be ahead of the pack, and that's where the SM is, far out: a *gran turismo* motorcar that takes 140 miles per hour out of an under-3-liter engine driving the front wheels, and delivers this stunning performance in a ride that's incontestably the most comfortable, over any kind of surface, available in a wheeled vehicle. And on top of the basics, the SM piles other small wonders: hydropneumatic suspension (plus, of course, hydraulic-powered brakes and steering), height adjustment that keeps the car level under any load condition and allows wheel changing without jacking, and six quartz-halogen headlights, two of which peer around corners as the front wheels turn. (It appears that the Stone Age idiocy that allows each of the fifty states to legislate its own traffic laws will for the present deprive the American market of the SM's advanced lighting system.) Turning those front wheels, by the way, is done in a fashion unique to the SM: the steering ratio is two turns, lock to lock. Obviously, it would be impossible to park such a manually steered car carrying 1985 pounds on the front wheels, and ordinary power steering, at that ratio, would be so twitchy as to be dangerous, even for an expert. The Citroën solution is variable power: the battalions of gremlins that run the overall hydraulic system—a true plumber's nightmare, but it works and keeps on working—pour in full assistance at low speeds and take almost all of it away when the car is running fast. Parking and maneuvering are effortless, but at speed, when quick *and* soft steering can put you into the boonies in a flash, the car's tendency is to run dead straight, and reasonable effort is needed to make it do anything else. Further, self-centering of the steering is also hydraulically aided. The total effect may not build to a perfect solution, but it's close, very close. Some testers have entered dissents, on the ground that this power steering, like almost every other, deprives the driver of the "feel" at the steering-wheel rim, the subliminal vibrations—Stirling Moss used to say that he could hear them—that telegraph the behavior of the front wheels, warning, for example, when they are about to lose their grip on the road in a corner. But the governing fact is that very few drivers ever push a car to the cornering limits that produce these signals, or could read them if they did, while low-effort low-speed steering is in universal demand.

The days of the great automobiles—exotic, individualistic, high-performance—are surely numbered; the trend toward governed uniformity has been for years as visible and as predictable as the flow of lava down a mountainside. The more to be marked and enjoyed, then, are those few originals, the ones that resist the bureaucratic crunch and come, as the SM does, of proven lineage. Maserati and Citroën both draw from long books of experience—nearly sixty years long. Citroën began as a gear maker in 1913. The Officine Alfieri Maserati, a Bologna repair shop, took its first *lire* across the counter a year later.

André Citroën was the fifth and last son of a Dutch father, a diamond merchant, and a Polish mother; there were six Maserati brothers—Carlo, Bindo, Alfieri, Mario, Ettore, Ernesto—whose father was a locomotive engineer. Except for Mario, an artist, they all gravitated, as if by instinct, to the emerging world of the automobile. Carlo, the oldest, built a motorcycle before he was out of his teens and raced it for the Italian bike maker Carcano. At twenty he was head of Fiat's test department and in the next six years he was tester and team driver for Bianchi, Isotta-Fraschini, and Junior of Turin, where he became managing director. He died when he was thirty.

Bindo Maserati was chief tester for Isotta, Alfieri a racedriver. Ernesto flew with the Italian Air Force during World War I. Afterward, the Officine Maserati picked up an order to build a race car for Isotta and in 1921–1922, with Alfieri driving and Ernesto riding mechanic, it won a lot of races for Isotta, although it was solid Maserati—the first, in fact. In 1923 they went to auto maker Diatto, stayed until 1925, and a year later built the first car to bear their name and their trademark, the trident Maseratis still carry (they took it from the statue of Neptune in Bologna's city square). They called the car the Tipo 26 (for 1926). It was a two-seater race car with a 125-horsepower 1491-cc engine. They ran it for the first time on April 25, 1926, in the Targa Florio, the classic Sicilian roadrace. It won its class, Alfieri driving and Guerrino Bertocchi in the second seat. Bertocchi was Maserati's first employee and is still with the firm—as chief mechanic and test driver.

By 1928 the name Maserati rang loudly enough in European racing to bring in drivers who were coming to the top of the first rank: Luigi Fagioli, the first of a long line that would include Achille Varzi, Tazio Nuvolari, Wilbur Shaw, René Dreyfus, Alberto Ascari, Juan Manuel Fangio, Jean Behra, Stirling Moss, Masten Gregory, and Dan Gurney. The firm by then had a staff of about thirty mechanics and was off and running. Maserati turned out a 4-liter supercharged V16 race car in 1929 and took the world ten-kilometer record during a race, without really trying. Later they laid two V16 engines together to make a 32-cylinder monster, which proved something of a Pyrrhic victory: it had too much twist (700 horsepower) for any chassis the state of the art could then produce. It went into a record-breaking unlimited-class boat. Nuvolari won the Grands Prix of Belgium and Nice for Maserati in 1933, but by the next year, the Germans were in charge, with the almost unbeatable government-backed Auto Unions and Mercedes single-seaters, and three years later, the Maserati brothers, Ernesto, Bindo, and Ettore—Alfieri had died in 1932—sold out to the Modena industrialists Orsi. The contract was to run for ten years and the three Maseratis went with it. The first Orsi-Maserati was the great Tipo 8CTF with which Wilbur Shaw took it all at Indianapolis in 1939 and 1940. (Under the hallowed Indy custom, the car ran under its sponsor's name as the Boyle Special.) The 8CTF was a supercharged straight-8, 3-liter that could pump out 350 horsepower at 6000 rpm. As late as 1947, it was still competitive: Louis Unser won the Pikes Peak hill climb with an 8CTF that year.

When the Orsi-Maserati contract ran out in 1947, the brothers packed up, went back to Bologna, and founded Osca. Under the terms of the deal, they had to leave their name behind in Modena. Orsi pressed on with other engineers—Massimino, Colombo, Bellentani. Ascari won the 1948 Grand Prix of San Remo for Maserati, Fangio repeated the next year and took the Albi G.P. as well, but Alfa-Romeo and Ferrari, trying harder and running newer designs, got away with most of the money. Things began to look up in 1952, when Omer Orsi took personal charge of the Maserati operation, which had become something of an orphan in the Orsi complex. A new model—the A6GCM—won the G.P. of Italy in 1953, Fangio won the Argentine and Belgian G.P.s in 1954, Moss the Italian again in 1956. The following year, Fangio led three other Masers across the finish line in the Argentine G.P., a 4.5 sports model won the Sebring 12-hour Race and the firm announced that it was retiring from competition as a house, although it would continue to back private entrants. And Maser engines powered the British Cooper Grand Prix machines that foreshadowed, in 1959, the rear-engine revolution of the sixties.

The Maserati brothers were race-car builders all the way; unlike some of their contemporaries—Alfa-Romeo and Bugatti, for example—they had no interest in the more profitable passenger-car field. Production sports-model Maseratis didn't appear until 1948, the first one a 1.5-liter 6-cylinder of modest output: 65 horsepower. It came up to 2 liters the next year, still nothing extraordinary. But the direction had been marked, and in 1953 Pinin Farina built three *grans turismos* for Scuderia Centro Sud. Another, the two-seater A6G 2000, came in 1954, bodied by Frua, Zagato and Allemano. Maserati sports cars won the 1000-kilometer races at Buenos Aires and the Nürburgring in 1956. The chassisless "birdcage" Maserati appeared in 1960, a tangle of small-diameter tubing so complex it seemed a marvel that an engine could be fitted into it, and won the Nürburgring twice—Gurney/Moss in 1960, Casner/Gregory in 1961. The birdcage was effectively the end of the line in Maserati competition cars. The firm moved on to *gran turismo,* 140-plus over-the-road machines, and they are its main concern today: the Quattroporte of 1963, a stunning departure from ordinary *g.t.* practice—a 150-mph four-door sedan, the Mistral and the Sebring, the Mexico, the Ghibli, the Indy. Maserati, Ferrari, and Lamborghini of Italy and Aston Martin of England are the four paramount names in the *gran turismo* world. These are superlatively constructed road cars, deluxe to the level of air conditioning, electric windows, power steering, and so on, and capable of an easy, unstressed 150–175 mph with acceleration—on the order of 0–100 mph in twelve seconds—to match. They're not cheap: the Maserati Ghibli is ticketed at $21,000–$22,000 in the United States.

Choice of a Maserati engine for the SM was a matter of economic as well as engineering logic: Maserati has been controlled by Citroën since 1968—as Citroën has been part of the Michelin tire complex since 1934.

The Maserati brothers' beginnings in mechanics tended toward the empirical and mechanical, but André Citroën was a scholarly sort of youth, a brilliant graduate, in 1900, of the famed Ecole Polytechnique in Paris. Ten years later, he was in charge of production for Mors, where he boosted the output ten times, from 120 cars a year to 1200. His career really began in Poland, on a vacation trip, when he acquired from a member of his mother's family—or, according to another story, from a country blacksmith—the idea of silent-running helical gears. He set up a small factory of a dozen people to make these gears, licensed the rights to Skoda of Czechoslovakia, and began to make serious money.

World War I stopped him; he was a lieutenant in the reserve artillery. At the front, he found the duty frustrating—and perilous: the German guns were outshooting the French five to one. French artillerists had been, since Napoleon, among the best in the world, but in 1914, although they had excellent guns, they were short of shells. The standards of the French armaments industry suggested that 5000 rounds was a good day's work. Citroën thought 50,000 might be more reasonable and told the brass he could make that many. Oddly enough, instead of busting him to private for his temerity, the war ministry gave him a chance—and sent word to the banks ahead of him. He built a factory in six weeks and within a year was producing shells at a 55,000 daily rate. Before the war was over, Citroën was suzerain of the French war industry, his reputation that of an innovator who got things done.

By war's end, he had a paid-for factory, lots of machinery, and thousands of trained workers. He would make something else. He thought about it. Stoves? Boats? Farm equipment? He couldn't see much future in such mundane stuff. But the automobile—that was a device of the future, he decided, a growth industry if ever there was one. Citroën was no Bugatti, no Maserati, no lover of the motorcar for its own sake. He was an industrialist, a rational man, at least in business. He knew about mass production and he knew that the Americans knew more about it. So he took a trip to the United States and studied with the master, Henry Ford. Indeed, Citroën took back to Paris a framed photograph of Ford and it stood on his desk as long as he sat behind it. Before Citroën, European design practice tended to be one-man. He changed all that. His cars were designed by specialists responsible only for components, with final decisions at the top, as in the American system.

So it came to pass that in May 1919, Europe's first mass-produced automobile came off the line, the simple, sturdy, 18-horsepower. Type A open touring car. It was cheap and solid and welcome. By 1924 the factory was cranking out 300 cars a day, to the astonishment of veteran industrialists who had assured Citroën that even if he *could* build 100 *voitures* a day, he couldn't hope to unload them on a skeptical populace. In 1922 he had modified the design a bit, put a full sedan body on it, and practically cornered the French taxicab market.

A Citroën classic, the C3 Trèfle (Cloverleaf)—a three-passenger touring car, two seats in front, a narrow slot between them to allow access to the third, sited dead in the middle of the rounded-off stern—was a smash in 1923. The Cloverleaf had a marked elfin appeal—it still does—and Citroën flogged off 20,000 of them a year until 1926.

André Citroën was a notable innovator and one of the first tycoons really to understand publicity. In his time, the phonograph was as much a fixture in every bourgeois home as the dining-room table, yet no one before him had thought of distributing records on which living voices told of the wonders of the product. The Eiffel Tower had been standing in Paris since 1889, but it was Citroën who bought the advertising rights to the structure, all 984 feet, and screwed 250,000 bulbs into it to spell out his name, in letters ten feet high, the whole array so visible so many miles away that aviators homed in on it, Lindbergh among them (it wasn't until he saw the tower that Lindy really knew he had made it). Skywriting was another of Citroën's notions and, in those airplane-mad days, a very good one. It foundered, however, on the flinty face of French bureaucracy, which was willing enough to let Citroën put his name across the sky in letters a mile high— providing he paid for the air he used, per cubic meter. It happened after his death, but Citroën would have appreciated the mad stunt of the restaurateur François Lecot, who lived halfway between Paris and Monte Carlo. Every day, for 365 consecutive days, Lecot drove his Citroën to Paris, then to Monaco, then home, a neat total of 400,000 kilometers, say 248,000 miles, a record no one has since broken.

A Franco-Russian half-track system called Kégresse had come to Citroën's attention. He acquired the rights and built half-track Citroën trucks for Georges-Marie Haardt and Louis Audouin-Dubreuil, who were planning the first trans-Sahara crossing by automobile. The expedition ran from December 1922 to March 1923, was a tremendous *succès d'estime*. Between 1923 and 1934, three more Citroën-Kégresse expeditions were made, across Africa, across Asia, and into the arctic. They brought to Citroën both publicity that drove his competitors to despair and recognition as a benefactor to science and technology of the first order.

Really rolling now, Citroën pulled off, in 1934, the coup that was to assure his place among the immortals of automobilism: the Traction Avant Citroën, the front-wheel-drive car. Front-wheel drive was no new thing. Indeed, the first vehicle to move under its own power, Cugnot's steam carriage of 1769, ran on front-wheel power; the American Christie and the Frenchman Grégoire had made demonstrable use of it, too. But in Citroën's first front-wheel-drive automobile, the drive system was only part of an overall design so farseeing and so well integrated that it stayed in production without basic change for twenty-three years, a record that ranks it with the Model T Ford, and the Silver Ghost Rolls-Royce—properly so, for the Series 11 Citroën was years ahead of its time: the body and chassis were unitized, the suspension was torsion bar, the steering rack-and-pinion, the 4-cylinder engine running overhead valves. The vehicle was so low it needed no running-boards and the pedals were suspended, a system thought sophisticated twenty years later. The Traction Avant's road holding, springing out of a low center of gravity, torsion bars and front-wheel drive, was, for 1934, extraordinary, even revelatory, and early professional testers made no attempt to bury their enthusiasms. Fifteen years later, it was still thought exemplary.

The Traction Avant was Citroën's greatest triumph—and his downfall. Development and tooling costs had run into millions of francs and the company was deep into the banks. There must have been days when Citroën thought bitterly of the piles of 1000-franc plaques he had thrown across the tables of Deauville. He was desperately ill, too, with cancer of the stomach. For a time, tossing money from one account to another like a virtuoso juggler, he managed to survive, but the wolves were on the watch and the secret didn't keep. A major supplier panicked and called a demand note. That tore it. The money wasn't in the box. For Citroën, the alternatives were to sell out or to go bankrupt. Michelin took 57 percent of the stock. The following year, in July of 1935, Citroën died, but the thrust he had put into his enterprise followed on like a jet stream. The original 4-cylinder Traction Avant, the 11, was increased in power from the original 45 horsepower to 59 and a 6-cylinder version, the 15, ran to 76 horsepower. In the last of the 15s, Series H, the rear was sprung by a hydropneumatic system presaging the notably far-out suspension of today's SM. Innovation pressed on innovation. In 1937, the Citroën works had on the road a vehicle—it was a little much to call it an automobile, although technically it certainly was —called the 2CV, for *cheval-vapeur,* or steam horse, the French horsepower unit. The 2CV was basic transport of an ilk the world hadn't seen since the Model T Ford: a cheap, indestructible, go-anywhere device. It didn't appear in quantity until 1948, when it was in such frantic demand that for a long time, a good used *deux chevaux* brought as much on the market as the list price of a new one, and sometimes more. The 2CV ranks in a dead heat with the Chrysler Airflow and the "tank" Bugatti race car as the ugliest motor vehicle ever built, but its virtues soared far above mere esthetic values. The 2-cylinder air-cooled engine churned out just enough power to produce 50 mph downhill and 40 on the level, but it was well made of premium-grade materials. The ride was surprisingly comfortable, almost indifferent to road surface; the seats were quickly removable and the cloth roof rolled back, accommodating the 2CV to almost any odd-shaped load—a farmer could stuff a half-grown calf into it, for example. The *deux chevaux* was primitive but well thought out. If a half-ton of something in back pointed the headlights to the sky, a wheel under the dash would crank them down—useful in fog, too. The windshield wipers were economically driven off the speedometer, so that they went fastest at high speeds, but if the rate was too slow for traffic, a hand crank could be cut in. Eventually, there was a two-engine, four-wheel-drive 2CV, the Sahara, highly regarded by desert travelers.

As big a noise as the original Traction Avant had made came out of the 1955 Paris salon. The Citroën company, always a bear for preannouncement security of new models, had an obvious sensation—obvious because, by nightfall on opening day, there were 12,000 orders for it on the books. This was the DS 19, a superlatively refined treatment of the 1934 groundbreaker. Power came out of a 73-horsepower version of the 1934 4-cylinder engine, but everything else was startlingly new: the stretched, shark-nose shape, much glassed, the sensuously comfortable and roomy interior, the first disk brakes on a production touring car and a multipurpose hydraulic system that provided suspension, shock absorption, level ride, jacking, power steering, power brakes, and actuation of clutch and transmission. Early onlookers of a technical turn of mind were doubters. They thought it most unlikely that nitrogen gas and hydraulic fluid, in such a welter of reservoirs, lines, and valves, could successfully be combined into the kind of genie Citroën was claiming. They were wrong. The system is into its sixteenth year now and even under the heavy demands of Paris taxi service, it has soldiered on. And as for comfort and roadability, a second generation of test drivers had to go to the thesaurus for new superlatives. One respected technician claimed that at 50 miles an hour, he couldn't detect a foot-wide, six-inch-deep pothole. A cheaper version of the DS 19, the ID, came along a year later; it had a simpler interior and manual controls. The DS 19 got an all-new engine—with a displacement of 2.2 liters—in 1966, when the model designation went to DS 21.

The Light 11 and the DS 19 were father and mother of the Citroën SM, the engine aside, that being a direct descendant of the 1929 V16 Maserati. It's a mark of the white-water rush of technology that the V16, thundering and shaking, would push a race car 150-odd mph and the 1971 V6, a bit over twelve inches long and 300 pounds in weight, will move a full four-seater coupe at 140 in near silence. The SM's fishlike slipperiness offers part of the answer. The Citroën body designers lay down their base lines on air-tunnel data, not on their concept of projected public taste. (The car is eight inches wider in front than in the rear.) The driver commands this power from a seat adjustable seven ways, single-spoke oval wheel in hand, through a five-speed gearbox on which fourth *and* fifth are overdrive. The French like to call a fast car a *bolide,* a thunderbolt, but the SM is more than that, really a sports/limousine, a very fast, elegant motor carriage.

—1971

The
Jaguar
Story

Four in the afternoon, a cold day, a soft rain falling
out of clouds almost low enough to touch the spires
of the church: the cathedral in Coventry, England. It
had been burned and blown into rubble on the night
of November 14, 1940, by 500 *Luftwaffe* bombers in
the longest raid England took during the war. Work
to rebuild began the next day, the architect Sir Basil
Spence planning the new cathedral on the site of the
old, forming some of the standing ruins into it; the
cornerstone was laid by the queen sixteen years and
a bit later. It's a starkly, strangely beautiful building
in stone-and-concrete verticals, angular bronze, incredible spreads of stained glass (one window eighty
feet high, fifty wide), carvings and sculptures (Jacob
Epstein's last religious work), and the biggest tapestry
ever woven.

That cold rainy day I was there, the hush of the
place was oddly broken by an organ tuner striking
again and again a booming chord in E-flat and shouting across the nave to his apprentice; outside, the
traffic's remote rumble. Coventry is in the Midlands,
and in the Midlands they make machines. That was
why the Germans went there in 1940, and that's why

people have gone there since: to bring dollars, kroner, francs, lire in exchange for machines and, if they think of it, to look at the cathedral as they go away. But they go for machines. Automobiles, many of them, and best known among these, the Jaguar.

It's close to fifty years now since the Jaguar's beginning—as a motorcycle sidecar built at the rate of one a week by a William Walmsley, who put the thing together, and his sister, who upholstered it. Walmsley's sidecar was a good one, octagonal in form, polished aluminum over ash, and it attracted a partner, William Lyons. They incorporated as Swallow Sidecar, projected the prodigious output of ten units a week, and hit the banks for £1000. They prospered, and when they abandoned the sidecar business, they had pushed production to 500 a week.

In the middle twenties, to reduce the thing to absurd simplicity, there were two kinds of automobiles: custom-built luxury cars, dazzling in the elegant variety of their bodywork, and the rest. The rest were off-the-peg sedans and touring cars, for the most part—utilitarian, good value for money, some of them, and ugly as sin. Obviously, there was a nascent market among upward-strivers who couldn't afford a Rolls-Royce, nor the two front wheels and the radiator off one, if it came to that, but who deplored the small status conferred by ownership of an Austin Seven. To buy cheap chassis and build attractive bodies on them was a notion that had occurred to others besides Walmsley and Lyons, but not many were to do it as well as they did. They built on the Austin, Fiat, Standard, and Swift chassis, and flourished. When the Depression of 1931 hit, they picked up a new segment of trade: people who had to come down an economic notch or two but hated to be obvious about it.

The bodies were attractive—they ran to split windshields, external sun visors, wire wheels, and good options in two-tone paint jobs—but the running gear under them was never up to the performance the coachwork seemed to promise. Lyons made a deal with the Standard Motor Company for its 16-horsepower Ensign model, which ran a 2-liter engine of adequate if not stunning performance. Standard agreed to modify the 16 by adding three inches to the wheelbase and stuffing in a higher axle ratio for more top speed—and, of course, less acceleration. The frame was underslung and the engine was set back seven inches. The first body Lyons erected on this chassis was a tight-fitting four-passenger two-door hardtop coupe, blind rear quarters carrying fake landau irons. The hood was tremendously long and this alone, according to the fashion dictates of the time, spelled potency. In fact, the car was deplorably slow getting under way and would do just 70 miles an hour flat-out in fourth gear. But that didn't matter. It looked great and the price was almost incredible: £310, then worth $1400. This was the SS-1, the sensation of the 1931 London auto show and sire of the *Wunderwagens* that were to follow it—the XK-120, the C-type, the D-type, the XK-E, the XJ-6, and the new 12-cylinder just now on the world market.

The SS-1 and SS-11 passenger cars were backed up by sports models—SS-90, SS-100—because Lyons, whose grasp of the fundamentals has never been less than brilliant, knew that competition effort was vital to sales, particularly in Europe and particularly then. A good SS-100 would do 100 mph and the model had notable successes in rallies, hill climbs, and sports-car races. An SS-100 won the International Alpine Trial of 1936 (and again in 1948) and the 1937 Royal Automobile Club Rally. The car would not only run, it had visual appeal to burn—a happy amalgam of the design points that were the desiderata of the day: big flat-lens headlights, flaring fenders, louvers all over the hood, curved dashboard carrying saucer-sized main instruments, a saddle gas tank hung astern. Only a few SS-100s were made and the survivors are classics.

In the middle thirties, Lyons decided (Walmsley had retired) that the cars needed something more than SS for identification. (Incidentally, no one now remembers what SS stood for: Swallow Sidecar or Standard Swallow or Swallow Special.) Animal and bird names were in vogue at the time, and he chose Jaguar for that reason and because it had been the name of a good aircraft engine. The cars were SS Jaguars from then until after the war, when Nazi Germany had given the initials *(Schutzstaffel)* an unhappy connotation. The car has been Jaguar since. To give the first SS Jaguar the performance its appearance called for, Lyons had asked the designer Harry Weslake to modify Standard's side-valve engine into an overhead-camshaft unit and had brought in W. M. Heynes to oversee engineering, the beginning of an enduring association with the company for both men. Heynes was a vice-chairman when he retired, full of honors, in 1969. Like the SS-1 that had gone before it, the new SS Jaguar sedan looked more expensive than it was: a poll of dealers at its introduction showed an average price guess of £632, but the sticker was only £385 ($1885). The model was another smash success (it was called the poor man's Bentley, sometimes admiringly, sometimes not), and when everything stopped in September 1939, the firm was turning out 250 cars a week.

When war work was over (repairing bombers, building the fuselage for the Meteor, Britain's first jet, making army sidecars, 10,000 trailers, and so on), Lyons got back into automobile production quicker than most, being under way in July 1945. The factory had been bombed, of course, but not wiped out. First cars off the line were prewar models and it was 1948 before a new one came along: the Mark V, sedan or convertible, 2.5- or 3.5-liter engine. It was the first Jaguar to have independent front suspension and hydraulic brakes; it was the first Jaguar most Americans saw, and they liked it. It was no ball of fire in performance and it had irritating detail flaws (for one, a heater that couldn't cope with a brisk autumn day in Connecticut, never mind a Minnesota winter). Still, the imported-car mystique was new and wonderful then and, like all the Jaguars that had gone before it and most of those that were to follow, it lifted the psyche, roused the spirits, and made Buick owners feel somehow slobby. But the Mark V was really an interim device. Long-laid plans were about to spring into reality.

The XK-120 Jaguar was first seen in the London auto show of 1948. Competing makers looked and knew despair. They wished they had left their things on the transporters. In John Blunsden's history of Jaguar: "Overnight it rendered obsolete all previous conceptions of what constituted a mass-produced sports car . . . by combining refinement and comfort with outstanding good looks and a brilliant performance, all at the staggeringly low price of £998 [$4000] . . . it couldn't fail to become one of the great sports-car successes of all time."

A new car, a really new car, is a rare thing. Sheet metal curved up instead of down or in instead of out has masked many an old bucket, and new technical features are usually only so-called: the historians will tell you, and prove it, that the Himmelstadt had a three-way bronze-bushed gitzel valve in 1908. The XK-120 was a new machine not just in single variants on ancient themes but in total being: it was a high-performance automobile, good-looking, and comfortable, purchasable for less than half the $10,000 that equivalent performance alone was supposed to cost. And it was remarkable, in a way, that it had surfaced in England, home of generations of drivers who were prepared to pay for speed and handling in agonies of cart springing, wind in the face, wet feet, and mind-splitting unreliabilities —and swear, even as they bled, that they loved it all and would be content with nothing else. The British ultraenthusiast turned a stone face to everything that made motoring easier and thus more accessible to the masses, from synchromesh gears and the centrifugal spark advance to the abominable automatic transmission. The XK-120, if it didn't go all the way in the other direction, at least pointed out the path.

On the other hand, perhaps what William Lyons had done wasn't all that new. Certainly he was following the precept of the original earthshakers, Ford and Austin: make it cheap and sell it by the boatload. Jaguar has never exported less than 50 percent of its output, in some years has run as high as 80 percent, and does business in 100-odd countries. Lyons's worst enemies would not deny that the figures reflect his determination to avoid the parochial like typhoid, to build for world taste. Not all U.K. manufacturers have shared his insight.

Heart of the marvel that was the XK-120 was the 6-cylinder, 3.4-liter double-overhead-camshaft engine, rated at 160 horsepower. Susceptible to apparently endless modification and improvement, it was to prove out as one of the longest lived of automobile power plants. Its longevity was the root secret of the Jaguar price policy: the initial tooling costs on the XK engine were paid for so long ago that only the accountants remember, and they're not sure. The engine had been in work since just after the war, the creature of Heynes and Walter Hassan, long a legendary figure in high-speed design. First double-overhead-camshaft hemihead engine to be made on a production-line basis, it showed more horsepower per liter than any other such, and its estimated top speed in the two-seater chassis—120 mph —was conservative: Run through a flying mile in Belgium, it did 132.6.

Competition drivers couldn't wait to lay hands on XK-120s. In August 1949, Leslie Johnson's roadster won the Silverstone production-car race; in 1950, Ian Appleyard won the Alpine Rally, Peter Walker took the Shelsley Walsh hill climb, Stirling Moss won the Tourist Trophy, and Phil Hill won at Pebble Beach, the first big U.S. victory for the XK.

These were private-owner efforts. The factory's own program, headed by the legendary F. R. W. "Lofty" England, was pointed to the Le Mans 24-Hour Race. Le Mans, though it was a French race, was important to British car lovers; it was famed in song and story as the site of the glorious Bentley triumphs in the '20s and '30s: they won it five times. It was plain that stock XK-120s would be overmatched at Le Mans in 1951 against the quick Ferraris and the big Chrysler-engined Cunninghams. A *pro forma* two-seater body was put on a light tubular chassis, the engine an XK-120 boosted to 210 horsepower. This was the C-type Jaguar. Three were entered. An identical oil-pipe failure put two out, but the third, Peter White-head and Peter Walker up, won at a new record rate, 93.49 mph for the day and night of running. The C-type won again in 1953, first and second place; the leading car was first ever to average over 100 mph at Le Mans. Ferrari won in 1954 by two and a half minutes over a new competition Jaguar, the D-type. The XK engine was now putting out 250 horsepower and the D-type, which won at Le Mans the next year, had 285. Privately entered D-types won in 1956 and 1957 to give the Jaguar an equal standing with the Bentley as a five-time Le Mans victor. The big year was 1957: first, second, third, fourth, and sixth, a wipe-out.

The all-conquering D-type was a stark sports-race car, thoroughly unsuitable for everyday use; but so many people wanted one that the factory put into work a roadable version, the body equipped with reasonable amenities and the bumpers, lights, and so on that would see it through licensing inspection. Even with the engine tamed by 35 horsepower in the interest of tractability, the XK-SS would reach 100 mph in fourteen seconds and touch 144 at the top end. It was an export-only item and sixteen had been built, twelve for the U.S. market, when a fire destroyed nearly one-third of the Jaguar factory. Disastrous block-square fires were an old story to people who had lived through the blitz; they began to rebuild as soon as the rubble cooled. The factory was back to normal in six weeks, but the XK-SS was a permanent casualty.

In 1956, the year William Lyons was deservedly knighted, Jaguar abandoned racing. The bill had been around $3 million and worth it. The publicity return had been prodigious; it had sold not only thousands of XK-120s, 140s, and 150s but thousands of sedans, too. The Mark VII of 1950 had been called as much a breakthrough as the XK-120: a big sedan, sized for the U.S. market, the XK-120 engine giving it a true 100 mph and roadability to cope with it. It was a luxurious car, loaded with the leather and the genuine tree-wood without which no quality British car has a chance, even today, on the home market. It could be used as a limousine, but still it turned out to be a useful rally car, winning the brutal Monte Carlo in 1956, and it could be raced. Stirling Moss ran one in a production-car race at Silverstone the year after it came out, and while a contemporary photograph shows it heeled hard over, indeed, in a corner, precariously hanging in there, still it did win.

Not the best loved of all Jaguars, the Mark VII plagued many owners with small annoyances: electrical problems, persistent starting difficulties, and other such nuisances. In the late forties and early fifties, British car makers heavily dominated the U.S. market; but the Volkswagen blitz, emphasizing rigidly schooled mechanics and warehouses full of parts, changed all that, and some cars that had sold well—the Austin A40 comes to mind —practically disappeared. Jaguar had an advantage in its first U.S. dealer, M. E. Hoffman, who is a supersalesman in the classic mode. (A customer said, "If you told Hoffman New York was going to be atom-bombed in five minutes, he'd say, 'It's not important. I'm going to show you the greatest automobile in the world. You will see. Come.' ") He moved a lot of Jaguars.

The Jaguar sedans went through various permutations up to the Mark X, with 2.4-, 3.4-, 3.8- and 4.2-liter engines. In 1968, a redesigned sedan, the XJ6, was announced—prematurely, as it turned out. Production difficulties, obvious bad planning, and wildcat strikes so delayed the car that it is only now coming into the showrooms in reasonable quantities. For a long time, it commanded a black-market price as high as £1000 ($2400) over list. One enterprising character was discovered to have got his name on the top of the waiting list in sixteen dealerships. I drove one around England for a week in May 1968. I admit, more or less cheerfully, that I loathed every Mark VII I ever sat in; but the XJ-6 is something else again, quiet, fast (120 mph), and sure-footed on the road to a degree still uncommon in comparable American cars. It has a heater that heats and an automatic transmission that does automate, if without the turbinelike, notchless smoothness that is taken for granted in the best Detroiters. (The heater and the automatic transmission, for reasons that baffle me, at least, seem to have been the two things European makers have found hardest to master.) The XJ-6 spreads out a splendid impression of luxury, not more nor less than, say, a Cadillac, but of a different sort. It's classic luxury, a virtuoso treatment of the solid-leather, polished-walnut, big-round-instrument theme. You can't get an XJ-6 upholstered in a sculptured fabric shot through with silver threads, and perhaps that's just as well; it would probably make the car look, as the British say, tarted up.

The XJ-6, stickered at $7000-plus, runs, in the export version, the same 4.2-liter engine that gave the famous E-type its blistering performance. Slinky, slippery-looking as a shark, the "Lyons line" all over it, the E-type two-seater was Jaguar's 1961 gift offering (at around $5600) to its devoted clientele. Few better-looking cars were ever built. The E-type was, one might say, irritatingly faithful to what was now becoming the tradition: it looked great, went like the hammers of hell—100 mph in twenty-two seconds, with lots left—and it handled impeccably, stopped imperatively on eleven-inch disk brakes in front and ten-inch in the rear.

But the ghost of the long-suffering British enthusiast still rode beside the driver: no synchromesh on first gear, windows-up ventilation? forget it, outside door handles sized for ten-year-olds fingered small for their age, heavy clutch, convertible tops that leaked, dimmer switch on the dashboard, an interior that might have been designed by the mechanics who made it. But, going, it was some sensational $6500 worth (after all, you could challenge $18,000 Ferrari things; you might not win, but you wouldn't look like a clown); and until so many were sent to this country (95 percent of production in some years) that an E-Jag became almost an ordinary possession, it was a big draw at curbside.

For years the elves of Coventry hinted that the wizard Heynes had on his drawing board a new engine to replace the ancient device that had pushed the XK-120 to glory. The old one had been bored, fiddled, and breathed upon to churn out 125 more horsepower than it was born with, but there had to be an end to it somewhere. Heynes told me three years ago, under binding oath, that there was, indeed, such an engine and that it was a V12. There is a certain amount of magic in that number (obviously, since most models of the Ferrari have been V12s). The V16 Cadillac and Marmon engines of forty years ago were delightfully smooth. A V12 engine, for reasons mechanical and unenchanting, is inherently in balance. It can idle quietly, accelerate briskly, run at top speed without unseemly hubbub. A V12, 314-horsepower engine is in the car that will replace the E-type as the E-type replaced the XKs. This engine produces the sensation, and the forward motion to go with it, of an E-type engine set up for racing, and with about as much tumult as a Waring blender. It will jump 0–60 in 6.8 seconds and it will run 140 mph (the theoretical top is nearly 150) with dignity. That last is important. There isn't much point in going fast if it's all an adventure. That's for stock-car racedrivers, who know what Parnelli Jones meant when he said, "If the thing's in control, you're not going fast enough."

A plan, later aborted, to go to Le Mans again in the sixties was the root of the V12. It was a team project: Heynes, chief engineer C. W. L. Bailey, Walter Hassan, and chief designer Harry Mundy. The race engine was rated at over 500 horsepower so it's obvious that the production V12, like the old XK-120, will accept any amount of future modification. Incidentally, the 4.2 Series 2 E-type engine continues in production, although the car itself does not, and it can be had as an option in the Series 3.

There are lots of important little things in the V12 Jag, like fully transistorized ignition (no points to get out of whack). Detail improvements in the new model take pages to list. In front, it has a wider front track than the old E-type, antidive suspension, ventilated disks. It runs on six-inch rims, Dunlop radial tires on the pressed-steel wheels. Wire spokes can be had.

So, Sir William has done it again. A car that doesn't look like anyone else's, things on it that can be called new! new! new! and released with perfect timing—when the market for the old one had been worked out. He's won the half-price war again, hands down: for the price of a car of comparable usable performance and status rating, you can have two V12 Jags (they go for about $7300 each) and maybe a dune buggy and a good bike thrown in. For consistency's sake, there are a few grubby things: occasional body noise, road rumble, easy bottoming at the rear. The heating system is a lot better, but the switches are still Mickey Mouse and obscure, you still go to the dashboard to dim the lights and you still jam your fingers in the outside door handles. On the first cars to come into this country, at least, the original right-drive layout was obvious in such things as switch placement. The selector lever for the Borg-Warner automatic (better than before, but it still chirps and tells you everything it's doing) has the detents on the left side of the slot, where a driver sitting on the right, as in England, will naturally push the lever to the left and engage the notches. But since there are no detents on the other side of the slot, it's dead easy for a left-side driver to stuff the stick from second straight into reverse, an event that, at 60 mph, would produce calamity, if not something serious. But the underbonnet view would move a heart of stone, and the engine response, the sheer spinning surge of it, is marvelously exciting, and terror-free, too, because for all its capability, the thing is as sturdy as a set of bar bells.

Each V12 Jaguar is eight weeks in the making. I don't know if that's a tribute to old-world craftsmanship (I devoutly doubt it) or the brutal intransigence of British union leaders or other, weightier factors beyond my ken. Still, the last of eight coats of paint is not laid on until the car has been road tested. That, no argument, suggests a strictly first-cabin attitude going in. Or, rather, coming out.

—1971

The
Porsche

The Le Mans 24-Hour Race in France is a brutal
competition. It begins at four o'clock on Saturday
afternoon, ends at four o'clock Sunday afternoon, and
in those twenty-four hours the winning car may cover
more than 3,000 miles. The Le Mans course is not a
round-and-round track like Indianapolis: it's 8.3
miles of ordinary two-lane highway except for a short
stretch running past the grandstands, and on this
highway drivers often reach speeds of 230 miles an
hour—even at night, in fog and pouring rain, because
the Le Mans race is never stopped, no matter what the
weather.

One of the most exciting sights in racing can be seen
at dusk at Le Mans, when the cars begin to scream
down the road with four big quartz-iodine head lamps
throwing long shafts of blue-white light ahead of
them. Last year when nightfall came, it was raining,
the road glistened jet-black, and the cars traveled in
clouds of spray, throwing big rooster-tails behind
them, so that close-following competitors were running in a steady waterfall. All at 200 miles an hour!

A ride around Le Mans at racing speed is a truly
unforgettable event. The start is stationary, not roll-

ing. The cars, as many as fifty-five of them, are lined up in front of the grandstands at an angle of about forty-five degrees to the road, the fastest ones at the head of the line. On the precise second of four o'clock, the starter's big French flag falls, and people standing close clap hands over their ears and watch fifty-five automobiles disappear in a cloud of blue exhaust- and rubber-smoke.

Less than four minutes later (the lap record is three minutes twenty-one seconds), the leading car appears at the head of the grandstand straight and howls past into the bend at the end of it, going about 160 miles an hour. There's a famous bridge over this bend, called Dunlop Bridge, built in the shape of a tire. This is followed by a short straightaway, then a double left-right bend called The Esses, another short straight—and the cars, doing about ninety now, come out onto the public road at Tertre Rouge.

This is the beginning of the longest straightaway in the world, the Mulsanne Straight, nearly four miles long with only two very slight bends in it. The fastest cars are doing 230 when they start braking for Mulsanne Corner, a more-than-right-angle corner that cannot possibly be taken faster than 35 miles an hour. About 400 yards away from it, in fourth gear, the driver puts on the brake with his toe, and uses his heel to blip the accelerator as he shifts to third, then to second, then to first, the brake hard on all the time. If he comes into the corner too fast, he will slide into a big pile of sand on the outside of it, and there he'll stay until he can dig himself out. (Help from anyone is forbidden by the rules.) If he comes into the corner too slowly, someone who has done it just right will pass him going out. He then accelerates violently, up to perhaps 170, until he comes to hard-left and hard-right corners—Indianapolis and Arnage—along another straight with a pronounced bend (White House Corner) in the middle of it, into a hard left-right at the top of the grandstand straight.

This is an artificial corner called Ford Chicane, designed to slow the cars through the straight, between the crowded pits on one side and the jam-packed grandstands on the other. (In 1955 a Mercedes-Benz went off the road into the crowd, killing the driver and 118 spectators, the worst automobile accident in history.) The Ford Chicane hasn't slowed the cars very much. They can go through it at 50–60 mph and be doing 100 miles an hour more than that a few hundred yards down the straight. After all, some of them weigh less than a Volkswagen, have 600 horsepower, and can reach 100 mph from a standing start in five seconds.

No one could be expected to drive like that, flat-out in traffic—the fastest cars pass the slowest at speed differentials up to 100 mph—for twenty-four hours, so each car has two drivers who relieve each other every three or four hours. And, of course, the cars must come into the pits at frequent intervals for gas, tires (when it begins to rain every car is changed from dry- to wet-weather tires), and sometimes for minor repairs. The pit crews are expert and incredibly quick. They have to be, because a car leading the race by three minutes can lose everything in a four-minute pit stop.

As many as 300,000 people watch the Le Mans race, although few of them see all of it. There's a big midway section behind the stands, with carnival rides, restaurants of all kinds—from hot-dog stands to deluxe establishments—beer halls, sideshows, and exhibits. Anything is available, including church services on Sunday morning. Not everyone watches from the grandstands. There are spectators everywhere along the 8.3 miles of road. Two of the choice viewing points are in a pair of restaurants in a village called Hunadiers, halfway down Mulsanne. They are so close to the road—a few feet—that the windows rattle and the buildings shake when the big cars boom past.

The 1970 Le Mans was completely dominated by the great German sports car, the Porsche, which took first, second, third, and sixth places. Le Mans is one of the nine races counting toward the International Manufacturers' Championship, which is the world championship, and Porsche won seven of them—an accomplishment certifying it as the most competitive sports car in existence. Porsche also won the International Rallye Championship: it dominated all other makes in the all-day/all-night European rallies, some of them run in the dead of winter over ice-covered mountain roads.

As automobile makers go, Porsche is a young firm: Mercedes-Benz began in 1901, Cadillac in 1903, Rolls-Royce in 1904. But in only twenty-one years of competition, Porsche has won more than a thousand major races, and many thousands of lesser events, sometimes more than a thousand in a single year.

Although the Porsche dates only from 1949, its true beginnings run much further back, perhaps fifty years further, when Ferdinand Porsche was twenty-five years old. He was an Austrian, the son of a tinsmith, and very gifted mechanically. Before he was out of his teens, he had designed, built, and installed an electric-light system in his father's house, the first in the little town of Maffersdorf. In 1898, when he was twenty-three, he was working as a designer for one of the earliest auto makers, Jacob Lohner, and in 1900 a car of his design was a sensation at the Paris Auto Show. The Lohner-Porsche was an original: it was an electric car, but instead of one motor it had two, one mounted in each of the front wheel-hubs for better cooling. It would do 23 mph, fast for the time. From then until his death in 1952, Ferdinand Porsche's inventive genius never flagged.

"The range and scope of his capacity were staggering," A British authority wrote. For the Austrian Army Porsche built the first practical "go-anywhere" prime mover, a vehicle that produced electricity with a gasoline

337

engine and fed it to motors in the wheel-hubs of as many as ten trailers. He built the classic Prince Henry touring car for Austro-Daimler. Moving to Germany after World War I, he designed the legendary S, SS, SSK, and SSKL Mercedes sports-touring cars. He built engines for airplanes and dirigibles, and flew the aircraft himself. He made diesel trucks and air-cooled shaft-driven motorcycles.

He worked constantly, slept little, often had to be reminded to eat lunch: an apple and a roll, out of his pocket.

For the German Auto Union company he built a 16-cylinder Grand Prix racing car that remains a bench mark in the history of competition: its engine, the size of a Chevrolet, put out 520 horsepower. The engine was mounted in the rear—in 1931—and the Auto Union would do 113 mph in second gear, 200-plus in fourth. Today all racing cars have rear-mounted engines. He designed the formidable Tiger tank, one of the best armored vehicles of World War II. And he designed the all-conquering Volkswagen, as efficient an automobile as the world has known.

Project No. 356 of Ferdinand Porsche's design company was an outgrowth of the Volkswagen and, like the VW, had an opposed flat 4-cylinder rear-mounted engine. The prototype Porsche was made in 1948, and for a long time the production rate was five cars a month, each body hand-hammered out of the sheet metal by one man! Today the rate is still low, about eighty cars a day, not enough to meet world demand, but as many as Doktor-Ingenieur Porsche, the founder's son, considers can be built properly in the present plant, under the strict standards that have become traditional: new engines flushed with oil at exactly 176° Fahrenheit; doors, trunks, engine lids fitted to exactly one-millimeter clearance; and so on down a long, long list.

There is no such thing, and there never has been such a thing, as a handmade automobile, but the Porsche comes very close to this legendary ideal. (Actually, a handmade car wouldn't be a very good car because modern machining methods are more precise than anything a workman could duplicate without spending half a lifetime at it.) The Porsche is, however, virtually hand-assembled. Each engine is put together by one man, and strict records are kept, so that the factory can, in a few minutes, find the name of the man who assembled Engine Number so-and-so in December of 1965. For a long time each engine was signed: the mechanic who assembled it stamped his initials into it.

Porsche engines still are just as carefully put together as they used to be. One of the first things that strikes one on entering the Porsche factory at Stuttgart is the quiet of the place. Most automobile factories sound like old-time boiler works, the walls vibrating with incessant clangings and bangings. The Porsche shop is quiet because hand files and similar tools just don't make much noise. Parts are carefully fitted together—nothing is forced. Assembled engines are run on dynamometers that measure their horsepower. An engine that fails goes back to be torn down and rebuilt. Finally, the completed automobile is given three separate road tests by three different drivers, the final test being run over parkways, or *autobahnen,* on which there is no speed limit.

The result of all this painstaking care is an automobile that is remarkably long-lived and trouble free. Many Porsche owners say that their engines are just as good after 50,000 miles of hard use as they were brand-new. And nearly all Porsches are driven hard and fast, because they invite it: they handle beautifully, stick to the road as if glued to it, and have tremendous braking power.

From the beginning, Porsche engines have been air-cooled, which frees them from the danger of boiling in summer and freezing in winter, at the slight cost of some additional noise. (The water surrounding a conventionally cooled engine makes a good sound barrier.) Until recently all Porsches had rear-mounted engines, which in part accounted for their superior traction and stability on slippery roads: the weight of the engine is directly on the driving wheels. Currently one model, the 914, following the practice for racing sports cars, has the engine mounted in the middle of the car, directly behind the driver. This position gives excellent all-around balance and, as a bonus, two trunks, one in front, one in back.

Most of the machines we use today are stamped out by the thousand and hardly touched by human hands in the process. The Porsche is an exception, a kind of survivor from the days of custom craftsmanship, slowly and carefully put together by people who would rather do it right than do it fast

—1971

Mr. Royce
and
Mr. Rolls

Has another business firm, a mere corporate entity, ever operated on the lofty level where Rolls-Royce lived for so long? Maybe, but alternatives don't leap to mind. Rolls-Royce was much more than the name of an automobile. It transcended mere commercial eminence, it seemed to be, with the Throne, the Royal Navy, the Bank of England, a pillar of empire. Hadn't Lawrence of Arabia campaigned in Rolls-Royce armored cars, and didn't the RR Merlin engine power the Spitfires and Hurricanes that won the Battle of Britain? Wherever wheels rolled, and some places where they didn't, the words Rolls-Royce were *lingua franca* for ultraquality, mechanical perfection, triumph of hand craftsmanship over the machine age, and the glory of tradition maintained. When, without more than a preliminary rumble, the company went bankrupt a few months ago it was as if the dome of St. Paul's had fallen in, or Prince Charles had renounced his claim to the throne to join a hippy commune: it was not to be believed. And worse: the British government didn't think it worthwhile to save Rolls-Royce. And worse again: the company hadn't been put to the wall by agents of evil or uncontrollable circumstance: its executives stood accused of incompetence, and words like stupidity and mismanagement were heard in the land. The debacle seemed to be complete.

But two facts, one obvious and one obscure, were generally overlooked. Rolls-Royce's aero-engine division had gone down, but the car division was merrily making money, as it usually had; and while news that a factory is in trouble has nearly always meant that its cars become pariahs, word of Rolls-Royce's bankruptcy brought a run on the showrooms. Clearly, people were thinking, "If I don't get one now I never will." The most prestigious motorcar the world has seen was still just that, bankrupt company or not.

Best-informed opinion in London was that the root of the trouble might have been the thing that had made it great: dominance by engineers. The founder of the company once signed a guest book "Henry Royce, Mechanic." That was how he thought of himself, and in his organization men who could shape metal always stood above those who merely made decisions. Sadly, it was the determination of engineers to make the best jet engine in the world that pulled Rolls-Royce down.

The engine was typed the RB-211. It was planned to be lighter than its competitors, have fewer parts, and produce more thrust, and in fact it met these specifications. It was a disaster nevertheless.

The biggest order in sight for the RB-211 was for Lockheed's Tristar, 540 units. Rolls-Royce put on a blitz, the biggest and most costly sales campaign any British firm had ever done. In eighteen months of trying, the company's task force of twenty-odd people racked up 230 transatlantic crossings—cost, $200,000—produced a stack of literature two feet high, and spent, in all, over $1 million. But Rolls-Royce got the order, estimated to be worth $2.4 billion dollars, and David Huddie, the engineer who led the effort, was knighted for it. In the executive offices the picture seemed rosy indeed, but back at the foundry it was rather less so.

Determined to replace Pratt & Whitney as the world's number-one jet-engine producer, Rolls-Royce had taken the Lockheed contract on tough terms. And while the RB-211 engine was, overall, brilliantly conceived, it was rushed. For example, it was designed to use turbine blades of pressed carbon, far cheaper than the usual titanium, but untried in service. Too late, testers found that carbon blades would not stand up to two common flight hazards—a deluge of rain or hail, or a bird sucked into the fans. With the engine already in production, the cost of switching to titanium was fearful. There were other similar gaffes. But the engineers pressed on, knowing that in the end they were certain to come up with a great engine. And Rolls-Royce's cost-accounting methods, admittedly stone-age, lighted the looming disaster only dimly. The company arranged to borrow $100 million from the government, $43 million from private sources; but curious outside accountants came with the deal. Unromantic, indifferent to anything but the numbers, it was they who came up with the definitive bad news: the 540 engines were going to cost, each of them, more than $264,000 over what Lockheed had agreed to pay. The answer was either bankruptcy or massive government financing. The government declined, the roof fell in, a receiver was appointed, and a Tory government, dedicated to damming the socialist tide, found itself nationalizing one of Britain's proudest private enterprises. A separation between the failing aero-engine division and the profitable car division was arranged; a new company, Rolls-Royce Motors, Ltd., took over and automobile production went on, having hardly skipped a beat through the whole upheaval.

I visited the factory at Crewe on the day the new company was announced. No faint sign of crisis marred the accustomed hushed serenity. A limousine waited at the railway station; the reception room still seemed vaguely churchlike, quiet and remote, one of Sir Henry Royce's favorite maxims on the wall: *Quidvis recte factum quamvis humile praeclarum.* ("Whatever is rightly done, however humble, is noble.") Luncheon was in the civilized mode of British business: a preliminary relaxation abetted by an adequate flow of sherry, excellent food, suitable wine, and a minimum of shop-talk by the executives at the round table. The page-one headlines in every significant newspaper in the United Kingdom appeared to have left Managing Director D.A.S. Plastow determinedly unmoved: "The position of the Company is more nearly unique now than it ever was before," he said. "Rolls-Royce once had competitors—Hispano-Suiza, Lanchester, Bugatti —but we are now the only manufacturer in the world concentrating on large high-quality saloon cars . . . we intend to improve them, concentrating on refinement, elegance, and longevity, and at the same time to produce, every year, a few more."

It was an attitude Sir Henry Royce would have appreciated. Few men can have been more single-minded than he was, more rigid in refusal to allow nonessentials to divert him from his primary purpose.

For most of his life he was profoundly uninterested in anything but work, food and sleep included, and he was driven always by a furious pursuit of unattainable perfection.

Royce seemed poorly prepared for his role as creator of the best thing of its kind in the world. He had little education, not always enough to eat, and he was working hard selling newspapers, running telegrams, and the like before he was into his teens. He was apprenticed to a railroad locomotive shop when he was fourteen. The apprenticeship cost £20 a year, but he couldn't afford to finish it, and got a job with a tool maker at eleven shillings a week. The work week was fifty-four hours, but he found time to go to school at night. By the time he was twenty-one he was a specialist in electricity and he set up a company to make electric cranes. They were good cranes and the firm made some money, enough to put Royce into the select company of those who could afford a motorcar. His was a 2-cylinder Decauville. It wasn't at all a bad car, but it seemed to Royce that he ought to be able to make a better one. On April 1, 1904, Royce's own motorcar was running.

It is probable that more nonsense has been spoken about the Rolls-Royce than any other car, beginning with the first one. It was not an innovative wonder. Royce never claimed eminence as an inventor. He was a good practical engineer, not more. His great strength lay in a nearly unerring ability to find the best way of doing something, backed by a flinty refusal thereafter to do it in any other way. His first engine was finely finished and balanced, so it was notably quieter than contemporaries. His electrical system, then—and now—the primary cause of the internal-combustion-engine breakdown, was superior; and because he had taught himself a good deal about gas flow, his carburetor was excellent: it was the first one that would allow an engine to pick up instantly and smoothly from idling, and without a lot of fiddling with spark- and air-control levers. The car was heavy for its size, it was an open two-seater, but it had respectable performance nevertheless. Royce made a second and a third. He had no facilities for effectively marketing them, however, and if he had not, reluctantly, met Rolls, he might not have gone on.

Rolls, Charles Stewart, the third son of Lord Llangatock, was rich and an aristocrat. In his time—he was born in 1877—the emerging concept of mechanical travel was as exciting as space exploration is today. Rolls was fascinated by it, and he had the means to indulge his interest. He was one of the first British balloonists and airplane pilots; he was well known as an automobilist while he was still a Cambridge student, when there were more than merely mechanical hazards involved: the law of the land specified a speed not to exceed 4 miles an hour, the vehicle to be preceded by a man on foot carrying a red flag to warn other road users of the imminence of mortal danger. Rolls, sensible of the privileges of birth, consistently drove his Peugeot over the limit, and without a flagman, his purpose not merely to flout an absurd regulation but to create a test case. He never succeeded, the police apparently finding him invisible. The phenomenon persists: when England set up a 70-mph limit a few years ago a friend said to me, "My dear man, this country is run by and for the 5 percent of us who matter, who are, in one way or another, aristocrats. I shall drive as fast as I please, where I please, and when I please, and be damned to their silly speed limit!"

The 4-mph limit was, in 1896, raised to a blistering 12, and in celebration of what was called Emancipation Day the first London-to-Brighton run was organized. Rolls was a prominent entrant. Four years later the Automobile

Club of Great Britain and Ireland ran a 1000-mile trial, and he won it in a Panhard et Levassor. With Claude Johnson, the secretary of the Automobile Club, he set up a London dealership, selling the Panhard and the Belgian-made Minerva, but no British cars. One of Royce's associates, a Henry Edmunds, thought Royce's car could properly fill the gap, and undertook to bring the two men together. It wasn't easy. Royce was shy, taciturn, disliked meeting strangers, and flatly refused to go down to London from Manchester. Rolls was accustomed to have people come to him, but he went to Royce. He knew the car for what it was as soon as he saw it, and so did Claude Johnson. A deal was worked out, money was found, and C.S. Rolls & Company undertook to sell all the cars Royce could make. Logic indicated that on the basis of weight of contribution the name should be Royce-Rolls, but the reality situation was that Rolls's name was well known in the motoring community and Royce's was not. So much for the name. But to call the car a Rolls has always been to utter a vulgarism, although to call it a Royce is acceptable—among factory people and second-generation owners. The famous slogan, still the base of the company's advertising, "The Best Car in the World" was picked up from a journalist later on. The hallmark radiator, essentially unchanged from the beginning, was probably derived from a short-lived automobile called the Norfolk, but Royce improved it, taking advantage of the principle of entasis: the human eye sees a truly flat surface as concave, so to make it *appear* flat, it must be slightly convex. The squared radiator shell demands to be handmade and finished, and this accounts for the price difference between the Rolls-Royce and the otherwise identical Bentley, which carries a die-formed shell.

The first Rolls-Royce, a 4-cylinder, four-passenger open touring car rated at 20 horsepower, was on the floor at the 1905 London motor show. It was priced competitively with cars of similar pretension. Knowing viewers noted the heavy, rigid chassis, the meticulous detail, and, when the car was run, its remarkable sound level. The strength of the chassis was evidence of Royce's characteristically long view. The coachwork of the day, mated with light, flexible chassis, soon developed distortion-made squeaks and rumbles. Chassis rigidity was the answer, that and stringent control over the ways the coachbuilders attached their bodies. (Until 1951 Rolls-Royce built chassis and engines only, all bodies were custom-made.)

The Rolls-Royce troika management, Royce, Rolls, and Johnson, showed a rare conjoining of abilities. Royce created, Rolls drove the cars brilliantly and successfully in competition, Johnson had a most perceptive grasp of publicity and promotion. In 1907 a 6-cylinder model designated by the factory as the 40/50 hp, 6-cylinder came out, a nearly flawless automobile destined to be a legend and an imperishable classic. Johnson took the thirteenth 40/50 produced, had it finished in aluminum and silver-plated hardware, gave it a sterling-silver dashboard plaque naming it "Silver Ghost." With suitable fanfarade he had it run 14,371 miles over ordinary roads under strict Royal Automobile Club observation. Stripped, it showed zero wear in engine bearings, transmission, or cylinder bores, and to bring it back to new cost less than £3 in coin of the realm, an outcome that shook the opposition and impressed motorists who had thought of breakage and warpage and general delapidation as part of the game. Later Johnson caused a slightly more powerfully engined Ghost to be run from London to Edinburgh and return in top gear only, a feat probably beyond the capability of any other automobile then purchasable. In all 7876 Silver Ghosts were made from 1907 to 1926; 1703 of them in the Springfield, Massachusetts, branch factory, a 1919–1926 experiment in tariff reduction which failed because it lessened the car's snob value. The Silver Ghost had the second-longest single-model run the industry has seen, one year more than the Model T Ford, four years less than the Citroën Traction Avant. The original Silver Ghost still exists and, with 500,000-plus miles on its odometer, still runs in the smoothness and near silence it was born to. The 1971 value of mint-condition Ghosts is in the area of $50,000 but they are a market rarity.

About twenty models of Rolls-Royce were built before World War II, including, in 1905–1906, a V8 and a 3-cylinder, but the Ghost, the 6-cylinder Phantom I and Phantom II, and the 12-cylinder Phantom III were the cars on which the RR reputation prospered. New designs showed few startling innovations; change was gradual if inexorable and never for novelty's sake. A 1931 looks remarkably like a 1921 and the resemblance is not due entirely to the radiator shells.

Royce's engineering was not universally applauded by his peers: accusation of overweight, for example, was common. But if weight was partially responsible for the sheer durability of the vehicle, then it had to be accepted. The Silver Ghosts seemed almost indestructible. For World War I armored bodies were put on Ghost chassis, often well-used chassis at that, weighing more than twice what the car was designed to carry. Even in desert warfare chassis did not give way, springs did not break, and engines ran for miles on the boil when bullet-proof radiator slats were closed. Only tires created trouble, T.E. Lawrence reported afterward. (Someone once asked Lawrence what he would like most as a gift. A Rolls-Royce, he said, with tires and petrol to run it forever.)

The cars ran that way because Royce had decreed it. For him, the best was only marginally good enough. His steel was smelted and rolled to his specification, and he kept inspectors in Sheffield to see to it that no one slipped. (Old Rolls-Royces are remarkably rust-free, even those that were sold in the home market and worked for years in one of the dampest climates in the world.) To be doubly sure, a test piece, or "ear," was formed in every part at the factory, broken off, numbered, and sent to the laboratory. An adverse report meant that the part, and perhaps the entire batch, would be discarded. Royce devoutly believed in testing. One device in which he put great store was called the bump machine, a simple enough rig made of big irregularly formed wheels set into a floor. A finished car would be chained down over them, and the power turned on, with an effect far more wracking than 40 mph over the roughest kind of road. Company engineers claimed that the bump machine would break up quite good automobiles in a few minutes; their own cars were expected to take it indefinitely. Assembly methods were meticulous: chassis members, for example, were bolted together, the bolts tapered, set into hand-reamed holes, and tightened by torque-wrench. The locking hub-fasteners were costly and complicated, but no Rolls-Royce ever had a loose wheel, and so it went. Some of the things Rolls-Royce engineers insisted upon were surely overdetailed and unnecessarily expensive, but they had Royce behind them: "Quality will be remembered," he said, "long after price has been forgotten."

The car lasted longer than the men. Charles Rolls was killed in an airplane crash in 1910. He was a national hero by then—he had made a ninety-minute round-trip Channel crossing when it was infinitely more hazardous than doing the Atlantic solo today. Flying a Wright biplane in a short-landing contest at Bournemouth, he came in a bit too high and apparently overstressed an elevator component in a correcting dive. The plane dropped an estimated twenty-seven feet, Rolls was thrown free, and died almost instantly. He had, by this time, lost interest in automobiles, and he had probably even sold his stock in the company.

A year later Royce had a complete physical collapse, clearly the result of years of overwork and actual malnutrition. From the beginning he had worked obsessively, often twenty hours at a stretch, and he grudged taking time off even to eat. If he hadn't remembered to put an apple or a roll into a pocket, he wouldn't bother to eat. He truly could not understand men who labored to lesser standards. In the early days, when he handed out the week's pay on Saturday morning, he would often tell a man, "You don't deserve it if you're not going to work this afternoon." Since he was probably going to work until midnight, it seemed a reasonable enough observation to him. The doctors could find nothing organically wrong, so they fell back on the recommendation of "a change of air." Egypt was favored for the purpose then, and Claude Johnson took him there with all speed. It didn't seem to make a lot of difference.

On the way back from Egypt they wandered in the south of France. In Le Canadel on the Riviera Royce remarked that it might be pleasant to have a house in France. Johnson immediately bought land and had two villas built, one for Royce, and a smaller one nearby for a staff. During the waiting interval, in England, Royce fell seriously ill, there was surgical intervention, probably for an intestinal malignancy, and he was never really well for the rest of his life, most of which he spent in Le Canadel, working. He had a housekeeping staff, a nurse, draftsmen, and secretaries. A steady stream of directives, ideas, designs began to flow to England, and it never stopped. He rarely saw the factory again, but he dominated everything that happened in it until his death in 1933. He was Sir Henry Royce by then, indisputably a titan. He is hard to place as a personality.

Royce was a kind man who could raise tremendous loyalty in his employees, but he was irascible and short-fused too. Someone who was with him when he heard a workman remark that a certain part was "good enough," said that "he carried on in an alarming manner." He had small talent for recreation. Sometimes he played the flute. He liked flowers—but even his garden was artificially lighted, because he couldn't find time to dig in it by day. In the literal sense, he was a workman.

Claude Johnson, who had held the company together and had been helmsman from the beginning, died in 1926, plainly a victim of overwork and exhaustion. The production of aircraft engines during World War I, at small profit and in the face of incessant interference by an ignorant bureaucracy, had hurt him most.

After World War II, in the 1950s, it was sometimes said that the cars were not really as good as they had been. It wasn't true. Standards hadn't been lowered. Today, at Crewe, one still sees painstaking thoroughness: binned parts, stub-axles for example, covered in protective plastic, partially to prevent their scratching each other, but more importantly, as an engineer told me, "for discipline." Oil-pump parts are individually inspected, and after assembly the whole unit is checked. At this point, in the ordinary manufactory, it would go into the car. Rolls-Royce hooks it to a test-rig, where it must pump oil in rated volume for a specific time. Some disk brakes are noisy because of bell-like resonance in the metal-mass. RR disks are muted: a groove is machined all around the periphery, a soft iron wire fastened in, the whole covered with a strip of stainless steel. Cars on the production line still move only about once an hour, and not far, and by manpower. Engines are still bench-run under a constant wash of fresh oil and every car is taken on the road by a tester before going to the paint shop for finishing. He is far more knowledgeable than the fussiest customer, and more critical, too, because that's his job. This systematic over-kill largely explains why, of around 50,000 Rolls-Royces that have been built, some 25,000 are still running, probably the highest survival rate of any production automobile. Too, it explains why the Rolls-Royce is one of the cheapest cars to run: overall, maintenance cost is low, and resale value very high.

It is true that the Rolls-Royce of 1950 or so was not so notably superior to its competitors as, say, the Silver Ghost had been. Silver Ghost devotees believed that their cars had no peers. They might grudgingly have conceded that the Napier was a fair motorcar, but that would be the limit. In 1910 few makers were willing to spend as much in effort and money as Royce was, and nothing else would do.

In time, technology overcame handcrafting. Rivets banged into place in a few seconds held a chassis together as well as tapered bolts; hexagonal nuts could pin a wheel as tightly as a splined and machined hub-fastener, and for pennies instead of pounds. It's an old, old story: the English longbow-man was the terror of Europe because he was a deadly shot, childhood trained, with a sightless and subtle weapon that had to be aimed instinctively and could be handled only by a strong man. Technology produced the gun; ninety-seven-pound weaklings could master it in a month, and the longbow went for firewood.

The fabulous variety of custom coachwork beguiled one into thinking the older cars superior, too. Every Rolls-Royce today looks much like every other. Not so when there were more than fifty bespoke body-makers at work and a man had his motorcar tailored to his taste exactly as he did his suit. He could order a tourer, a roadster, a coupe in any form, or a landaulette, a phaeton, a salamanca, a cabriolet, a sedanca de ville, a drop-head sedanca, a two-door sedan with a blind rear quarter, a torpedo, a boat-decked sports tourer. And these were merely body shapes. It was interiors that offered individuality, or eccentricity, full rein. Choice of fabrics, leathers, cabinet timbers was limited solely by the world market. Gold or silver plating, Venetian blinds, running water, extra instrumentation, double-glazed windows, cocktail sets electrically lifted to lap level, miniature elevators built into the running-boards—even toilets were not unknown. They were usually arranged to disappear into the trunk, and one lady of rank stipulated a seat of best ivory. The Nizam of Hyderabad liked foot-wide sterling-silver crests on his Royces; he was said to own sixty. The Dowager Queen Mary was less demanding, requiring only a horn sounding like no other, and a recording speedometer in the passenger compartment so she could be certain that at no time her chauffeur exceeded the slow rate of travel she enjoyed.

Although customer choice was wide, I can recall only two really ugly Rolls-Royces. One was a bulge-sided horror on a Silver Wraith chassis built for Nubar Gulbenkian, the other a fearsome streamlined thing with round doors done by Jonckheere, a Belgian coachmaker, for a party or parties unknown. I presume most Rolls-Royces were good-looking because British custom body-builders, like British custom tailors, would allow a client only so much latitude in taste before suggesting he might be happier elsewhere.

Many extraordinarily pretty bodies were erected on the 1929–1935 Phantom II chassis, the last car of Henry Royce's own design, perhaps because its 200- or 206-inch chassis lent itself to long and low coachwork. A two-seater roadster on a P-II was certainly a splendid example of conspicuous consumption. The P-II engine was a 6-cylinder, Royce's favorite configuration, and big—7.6 liters. (It took eight quarts of oil and nearly seven gallons of water, two of the reasons RR engines didn't often overheat. One was run from England into Africa and back without water added.) The engine carried good things: overhead valves, a seven-bearing crankshaft, double ignitions systems (coil and magneto, used together), a double-sequence silent starter, and a constant-speed control of the kind that has lately been an option on some U.S. luxury cars. Brakes were powered on Rolls-Royce's well-tried system, based on Hispano-Suiza and Renault patents, the amount of pedal assistance increasing precisely in ratio with the speed of the car. Chassis lubrication was by oil controlled by a driver's pedal, only the propeller-shaft universals needed rack lubrication; even Rolls-Royce ingenuity couldn't find a way to squirt oil into them while they are spinning. A slightly modified P-II, the Continental, took twenty-three seconds to accelerate its two-and-a-half tons to 60 mph and would do 90–95 on top. The Continental was an ideal carriage for long-distance touring in the grand manner, and many were bodied with nested trunks and valises astern. It did not occur to anyone that they might be stolen—because they wouldn't be. What might be stolen was the so-called mascot, the Flying Lady figure adorning the radiator; a plain cap was provided for use when the car had to be parked in dubious security. (Today the big prewar German silver mascots bring $100–$150.) Charles Sykes, a noted sculptor of the time, did the mascot in 1910 and titled it "The Spirit of Ecstasy" after a ride in a Silver Ghost, the company likes to say. That Sykes modelled the statuette from life is usually not mentioned; the lady was the mistress of a titled Rolls-Royce owner.

At the other end of the spectrum were the little 20-horsepower and 20/25 cars, sometimes inelegantly called Babies. They made lovely town carriages and they were great favorites with doctors, combining elegance with economy. Some thought their performance derisory—they were flat-out at around 65 mph—but then as now 65 is more than adequate on most roads, and a 20/25 would do it silently and gracefully and practically forever. The authorities Anthony Bird and Ian Hallows cite a 20-horsepower owned by a woman who could not, or would not, learn to shift gears. For twenty-five years she ran the car in fourth gear, starting, honestly, uphill and down. It ate clutch plates like popcorn, of course, but the engine imperturbably took the beating. The lady should have taken the course the factory used to offer for chauffeurs and the occasional owner-driver. It ran twelve days, three of which were given over entirely to gear-shifting. I have ridden with seasoned graduates of this instruction, and it is true that the automatic transmission which can shift as nearly imperceptibly as they did has yet to be devised, never mind such niceties as releasing the brakes completely about six inches before the car stopped, so that it would "die" without rippling the water in a glass.

Rolls-Royce believes in the survival principles established by the Vatican: among them, change when it's necessary—but not before, and not much. Postwar realities doomed the custom coachbuilder, so the company began to deliver complete cars instead of chassis only; they were smaller, and more of them were made to be driven by their owners. Innovations like the automatic transmission—a reworked GM hydramatic—a V8 engine, and twin headlights were taken on over screams of rage from the old guard who saw in them nothing but transatlantic cheapening of the sacred vehicle. But the company had no intention of abandoning the thrust that had brought it greatness, and ultraluxurious carriages were still on the stocks: the Phantom IV limousine was available to heads of state only in a production run of eighteen cars. The P-IV was the first Royce used in procession by the royal family, Daimlers having previously been preferred. The even bigger P-V had a run of 510 at around $28,000 each, and would do 100 mph. British motoring journalists, usually gentle with the home product and deferential to Rolls-Royce, nonetheless suggested that for all its air of pasha's luxury, the road-holding, the ride-comfort factors, and the steering left a lot to be desired. They also pointed out that it did seem extreme to have to take off the right front wheel to get at the spark plugs on that side. As a processional carriage, of course, doing 10 mph on a boulevard, a P-V was a moving house of immense dignity, beauty, and impressiveness. Mechanically, it had fallen behind the times. Bemused by the purple prose in which Rolls-Royce has so long been imbedded, drivers new to the make are usually disappointed when they first try one of the Phantoms.

Expecting a magic-carpet sensation, they're surprised to find a firm ride, heavy steering, leisurely acceleration. They would be equally upset by the legendary Duesenberg. Fastest luxury vehicle of its day, it makes a distinctly trucky impression now.

The current RR is the Silver Shadow, a 308-cubic-inch V8 of around 275 horsepower. (For no apparent reason save snobbism, Rolls-Royce never discloses horsepower figures, but they have usually been modest, if steadily increasing, since the postwar Silver Dawn's 125.) The company anticipates making about 2500 Shadows this year and selling 610 of them in the United States, 110 over last year's quota, in the range of $23,800 to $34,600. Brakes are disk on all four wheels, with three systems available, and suspension is fully independent, a refinement the company resisted for longer than seemed justifiable. Few amenities have been omitted. Seat adjustment, door locks, gear selection, gasoline filler-flap, for example, are all electrically operated. Ten cowhides are required for upholstery, each the survivor of hundreds rejected for insect bites, barbed-wire scars, and the like. A cabinet-maker of formidable skill spends a week on the woodwork, and if the customer doesn't care for Circassian walnut, he can command Persian burr, paldao, rosewood, coromandel, tola, birdseye maple, myrtle, or sycamore. I remember a striking drop-head coupe in which white leather had been happily combined with coromandel, a figured ebonylike timber. Should the woodwork ever be marred in use, it can be replaced by precisely matching veneers cut from the same log, set aside in permanent storage.

There are four models of the Shadow: a standard sedan, a chauffeur-driven long-wheelbase sedan, a coupe, and a convertible, all also available under the Bentley label at a miniscule discount. (When Rolls-Royce took over the Bentley in 1931, it was a hairy, powerful sports car, famous for having five times won at Le Mans. The current model, the Bentley T, is identical with the Silver Shadow, radiator shell excepted, and is made in small quantity. It appeals chiefly to buyers who are diffident about the view of Rolls-Royce ownership Zero Mostel laid down in *The Producer*: "If you've got it, flaunt it!")

The coupe and the convertible are type-named Corniche after the famous cliff roads of the French Riviera and show three fairly stunning departures from Rolls-Royce tradition: the radiator shell has been widened by a half-inch, the only significant change in it since the name-plate enamel was changed from red to black with Sir Henry Royce's death;* the instrument panel carries a tachometer, a suggestion of performance capability the company has not often wished to emphasize, and for the first time ever the model name appears on the trunk lid, a similarity with such things as the Duster that has lifted eyebrows from one end of Pall Mall to the other. Detroit may have ordained that the rag top is as dead as the rumble seat, but the Corniche convertible is the top of the Rolls-Royce line at $34,600. Silver Shadow sedan bodies are standard steel stampings; the Corniche is coachbuilt by H.J. Mulliner-Park Ward, a wholly owned subsidiary formed by combining two old bespoke houses. Panels are hand-formed, six weeks are spent painting the car, and the convertible top, a week's work, from a little distance defies detection as a folder.

The Corniche will do 120 mph in dignity, but like all postwar Rolls-Royces, it demonstrates more roll, tire-squeal, and understeer in hard corners than is acceptable under 1971 *gran turismo* standards. Still . . . when the bankruptcy notice was posted ten months ago, there were those who

---

*Or because the directors decided that red was simply too flamboyant for the vehicle.

counselled that the company should abandon ship altogether, or sell out to one of the giants, or "rationalise" with a line of mass-produced cars like everybody else. Instead, Rolls-Royce came up with the Corniche, a *beau geste* indeed, and not the less so because the decision had been taken before the dam broke. Still, it represented justifiable optimism. After all, the car division's 8500 workers had made a $19-million-dollar profit on exports alone in 1970, and the Congressional decision to bail out Lockheed's Tristar program, March-to-August cliffhanger though it was, saved the RB-111 engine as well.

Is the Rolls-Royce still the best car in the world? No. That pride of place has gone to Mercedes-Benz, with cars that are as comfortable, mechanically more advanced, more roadable by far, faster, and, in the case of the 600 seven-passenger, even more massively sized.

Is the Rolls-Royce still absolutely unique, a hallowed name carrying an indefinable cachet born of stoutly maintained tradition, and of ownership by the world's eminences for nearly seventy years? Yes, and as nearly as one can tell, that will be true until they shut down the line and padlock the doors at Crewe.

—1971

The Playboy Stable

The assemblage of a gentleman's stable of motor-cars, utility and esthetics the only considerations, calls for an imaginator in good form—and an open-ended bank account. Still, in the mind's eye it is as easy to create the one as the other, a list of desirable possessions is amusing to make and may be handy to have, since one never knows when emergency will strike: a New Jersey man was recently obliged to accept two $250,000 lottery prizes in succession and, not having considered the contingency in advance, had to put the stuff into a bank for lack, one must presume, of something better to do with it. One should be on guard against this sort of thing.

PLAYBOY has in the past named ideal *scuderia* but while most, if not all the choices are still valid, others, because the total must be limited, have been squeezed out by the passage of time, although they are still enviable properties: the Mercedes-Benz 300SL for example, or the Lancia GT 2500. So, once more into the breach. . . .

Range is the name of the game. Diversity. The ideal: a garageful of vehicles so selected that no situation will find one other than suitably mounted. When there were five or six hundred automobiles on the world market, the selection might have been easier: one could have had a steamer or an electric, for example. On the other hand, we are probably at this moment in the golden age of the automobile—history is difficult to assay close up—and in future the creation of a stable may be impossible, because it is clear that society is gathering itself to insist upon mass public transport for most of the population, with small, uniform automobiles taking up what slack there will be left. (Starkly significant in this connection, with the cancellation of the 1971 Frankfurt Motor Show on the ground that the European motorist is not interested in utility, not exotica.) The trifling matter of exhaust pollutants is not the problem, it's a symptom. The problem is proliferation. When the United States census hits 250 million, the idea of a three-car family will be plainly insupportable, ludicrous. We already have one mile of road for every square mile of land we own; we can't pave the whole country.

The PLAYBOY Stable, then, for 1971: a Wankel, a dune buggy, a *gran turismo,* a deluxe town carriage, an antique, and the biggest—and fastest—limousine ever put upon wheels.

The Wankel-engined car is Toyo Kogyo's Mazda RX2, its function in the line-up to serve as urban and short-haul country transport without being limited to those uses.

The rotary internal-combustion engine has been called the only all-new power plant of our time and in its present useful form it is new, although the idea on which it's based is a very old one. It's largely trouble-free: the magazine *Road Test* ran a Mazda R100 30,000 miles without changing the plugs or points or touching the carburetor. The engine maintains its tune, stays on the road and out of the shop. It does, indeed, have a lot going for it.

Reasonably diligent research has failed to turn up Toyo Kogyo's reason for naming its cars Mazda,* except that it has nothing to do with the old General Electric lightbulb. (Owners occasionally report being asked if the thing is battery-run.) The RX2 is beguiling: a good size for city use, dependable, cheap to buy ($2850) and to run (eighteen to twenty-three miles to the gallon of no-octane), and amusing to drive. There is acceleration sufficient to blow off most things its size, and a 110 mph top. Handling is not in the sports-car bracket, but it's predictable and adequate for the tasks the car should normally be set. Pleasure in using the car derives from its uncanny smoothness and from its satisfying snob-value: it's a rarity, after all, and will be for some little time yet. The ordinary amenities are available, including

---

*The authority Jan Norbye has suggested that it's an anglization of the name of the designer, Matsuda.

air conditioning, a good idea since the ventless front windows create an irritating tumult wound down at highway speeds. There's one splendid refinement, a five-function single stalk on the steering column: it commands the directionals, washer, wipers, headlight flasher and dimmer.

The dune buggy is a phenomenon—loathesome or lovely, depending upon one's prejudices—out of California, spawning ground for most innovative wheeled things since World War II. Specifically the dune buggy can be laid at the door of Bruce Meyers, whose Meyers Manx established the basic pattern: fat tires, glass body, VW running-gear. The Manx was, in the view of James T. Crow, an eminence of the authoritative journal *Road & Track,* the most imitated design in automotive history, and it was also responsible, when the craze it set off crested, for the theft of Volkswagens in such numbers that the elves of Wolfsburg were hard put to ship replacements fast enough. California teenagers have always been adept with plier and jack-handle; there were some who could spot a black VW parked in Sausalito and have it storming the dunes thirty-six hours later, bright in Fire-Mist Lime, a whippy ten-foot flagpole heralding its coming from afar.

The dune buggy sired a generation of all-terrain and off-road recreational vehicles, including the snowmobile. They have made one thing possible and another practically impossible: they have opened the great outdoors to people who would never have known anything about it had they been restricted to leg-power, and they have almost guaranteed that one cannot get far enough into the boondocks to escape the howl of the internal-combustion engine. That is the barest statement of the case, and I don't propose to amplify it.

At the right time and in the right place, a dune buggy is a formidable fun-generator, and running one really can be what it seemed to be if you remember watching Steve McQueen and Faye Dunaway in *The Thomas Crown Affair.* There are times when only a dune buggy will do it for you.

There's a drawback, though—range limitation. The dune buggy is great on its own terrain, and tolerable as an open town runabout. But if one lives any distance from dune-buggy country, the thing is a bore because it's geared for power to run up the side of a cliff, fat-tired for flotation on soft ground, and open to the crisp fresh air on every side. After 100 miles on a parkway, all but terminal nut-cases are ready to trade it for a pogo stick.

The Meyers Tow'd [the word is a copyrighted trademark] is craftily cast to negate this lamentable built-in characteristic with a gimmick as simple and as workable as a paper clip: there's a tow-bar telescoped into it. Hooked to a standard trailer-hitch on the back of a roadcar, the bar lifts the Tow'd front end off the ground and away you go. The Tow'd is sold as a kit—about $440 standard, $550 deluxe—and the package has everything but power and accessories. For these, a 1955–1970 VW is required (you can use a Corvair engine if you're eager) plus a few hours with wrench and screwdriver. Well, a few hours if you're good at it. If you're one of those who need twenty minutes to wire up a wall plug, if you're an instruction-sheet lip-reader, a few days, maybe. In that case, seek out a knowledgeable teen-ager and contract him to bolt your Tow'd together for a flat fee, a bonus for celerity, and the privilege of the first ride. (In England, where the kit idea originated, this procedure is highly illegal, the law requiring that only the owner and his friends can do the work. However, the term "friends" is subject to generous interpretation.)

To fill the *gran turismo* slot in our 1971 garage we are citing the Ferrari 365 GTB/4, the Daytona. Calling this vehicle a *gt* is probably an understatement of some dimension, because it is a motorcar of awesome power, one of the fastest roadcars we have yet seen, fast enough to be taken direct from the dealership to the race circuit with perfect confidence. Luigi Chinetti and Bob Grossman did just that, running a Daytona in the 24-Hour Race at Le Mans this year and bringing it in fifth overall.

We have here a $20,000 two-passenger fastback coupe by Pininfarina/-Scaglietti mounting a 12-cylinder, four-camshaft, 400-horsepower engine, five-speed transmission and eleven-inch power-disk brakes. The speedometer reads to 180 miles an hour, and the needle will go there. Bill Harrah told me he thinks the Daytona the "strongest" automobile he's ever touched, a statement of some weight when one thinks of the hundreds of cars he's handled down the years. I found driving it a stunning experience, out of range of anything I could recall. The thing doesn't *feel* like an automobile: it's a locomotive. I took it out on a lamentably rainy Sunday morning in Reno. I'd been driving a good 275 Ferrari daily for two weeks, but I can't say that was any real preparation for the Daytona, which will do 85 in second and get to 100 in twelve seconds some fast motorcars take to reach 60. The sheer pull of the engine straight up to 7500 rpm is fabulous, and for the first few miles there is a soul-stirring conviction, every time one shifts, that the thing is running away, in someone else's control, like a moon rocket. I never came near the honest 173 miles an hour the same car had done in other hands. At 135 I convinced myself—it didn't take much doing —that the steady rainfall interdicted a higher speed in a $20,000 motorcar loaned, and voluntarily at that, by a friend. In any case, this is a car that demands respect—and, for an already well-schooled driver, about 250 miles of familiarization would be a good idea, too.

While the Daytona's shattering capabilities in the maximum ranges obviously qualify it as a race car, it still is a tourer: it idles without argument around 600–700 rpm, and in fifth gear it can be backed off to a neat and steady 40 miles an hour. It doesn't foul plugs, it doesn't overheat in traffic, it's comfortable, there's more than adequate luggage space for a month's travel, and its stunning good looks guarantee first-cabin reception wherever it stops, from filling station to the *porte-cochere* of The Beverly Hills Hotel. Characteristically, the frill features—air conditioning, electric windows, and so on—perform dimly. I say characteristically because I can recall the same faults in other Ferraris. I remember one with 6000 miles on the odometer, the driver's window stuck half-open, the hand brake useless, the fuel gauge registering full at all times. In limited production it's hard to enforce quality in bought accessories, and in any case many Italians remain to be convinced that anything but sheer go matters. In a car like the Daytona, unique in bloodline and performance, perhaps they're right. They *shouldn't* be right, but maybe they are.

Cadillac's placement in the chronicle of U.S. luxury town cars is unchallenged. A great many competing makes have come and gone—Packard, Lincoln, Duesenberg, Pierce-Arrow—since the first Cadillac took the road in 1902. Only the Mark IV Continental, descendant of the Lincoln, remains to challenge it. Oddly, both cars were created by the same man, Henry Leland, a Vermont engineer of passionate devotion to detail perfection. Leland named the Lincoln after Abraham Lincoln, a lifetime idol. The Cadillac was called after Antoine Laumet, who in 1901 founded Detroit, and who titled himself Cadillac for reasons that remain obscure. There was a Duc de Cadillac in the French nobility, but a connection between him and Laumet has not been established, and the Duc's coat of arms does not resemble the badge all Cadillacs since the first one have carried: apparently it was someone's original creation.

The Cadillac was a good car from the first single-cylinder Model A onward. In 1907 its excellence was demonstrated in a publicity coup by Fred Bennett, the British distributor. Visiting Detroit, Bennett had been struck by the accuracy Leland was enforcing in parts-machining: tolerances of 1/1000th of an inch. In London, he proposed that the Royal Automobile Club supervise a contest in which three cars of any entering make would be stripped, the parts jumbled, and new cars reassembled out of them. As Bennett had suspected would be the case, only Cadillac tried it. Three cars were stripped, the parts thoroughly mixed, some of them removed at random and replaced from the stock-bins, and the cars reassembled with hand tools only, and under close RAC supervision to be sure there'd be no surreptitious filing or forcing. Set up, the cars started instantly and ran perfectly. Cadillac won the prestigious Dewar Trophy and the foundation of a great reputation.

Down the years Cadillac has been remarkably original, first with a good electric starter, hydraulic valve-lifters, synchromesh gears, quick-drying enamel, chrome plating, and so on. The first high-speed V8 engine was the 1915 Cadillac, and the great V12s and V16s of 1930 et. seq. were bench marks. Another was the front-wheel-drive Eldorado of 1967. Before the Oldsmobile Toronado, and the Eldorado, it was held gospel that a really big engine could not be used in the front-wheel-drive configuration—there simply wouldn't be room, the car would understeer madly, and so on. The registered attempts, Bucciali's, for example, had been less than winners. The advantages were tempting: good traction due to engine weight over the driven wheels, and the roomy interior deriving from a flat floor; the big drawback, steering the driven wheels, had been negated by technological advances and power steering. The extent of the Eldorado's success with front-wheel drive can be judged by its 8.2-liter engine, the biggest in world production today, and by the fact that it's practically impossible to detect on the road which set of wheels is getting the power. The standard test, backing off the throttle in the middle of a fast curve, has no discernible effect on the vehicle. Correctly estimating the interest of its clientele in things mechanical at just under *nil,* the Cadillac makes minimal reference to the drive, and there are Eldorado owners who don't know where the power is going. I met one of them in a garage two winters ago, having chains put on his rear wheels. I presume the officiating mechanic knew but for some reason preferred to keep it to himself . . . maybe that was how he got his jollies that day.

The 1971 Eldorado is an informal four-place town car of great distinction and refinement, a splendid parkway touring car as well. I inject the caveat because the awesome impression of width from the driver's seat and its suspension are at least partial disqualifiers for country roads and byways. On boulevards and superhighways it's as good as anything in the world, the mammoth engine almost dead silent until the whip is laid on, the ride better, to my taste at least, than Rolls-Royce's. Hitting obstructions like big frost-heaves, the thump is audible, the driver knows that work is being done down there, but next to nothing at all comes through the upholstery.

This is an unobtrusively fast machine, too. I have a standard fifty-mile stretch over which I have run many cars. It includes city driving, parkway, country road, a long straight, and a small town. In a light-traffic time of day I made this run in fifty-five minutes without doing anything dramatic or conspicuous. The Eldorado is automated to a point requiring the driver to do little more than start it and steer it: temperature control, cruising-speed control, the best automatic transmission extant, electric locks, both-sides interior-controlled mirrors, signal-seeking stereo, electrically adjustable seats, on-off indicators for all running-lights, automatic parking-brake release, and so on through a list long enough to boggle a maharajah. There are a few negatives, of course: showing 5800 miles, the last Eldorado I drove had an unacceptable level of body noise, far more than my 35,000-mile Pontiac Grand Prix, a vehicle I've never thought quiet. If one's much over

5′10″ one's out of rear-seat headroom; hatted, I'd say the limit might be 5′7." The fake wood liberally used up front is the fakest I've ever seen, so patently fraudulent that in a perverse way it's amusing. However, not to grumble. We live in parlous times, and what do you want for $7000—gold plating? The Eldorado remains, in the essentials, an admirable device.

There are occasions that can be happily enlarged by a really unusual motorcar: I recall a picnic in England done in an Edwardian mode that was twice as enjoyable as it might otherwise have been because the party travelled in a Rolls-Royce Silver Ghost touring car fitted with a mammoth wicker basket, food, wine, china, and silver in a service for six. And a summer wedding, the bride and groom carried from the church in a torpedo-bodied Bugatti. For this kind of laudable endeavor, something pre-1940 is indicated, and since, when pure pleasure is the primary purpose, we incline to think of a small car, something in the two-seater configuration. In this overview the range is tremendous. A Henley Rolls-Royce roadster? A Stutz Bearcat? A 1750 Zagato Alfa-Romeo? A chain-gang Frazer Nash? Or go to the top of the pile and take a T-head Mercer Raceabout?

The Mercer Raceabout circa 1910–1915 is probably the most sought-after of U.S.-built automobiles. There are fewer than thirty of them extant, and the market on them, established by a single sale every couple of years or so, is in the area of $35,000–$50,000. The original sticker was $2500.

As was the case with every great motorcar, the Mercer was built by men much less concerned with profit than with quality and the charm of the Mercer in the T-head models (so called after the configuration of the engine) is soon stated: it was soundly and strongly made of the best materials; the performance it offered was startling; and its stark simplicity—the thing was all automobile, completely unfrilled—was esthetically most appealing. Some owners even dispensed with the eighteen-inch "monocle" windshield as an encumbrance!

There were other models in the Mercer production of about 5000 cars before the company abandoned ship in the 1920s, but the T-head Raceabout was the best, and deserves its compulsory inclusion in any list of the dozen greatest sports cars we have known since the beginning.

As far from the Mercer as one could get and still be on four wheels is the Mercedes-Benz 600. This does appear to be, in all sooth, The Ultimate Limousine. History makes liars of us all, but, in the present state of the art, it is hard to think of something better than an almost-dead-silent seven-passenger automobile offering comfort that begins where other luxury vehicles leave off—and still capable of 0–60 acceleration in under ten seconds and a top speed of 125-plus mph. In its combination of comfort and performance capability the 600 is unique. On a winding road, only a really good sports car can stay with a 600. This is not surmise or estimation: Stirling

359

Moss once loaded a 600 with six passengers and took it around the short and difficult Brands Hatch circuit at a rate a little less than five seconds under the racing-sedan record for the course! Beyond all doubt, any other limousine in the world, trying to stay with him, would have been into the bushes, probably upside-down, in the first half-mile.

No arcana, nothing of the occult, goes into the 600. It is an automobile made by men using machine tools like any other, except that it was designed to be best, and great pain is taken with it. It is made to individual order only, on a separate production line. The engine is a fuel-injected 6.3-liter V8 of 300 horsepower in a 126- to 153-inch-wheelbase chassis, air-suspended with driver-adjustable hydraulic shock-absorbers. Transmission is automatic and the power steering is unusual in offering the front-wheel "road-feel" without which really fast driving is difficult. In brief, the running gear is of the quality its clients expect from the oldest motorcar manufactory in the world, with the longest competitive history. It is in the amenities that the 600 breaks new ground.

Three bodies are available: five- and seven-passenger four-door, seven-passenger six-door. Because electric motors cannot be absolutely silenced, a hydraulic system actuates the window lifts, the six-way front-seat adjustment (vertical, horizontal, and back-angle), the four-way (horizontal and back-rest) rear seat, the sliding roof, doors, trunk lid, windshield wipers, and so on acting through twenty-three push-buttons variously distributed. Electronic temperature control is standard, with inside- and outside-temperature gauges, so is air conditioning, stereo, and heated rear window. There are seventeen interior lights in the car, those in the passenger compartment set for thirty-second time-lag turn-off. Basic design of the passenger seats was done by orthopedic specialists, and the seat springs are tuned to the suspension to eliminate sympathetic vibration at any speed.

The rear windows, are curtained, an oddly old-fashioned touch that is beguiling and useful in practice.

Because each 600 is built to order, variations in such things as seating arrangements are possible. So are folding tables in various cabinet woods, bars, tape recorder, television, vanity sets, electric razor, and so on. A six-piece set of fitted luggage can be nested in the trunk. These trifles will add the old penny to the basic $28,500 price, but what of that? You are buying a motorcar that is the current choice of the sheiks of Araby; the cost of travelling like a *raj* has never been low.

As far as is known to me, Mercedes has refused only one client request: to finish a seven-passenger six-door completely in black, end to end, not a hairline of chromium showing anywhere. But the buyer had his way: he shipped the car to England and had the work done there. Occasionally one sees it in New York, marvelously funereal and gloomy looking. A reversal of the specification, to produce twenty feet six inches of solid chromium, would have made an effect only a little more bizarre.

Thus The PLAYBOY Stable, 1972, six motorcars varietal to a degree in purpose and appearance. To assemble them for photography required only a telephone call to the amiable curators of Harrah's Automobile Collection in Reno. To reassemble them in duplicate? Say $125,000 for openers, much persistence and . . . good luck.

Acknowledgments

The Brothers Chevrolet originally appeared in *Sports Car Illustrated*, March 1959. Copyright © 1959. Reprinted by permission of the publisher.

Pat Moss Carlsson by Ken W. Purdy, using the pseudonym Karl Prentiss, originally appeared in *Holiday*, September 1969. Reprinted with permission from *Holiday*. Copyright © 1969, The Curtis Publishing Company.

The Day They Dug Up Babs by Ken W. Purdy, using the pseudonym Karl Prentiss, originally appeared in *Holiday*, February 1970. Reprinted with permission from *Holiday*. Copyright © 1970, The Curtis Publishing Company.

Like a Collapsed Balloon by Ken W. Purdy, using the pseudonym Karl Prentiss, originally appeared in *Holiday*, March 1970. Reprinted with permission from *Holiday*. Copyright © 1970, The Curtis Publishing Company.

The Mercedes-Benz C-111 by Ken W. Purdy, using the pseudonym Karl Prentiss, originally appeared in *Holiday*, December 1969. Reprinted with permission from *Holiday*. Copyright © 1969, The Curtis Publishing Company.

The Body Beautiful by Ken W. Purdy, using the pseudonym Karl Prentiss, originally appeared in *Holiday*, September 1970. Reprinted with permission from *Holiday*. Copyright © 1970, The Curtis Publishing Company.

Blood Sport originally appeared in the *Saturday Evening Post*, July 27, 1957. Reprinted with permission from *Saturday Evening Post*. Copyright © 1957, The Curtis Publishing Company.

363

ACKNOWLEDGMENTS

A Guy Named Gurney originally appeared in the United Air Lines' *Mainliner* Magazine, June 1970. Reprinted by permission of the publisher.

The Porsche originally appeared in *Boy's Life,* August 1971. Reprinted by permission of the publisher.

The Mercer originally appeared in *Boy's Life,* October 1966. Reprinted by permission of the publisher.

The Duesenberg originally appeared in *Boy's Life,* January 1967. Reprinted by permission of the publisher.

Targa Florio originally appeared in *Boy's Life,* August 1967. Reprinted by permission of the publisher.

Model Cars originally appeared in *Boy's Life,* December 1968. Reprinted by permission of the publisher.

Wonderful Chain Gang Car originally appeared in *Boy's Life,* July 1968. Reprinted by permission of the publisher.

Three Wheels Are Enough originally appeared in *True,* December 1952. Reprinted from *True* Magazine. Copyright © 1952, Fawcett Publications, Inc.

Change of Plan originally appeared in *The Atlantic Monthly,* September 1952. Copyright © 1952, by Ken W. Purdy. Reprinted by permission of the publisher.

At Ten-Tenths of Capacity originally appeared in *The Atlantic Monthly,* July 1965. Copyright © 1965, by The Atlantic Monthly Company, Boston, Mass. Reprinted with permission.

Diesels originally appeared in *The Atlantic Monthly*, May 1966. Copyright © 1966, by The Atlantic Monthly Company, Boston, Mass. Reprinted with permission.

Classics of the Road originally appeared in *The Lamp,* June 1955, published by Standard Oil Company (New Jersey). Reprinted by permission of the publisher.

Masten Gregory Lives originally appeared in *Esquire,* January 1969. Reprinted by permission of *Esquire* Magazine. Copyright © 1969 by Esquire, Inc.

The Marvel of Mantua originally appeared in *Sports Illustrated.* Reprinted by permission from *Sports Illustrated,* "Yesterday," October 14, 1957. Copyright © 1957 by Time, Inc.

What Makes Men Race? originally appeared in *Ford Times,* September 1966. Reprinted by permission of the publisher.

The Lady or the Bugatti originally appeared in *This Week,* January 25, 1959. Reprinted by permission of the publisher.

Elisabeth and the Racing Mog originally appeared in *This Week,* October 25, 1958. Reprinted by permission of the publisher.